Social Evolution, Political Psychology, and the Media in Democracy

"This is a brilliant and truly intellectual book worthy of a hundred conversations on contemporary civilization."
—Edward O. Wilson, *University Research Professor Emeritus, Harvard University*

"If I were to tell you that someone has written a book that melds together ideas about information dissemination consumption, evolutionary psychology, and a normative critique of the American media, you might not believe it was possible. But you'd be wrong. *Social Evolution, Political Psychology, and the Media in Democracy* explains how humans think, what they believe, what they hear, and why it is often bad for American democracy. But he also offers us a way forward through a comparison with other countries. In today's politically deteriorating environment, we need a book like this."
—Brian Rathbun, *Professor of International Relations at University of Southern California, and author of* Reasoning of State: Realists, Romantics and Rationality in International Relations

"In this quirky, clever, and creative work, Peter Beattie leads us on a wild romp through evolutionary biology, social psychology, history, politics, literature, and philosophy to understand why democracy is failing and the human race is flirting with extinction—and what, if anything, can be done about it. No questions could be more important for us to ponder at this time."
—John T. Jost, *Professor of Psychology and Politics, and Co-Director of the Center for Social and Political Behavior at New York University*

"We are what we got fed by the news media, to a great extent. Armed with a social evolutionary approach toward artificial selection in the marketplace of ideas, Peter Beattie has ably shown that psychology tends to prime us into accepting and rejecting certain ideas and how the news media tends to supply those ideas that fit into our biases. A penetrating critique of the news media today and a passionate defense of a new marketplace of ideas for democracy."
—Shiping Tang, *Distinguished Professor of International Relations and Public Affairs at Fudan University, and author of* The Social Evolution of International Politics

"Corrupted by corporate interests and vulnerable to easy manipulation, our news media system is failing us. Beattie makes an urgent and compelling case for bringing it under democratic control—for the sake of preserving democracy itself. This book couldn't be more timely. In an era of dangerous political instability and ecological breakdown, we need media that delivers critical, fact-based communication now more than ever before."

—Jason Hickel, *Lecturer of Anthropology at Goldsmiths, University of London, Fellow of the Royal Society of Arts, and author of* The Divide: A Brief Guide to Global Inequality and its Solutions

Peter Beattie

Social Evolution, Political Psychology, and the Media in Democracy

The Invisible Hand in the U.S. Marketplace of Ideas

Peter Beattie
The Chinese University of Hong Kong
Shatin, New Territories, Hong Kong

ISBN 978-3-030-02800-8   ISBN 978-3-030-02801-5 (eBook)
https://doi.org/10.1007/978-3-030-02801-5

Library of Congress Control Number: 2018959735

© The Editor(s) (if applicable) and The Author(s) 2019
This work is subject to copyright. All rights are solely and exclusively licensed by the Publisher, whether the whole or part of the material is concerned, specifically the rights of translation, reprinting, reuse of illustrations, recitation, broadcasting, reproduction on microfilms or in any other physical way, and transmission or information storage and retrieval, electronic adaptation, computer software, or by similar or dissimilar methodology now known or hereafter developed.
The use of general descriptive names, registered names, trademarks, service marks, etc. in this publication does not imply, even in the absence of a specific statement, that such names are exempt from the relevant protective laws and regulations and therefore free for general use.
The publisher, the authors, and the editors are safe to assume that the advice and information in this book are believed to be true and accurate at the date of publication. Neither the publisher nor the authors or the editors give a warranty, express or implied, with respect to the material contained herein or for any errors or omissions that may have been made. The publisher remains neutral with regard to jurisdictional claims in published maps and institutional affiliations.

Cover design by Thomas Howey

This Palgrave Macmillan imprint is published by the registered company Springer Nature Switzerland AG
The registered company address is: Gewerbestrasse 11, 6330 Cham, Switzerland

Dedicated to young women and men
...*very wise men, perhaps quite worthy to govern, have written in France, Spain and England on the administration of states. Their books have done much good: not that it corrected the ministers who were in office when the book appeared, for a minister does not and cannot correct himself. He has reached his full status. No more instruction, no more advice. He has not the time to listen to them, the tide of business carries him away. But these good books form the young men destined for office, they form the princes, and the second generation is educated.*
—Voltaire, *Philosophical Dictionary*, "States, governments: which is the best?"

Acknowledgements

I'd like to thank Rowan Fortune for his help with editing, my classmates at UCI for the time we spent together and the conversations and debates we had, my incredible co-workers at PLI, my students over the years, and all my friends and family. I was lucky to have discussions, debates, guidance, and suggestions from a great many people: Shawn Akbari, Stefano Albertini, Gabriel Anderson, Marguerite and Paul Beattie, Karim Bettache, Keane Bhatt, Marc Chattah, Chuansheng Chen, Rosalie Chen, Chi-yue Chiu, Pete Ditto, Jeffrey Friedman, David Graeber, Siba N'Zatioula Grovogui, Nabila Habbida, Kamil Hamied, Brian Hansbury, Pyong-su Kang, Ielnaz Kashefipour, Albert Kim, Saadi Lahlou, Francis Lee, John Mage, Tali Mentovich, Hugo Mercier, Jovan Milojevich, Charmaine Mirza, Karen Monroe, Alessandra Montalbano, Robert Moyzis, Alex Paykin, Assal Rad, Annamaria De Rosa, Shawn Rosenberg, Kyle Sanford, Nicholas Scurich, Ruchi Shroff, Sean Starrs, Thomas Taylor, Michael Tesler, Ana Tomicic, Oliver Traldi, Francesco Tripoli, Luciana Vega, Jingguo Wang, Jake Witlen, Shangqiu Zhang (谢谢你的 '美国特色审查')... My apologies to all those I have forgotten to mention; drinks are on me for the omission. Lastly, I'd like to thank Edward Herman and Noam Chomsky for introducing me to political economy of media, and especially their critics, whose conspiratorial misreading first suggested to me that psychology needed to be added to the picture.

Contents

1 Introduction: Why Democracy Is Not Working   1

2 Information: Evolution, Psychology, and Politics   17

3 Evolution: How We Got the Minds We Have Today   63

4 When Our Evolved Minds Go Wrong: Social Psychological Biases   115

5 The Transition: Information from Media to Mind   165

6 The Supply Side: What Affects the Supply of Information Provided by the Media   219

7 Comparing Media Systems: What a Difference Supply Makes   273

8 Conclusion: The Invisible Hand and the Ecology of Information   309

Index   355

CHAPTER 1

Introduction: Why Democracy Is Not Working

> "*What kind of truth is this which is true on one side of a mountain and false on the other?*"
> —Michel de Montaigne, *Essays*

Planes struck the towers while I was in the shower. A roommate was downtown taking photographs and, in the rudest way, received information about what would later be called "9/11"; he witnessed dozens of people choose the brief terror of jumping over the prospect of burning alive. I was blissfully ignorant for an hour. As I walked from Alphabet City to Washington Square, two miles from the World Trade Center, I missed the relevant information—"change blindness" prevented me from noticing the Twin Towers were missing from the skyline. Even as I witnessed streams of businesspeople walking north, truth eluded me. (Those whose proximity to the collapse had covered them in soot were further downtown.) It was the day of the mayoral primaries, and I interpreted the unusual migration as a trip to the polls. What a turnout, what a day for democracy!

Information about the attack only reached me from fellow students as I arrived at class and even then, much was false: Planes had hit the White House! Another attack was on the way! I tried to call my father, in the Financial District for a conference, but the cell phone network was overwhelmed. Instead, I walked to an apartment near Union Square, where, uncoordinated, friends were converging. There, as most of them walked to a nearby hospital to donate blood (there were too many would-be

© The Author(s) 2019
P. Beattie, *Social Evolution, Political Psychology, and the Media in Democracy*, https://doi.org/10.1007/978-3-030-02801-5_1

donors), I saw CNN's coverage of what had happened two miles away. For billions, the news media would be their *only* source of information.

I remember the week after 9/11 as an unusual time. Strangers made eye contact and daily interactions were gentler. The stress of daily life was subdued, not augmented, by the mass murder. It was as if the toxic smoke from the ruins were soporific. Parks were filled with spontaneous memorials, chalk drawings, and posters with a theme so common I only found it remarkable later[1]: peace. I saw calls for resilience, understanding, to avoid violent retribution, remembering and honoring the dead by putting an end to violence.

Not so on television. The news was jarring, like entering an alternate universe where mourning and the desire for peace were replaced by rage and the desire for retribution. And fear, pervasive fear. The fear spread by the news media took root across the country, creating a sharp distinction between how New York City and the United States reacted. (Fear even snuck into my apartment—a month later, I bought gas masks for roommates and myself, should a poison gas attack force us escape across the Williamsburg Bridge.) This was my introduction to the media's power, my first intimation of the difference between mediated and unmediated reality.

There was a question on everyone's mind: Why do they hate us? The easiest answer, one found with only a remote control, was *freedom*. "They" hate "us" for our freedom. As a college student, I had the time and resources to engage in more effortful searches. The answers I found in books, magazines, the alternative and international press, community radio, and documentaries were less pat than freedom-hatred. These answers attacked my identity, how I saw myself as a member of a nation devoted to justice and democracy. They were answers—true or false— that never reached more than a small minority of my compatriots.

But why did this information reach me and not everyone? How did so many others around me come to have ideas so different from mine? These questions made me look at ideas anew. What are ideas? Fundamentally: information. Ideas are bits of information generated in or communicated to human minds, which combine, change, and spread. One's beliefs are simply ideas—often what one was taught as a child. The mind may be mysterious, but it is not magical: it cannot survey all ideas and choose the best. The mind can only embrace ideas it is exposed to by others, or create new ideas from pieces of other ideas. Gore Vidal once put it that Montaigne wrote "about what he had been reading *which became himself.*"[2] Who we are—our identities and beliefs—is largely information we absorbed from our environments. Hence the distribution of the world's religions: Catholics are disproportionately those whose parents were Catholics, Hindus those who were raised Hindu and so on.

It is not only religious ideas that we hold for reasons of geographical accident. There are few French nationalists among those born and raised in Ethiopia, just as there are few monarchists born and raised in the USA. Our political ideas, like our religious ideas, are powerfully influenced by mere geography.

Why do we believe what we believe about politics? Our parents are a primary influence, as are schools, churches, and friends. And, finally: the books and newspapers we read, the television we watch and internet sites we visit. Outside of these sources, what do we have? The news media provides the majority of us with nearly all the information we have about the world outside of our social circles. Whether that information is worthy of trust depends on the nature of the media system we have access to; citizens of North Korea would be wise to distrust information coming from their media system, while citizens of the United States can be confident that a far greater percentage of the information from theirs trustworthy. After all, the U.S. government does not actively censor the press and journalists are trained to be as objective as possible. Yet there are reasons for doubt. There need not be a conscious, coordinated policy *à la* North Korea for a media system to display a propagandistic character. Unconscious or unintentional mechanisms abound: political-economic pressures, ideological uniformity among the owners of media companies or journalists, and a reliance on government sources for information are candidates. Even "culture" is a candidate: norms, routines, common sense, conventional wisdom, and what "it just wouldn't do to say" or write. Hence even in relatively free and open media systems, healthy skepticism is required.

Such unconscious mechanisms are capable of producing bias that eerily mimics conscious propaganda. Before and during the second US war on Iraq, the U.S. public largely believed the war justified because Iraq posed a serious threat to national security. Yet the majority of the world's people outside of the United States believed the war unjustified. Simply, the U.S. media was more accepting of the U.S. government's position than media systems globally. The result: the U.S. public believed falsehoods and most of the rest of the world did not.[3] What was true on our side of the Pacific and Atlantic was false on the others—and, as recognized by even Republican candidates for president in 2016, our "truth" was false.

Such dependence on the news media strikes us as unpleasant, even embarrassing. The more comfortable and reassuring thought is that we choose what to believe. And we do, but we are *not* free to accept or reject ideas we never see or hear. Herein lies the power of the news media.

A commonsense rebuttal to claims about a powerful media is that there is no evidence of any conspiratorial cabal using the media to mislead the public; rather, the U.S. media (among others) is composed of fair-minded professional journalists able to write and speak freely; that they are often adversarial toward government and corporations and tend toward the liberal side of the U.S. political spectrum; that the United States is an open society without censorship, in which citizens can read, watch, say, or believe what they please. Therefore, those concerned about media power are likely to be adherents of ideological persuasions outside the mainstream, upset their ideology has failed to gain wider acceptance. Each of these points of rebuttal is correct. Only, they are correct in themselves but do not constitute a rebuttal. This book explains why.

It explains how an "invisible hand" creates a *de facto* propaganda system within the American marketplace of ideas. A conspiracy is unnecessary to explain the constricted supply of information within our open society: psychological, commercial, and political pressures suffice. As Adam Smith might put it: "It is not from the malevolence of the politician, the journalist, the media owner, or the audience that a propaganda system is created, but from their regard to their own interests—and, from their psychology."

This book will argue that the news media has a power rivaling any branch of government. It suggests that to be consistent with democracy, the power of media, like the power of government, must be submitted to democratic control—and not merely to the polyarchic plutocracy of the market. Otherwise, we must admit that ours is a sham democracy disguising an oligarchy. Or, simply a democracy in disrepair.

Explanations for this sorry state can be grouped into two broad categories. The Right insists human nature is profoundly flawed: "out of the crooked timber of humanity no straight thing was ever made," according to Immanuel Kant. Our ideal forms of government cannot help but fall short of their goals, because human nature is corrupt, selfish, and tainted with evil. Hence democracy, which Churchill called "the worst form of government, except for all those other forms," is failing of necessity. Our fallen nature can do no better, though it could do worse.

On the Left, it is argued that democracy fails only when impeded by external forces. Human nature is suited to self-government and would produce wonderful results if allowed time to flourish under true democracy. The Left's diagnosis for the present democratic deficit is the impediment imposed by wealthy individuals and corporations. This, not any failings of human nature, is what is preventing democracy from achieving its potential.

Evolutionary and social psychology have shown that we are animals that evolved to cooperate with members of our groups and compete with other groups. Our brains are designed with biases and prejudices to facilitate this cooperation and competition—not to think with the rationality and objectivity of philosophers. We know that humanity is crooked timber: far from the liberal ideal of rationality, *Homo sapiens* has an evolved mind riddled with biases that skew perceptions and political thinking. But while our nature seems fallen by comparison with an imagined, Edenic ideal, it does not warrant the Right's pessimism any more than the Left's optimism. Our nature is Janus-faced: we have a competitive, selfish heritage from our distant simian forebears and a cooperative, group-focused heritage that emerged when our lineage diverged from that of chimpanzees. What separates our species from our closest relatives is an impressive ability to cooperate, but we still share much of their selfish and competitive instincts.

A diverse array of scientific studies provides an understanding of how the media[4] exerts political power. Unlike in the realm of law, where successful arguments are built on persuasive reasoning and the accumulated authority of judges and legislators, scientific study is constrained only by what we can observe. When a chemist says that two chemicals produce an effect if combined, we are not constrained to believe on the strength of the chemist's authority; we are invited to see for ourselves. Hence the motto of England's Royal Society: *nullius in verba*, "nothing in words" or "take no one's word for it." Not all science is as simple as chemistry, however; more complicated areas of study, like human societies, do not allow for pure experiments. There are always extraneous, uncontrolled factors in even the most careful social psychological experiment. And many social questions do not allow experimentation, in which case "science" refers to its older, broader definition: a systematic study that creates knowledge to explain or predict aspects of the world. Regardless, as much for chemistry as sociology, how we *interpret* science, and what our interpretations tell us about how we might better organize ourselves socially, politically, or economically, is open to debate. I mean to build here only a *prima facie* case for the power of media in politics, using the findings of scientists from several fields. Though I have not yet encountered one, a counterargument could be made that reinterprets the same findings, and others, weaving them into an opposing narrative that more satisfyingly explains the whole. (I would welcome such a counterargument, especially if it provides reassurance that democracy, in a form substantially faithful to its ideal of citizens sharing equally in political power, presently exists in the United States.)

To make this argument, first a theory of information in society—ideas, beliefs—is needed. The first chapter explores three such theories: social evolution, which ties *social* information to broader conceptions of information at the root of physical existence and the evolutionary process; schema theory, which conceptualizes how the human brain absorbs, processes, and stores information; and social representations theory, which explains and explores how large chunks of socially shared information disseminate through a population. These approaches cover three ascending levels, from the individual bit of information, to the information within an individual brain, to the sets of information widely shared within a society. Combining them, the resulting approach views ideas as bits of information that evolve and spread, in an ecology of information featuring selection pressures of various sorts: psychological, cultural, political-economic.

The first chapter explains why this perspective is reasonable, and what explanatory benefits it has for an understanding of politics. While it illuminates much about the realm of ideas, it cannot predict or even fully explain why some ideas spread widely and other ideas do not. This theoretical approach can only sketch the complex system that is the world of ideas or the ecology of information. But to understand the system overall, it is necessary to investigate the main forces in operation *within* the ecology of information.

The forces at play within the evolution of political ideas can be divided into categories of demand and supply. "Demand" encompasses everything about the human brain that makes some ideas likelier to be absorbed or accepted, retained and retransmitted. For example, memory would be a demand force or bias: *ceteris paribus*, a small amount of information is likelier to spread than a large amount. (Accordingly, the understanding of a "meme" as an entertaining picture-and-joke on the internet has spread further than the definition of the meme as the basic unit of the evolutionary algorithm as applied to the realm of ideas.) "Supply" encompasses any influence making some ideas likelier to be disseminated by the biggest supplier of information, the media (or smaller suppliers, from churches to schools). For example, libel laws are a supply force or bias: *ceteris paribus*, information that carries the risk of a libel lawsuit is less likely to be disseminated than information carrying no such risk.

To understand demand biases, we need to understand the human mind, how it evolved, and how its evolutionary history affects political cognition. To understand our psychology, the second chapter begins with the emergence of hominids, through the point when our species branched from our hominid cousins, to our development of sedentary agriculture and large civilizations. This chapter describes the marks evolutionary history left on our psychology, including our capacity for morality and political cognition. One of the most striking anomalies of human evolution was the emergence of large-scale cooperation (eusociality), a phenomenon common in ants and wasps but few other species. To produce this anomaly, unique ecological conditions were required and several psychological capacities had to develop. Once in place, these capacities produced their own ecology of human minds in which information (ideas, technologies, languages, and religions) could evolve. These distinct but interlinked evolutionary systems—the biological and the informational or ideational—have produced everything that makes us human. This includes political ideologies: gene-culture coevolution has produced predispositions—weak though they may be alone—that make some inclined toward left-wing ideas and others to right-wing ideas. That is, our genes help to produce a *psychological* Left and Right, or "elective affinities" toward certain ideas. Thereby, our evolutionary history lives on in the design of our minds, producing an "evolutionarily stable strategy" helping some ideas, practices, and institutions to persist (the psychological Right), while providing a laboratory of innovation for potential improvements (the psychological Left).

The third chapter examines more direct demand biases, exploring what the field of social psychology can tell us about our psychology on matters of social and political importance. Today's globally dominant political philosophy is liberalism, born before evolutionary theory and psychology. Liberalism's view of human capacities looks naïve today[5]: in contrast to the liberal assumption of human rationality, our psychology is ridden with irrational biases that interfere with an ideally rational way of learning and thinking about politics. This chapter focuses on biases likely to affect how we construct our political worldviews using the information about the outside world we receive from the media: from in-group bias to the system justification tendency. Even if our media systems were designed to offer an objective and bias-free *supply* of political information from diverse perspectives, demand-side biases may nonetheless distort the way information from the news media is received, processed, and remembered. Hence a democracy-appropriate media system must present information in a way that mutes or reduces our social-psychological biases.

Arriving at the question of media power, the fourth chapter surveys what we have discovered about how information moves from the news media into our minds. The conventional wisdom for decades in social science was that the media produces minimal effects on opinions. But if the theoretical approach laid out in the first chapter is correct, this cannot be: information is physical and must be transported from where it originates in political events, legislation, and research before it can reach our minds. As such, the media's effects simply cannot be minimal. The overwhelming weight of recent research demonstrates this: that the media has a pervasive sway on political opinions and understandings. From advertising and entertainment programming to the news, it shapes what we believe about the wider world. It can persuade, prime, frame, set the political agenda, and shape political opinions. It can facilitate or impede spirals of silence, ideological segregation and polarization, and the acquisition of political knowledge. While the media is far from a brainwashing "influencing machine" or a hypodermic needle capable of injecting ideas into our minds, it is nonetheless the greatest influence on public opinion, as it is the conduit through which the building blocks of public opinion are transported. Therefore, biases in the *supply* of information are likely to translate into biases in our political knowledge, from which we construct our understanding of the political world and act in it.

Whereas the second and third chapters examine the "demand side" of political information, the fifth chapter examines the "supply side." It investigates the political economy of media: the factors by which information is included in, or excluded from, the supply offered us by the news media. Regardless of whether we are perfectly rational or systematically biased, what determines the *supply* of information can affect the understandings we end up with. Beginning with a short history of the media and how it developed, this chapter concludes that while the media ideally should provide a free "marketplace of ideas" or an open public sphere, several political-economic forces frustrate that ideal. These include ownership concentration, an economic process of creative destruction currently light on creation, ideological bias, commercial and political pressures, and cultural and institutional influences. In combination, these supply-side biases produce a media system that not only fails to counteract our evolved psychological biases, but compounds them.

If the United States were the only country in the world, we could draw little from examining its media system: innate psychological limitations might make ideal conceptions of a public sphere or marketplace of ideas impossible dreams of political theorists. The variety of media systems globally allows us to compare their outcomes, further testing the causal link between the media and political ideas. The sixth chapter examines the ways different countries have designed and regulated their media systems. It traces differences between levels of political knowledge across countries to differences in how their respective media systems have been structured, particularly regarding the degree of commercialization and level of investment in public service media. These comparisons suggest best practices to make media systems better live up to the ideal role they should play in a democracy: providing a free, fair, and open marketplace of ideas.

Finally, the conclusion analyzes how deficiencies in the US media have translated into deficiencies in political practice. As people have often said about communism, democracy is a wonderful theory, but in practice it is doomed to failure—without a well-functioning media system.

The question of the media is of the utmost political importance. The news media is our lifeline to participation in the political realm; it is the telescope through which learn about our place in the universe, or the microscope through which we learn of what we are made. A network of salons, coffee shops, and a community of the literate comprised the first public sphere, which provided the impetus and the foundation for the rise of liberal democracies. Today, the public sphere has enlarged and diversified along with the franchise, and the modern mass media is its primary constituent. Dire social problems can be solved in a dictatorship, so long as the dictator is benevolent, well informed, and has the power to enforce policies. In a democracy, however, a majority of voters must be knowledgeable or problems can go unaddressed or intensify. Yet informed observers warn that "[t]he political ignorance of the

American voter is one of the best-documented features of contemporary politics..."[6] The invisible hand in our distorted marketplace of ideas is malfunctioning.

As *Homo sapiens*, we face dire political problems that may, if unaddressed, prove fatal. There are enough nuclear weapons on the planet to destroy most forms of life, and their use remains just one serious provocation or accident away. The threat of non-nuclear warfare is not so profound, yet one is hard pressed to find a war anywhere that is not a fundamentally senseless loss of life and cause of unjustifiable suffering. The way we organize ourselves economically is such that tens of thousands die every day due to lack of food, a mere distributional problem that nonetheless claims more lives in a day than terrorism does in a year. Meanwhile, even in those limited geographical areas favored by the global distribution system, where food grows on pace with asset prices, despair abounds with suffocating poverty amidst unprecedented wealth.

And then there is perhaps the greatest threat, climate change, jeopardizing the lucky condition in which our species encountered the world by threatening to make our planet uninhabitable (for us). Even without significant expertise in climate science, one cannot help but be impressed by the accumulated evidence and overwhelming scientific consensus. One has every right to be skeptical about any scientific theory, no matter how well supported, but serious criticism can only be made using the scientific method, proposing an alternate theory with even better evidentiary support. Even approaching climate science from a more skeptical perspective, the principle of precaution would urge us to take immediate steps to avoid even a *potential* harm of such magnitude. Yet, we do nothing—or what amounts to nothing. Increasingly, past predictions of climate scientists come to seem less alarmist, and more conservative—too conservative, as we quicken the process by which the planet becomes inhospitable, and *Homo sapiens* flirts with extinction.

Information, particularly a lack of information, lies at the heart of these problems. These problems are not information "all the way down"—they are more than merely a lack of information, there are resource constraints and psychological biases too. Yet, their solutions *could* all be based fundamentally on information. Voters *could* make immediate action on climate change a prerequisite for holding political office. With fuller information on the global economy, along with proposed reforms, voters *could* make devastating status quo policies taboo and put an end to the career of politicians without a serious reform proposal. Whether they *would* is another question; perhaps they would find criticisms of the proposed solutions more persuasive, accepting the belief that such proposals would only make things worse. But without mere *knowledge* of the proposals, they cannot do either. Without awareness of options, choice is impossible.

And for war, information is a prophylactic. For as long as Europeans have been known as Europeans, they have slaughtered each other (and non-Europeans) with regularity—only the justifications and weaponry change. Arguably, they have recently become civilized: witness over a half century of relative peace after the unsurpassed barbarity of World War II. And no explanation of *why* Europeans have not relapsed into mass, mutual slaughter could exclude *ideas*. Europeans are better educated than at any time in their history, and it is hard for an educated mind to be duped by rationalizations and justifications for risking one's life while killing unknown others. Today's Europeans disdain aggressive nationalism more than ever and have adopted pacifism to a reassuring extent.[7] The information contained in enough Europeans' minds has prevented the outbreak of that to which Europeans had formerly been as enthusiastically attached as they currently are to football: war.

Manuel González Prada wrote:

> Only a perverse morality can make us regard as bandits six shirtless men who hang about the outskirts of a city and as heroes six thousand uniformed outlaws who invade the neighboring country's territory to steal away lives and property. What is bad in the individual we judge to be good in the collectivity, reducing good and evil to a simple question of numbers. The enormity of a crime or vice transforms it into a praiseworthy action or into virtue. We call the robbery of a million "business" and the garroting of entire nations "a glorious deed." The scaffold for the assassin; apotheosis for the soldier.... When man leaves behind his atavistic ferociousness, war will be remembered as a prehistoric barbarity, and famous and admired warriors of today will figure in the sinister gallery of the devil's children, by the side of assassins, executioners, and butchers. Napoleon's skull will be stacked next to that of a gorilla.[8]

Unhappily, there is still quite a lot of museum space between gorillas and Napoleon. But this is not due to a perverse morality in which small crimes loom large while large crimes are transformed through moral algebra into glorious feats. That is, this flawed morality does not recognize its perversity: it views large crimes as the unfortunate but only-available means to accomplish great feats. And as the evidence discussed in the second chapter reveals, such a museum placement would be unfair to the gorilla: war is a relatively recent invention, and it is uniquely human. (Or nearly so—we share it in common with ants.)[9]

While early empires like the Roman[10] and Mongol[11] had ideological justifications of some divine sanction granted to the emperor or Khaqan, more recent empires have felt the need to excuse great crimes as the only available way to achieve a greater good.[12] Spain's empire in the Americas was vicious, but its defenders argued that it benefited Indians, civilizing them and saving their souls from eternal torment. Britain's blood-soaked empire was also a noble mission to bring the light of civilization to the barbarians; France eagerly adopted its own *mission civilisatrice*. Nazi Germany was merely trying to save Europe from contamination by inferior genes and Imperial Japan saving Asia from Western imperialism to create a prosperous East, guided by Japan like a wise father. Likewise, the United States merely promotes democracy, freedom, and open commerce. Later empires never seemed to engage in anything other than just, even selfless wars. (As Wyndham Lewis quipped, "what war that was ever fought was an 'unjust' war, except of course that waged by the enemy?")[13]

Why is it that the more recent, post-printing-press empires felt it necessary to present fairly simple power grabs as noble and selfless missions? Why not revel in one's superior power and the maxim that might make right? But no; such thoughts tend to be restricted to "the closed and hushed councils of power, or in the concealed psychological depths of individual men and women."[14]

The definitive reason may never be known, buried in millions of years of evolutionary history interacting with thousands of years of intellectual history and social evolution. But what is important is that for whatever reason—the psychological adaptations that arose to produce large-scale cooperation, and/or institutional and intellectual evolution—naked theft, murder, and exploitation are frowned upon. As Martin Luther King Jr. said, "[i]t seems to be a fact of life that human beings cannot continue to do wrong without eventually reaching out for some thin rationalization to clothe an obvious wrong into beautiful garments of righteousness."[15] But since doing wrong can be *individually* beneficial (or adaptive), this forms a selection pressure for ideas to rationalize and justify predatory behavior; yet in the ecology of the human mind, such rationalizations are always vulnerable to the predation of contrary, critical ideas. Who today accepts any of these empires' justificatory pronouncements? Who does not cringe when reading an imperialist's rationalizations, like this gem from Winston Churchill:

> I do not agree that the dog in the manger has the final right to the manger, even though he may have lain there for a very long time. I do not admit that right. I do not admit, for instance, that a great wrong has been done to the Red Indians of America, or the black people of Australia. I do not admit that a wrong has been done to these people by the fact that a stronger race, a higher grade race, a more worldly-wise race, to put it that way, has come in and taken their place.[16]

All but one of these empires fell apart, for a variety of reasons. But one is surely that the ideas undergirding those empires failed to gain and retain the consent of sufficient people—among the rulers or the ruled. As Marie von Ebner-Eschenbach put it: "but little evil would be done in the world if evil never could be done in the name of good."[17] Perhaps our increasingly interconnected societies are inching toward such a state where evil-in-the-name-of-good becomes too difficult to sell.

Hence the promise of a well-functioning media and the marketplace of ideas supports and maintains: through open intellectual competition, harmful ideas stand little chance of surviving for long. Few could disagree with John Stuart Mill that "[i]t is a piece of idle sentimentality that truth, merely as truth, has any inherent power denied to error,"[18] but one can hope that there is an ever-present selection pressure in the ecology of the human mind for ideas conducive to a better life for humankind. This is a hope, and fundamentally a guess—albeit, an educated one.[19] A desire to avoid human suffering and promote human happiness is not the *only* selection pressure, guaranteeing with the passage of sufficient time a beneficial outcome. Yet it is deep-seated, arising from the suite of adaptations that first created our species. If Antonio Gramsci could write about having pessimism of the intellect, but *optimism of the will* while dying in Mussolini's prisons, those reading this can afford to be hopeful too.

However, there is ample reason for the intellect's pessimism. The following chapters provide additional reasons, at least for any who comfort themselves with soothing ideas about how the media and democracy currently work. Yet even arch-pessimist Harold Bloom ends *The Lucifer Principle*, his iconoclastic romp through the cruelty and misery of human history, with a similar hope:

We must invent a way in which memes and their superorganismic carriers—nations and subcultures—can compete without carnage. We may find a clue to that path in science. A scientific system is one in which small groups of men and women cohere around an idea, then use the powers of persuasion and politics to establish that idea's dominance in their field, and to drive rival hypotheses – along with those who propound them – to the periphery.[20]

This is the promise of a *functioning*, free-marketplace of ideas. Such a possibility looks distant, but as this book will demonstrate, the evidence inclining us toward hope outweighs that tending toward despair. That is, *if* we keep in sight the timescale appropriate to social evolution.

Pierre Teilhard de Chardin was a Catholic priest, scientist, and theologian who crossed evolutionary theory—down (or up) to the ideational, cultural level—with Catholic theology.[21] He knew that whether we think of the future as pessimists or optimists, we intuitively consider only a time period corresponding to our lifetimes (or a year, or the next quarter). As such, the pessimists seem to have the upper hand. But Chardin pointed out that the better way to decide whether to be optimistic or pessimistic is to adopt a timeframe appropriate to social evolution:

> [H]alf a million years, perhaps even a million, were required for life to pass from the pre-hominids to modern man. Should we now start wringing our hands because, less than two centuries after glimpsing a higher state, modern man is still at loggerheads with himself? Once again we have got things out of focus. To have understood the immensity around us, behind us, and in front of us is already a first step. But if to this perception of depth another perception, that of *slowness*, be not added, we must realize that the transposition of values remains incomplete and that it can beget for our gaze nothing but an impossible world. Each dimension has its proper rhythm. Planetary movement involves planetary majesty. Would not humanity seem to us altogether static, if, behind its history, there were not the endless stretch of its pre-history? Similarly ... we cannot expect to see the earth transform itself under our eyes in the space of a generation. Let us keep calm and take heart.[22]

While keeping calm and taking heart is as good advice as having optimism of the will, the question is whether the "omega point" de Chardin described—a convergence with the Divine to which human evolution is purportedly directed—will come in the life, or death, of *Homo sapiens*.

Will our species take advantage of our exponentially increased ability to communicate and inform, or go extinct? In the absence of a benevolent dictator to guide us, our only chance is a free marketplace of ideas, a functioning public sphere. Let us hope we have time enough to create one.

NOTES

1. Some of these have been preserved in: Martha Cooper, *Remembering 9/11* (Brooklyn: Mark Batty Publisher, 2011).
2. Gore Vidal, *United States: Essays: 1952–1992* (New York: Broadway Books, 2001): 510, emphasis added.
3. Stephan Lewandowsky et al., "Misinformation, Disinformation, and Violent Conflict: From Iraq and the 'War on Terror' to Future Threats to Peace," *American Psychologist* 68, no. 7 (2013): 489.
4. Due either to the poverty of the English language itself or my impoverished ability to use it with unfailing accuracy, much of the discussion in this book will use words that imply intentionality to describe mindless processes, or aggregate outcomes of many conscious (and unconscious) choices none of which individually *intended* to produce the aggregate outcome. For instance, evolutionary "selection"—clearly, there is no actor, Nature, that consciously *selects* some traits or populations for survival and others for extinction. This is a problem that may lead to misinterpretation, as when Richard Dawkins' use of the word "selfish" to describe how mindless bits of DNA replicate led many readers to erroneously infer that our genes evolved to produce selfish individual organisms. Nowhere in this book, however, is language that often *implies* intentionality actually *meant* to suggest that conscious intent is in any way involved outside of human consciousness. On a less important note, I most commonly use the Latin loan word "media" in the singular, although in its original Latin it is plural. "The media" is meant to refer to the modern means of mass communication and the institutions that wield them: newspapers, magazines, radio, television, and the internet.
5. Shawn W. Rosenberg, "Against Neoclassical Political Economy: A Political Psychological Critique." *Political Psychology* (1995): 99–136; However, see also Olivia Newman, *Liberalism in Practice: The Psychology and Pedagogy of Public Reason* (Cambridge, MA: MIT Press, 2015).
6. Larry M. Bartels, "Uninformed Votes: Information Effects in Presidential Elections," *American Journal of Political Science* (1996): 194.
7. Raphael S. Cohen and Gabriel M. Scheinmann, "Can Europe Fill the Void in US Military Leadership?" *Orbis* 58, no. 1 (2015); James Sheehan, *The Monopoly of Violence: Why Europeans Hate Going to War* (London: Faber and Faber, 2008).

8. Manuel González Prada, "Priests, Indians, Soldiers, and Heroes," in *The Peru Reader: History, Culture, Politics*, ed. Orin Starn et al., 199–206 (Durham, NC: Duke University Press, 1995): 201–202.
9. Mark W. Moffett, "Ants & the Art of War," *Scientific American* 305, no. 6 (2011).
10. Clifford Ando, *Imperial Ideology and Provincial Loyalty in the Roman Empire*, Vol. 6 (Berkeley, CA: University of California Press, 2000): 19–48.
11. Michal Biran, "The Mongol Transformation: From the Steppe to Eurasian Empire," *Medieval Encounters* 10, no. 1–3 (2004): 340–341.
12. See, for instance, Anthony Pagden, *Lords of All the World: Ideologies of Empire in Spain, Britain and France c. 1500-c. 1800* (New Haven, CT: Yale University Press, 1995).
13. Wyndham Lewis, *Rude Assignment: An Intellectual Autobiography*, ed. Toby Foshay (Berkeley, CA: Gingko Press, 1984): 45.
14. Uday Singh Mehta, *Liberalism and Empire: A Study in Nineteenth-Century British Liberal Thought* (Chicago: University of Chicago Press, 1999): 87.
15. Martin Luther King Jr., "The Church on the Frontier of Racial Tension," mimeographed transcript taken from taped recording of address given by Dr. Martin Luther King Jr., as the James B. Gay Lectures (April 19, 1961): 2.
16. Quoted in Arundhati Roy, *War Talk* (Cambridge, MA: South End Press, 2003): 58.
17. Kuno Francke and Isidore Singer, eds, *The German Classics: Masterpieces of German Literature Translated into English*, Vol. 8 (New York: The German Publication Society, 1914): 435.
18. John Stuart Mill, *On Liberty* (London: Longmans, Green, and Co., 1865): 17.
19. For example, Hugo Mercier and Daniel Sperber, "Why Do Humans Reason? Arguments for an Argumentative Theory," *Behavioral and Brain Sciences* 34, no. 2 (2011).
20. Howard K. Bloom, *The Lucifer Principle: A Scientific Expedition into the Forces of History* (New York: Atlantic Monthly Press, 1997): 328–329.
21. See, for orthodox criticism, Scott Ventureyra, "Challenging the Rehabilitation of Pierre Teilhard de Chardin," *Crisis Magazine* (January 20, 2015).
22. Pierre Teilhard de Chardin, *The Phenomenon of Man* (New York: Harper & Row, 1959): 254–255.

CHAPTER 2

Information: Evolution, Psychology, and Politics

> "*The most merciful thing in the world, I think, is the inability of the human mind to correlate all its contents. We live on a placid island of ignorance in the midst of black seas of infinity, and it was not meant that we should voyage far.*"
> —H.P. Lovecraft, *The Call of Cthulhu*

Information has been evolving on earth for billions of years. While the naïve view of information is of something ethereal, formless, weightless, immaterial, and the rest, in reality information never exists outside of some physical substrate. César Hidalgo explains:

> …information *is* physical. It is as physical as Boltzmann's atoms or the energy they carry in their motion. Information is not tangible; it is not a solid or a fluid. It does not have its own particle either, but it is as physical as movement and temperature, which also do not have particles of their own. Information is incorporeal, but it is always physically embodied. Information is not a thing; rather, it is the arrangement of physical things. It is *physical order*, like what distinguishes different shuffles of a deck of cards.[1]

Information can exist in patterns of ink on paper, sound waves, electrical pulses, radio waves, magnetic flux patterns, neuronal connections, molecules, or notches on a stick. One theory of quantum physics even proposes that the most fundamental physical unit making up our universe is information.[2] At a physical level, information is the inverse of entropy or uncertainty. Information theory defines it as the reduction of uncertainty; the "information" transmitted by a landline or wifi signal is a reduction in the listener or recipient's uncertainty about some aspect of the world. The more information we have about a physical system, the less entropy there is, and the more uncertainty a message reduces, the greater its informational content.[3] Information's two meanings—as a reduction in uncertainty, a subjective state, and as a physical reality, the organization (non-entropy) of matter—combine into one when we discuss information in our daily lives. Information that reduces our uncertainty is physical, ordered matter; it can take many forms, from sound waves to neuronal connections, but information in both senses is physical.

However, *information* is distinct from *meaning*; information is what a book or fiber optic cable transmits, while meaning is the human interpretation.[4] Throughout the physical world, "meaning emerges from interactions between system states. If there are no interactions, there is no meaning. For meaning to be present, particular states of one system must have particular effects on another system"[5]—as when information we receive changes our behavior (e.g., when we read an article about a politician's history of corruption and vote for her opponent). Hence Henry Plotkin's insight that "adaptations are biological knowledge, and knowledge as we commonly understand the word is a special case of biological knowledge."[6] Everything in the biological (plants, animals) and intellectual (technology, ideas) realms is made of information—or "knowledge" in Plotkin's sense. The evolution of information in the biological realm accommodates slow changes in the environment (e.g., thicker fur in a steadily cooling climate), and the evolution of information in the intellectual realm accommodates faster changes (e.g., various types of warm clothing).[7]

For the majority of earth's history, the only form of information to have evolved was in the form of molecular organization, DNA and RNA. Over billions of years, this information has increased in amount and complexity through a simple process, the evolutionary algorithm: a mixture of variation, replication, and selection. Whenever these elements are found in a system, the inherited properties of the evolving entities will inevitably become ever more adapted to whichever criteria determine reproductive success.[8] (This does not mean "better"—only more adapted to often shifting criteria.) The evolutionary algorithm has shaped DNA and the history of life. Its three components are instantiated in biology by self-*replicating* molecules, which change and *vary* due to processes like random mutation, and are *selected* by their differential survival. At their core, DNA molecules are information, instructions for making proteins—and in the aggregate, they code for the development of everything from bacteria to blue whales, our bodies and minds.[9]

In a universe marching inexorably toward greater entropy, the evolution of information occurs only under certain circumstances, but when it does, it produces the opposite of entropy: ever-greater physical order.[10] Therefore, "[w]e can think of our planet as a little whirlpool of information in an otherwise vast and barren cosmos."[11] The requirements for information to evolve are energy flows in non-equilibrium systems like our planet, the storage of order in solids (which protect against entropy), and the ability of matter to process information or compute.[12] The ability of matter to process information is different from the simple order we find throughout the universe: in solar systems, crystals, waves, weather patterns, and other processes produced by physical and chemical laws.[13] The way matter processes information is the evolutionary algorithm, or the "engine of complexity," a mindless yet powerful means of producing greater order:

> All evolutionary systems rely on stored information, and all modify, add to, or delete from this body of information by following a well-defined information processing strategy. At the core of every evolutionary system is a probabilistic computation that has the remarkable property of extracting purposeful information from randomly occurring events. When this computation is employed to assemble instructions for making something useful, a positive feedback loop can be established in which any change in the instructions that causes an improvement in the structures or actions specified by the instructions serves as the basis for future improvements to the instructions and their outcomes.[14]

While the popular understanding of the evolutionary algorithm is usually traced to Darwin's *On the Origin of Species* in 1859, evolutionary approaches to information began nearly a century earlier with attempts to search for the origin and "common descent" of languages.[15] Six years before Darwin introduced biological evolution (or the evolution of biological information), German linguist August Schleicher published tree diagrams of languages to recreate a common ancestor of languages. Interestingly, one of the first people to recognize the importance of the evolutionary algorithm outside biology was the psychologist William

James, who noted a "remarkable parallel, which I think has never been noticed, obtains between the facts of social evolution on the one hand, and of zoological evolution as expounded by Mr. Darwin on the other."[16]

Before the twentieth century, the concept of "gene" did not exist; Darwin referred to "gemmules" as a theoretical unit of inherited biological information. Today, in the realm of social evolution, there is no universally accepted theoretical unit of information. Early anthropologists broke down aspects of culture into various units and studied their spread and evolution: Edward Burnett Tylor called them "institutions" and "customs"; Franz Boas "elements" and "traits of culture," and the empirical manifestations of such units "incidents"; the German diffusionists referred to "trait complexes," and conceived of traits as general ideas rather than specific empirical units; and A.L. Kroeber studied the diffusion and origin of "culture traits."[17] Today's research into social evolution (or cultural evolution) more commonly adopts the term "meme," finding it to be "a timely lable for an established and respected approach to the study of cultural evolution and transmission."[18]

The analysis of social evolution took a mistaken and harmful detour through the Social Darwinism of Herbert Spencer and particularly his followers. Instead of viewing social evolution as the joint product of biological evolution and the evolution of information in society, Social Darwinists viewed social evolution as merely the product of biological evolution writ large. Ironically, it was Social Darwinism's blindness to the importance of social information—and its ignorance of how environmental influences affect physiological and psychological development—that doomed the project. But before Social Darwinism became extinct, it spread virulently in the United States in the 1880s and '90s, receptive as that environment was to justifications for competition, individualism, territorial expansion, and plutocracy.[19] Its ties to eugenics and right-wing ideology in the early twentieth century made later attempts to apply evolutionary theorizing to the social realm anathema to many social scientists.[20]

Gabriel Tarde, possibly the first precursor of the modern view of social evolution, offered a cogent, contemporary criticism of Social Darwinists.[21] He perceived an unjustifiable conflation of biological and social evolution in their use of the term heredity: "They use this word indifferently to express the transmission of vital characteristics through reproduction and the transmission of ideas and customs, of social things, by ancestral tradition, by domestic education, and by custom-imitation."[22] In Tarde's view, like those today who study gene-culture coevolution, the evolution of biology and culture are separate and complementary. While the reactionary applications of Social Darwinism (eugenics, racism, militarism) have led many well-intentioned people to scorn evolutionary approaches to society, Tarde explained nearly a century ago why this is mistaken:

> But we may accord to the biological side of social facts the highest importance without going as far as to maintain that there is a water-tight bulkhead between different races…. Taken in this false and unjustifiable sense, the idea of race leads the sociologist who has taken it for a guide to conceive of the end of social progress as a disintegration of peoples who are walled about and shut off from one another and everlastingly at war with one another. This kind of naturalism is generally associated with a defence of militarism. On the other hand, if we take the ideas of invention, imitation, and social logic as a guiding thread, we are led to the more reassuring perspective of a great future confluence – alas, that it is not immediate – of multiple divisions of mankind into a single peaceful human family.[23]

In other words, while Social Darwinism views social evolution as the product of vicious survival of the fittest between different human "races," an accurate view of modern human evolution comprises two forms of evolution: one of biology and the other of ideas. And it is the evolution of ideas that promises not war and conflict, but confluence and cooperation.

Tarde's revolutionary perspective proposed that *ideas* are the principal "actors" in social phenomena. Ideas spread by imitation and counter-imitation and combine in novel mixtures to produce inventions, themselves imitated or copied. Ideas can be adopted through "substitution," a choice between alternatives (similar to a gene and its allele), or through "accumulation," a logical union of ideas. An idea's success is determined by the compatibility of that idea with the current environment of other ideas. Tarde even defined "reason" as a specific desire for coherence between accepted ideas.[24] That is, what a society considers reasonable—a selection mechanism—is merely that which does not contradict common ideas. Another selection mechanism Tarde notes is prestige, with ideas originating from or held by prestigious persons, classes, localities, or times spreading further. Interestingly, in modern democratic societies public opinion is cloaked with the same prestige formerly reserved for monarchs, such that the attraction of already-popular ideas is reinforced by the mere fact of their popularity—a phenomenon Tarde viewed with distrust. Moreover, Tarde's view of social evolution is not strictly teleological or deterministic, but probabilistic: just because ideas *could* be fruitfully combined, does not mean they will be. He illustrates with an example from ancient Babylon, which had books and bricks marked with the names of their makers using movable characters or stamps, yet without the thought of combining the ideas to create a printing press thousands of years ahead of its invention in China.[25]

Tarde adapted his evolutionary mechanism to explain political development. The conservative or right-wing faction maintains and conserves commonly accepted ideas, while the liberal or left-wing faction introduces newly combined or foreign ideas.[26] Both create a spiraling process in which the conservation of old, proven ideas gives way to the absorption and incorporation of new ideas, then the conservation of those ideas, and so on. Tarde wrote:

> The innovating party plays, then, in all of this, only a transitory, although an indispensable, part. It serves as a mediator between the spirit of comparatively narrow conservatism which precedes it and the spirit of comparatively liberal conservatism which follows it. (Consequently, traditionalism should no longer be opposed to liberalism. From our point of view, the two are inseparable.) *Without hereditary imitation*, without conservative tradition, any invention or novelty that was introduced by a liberal party would perish still-born, for the latter is related to the former like shadow to substance, or, rather, like a light to its lamp. The most radical revolutions seek to be traditionalised, so to speak, and, reciprocally, at the source of the most rigid traditions we find some revolutionary condition.[27]

Tarde's contemporary, Emile Durkheim, contested his view of social evolution as the aggregate of individual imitation, broadly conceived as encompassing education, copying ideas and behaviors, reading books and newspapers, etc.[28] For Durkheim, sociology could not be built up from the basis of inter-individual processes, because these were so little understood. Instead, Durkheim took a top-down approach, looking at collective influences operating on individuals: "Each social group really has a collective inclination for [an] act, quite its own, and the source of all individual inclinations, rather than their result."[29] Durkheim's notion of collective representations, rather than being spread individual to individual in an epidemiological process like imitation, involved already-commonly shared ideas in a community that help produce social cohesion. Tarde's ideas about imitation were a precursor to social evolution theory, and Durkheim's ideas were a precursor to Serge Moscovici's social representations. Today, there is no need for conflict between Tarde and Durkheim's progeny.

Tarde would be elated by the growth in cross-disciplinary work on evolutionary approaches to culture, and Durkheim might concede that the inter-individual processes that were so poorly understood are ready to provide the building blocks for a bottom-up view of society to complement his approach. This new research includes studies on the emergence of social learning, traditions, or proto-culture in nonhuman animals; the emergence of true cultural evolution among hominids during the Stone Age and its acceleration during the Upper Paleolithic period; the application of methodologies from evolutionary biology to social evolution and the parallels between biological and cultural evolution; and studies of "rational imitation" and "over-imitation" in children as the basis for the replication of cultural units of evolution.[30] Major advances have been made in evolutionary perspectives in sociology, archaeology, economics, international politics, and the social sciences more generally.[31]

The stage is set to develop what Lev Vygotsky outlined nearly a century ago:

> It is not, of course, that biological evolution has come to a stop and that the species 'man' is a stable, unchangeable, constant quantity, but rather that the basic laws and the essential factors which direct the process of biological evolution have receded to the background and have either completely fallen away or have become a reduced or sub-dominant part of new and more complex laws governing human social development. ... New laws, which regulate the course of human history and which cover the entire process of the material and mental development of human society, now take their place.[32]

1   MEMES OR SOCIAL EVOLUTION THEORY

"And is it not a dream which none of you remember having dreamt that built your city and fashioned all there is in it?"
—Khalil Gibran, *The Prophet*, "Farewell"

To understand the meme as a theoretical construct, we have to go back to the context in which it was introduced: in 1976 with Richard Dawkins' *The Selfish Gene*, a popularization of the theory that evolution acts only on the genetic (as opposed to the organism or group) level. The book tells an amazing creation tale, rivaling religious creation myths. It starts billions of years ago, when all of the matter in the universe was condensed in a small space of unimaginable density and temperature. Then, nearly 14 billion years ago, this mass of condensed, supercharged matter exploded, expanding into space. As it rushed out at incredible speeds, it aggregated into planets and stars, attracted by gravity into solar systems. On our planet, atoms were being attracted in different combinations, forming molecules. By the laws of physical attraction and repulsion, with influxes of concentrated energy in the form of sunlight, volcanic eruptions, and lightning, some combinations of atoms happened to make copies of themselves from the atomic and molecular matter bouncing into each other on a planet devoid of life. All it took was for one molecule or chain of molecules to arise that had the property of attracting bits and pieces of atomic material, which would then form into a replica of the original molecule: this was the first replicator. From this inauspicious beginning came biological evolution: great sequoias, dinosaurs, mushrooms, birds, whales, humans, and all the rest.

The evolutionary algorithm is the differential survival (selection) of imperfectly replicating (variation) entities displaying fidelity, fecundity, and longevity (retention)—and the algorithm is substrate-neutral, meaning that there is no reason it cannot be applied to a variety of domains.[33] In the biological domain, the self-replicating ancestors of DNA displayed fidelity (they would usually make accurate copies), fecundity (they made several copies, given the right raw material or molecular "food"), and longevity (they tended to survive long enough to make copies). Sometimes they replicated imperfectly. For the majority of flawed replications, the flaw or mutation was such that the resulting molecule could not, according to the laws of physics and chemistry, make additional copies. Those molecules would "die off" and drift into the lifeless sea. However, on some rare occasions, a copying error in a replicating molecule would result in a molecular structure that was still able to replicate. This is the "differential survival" part of the algorithm: some self-replicating molecules of different forms tended to make more copies. Some of these molecules may have been composed of more readily available atomic matter in their environment; others may have grown larger and more stable, allowing them to stay together longer. Whatever the case, at some point these self-replicating molecules evolved to build structures around themselves out of the available atomic material. The cell was born. Now, instead of self-replicating molecules flowing through the earth's oceans, accumulating atomic material out of which to make copies, there were self-replicating *cells*, carrying the descendants of the first self-replicating molecules: DNA. Single-celled organisms evolved into many-celled organisms, and multicellular organisms eventually evolved into animals and plants.

At the core of this creation, story is the evolutionary algorithm, a mindless process that guarantees results, given the right conditions.[34] However, rather than the evolutionary algorithm, the starring role in *The Selfish Gene* was given to the anti-hero pilot of massive biological robots, the gene. Hence, when Dawkins introduced the "meme" later in the book, many readers considered it a mere analogue of the gene, and its worth to hinge on the coherence of the gene-meme analogy. But as Susan Blackmore later described the most basic principle of meme theory: "genes and memes are both replicators but otherwise they are different."[35] Henry Plotkin adds that "all of memetic replication looks different from genetic replication: not much longevity except for core conventional meaning and startling detail; very little fidelity apart from simple memes; and a fecundity that probably varies from person to person as a result of differences in cognitive capacity yet to be understood."[36] Memetic evolution, while analogous to genetic evolution, is more complex.[37] This is where most criticism of meme theory flounders: by itself, the analogy to genetic evolution is inessential. What is essential is that the evolutionary algorithm or "complexity machine"— *in the abstract*—applies to information in the human mind as much as to information in DNA. They are separate instantiations of the same process, similar in some ways and different in others.[38] The evolutionary economist Stanley Metcalfe clarifies that this is not "intrinsically a matter of biological analogy; it is a matter of evolutionary logic. Evolutionary theory is a manner of reasoning in its own right, quite independent of the use made of it by biologists. They simply got there first...."[39]

A meme is the theoretical basic unit of informational/social evolution: it is information subject to the evolutionary algorithm and selected in a social environment. The meme is dizzyingly broad, encompassing a peculiar noise and a software virus; a chair, to your idea of a chair and instructions for making one; a joke, story, or technology. For large chunks of information like ideologies, legal arguments, and religions, "memeplex" can be used: a collection of self-reinforcing memes that tend to replicate together.[40] As a phenomenon for empirical investigation, the breadth of the meme concept threatens to make it useless; as Serge Moscovici warned about Durkheim's collective representations, "by attempting to include too much, one grasps little: grasp all, lose all."[41] However, for empirical investigations of memes, Pocklington and Best's definition avoids the problem of overbreadth:

> The appropriate units of selection will be *the largest units of socially transmitted information that reliably and repeatedly withstand transmission*. ... The two important characteristics of this definition are that a unit be large enough to exhibit properties that may covary with replication success and still be small enough to have robustly developing characteristics that reappear from host to host.[42]

2 What Meme/Social Evolution Theory Is Not

Critiques of meme theory have focused on the weakness of the gene-meme analogy.[43] This is a problem to the extent meme theory relies on analogy. But it is important to recognize that it is not a defining characteristic of the memetic perspective or theorizing about social evolution in general. What is important is that information in human society is subject to the evolutionary algorithm; even though there are significant differences between genes and memes, at the abstract level there are important ontological similarities.[44] Pierre Teilhard de Chardin observed that "[f]or a mind that has awakened to the full meaning of evolution, mere inexplicable similitude is resolved in *identity*,"[45] and Garry Runciman points out:

> Information is not a metaphorical term needing to be cashed into something else. It is the reality. Although much of the language of science is metaphorical and none the worse for it, there is no other thing for which theorists of cultural selection are using the concept of information transfer to stand proxy. However difficult it is, when behavior is the phenotypic expression of information transmitted by imitation or learning, to say what exactly are the units or bundles of information passing from mind to mind that are competitively selected (or not), their mutation and recombination are no less a matter of literal fact than when computer scientists splice the codes for programs, cross them over, and see how the consequences work themselves out.[46]

The evolutionary algorithm has been usefully applied to computer software, creating self-improving programs.[47] Prions, antibodies, and computer viruses are other examples of evolving replicators.[48] These illustrate the substrate-neutrality of the evolutionary algorithm: it works for genes, memes, immune systems, prions, computer software, and viruses.

Today, it is ironic that one of the most cogent original criticisms of the meme concept was that, unlike genes, memes are insufficiently discrete and separable to be subject to the evolutionary algorithm. Yet developments in genetics over the intervening years have left the gene nearly as fuzzy.[49] According to bioinformaticians Sonja Prohaska and Peter Stadler, "the classical molecular concept of a gene as a contiguous stretch of DNA encoding a functional product is inconsistent with the complexity and diversity of genomic organization."[50] Another criticism of the meme focused on a different discontinuity in the gene-meme analogy: the ability of memes to change before being passed on, making them, in a sense, Lamarckian evolutionary entities. Today, evidence of an ability of organisms to change their DNA during their lifetime has inspired heated debate in genetics, with bacterial geneticist James Shapiro arguing that "[t]he capacity of living organisms to alter their own heredity is undeniable," and that the use of the term "'gene' gives the false impression of specifying a definite entity when, in fact, it can mean any number of different genomic components."[51] So much for the gene-meme analogy being inapposite.

Developments in cognitive science and linguistics have strengthened one aspect of the gene-meme analogy: sexual recombination. Gilles Fauconnier and Mark Turner's (explicitly evolutionary) theory of conceptual blending shows how the human brain routinely takes aspects of two or more concepts and recombines them into something novel—as happens to the DNA of a mother and father during meiosis.[52] This explains a key source of variation in social evolution: ideas do not simply mutate to provide variants for selection, but also combine in admixtures. Examples abound: metaphors ("digging one's own grave"), analogies ("social evolution is like biological evolution"), counterfactuals ("if I were you, I would…"), category extensions ("animal rights," "computer virus"), and countless inventions originating from devices meant for different uses (the fork from the pitchfork).[53] Conceptual blending, like sex, is an important contributor of variation needed for the evolutionary algorithm to function.[54] Interesting or useful blends spread, whether in popular culture (Minotaurs, Spiderman), science (disciplines "blending" by adopting methodologies or perspectives from other disciplines, as in political psychology and global political economy), technology (smartphones blending telephones and computers), law (intellectual property), institutions (the *brigade de cuisine* blending French military organization with the operation of a kitchen), etc.

A more useful critique of meme theory focuses on transmission mechanisms and imitation. Here, as Dan Sperber indicates, a simple form of imitation is not how information is normally transmitted.[55] Information transfer is mediated by attributing intentions, making inferences, linguistic rules, evolved dispositions, and other processes that decode and reconstruct messages with varying success. And at the neuronal level, even cultural attributes cause different patterns of brain activity when making the simplest perceptual judgments.[56] Therefore, is the copying fidelity of information too low to support the evolutionary algorithm? This has been addressed from a practical perspective by archaeologist Stephen Shennan: "even though there may be all sorts of things going on in the mind, the resemblance between the inputs and the outputs is often very striking, as the example of the continuity in many prehistoric pottery traditions clearly demonstrates."[57] There is variation: from direct and easy imitation or information transmission (as with pottery traditions, technological know-how, recipes, etc.) to information resistant to direct transmission or imitation (as with feelings, culturally specific understandings, etc.). As the biophysicist John Mayfield explains:

> The engine of complexity [evolutionary algorithm] works on a body of information that is evaluated in some way, requires a mechanism for copying and modifying this information, and operates in an environment that provides consistent selection favoring some, but not all, of the modifications. Society as a whole and most social institutions examined separately exhibit all these features. Controversies arise over the nature of the information and the mode of copying, but it is not all that mysterious.[58]

To avoid the problematic nature of imitation, Robert Aunger suggests the meme be redefined as "the state of a node in a neuronal network capable of generating a copy of itself in either the same or a different neuronal network,"[59] or "a configuration in one node of a neuronal network that is able to induce the replication of its state in other nodes."[60] Viewing memes as nodes in a neuronal network helps reveal that even if there are copying errors or information loss during interpersonal communication, the central tendency of the copies will still float around the original meme. Therefore, on a population level, the original or normative meme will be dominant and copying fidelity is high enough for evolution to occur.[61]

A review of current neuroscientific research supports but complicates this view.[62] There is evidence of concepts being encoded by individual neurons—the localist, "grandmother" or "Halle Berry" cell theory, with one cell coding one concept—but the evidence is inconclusive. Better supported is that individual concepts are encoded in representations distributed through a neural network. Concepts are grounded in perception and action, and their storage is distributed across sensory and motor areas of the brain—meaning that our representation of concepts depends on idiosyncratic experiences. Even abstract concepts are stored in neural networks that include memory traces from our experiences: "Complementing sensory-motor representations, abstract concepts such as 'to free', but also 'truth' and 'relationship' are typically strongly associated with emotions and may also include introspective information about internal states experienced in corresponding situations (e.g., in a situation, in which an individual felt freed in the past)."[63] Thus, at a fundamental, neuronal level, information does get copied more or less accurately from individual to individual (close enough for jazz, or for evolution to occur at the population level). But that information may *feel* different from person to person, depending on the memories tied into its neuronal encoding. Hence the distinction between information and understanding or meaning: two people may have the same information, yet understand it differently.[64]

Regardless of inter-individual differences in storing information, developments in our understanding of "mirror neurons" have supported the memetic view.[65] Although mutations are far more common in memetic than biological evolution, this does not make memes or social information an impossible candidate for the evolutionary algorithm.[66]

3 What Social Evolution Theory Provides

What is important about the meme concept is not that it represents a radically new scientific theory with testable predictions and surprising results. Memetics as a research paradigm, with its unique methodologies, has not yet achieved great,[67] only modest,[68] success. One can reasonably reject ontological claims of social evolution theory about the meme, remaining agnostic about the evolutionary process in the realm of culture and society. Nonetheless, the memetic perspective is valuable as a *perspective*. (As one philosopher put it: "Ontologies are jealous, exclusive. Points of view are not.")[69] It replaces our implicit, unexamined view of knowledge: it feels as though we have sought out the best, most accurate ideas and beliefs, as if we stood atop an intellectual Mount Olympus, with all ideas, beliefs, and ideologies within view, and picked among them according to our own (impeccable) taste and judgment. In contrast, the memetic perspective is explicit and humbling, reminding us that beliefs and knowledge are contingent on information we have been taught, indoctrinated with, or learned independently—at the least, the information we *have been exposed to*—and that there is no guarantee that it corresponds with the reality it purports to describe. This cuts through needless obfuscation and intellectual anachronisms to get at the key constituent of culture, politics, and social organization: information. This perspective teases us into looking at information as an agent that spreads through the human population, subject only to the constraints of the social and physical environment. And as an agent, one does not have to be Josef Goebbels to know that information is powerful.

Presently, "meme theory" may largely be a "mere superimposing of a new language on old insights."[70] Yet it has epistemological value, and it offers a hypothesis of the origin and development of human culture and the intellectual world. Philosophy has been somewhat silent on how we, a young species, came to have so many ideas in such a short time. Parmenides argued that change is impossible, so that in a sense all ideas must have always existed; Plato believed that at least some ideas were eternal.[71] Descartes and Leibniz thought some ideas are innate, which is reminiscent of Plato's view of knowledge as a recollection of ideas forever present in our souls.[72] Western philosophy has been reliant since its inception on the concept of the "soul," a spiritual or magical entity outside of the physical realm and responsible for conscious thought. Owen Flanagan explains that for most of Western history, "[m]inds and souls, not being physical, were not a proper object of scientific study"[73]—so they were left to the philosophers, who until recently were enjoined to reason in accordance with religious dogma, including the concept of the spiritual soul that creates ideas out of thin air. If we posit this hypothetical entity, we can facilely explain the development of a staggering array of ideas since our hunter-gatherer days in Africa. However, if we do not posit a spiritual or magical soul, our only explanation is the human brain, and we are left with the options of either merely ascribing to it the abilities of the soul[74] or deferring the question until (hopefully) neuroscience and psychology can answer it. Hence, to paraphrase Churchill, social evolution theory may be the worst explanation of how our species came to have such a wealth and diversity of ideas; except for all the others. Not only does social evolution theory explain the development of ideas in a manner consonant with available evidence and without resort to magic, but it is the only tentative explanation that answers, however provisionally, the question of why our intellectual realm is so densely and diversely populated.[75]

Social evolution theory offers a hypothesis for how our species developed such large brains with the capacity for culture and cultural evolution.[76] Models of evolutionary processes demonstrate that in an environment of memes with positive and negative fitness consequences, genes for increased imitative ability are progressively favored (even when such ability, if it requires larger brains, entails reduced fitness due to greater metabolic requirements and increased maternal mortality during childbirth). As imitative ability increases, a "mimetic transition" tipping point is reached, when brains have evolved an imitative capacity such that memes can spread like epidemics. This point may have been reached approximately 120,000 years ago, when evidence for cultural diversification accumulates first in Africa and then elsewhere as *Homo sapiens* spread throughout the planet.[77]

Also, as the critic Maria Kronfeldner suggests, the meme concept can serve and is serving a bridging function between disciplines, facilitating the cross-disciplinary study of social evolution.[78] The simplicity and all-encompassing breadth of the meme provides a common vocabulary for varied disciplines to share information and perspectives. It also anchors social evolution in a metaphor with biological evolution, which—while unnecessary—may help to keep the former from straying from the confines of the evolutionary algorithm. Most importantly, social evolution theory and the meme concept require us to recognize the physicality of information. One can choose to reject everything else about the social evolution perspective save the physical basis of information, and the resulting need to think in terms of information logistics and transportation.

4 Schemas

The concept of the "schema" overlaps considerably with the meme, yet in subtle but important ways, it is both narrower and more inclusive. The schema is a generic, abstracted knowledge structure, which also contains specific instances. ... [It is] an active, constructive process, rather than a veridical copy; abstraction over instances, rather than a collection of raw data; structure based on experience, rather than determined wholly by genetic factors or by the current environment; and organization in the service of adaptive efficiency, rather than accuracy.[79]

Schemas, like memes, come in as many forms as there are types of information relevant to human beings.[80] As a psychological construct, the schema is not pure, disembodied information, but *embodied* information. As such, many schemas are inseparable from emotion: we do not just think of "fear" abstractly, we think of "fear" and unavoidably *feel* it, however fleetingly. Schemas are conceptualized, unlike memes, as laden with affect.[81] Like memes, schemas are largely conceptual, encoded in the brain but lacking a precise description of that encoding. Schema theory is more concerned with the processes and dynamics of knowledge representations in the brain than their neurological basis. Neither is it concerned with a theoretical narrative explaining the development and modification of schemas. If social evolution is a theory in search of a unit of measurement, the schema is a unit of measurement in search of a theory.[82]

"Schema theory" may be weak on theory, but its empirical results are strong. The schema concept helps explain how we process information and guide its retrieval from memory.[83] For instance, reading someone's biography and then being told the person was a member of a social category makes us remember more information from the biography consistent with our schemas for that social category—in fact, it makes us more likely to "remember" schema-consistent information that was actually absent from the biography. In one experiment, experts and novices in baseball were asked to read a description of one half-inning and then tested for memory of it.[84] Although baseball experts and those who knew little had similar memory ability, baseball experts incorporated the information about the half-inning into their baseball schemas. As a result, they remembered more important details and recalled events in the correct order. The baseball novices remembered peripheral details, such as the weather, and failed at recounting the half-inning.

The effects of schemas on memory fit into five categories: selection, abstraction, interpretation, integration, and reconstruction.[85] Selection effects occur when information relevant to currently held schemas is better remembered than irrelevant information. Abstraction effects occur when we remember the gist, rather than full content, and the gist we tend to remember comprises schema-consistent information. When we try to recall details of messages that do not fit our schemas, we tend to make them up by providing inferences from our schemas. Interpretation effects occur when distortions and additions to information are encoded in memory. Integration effects occur when different pieces of information are combined into a unified schema, sometimes distorting and modifying it. Finally, reconstruction effects occur during the process of remembering rather than encoding, when we fabricate memories out of partial recollection and our general knowledge (schemas) of cause, effect, intention, attitudes, and theories.

In addition to affecting memory, schemas guide our attention to stimuli. For instance, when reading the Bible, those with extensive Calvinist schemas are likely to be drawn to the Parable of the Talents, whereas those with extensive schemas representing gross social inequalities are likely to be drawn to the Sermon on the Mount. Schemas sometimes direct attention to schema-*in*consistent information, unlike in the case of memory recall, where schemas direct attention to schema-consistent information.[86] Hence, the Calvinist reading the Sermon on the Mount may focus intently on it, to explain it away, and make it compatible with their schema that wealth is a sign of divine approval. Although relatively little research has been done on how schemas are developed, it may occur in situations where incoming information is not consistent with existing schemas and it is important to us.[87] When incoming information is difficult to categorize by schemas, and it is relatively unimportant, we shoehorn it into existing schemas, modifying or distorting in the process. However, when we encounter schema-inconsistent information that *is* important, we engage in more bottom-up, data-driven processing, attending to the details of the information rather than unconsciously categorizing it with reference to our schemas. These may be the situations in which we create new schemas.

The schema concept has been applied in fields other than psychology. In anthropology, schema dynamics have been used to explain how information is distorted during transmission from speaker to hearer, according to the hearer's schemas. In one experiment, American listeners of Eskimo stories tended to systematically distort the stories to better fit their cultural schemas of story structure.[88] This suggests an important wrinkle to the idea of memes spreading via imitation: transmitted information will be warped by the gravitational pull of recipients' schemas. In political science, schemas have been used to explain how citizens absorb political information from the media.[89] Those with well-developed political schemas are likelier to remember schema-consistent information (a Republican politician announcing support for a typical Republican policy), but also to misremember schema-*in*consistent information (a Democratic politician taking stereotypically Republican, hawkish foreign policy positions).[90]

Schema research, by focusing on salient and relevant bits of information of small to intermediate size and illustrating the dynamics affecting the use, processing, and storage of information, elaborates on the sparse picture painted by the meme concept. As Elizabeth Rice explains, schemas "represent more than mere descriptive devices; 'schema theory' is a theory of the comprehension process. Considerable research has already been undertaken into the role of [schemas] in the assimilation of information, in information storage and memory, and in recall and reconstruction."[91] Hence, schema and meme theory may be fruitfully combined: The meme foregrounds the informational and evolutionary nature of knowledge, and the schema foregrounds how such information is processed by our not-computer-like brains, explaining an essential part of the ecology in which memes evolve.

5   Social Representations

"[W]hat is very much lacking in social psychology today is concern with the strife of ideas."
—Serge Moscovici, "Ideas and Their Development"

Like schema and meme theory, social representations theory has been criticized as "mushy" and imprecise.[92] A similar critique of "they merely describe, but do not explain" shadows these different yet (implicitly) related perspectives. This may be less a weakness and more a truism about the inherent difficulty of subjecting social information to scientific scrutiny.

Schema and social representations theories concern social information; that is, information generated by (and relevant to) social interactions.[93] Like schemas, social representations also conceptualize information in memory with an organizational structure, explore cognitive shortcuts or heuristics, and examine the affective, emotional dimension. These similarities are expected, given the mélange of ideas and processes social representations takes as its focus. Social representations is an "open" theory that welcomes diverse methodologies and can be described as an all-encompassing concept, as it includes other psychological concepts like values and attitudes.[94]

The structure and function of schemas and social representations are also similar.[95] Schemas are organized around an exemplar or prototype, and social representations center on a nucleus or core. Both have effects outside of conscious awareness: schemas shape or distort incoming information and social representations affect judgment without thinking— much as "common sense" is rarely examined.[96]

There are, however, fundamental differences, particularly in scope. While schema theory encompasses more of the realm of information than social representations (due to the latter's restricted focus on *socially* generated, shared, and efficacious information), social representations theory encompasses more of the psychological realm. For social representations, psychological phenomena explain how socially shared information is formed and affects society. Information that comprises a social representation is also a schema, but some bits of information that comprise schemas may not be part of any social representation. Alternatively, the social psychology of in-group bias or system justification is outside schema theory's scope, but can form part of an explanation of how social representations operate.

More fundamental is the dissimilarity between focusing on the individual and social levels.[97] As Augoustinos and Innes explain:

> Unlike social schema research, social representations research does not limit itself to the study of simple cognitive structures but is predominantly concerned with complex cognitive structures such as belief systems and cultural value patterns. As such, it is a much more ambitious theory necessitating multidisciplinary endeavours.[98]

There are two implications. First, social representations theory concerns only socially shared groups of interrelated ideas. Second, this socially shared nature necessitates a larger fundamental unit than the schema. For instance, small chunks of information comprising simple ideas like "bicycle" or "chess" may be of interest in schema theory, but social representations theory concerns larger chunks of information, like belief systems, cultural values, even ideologies.

Social representations theory also helps fill in a gap left by schema research: how knowledge representations are formed.[99] The individualistic focus of schema theory might imply that as we pass from childhood to adulthood, we generate knowledge based on our experiences, but this is intuitively unsatisfying. Social representations theory (like social evolution) instead posits that the shared understandings and knowledge of our society are transmitted over the course of our development, rather than generated individually.

In 1961, Serge Moscovici introduced his theory of social representations in a study of psychoanalysis and how it was represented among segments of French society. His methodological pluralism (interviews, surveys, media content analysis) has characterized the field ever since.[100] This case study elaborated a theory not only of psychoanalysis or other scientific paradigms, but all social representations whatever their content: scientific, ideological, political, cultural, etc. Although Moscovici was reticent to provide a straightforward definition of a social representation, he explains more clearly what they *do*: they simplify and standardize sciences, ideologies, value systems, etc. whose full informational content may only be barely known by the masses, thereby "[r]esolving problems, giving social interactions a form, and supplying a mould for behaviors...."[101] That is, social representations are widely disseminated, abridged versions of anything from scientific disciplines to economic theories. In their full form, the latter are interrelated complexes of ideas comprising massive amounts of information, while their social representation variants (which are much more common among members of a society) significantly economize information. In some cases, these abridged versions are faithful to the gist of what they represent; sometimes, they are significantly distorted.

In a later article, Moscovici offered a broader definition focusing on function: "Social representation is defined as the elaborating of a social object by the community for the purpose of behaving and communicating."[102] Wagner and Hayes provide a more comprehensive, two-part definition of a social representation as the

> (a) structured, (b) cognitive, affective, evaluative and operative, (c) metaphorical or iconic 'portrayal', of (d) socially relevant phenomena. These can be 'events', 'stimuli' or 'facts' (e) of which individuals are potentially aware and which are (f) shared by other members of the social group. The commonality between people represents (g) a fundamental element of the

social identity of the individual. ... Second, the term 'social representation' identifies the process of the origin, change and elaboration of the iconic portrayal of things in the discourse of social groups....[103]

Most importantly, the abridged, widely disseminated social representations of large bodies of information like scientific theories and political ideologies exercise at least as much social power as the theories or ideologies in their "pure" form. Moscovici emphasized:

> the representation, and the attention it draws to psychical, physical or collective phenomena by functioning as a framework for the interpretation of those phenomena, becomes one of the constituent factors of reality and social relations. ... [T]hose relations and that reality are not 'concrete' on the one hand and 'represented' on the other. Their interweaving is total, and the analytic distinction between the two is fragmentary and artificial.[104]

For example, of what value is the distinction between the social representation of Catholicism—Catholicism as understood by large social groups—and Catholicism "proper" as understood by a theologian? The theologian would see more than an artificial distinction, but a social psychologist interested in organized collections of ideas on a population level would not. The "proper" view of Catholicism would entail a rejection of birth control, for instance, but the social representation for a majority of Catholics in the United States does not.

Moscovici also describes two processes involved in the genesis of social representations: objectification and anchoring. Objectification occurs when the abstract concepts of a science or ideology are made concrete, such as when the complexes and neuroses of psychoanalysis became commonly understood as diseases, just of a psychological sort. Anchoring occurs when such abstract concepts are inserted into a society's hierarchy of values, changing how things are *done*.

Apart from how these shared representations develop, Moscovici examined three patterns in how representations are spread via the media. These corresponded to the ideologies and goals of the media sources vis-à-vis the social representation they were spreading. For the mainstream commercial press in France, psychoanalysis posed no threat; rather, it was of increasing interest in intellectual circles and could be used to attract potential customers. Their approach Moscovici termed "diffusion," a conservative process characterized by neutrality, a lack of clear intentions, and no sustained orientation. The Catholic Church and its press organs, instead, viewed psychoanalysis as variously threatening and admissible. The way the Church disseminated a social representation of psychoanalysis was termed "propagation:" it sought to integrate psychoanalysis into its frame of reference and to sway society into adopting its preferred representation. Lastly, the Communist Party of France and its press organs viewed psychoanalysis as an inassimilable threat. Not only did psychoanalysis deny the materialist basis of reality, but explained social ills not as the result of class exploitation, but individual maladaptation to a presumably healthy society; furthermore, its popularity in the imperialist United States suggested it was a device to extend bourgeois hegemony. Therefore, the Communist press disseminated its own social representation of psychoanalysis Moscovici labeled "propaganda," an action- and goal-oriented elaboration of one group's representation of an object of conflict.

In an explanation of the importance of a social representations approach to political psychology, Elcheroth and colleagues observe, "what shapes social behavior is shared social knowledge."[105] That is, information shapes social, including political, behavior, and makes social life what it is. The social representations perspective implies respect for the power of "mere" ideas in people's heads. This recognizes that what gives ideas power is their shared, social nature and the individual knowledge of the fact that they are shared. "The biblical writer was already aware of this when he asserted that the word became flesh; and Marxism confirms it when it states that ideas, once released amongst the masses, are, and behave like, material forces."[106]

For example, in a study of social representations of economic issues, the unemployed tended not to identify their plight with other unemployed people; rather, they distinguished between the unemployed as a group (jobless as a result of unwillingness to work, unreasonable demands) and their own situation (blaming outside factors).[107] This illustrates the difficulty the jobless face organizing to protect their interests and improve their situation: their representation of the unemployed as a group is derisory and does not even include themselves. A study of social representations about capitalism in Western versus (formerly socialist) Eastern European nations found intriguing differences.[108] For instance, representations of "the market" in Britain and France had prominent positive (allowing freedom) and negative (imposing one's will on others) connotations, while representations in the formerly socialist Czech Republic and Poland had more uniformly positive connotations. Overall, the study detailed interesting correlations between countries' historical experiences with a capitalist economy and their people's social representations of it. A study of social representations in Israel described the development of a "siege mentality" deriving from representations of the Holocaust and anti-Semitism, which influenced the interpretation of Arab states' hostility to Israel ("it is similar to the preconditions for the Holocaust") and of the rest of the world's support for the Palestinians ("it is similar to historical forms of anti-Semitism").[109] The acutely felt need for security produces a selective receptivity to information: existing knowledge remains frozen and information about Palestinians' parallel needs for security is not absorbed. Hence, calls for the establishment of an independent Palestinian state are viewed as the first step in an encirclement and ultimate destruction of Israel. Across national and cultural contexts, social representations of history influence how people react to political developments.[110]

Another study applied a social representations approach to explain how Slobodan Milosevic's government cultivated ethnic distrust leading to war.[111] Shortly before war broke out in 1991, social representations of ethnicity in the former Yugoslavia had been characterized by positive views of "the other," particularly in the most multiethnic regions. However, what mattered most were not individual attitudes or the aggregate of individual attitudes, but social representations about interethnic hostility. At first, media campaigns to foster and stoke interethnic tensions were treated skeptically. But as politically organized violence *created* what propaganda had only *claimed*, people either relied on their individual representations of the ethnic "other" or based their actions on newly dominant *social* representations.[112]

Political battles today are largely won and lost in the public sphere, where information is power, public opinion the judge, and the winners are those whose version of reality is predominant. As Caroline Howarth explains:

> [c]ertain groups have different degrees of access to the public sphere and have different means with which to present and/or contest particular claims to 'the real'.... Those who 'win' the battle over meaning and so the social construction of reality ... are those whose versions of reality are, or come to be, reified and legitimized as what is socially accepted as 'reality'.[113]

While individualist, cognitivist research (including research on genetic correlates with political opinions) has its place, the social nature of politics requires a psychology emphasizing the social.[114]

6 MEMES AND SCHEMAS IN SOCIAL REPRESENTATIONS

"When one looks at the variety of representations in existence, one is struck by two things: man's obstinate rediscovery and reiteration of the same themes and his extraordinary prolificness in inventing ideas, urged on by a poetic instinct. A troubling phenomenon, for it sometimes looks as though neither society nor the individual were in full control of this invention. Perhaps an intrinsic power of the mind has been unleashed."
—Serge Moscovici, "The Myth of the Lonely Paradigm: A Rejoinder"

Although all share similarities, memes are pure information, schemas are information plus individual psychology, and social representations include information and social psychology. Of the three, social representations theory is the most concerned with the effects of ideas on people and society, while some social evolution theory is so taken with a vision of ideas as evolving abstract-entities-cum-agents that social structure and dynamics fade from view. As an evolutionary explanation of how humans evolved such a diverse and immense intellectual universe, the meme's eye view is breathtaking, but makes it hard to discern what is going on in society.

What Moscovici wrote about the schema could be applied to the meme: "it refers to a simplified representation and is less rooted in the social world."[115] Social representations theory excludes ideas too rare, unincorporated into a meaningful whole, or marginal to have social significance. Social representations are "holomorphic"—individual instances are functionally related as a part of the whole in a society—while individual representations can be "idiomorphic," idiosyncratic and largely unshared ideas held by individuals.[116] Social representations are composed of memes, but not all memes comprise a social representation. The ideas Jesus had were memes, but after his death formed a social representation that dramatically spread and evolved.

Owing to their common core—information—memes and social representations exist in human minds and in recording media.[117] Moreover, social representations are dynamic, mobile, plastic, and interdependent[118]—a description consonant with memes in their ecology. While describing the genesis of his concept of social representations in *Psychoanalysis: Its Image and its Public*, Moscovici introduced Kenneth Boulding's *The Image* as "a fascinating little book,"[119] and summarized Boulding's "image" concept in similar terms to the meme, only without the evolutionary theory. In illustrating the "image" concept, Boulding anticipated Richard Dawkins' meme-gene analogy by a decade:

> There is a close analogy here between the image and the gene. ... [I]t is by no means fanciful to argue that the automobile and other human artifacts are produced as a result of a genetic process in which an image plays somewhat the same role as the gene does in the biological world.[120]

Although after introducing the "image" Moscovici distinguished it from social representations, its imprint is clear from a subsequent passage reminiscent of memes: "It is as though they [experts' articles, books, lectures] were genes and atoms that circulate in our images, words and arguments."[121]

Dan Sperber's epidemiology of representations provides an ideal starting point for an incorporation of social evolution theory into social representations research. Sperber starts from the proposition that the same human mental capabilities that evolved to support culture must influence its content and organization.[122] In addition, existing representations influence the spread of other representations, and the available information technology will also affect the spread of representations. For instance, in a non-literate society without writing technologies, representations that spread will be limited to those easily memorized. Moreover, a representation that sharply conflicts with a prevalent representation is less likely to spread. And representations that fit well with evolved predispositions in the human mind are favored: representations of dangers in the environment and how to avoid them or representations that facilitate cooperation.

Second, he posits that the study of the spread of representations will focus on their transformation rather than replication or reproduction in the sense of precise copying. This owes to the fact that shared information is generally *reconstructed* rather than reproduced in the recipient's mind. Hence, an epidemiology of representations will more often have to explain why some representations become so widespread and stable as to become cultural, unlike epidemiology of disease, which only occasionally has to explain why some diseases transform during transmission. For political and scientific ideas, the stability and fidelity with which they are transmitted are likely due to information technologies that promote stable replication. Third, just as epidemiology is not an independent science covering an autonomous reality, neither is an epidemiology of representations: epidemiology studies the distributions of diseases, studied in turn by pathology. So must an epidemiology of representations have a similar relationship with the psychology of thought, for instance, schema theory (including an evolutionary psychology of innate schemas). They ought to have a relationship of mutual relevance and partial interpenetration. "[P]sychology is necessary but not sufficient for the characterisation and the explanation of cultural phenomena. Cultural phenomena are ecological patterns of psychological phenomena."[123]

Like Runciman's theory of cultural and social selection, Sperber's epidemiology of representations acknowledges that in modern societies, institutions are powerful influencers of the spread of memes and social representations. This is particularly the case in the spread of political ideas. Of all ecological factors (like already-widespread memes and social representations), institutions play the most important role in explaining the distribution of political beliefs. Institutions do not only affect the spread of representations, but are constituted by representations: "*an institution is the distribution of a set of representations which is governed by representations belonging to the set itself.*"[124]

To illustrate, Sperber cites the political belief that all men are born equal.[125] This is a reflective belief (or meme) and, unlike an intuitive belief or myth, was consciously originated by a few philosophers and deliberately spread through communication. It was likely understood in different ways, which helped it spread in different cultural ecologies. The most important factor was its visceral relevance to societies organized on the basis of birthrights, particularly to those of "low birth" or no title. There was, however, a serious risk in spreading this belief. And this risk originated in the institution of the aristocracy and monarchy, themselves composed of representations justifying their social role and giving them power—including the power to execute would-be revolutionaries, traitors, and regicides inspired by the belief that all men are equal and that society should be restructured to reflect such. The holders of the contrary, older belief in rank by birth eventually lost out, however, and their institutions fell apart along with the representations that supported them. (This, of course, also involved an immense amount of political action by adherents of both beliefs.)

Pléh illustrates the same point in the context of recent Chinese history in one pithy and evocative sentence: "The little Red Book of Chairman Mao was certainly cognitively easy to absorb, however, in the diffusion of its representations a more decisive role was played by a certain type of human ecology."[126] And so too did the representations in the little Red Book spread to saturation in Chinese society, driving contrary representations to near-extinction along with the institutions they upheld. The key to the success of such representations is the ecology of information: political, economic, psychological, religious, technological, geographical, and other factors that affect the spread of ideas.

Where does this leave the schema? It is an individual-psychological bridge between the purely informational meme and the exclusively *social* representation. Schema research fleshes out the psychological dynamics of meme acquisition, modification, and interaction within the individual mind. It fills in important details about how human psychology affects the ecology of information in which memes spread and social representations take shape.

Synthesizing these theories of information allows us to begin mapping a society's ecology of information: the variety of competing and complementary forces making some memes likelier than others to spread into human minds, determining what social representations can form. The ecology of information, like natural ecologies, is unlikely to be dominated by any one force or influence.[127] Still less can scientific "laws" apply—ecologies are complex systems impossible to accurately predict. Roy Bhaskar's application of scientific realism to the social sciences is relevant: in complex, open systems like information ecologies, statements of *laws* are unlikely to obtain and are more accurately conceived as *tendencies*, which "may be possessed unexercised, exercised unrealized, and realized unperceived (or undetected) by men; they may also be transformed."[128]

For instance, research has found that upbeat, high-arousal and surprising, useful, or interesting news stories are likelier to spread (go viral) on social media.[129] This is human psychology shaping the ecology of information. Take the regularity with which global economic elites have preferentially adopted economic ideologies supportive of their privilege. (The Frederick Engels of the world are exceptions proving the rule.) A specific ecology of information is at play: among other factors, self-interest makes policies beneficial to one's class more attractive, especially when such policies are congenial to one's ideology (itself built over a lifetime of ideational and experiential influences); additionally, homophilous social networks not only reinforce similar ideas but serve as a reference group from which to make judgments about economic policy for society.[130] When one's neighbors and friends are doing well, it can seem like *everyone* is.

From a three-level meme, schema, and social representation view, Sperber's illustration would look something like this. As a result of the interactions of ideas and representations in the heads of philosophers, the meme of human equality evolved. It spread through conversations and writing, facilitated by how it was viewed as beneficial to a majority in highly stratified societies ordered by birthright. It mutated as it spread, depending on the schemas of those to whom it spread. Here, it became a belief in the equality of light-skinned European males—especially in European minds with highly developed racial status schemas—there it became the belief in equality of all human beings—in minds without such schemas, and with experience-based schemas of being powerless in society, attached to sharp negative emotional affect. As it spread and accumulated a body of related ideas, arguments, and elaborations, it was shared sufficiently to be a social representation. It came to compete with other social representations extolling (and shaping behavior to create) the contemporary social structure. At this point, the social representation preferring a society of equality had dispersed disproportionately to different social groups—probably mostly among the bourgeoisie and some of the peasantry. Here, the competition between it and the social representations upholding the old society became a power struggle between the respective social groups adopting them. The battle of social representations was not only a struggle between bits of information for replication, but also between social groups motivated by conflicting representations. With the victory of the bourgeoisie, new institutions formed on the basis of their ideas, and their social representations spread to saturation within society.

Wagner and Hayes' discussion of the intransitivity of explanations is relevant here.[131] For example, while it is true that everything operates according to the laws of physics, it would make no sense to *explain* something like one's choice of a friend by physical laws. The matter comprising human bodies and minds may be subject to the laws of physics, but at each progressively higher or more complex level of organization, from chemistry, biology, psychology, to sociology, the explanations of the previous level lose relevance. Each level is to some degree an emergent phenomenon operating according to its own forces, regularities, and tendencies. Hence, it is theoretically possible to "explain" one's choice of a friend by reference to physical laws, but it would take an unimaginable amount of data, and even then, the "explanation" would be in a form no human could comprehend, recognize, or find satisfactory.

Here too, there is a certain intransitivity of explanations between the levels of memes, schemas, social representations, and political economy. An explanation of the end of feudalism based entirely on the battle between social representations is as unsatisfying as an explanation of the social representation of an equal society spreading throughout a proto-capitalist, feudal society based entirely on memes replicating in willing minds. But—as importantly—a description of social representations is unsatisfying without an explanation of how ideas emerge, develop, and change.

Likewise, that theories of social evolution cannot explain everything of interest in society, or make accurate predictions of future developments, does not make them useless. The evolutionary economists Geoffrey Hodgson and Thorbjørn Knudsen point out:

> Proposals for a generalized Darwinism are also unaffected by the claim that Darwinism or the principles of selection, inheritance, and variation are inadequate to explain social evolution. They are definitely inadequate. They are also insufficient to explain detailed outcomes in the biological sphere. In both cases, auxiliary principles are required. However, none of this undermines the validity of generalization at an abstract level. Insufficiency does not amount to invalidity. Furthermore, given the existence of complex population systems in both nature and society, a generalized Darwinism is the only overarching framework that we have for placing detailed specific mechanisms.[132]

7 Political Ideas

"Our knowledge can only be finite, while our ignorance must necessarily be infinite."
—Karl Popper, *Conjectures and Refutations*

Imagine one's political ideology as a constellation. The stars represent memes, facts of some political relevance; the imagined lines between the stars that make up the constellation represent the woven narrative that pieces together various facts into a political perspective or ideology. On a very clear night in the desert, there is a maximum of visible stars—and every constellation is traceable in the sky. However, no one's brain contains every single political meme in the world, or *every* fact of *any* relevance to politics. In the metaphorical night sky each one of us sees, clouds or light pollution prevent all stars from being seen—we all see a different assortment corresponding to our individual knowledge base. Hence, it is practically impossible for any one person to truly know every political perspective or ideology as well as its most well-informed adherent; many of the facts that comprise their narratives are invisible to us. (This has significant downstream consequences; for instance, lacking knowledge of the history of racism in the United States has been shown to make it harder to understand how structural racism operates today.)[133] It is easy enough to search one's own views to find the bits of knowledge that support them; it is far more difficult to search contrary views to find the bits of knowledge supporting them—since most likely, the searcher will be ignorant of, hence blind to them. Yet, learning new knowledge (like clouds dispersing, revealing formerly-hidden stars) can result in opinion change (drawing new constellations using the newly-revealed stars).[134] This is likely to happen only when, as Jeffrey Friedman argues, "a new consideration is so substantively different from old ones that it provides a plausible new interpretation of a great many deal of them – outweighing all of them combined, let alone any one of them – because it casts them all in a new and persuasive light that, in turn, makes incoming information that might falsify this interpretation suddenly seem implausible."[135] This is analogous to a cloud covering the stars of Ursa Major except for those comprising the Big Dipper; if those clouds recede, and the rest of the constellation becomes visible, the bear's outline becomes clear and the pot-and-handle interpretation loses coherence.

Arguments between adherents of different political persuasions are like two people trying to see the same constellation in two skies with a vastly different assortment of stars. The constellations one person sees comprise stars that are simply invisible to the other. The figures that well-known constellations are supposed to form are already somewhat difficult to imagine, even in the one, identical night sky we all see. So too, even with a broadly shared set of memes, it can be difficult to agree on the political narrative to weave with them. This is all the more difficult here, where the metaphor is strained too far: seeing the exact same stars is not equivalent to having the exact same schemas. At a neuronal level, one person's schema may be significantly different than another's, even if the meme—as disembodied, abstract information—is the same. If my schema for inequality does not comprise any neuronal memory of a negative experience had as a result of inequality, and your schema for inequality is neuronally coded with viscerally painful memories of being dominated and powerless, then… we do not really have the same schemas at all. Embodied information, in the form of individual schemas, can differ even when the abstract information is the same.

The way that we perceive our own knowledge may be largely similar to the way we perceive our field of vision. An explanation in the psychology of perception posits that our experience of perceiving a rich visual world whenever we look out into our environment is entirely illusory.[136] According to the theory, our eyes do not scan a field of vision, sending details to be recorded by the brain as it builds a complete, movie-like representation of the outside world—a representation modified in real-time as the eye reports movements and new additions or subtractions. Rather than sight being a passive process whereby a complete representation of the outside world is projected in our mind as the information from light streams through our eyes, we never actually form complete representations of the outside world at any given time. Instead, we are constantly building fleeting representations one at a time, "to order," of individual objects or features in our field of vision. Once our fovea, the part of the retina with the highest relative acuity, shifts focus to another object or feature, the previous representation dissolves into a haze of undifferentiated features. Our vision *seems* as if it is continuously capturing all or most of the richness of a scene, but this is only because our fovea, during the course of the many saccades our eyes make each second, can quickly attend to enough individual details to create the illusion of a consistent and complete stream of vision. Although it seems that we perceive all objects in our line of sight concurrently, this is an illusion. The outside world itself is the only representative model we have, and it is accessed only if and when it is needed by quick saccadic eye movements.

In a similar illusion operating in the way we perceive our knowledge, we feel as though we have a largely complete set of knowledge about the world. This is what has been called "naïve realism," the widespread belief that one "sees things as they are," without distortion or ignorance, an epistemological error which prevents the naïve realist from recognizing "that her own interpretation *is* an interpretation, as opposed to being the secular equivalent of a revelation."[137] Naïve realism is our default state; we are blind to the fact that "what seems to be a self-disclosing reality is actually a generalization from a partial vision of reality, the product of fallible, contestable interpretations of culturally mediated perceptions."[138] (True realism would instead recognize that the realm of unknown unknowns dwarfs that of known knowns, known unknowns, and unknown knowns or "tacit knowledge.") We may know of gaps, but they do not bother us much or dissuade us from considering our knowledge to be nearly, fairly, or at least *functionally* complete.[139] The gaps in our knowledge we are aware of are usually considered to be in unimportant, trivial areas. (Like when driving, we feel like the sky is part of our rich, movie-screen field of vision—we just choose not to focus on it.) Even ideas, political views, and ideologies we disagree with, we feel that we understand. In fact, we may feel that we understand them better than their (benighted) adherents do themselves—our superior understanding is, after all, what keeps us from being adherents ourselves.[140]

However, from the theoretical perspective outlined here, this perception is certainly an illusion. The memes we have, and the social representations we share, are never more than a miniscule fraction of the total in existence. (This is similar to *hypocognition*: the state of lacking a cognitive representation of a concept.)[141] Yet with the sort of unabashed pluck and overconfidence typical of human psychology, we tend to believe that the narratives we form to explain the world—from the world of our personal relationships to the world of politics—are the best possible explanations for the facts. *The* facts—not *our* facts, that restricted set of facts we know, or the memes that happened to reproduce in our brains.

These are the ideas that the philosopher Max Stirner appropriately termed "spooks"—abstract ideas about incomprehensibly large numbers of people and their complex relations. Kathleen Taylor calls them "ethereal ideas," which

> are so ambiguous that they are often interpreted very differently by different individuals (political theorists describe political ethereal ideas, such as liberty and equality, as 'essentially contested'). This ambiguity makes them hard to challenge with rational debate; participants in such a debate may, in effect, be talking at cross-purposes.[142]

The conflict between spooks and the realities they purport to describe is illustrated in the following example: "He who is infatuated with *man* leaves persons out of account so far as that infatuation extends, and floats in an ideal, sacred interest. *Man*, you see, is not a person, but an ideal, a spook."[143] The brains we have evolved are capable of entertaining various memes, including spooks such as "man," "democracy," and "free markets." But when our brains were evolving this capability, we lived in small forager bands tied in a cooperative structure by mechanisms of "aggressive egalitarianism." Spooks would have been rare: any idea that could evolve about "society" limited to describing a group small enough to sit around a bonfire. There would have been no ethnicities, "races," nations, or political philosophies—the only prominent spooks would have been religious. But once sedentary, agricultural societies emerged, spooks—ideas without perceivable referents—appeared. We can never be certain that spooks accurately describe a reality; at best, we can ascertain whether they are in accord with empirical investigations into social phenomena. And evidence, no matter how persuasive and copious, is incapable of perfect correspondence with the reality it describes. Moreover, we *never* obtain the full body of evidence, only that available to us; the majority of possible evidence has been ruled inadmissible, in that only a fraction of the total of relevant memes ever makes an appearance in the court of our minds.

8 Conclusion

If nothing else, the contribution of social evolution theory to an understanding of why people believe what they believe is this: information is physical, and as such, it must be fashioned within a human mind or transported there via some medium (speech, books, TV). Contrary to centuries of Western thought, knowledge and the minds that use it are not spiritual; information cannot float from where it originated, through the ether or the realm of the spirit, to arrive in our brains. If we are at a neighbor's house, we can learn exactly what that neighbor is doing simply by looking: photons bouncing off our neighbor into our eyes give us reliable information. If we are in our own house across the street, some information might reach us in the form of sound waves ("loud music and conversation – must be a party") or photons (if our neighbor is near a window with the lights on). If we live a few blocks away, the means by which information can reach us are far more limited. Perhaps we can use a cell phone to call our neighbor, so that the sound waves her vocal chords produce can be converted into electrical impulses, then into radio waves, back into impulses, and finally back into sound waves that transmit us information about what she is doing. The information content of this conversation is less than in the previous two examples, however: some uncertainty remains ("perhaps she is lying"). But if our neighbor has gone on vacation to an isolated cabin in the woods, we have *no* means of getting information about what she is doing save by traveling to the cabin, where our eyes and ears can pick up light and sound. Short of that, we can generate all sorts of ideas about what she *might* be doing, with greater or lesser probability—but the information content of these suppositions is miniscule. Sure, we might know that our neighbor likes to fish and so guess that she is currently fishing, but she could be reading, hiking, cooking, or any number of other things.

In the realm of politics, even if we live near a capital and work in government, we only get direct information from events we witness. We rely on communication technologies for the rest: principally newspapers, magazines, television, and the internet, involving channels of information distribution so complex as to make Walmart's or the US military's logistics seem simple. Just one news story about trends in income requires information from millions of people to be translated into a magnetic field on a hard disk or ink on paper, sent via photons in fiber optic cables or planes, trains, and automobiles carrying paper to a government server or office, processed by computers and tax agents into a summary readable by journalists, who analyze the same information spanning decades—and this, to report a few numbers. To provide meaning and context, the journalist must speak to experts, each of whom has spent years reading the condensed knowledge of hundreds of other experts in books and articles, and make judgments about what information to include based on a lifetime collecting information about the economy (and the trustworthiness of various kinds of experts) through her personal experiences and countless conversations. Foreign policy is an order of magnitude more complex: a greater variety of aggregated information than mere tax returns is required.

Ultimately, we cannot avoid the conclusion that we are radically reliant on the media. Such information is not dropped off by a stork or delivered by Santa Klaus on their ways back from the world's capitals, financial centers, and war zones; it comes the only way it can, through the work of journalists collecting it from its sources and delivering it to us. "Facts have no wings."[144] The media is first and foremost a provider of information logistics, arranging for the transport of physical information from its points of origin to millions of people. Our extreme reliance on the news media means it has tremendous power to shape our beliefs, at the least by determining what informational building blocks we have available to construct understandings. While other forms of power may be more obvious (armies, police, wealth), the power of information is supreme—a truth which evaded Stalin when he famously asked, "How many divisions does the Pope have?" As Sandra Braman observes:

> Informational power shapes human behaviors by manipulating the informational bases of instrumental, structural, and symbolic power. Informational power dominates power in other forms, changes how they are exercised, and alters the nature of their effects. Informational power can be described as 'genetic,' because it appears at the genesis – the informational origins – of the materials, social structures, and symbols that are the stuff of power in its other forms.[145]

This conclusion about the informational power of the media can be reached through conduits other than social evolution theory. Walter Lippmann, writing before the physical nature of information was understood, made the same argument.[146] More recently, Jeffrey Friedman has arrived at this conclusion through epistemology, noting that news consumers are "helpless to discern whether the ideas they find plausible are in fact worthless—a matter about which they are radically ignorant. Thus, members of the public will be captive to the worldviews created by the journalism, and the other cultural inputs, that they happen to have encountered."[147]

In natural ecology, there are stronger and weaker forces, but no laws or strict determinants. An abnormally cold year is a force operating against the growth of trees, but other forces—rainfall, soil conditions—can counteract (or exacerbate) the effect. In information ecology, the same principle of complex systems applies: no laws or determinants, but a variety of forces operating differently and producing diverse effects. Among the forces affecting the ecology of political information in society are: our evolved psychology, particularly its social (political) aspects, and how our brains process incoming information; institutions, particularly those of education and culture; the political economy of media, which describes the forces operating on media outlets influencing their selection and presentation of information; and currently widespread ideas and social representations.

No one force or selection pressure operates as if it were a law, strictly determining how ideas evolve and spread. Rather than Marx's conception of ideas *expressing* economic interests—which posits that the predominant, if not only, selection pressure on the ideas one adopts is one's economic status—Weber's conception of "elective affinities" better describes how people adopt ideas and ideas adopt people.[148] Just as chemical compounds exhibit varying affinities for water, being hydrophobic or hydrophilic, there exist elective affinities between people and ideas. Everything else being equal, a king is unlikely to be attracted to democracy or a nun to sexual libertinism; a sweatshop worker is likely to find socialism more attractive than a sweatshop owner, and a rich person is likely to find *laissez faire* more attractive than a poor person; few in North Koreans read *The Road to Serfdom*, and few in the United States *Das Kapital*; someone of limited mental ability is more likely to prefer a simple affirmation of the status quo to a complex critique of it; and, as Orwell noted, "The nationalist not only does not disapprove of atrocities committed by his own side, but he has a remarkable capacity for not even hearing about them."[149]

These examples also illustrate at least two interacting ecologies of information: there is the ecology of information inside one's mind, created by genes expressed in our developmental environment, life experiences, and a bevy of ideational influences from school to the media; and the ecology of information within society, the aggregate of individuals' information ecologies, plus institutional, political, economic, historical, and foreign influences. The fact that few North Koreans read *The Road to Serfdom* has more to do with their social ecology of information (censorship, poverty), whereas that few Americans read *Das Kapital* probably has more to do with their individual ecologies of information (ideational influences suggesting Marx was wrong and/or evil). The nationalist not disapproving of atrocities committed by fellow nationals is an effect of the individual ecology of information (rationalizing atrocities away as unfortunate but necessary), while not even hearing about them is an effect of the social ecology of information (the media giving less attention to such atrocities). But the two are interpenetrating, with individual ecologies of information nested inside a social ecology.

Most importantly, the application of evolutionary theory to society and the stuff of culture does not generate any predictions of how a population of ideas *will* evolve. As William Harms points out:

> It is not from the mere presence of variation, selection, and heredity that evolution tends toward higher fitness or greater adapted complexity. Critically, the way in which variation is introduced into the population and the way that selection pressures change over time determines where things go. In a nutshell, the mere applicability of the concepts of evolutionary

theory is fully consistent with a system that chatters chaotically, darting one way and another, vaulting laterally via huge nonrandom variations with no systematic behavior over time whatsoever. It is knowledge of the causal particulars which govern patterns of heredity, variation, and selection that warrants expectations regarding the behavior of an evolutionary process.[150]

These causal particulars—sources of variation and selection pressures—can be understood as the ecology of information and will be examined in the following chapters.

Human psychology is the first selection pressure operating on the evolution of ideas. Schema research has shown that we store information in organized, networked chunks subject to snowball effects: bits of information form concepts, linked to similar concepts and memories of individual experiences and feelings, and as a conceptual schema develops it becomes easier to add information. Contrariwise, information that does not fit or contradicts a schema is likelier to be rejected or assimilated in a biased fashion. Memes do not spread from brain to brain like computer files copied from computer to computer, without prejudice. They spread differentially, depending on the brain's preexisting schemas, and they are rough copies, linked to idiosyncratic memories and emotions in different brains. Hence, the information content of a meme in two minds may be the same, but the subjective understanding or meaning they engender may be different. And these subjective understandings, undergirded by memories and emotion, make some ideologies or social representations more or less likely to be adopted.

Notes

1. César Hidalgo, *Why Information Grows: The Evolution of Order, from Atoms to Economies* (New York: Basic Books, 2015): xv.
2. Luis Masanes et al., "Existence of an Information Unit as a Postulate of Quantum Theory," *Proceedings of the National Academy of Sciences* 110, no. 41 (2013); Tom Siegfried, *The Bit and the Pendulum* (New York: Wiley, 2000).
3. John R. Pierce, *An Introduction to Information Theory* (New York: Dover, 1980): 23.
4. Hidalgo, *Why Information Grows*, xvi. For more definitions of information and the different understandings they engender, see Sandra Braman, *Change of State: Information, Policy, and Power* (Cambridge, MA: MIT Press, 2006): 11–21.

5. John E. Mayfield, *The Engine of Complexity: Evolution as Computation* (New York: Columbia University Press, 2013): 41.
6. Henry Plotkin, *Darwin Machines and the Nature of Knowledge* (Cambridge, MA: Harvard University Press, 1994): xv.
7. Plotkin, *Darwin Machines*, 144–152, 243–244.
8. Mayfield, *The Engine*, 24.
9. John Maynard Smith, "The Concept of Information in Biology," *Philosophy of Science* 67, no. 2 (2000). There has been some controversy on the use of information theory in biology; Griffith's "parity thesis" sensibly proposes that evolutionarily-relevant information subsists not only in DNA, but in organisms' environments as well (Griffiths, 2001).
10. Hidalgo, *Why Information Grows*, xviii–xx.
11. Ibid., 30.
12. Ibid., 25–41.
13. Mayfield, *The Engine*, 15, 68–90.
14. Ibid., 22–23.
15. Donald T. Campbell, "Variation and Selective Retention in Socio-cultural Evolution," in *Social Change in Developing Areas: A Reinterpretation of Evolutionary Theory*, ed. Herbert Barringer et al., 19–49 (Cambridge, MA: Schenkman, 1965): 21; Francis Heylighen and Klaas Chielens, "Evolution of Culture, Memetics," in *Encyclopedia of Complexity and Systems Science*, ed. Robert A. Meyers, 3205–3220 (New York: Springer, 2008): 3206.
16. Quoted in Lucas McGranahan, "William James's Social Evolutionism in Focus," *The Pluralist* 6, no. 3 (2011): 80.
17. Lee R. Lyman and Michael J. O'Brien, "Cultural Traits: Units of Analysis in Early Twentieth-Century Anthropology," *Journal of Anthropological Research* 59, no. 2 (2003).
18. William F. Harms, *Information & Meaning in Evolutionary Processes* (Cambridge: Cambridge University Press, 2004): 65.
19. Walter G. Runciman, *The Theory of Cultural and Social Selection* (New York: Cambridge University Press, 2009): 18.
20. Campbell, "Variation," 23–26; Geoffrey M. Hodgson and Thorbjørn Knudsen, *Darwin's Conjecture: The Search for General Principles of Social and Economic Evolution* (Chicago: University of Chicago Press, 2012): 13–18.
21. Paul Marsden, "Forefathers of Memetics: Gabriel Tarde and the Laws of Imitation," *Journal of Memetics-Evolutionary Models of Information Transmission* 4, no. 1 (2000).
22. Gabriel de Tarde, *The Laws of Imitation*, trans. Elsie Crews Parsons (New York: Henry Holt, 1903): xv.
23. Ibid., xxiii.

24. Tarde, *The Laws*, 149.
25. Ibid., 153.
26. Ibid., 289–290.
27. Ibid., 295.
28. Eduardo Viana Vargas et al., "The Debate Between Tarde and Durkheim," *Environment and Planning D: Society and Space* 26, no. 5 (2008).
29. Ibid., 770.
30. Andrew Whiten et al., "Culture Evolves," *Philosophical Transactions of the Royal Society of London B: Biological Sciences* 366, no. 1567 (2011).
31. Marion Blute, *Darwinian Sociocultural Evolution: Solutions to Dilemmas in Cultural and Social Theory* (New York: Cambridge University Press, 2010); Hodgson and Knudsen, *Darwin's Conjecture*; Alex Mesoudi, *Cultural Evolution: How Darwinian Theory Can Explain Human Culture and Synthesize the Social Sciences* (Chicago: University of Chicago Press, 2011); Runciman, *The Theory*; Stephan Shennan, *Genes, Memes and Human History: Darwinian Archaeology and Cultural Evolution* (New York: Thames & Hudson, 2002); and Shiping Tang, *The Social Evolution of International Politics* (Oxford: Oxford University Press, 2013).
32. Lev S. Vygotsky, *The Vygotsky Reader*, ed. René van der Veer and Jaan Valsiner (Hoboken, NJ: Blackwell, 1998): 175–176.
33. Daniel Dennett, *Darwin's Dangerous Idea* (New York: Touchstone, 1995).
34. Ibid., 50–51.
35. Susan Blackmore, *The Meme Machine* (Oxford: Oxford University Press, 1998): 66.
36. Plotkin, *Darwin Machines*, 222.
37. Campbell, "Variation," 42; Heylighen and Chielens, "Evolution."
38. Hodgson and Knudsen, 2012, 22–23.
39. J. Stanley Metcalfe, "Evolutionary Concepts in Relation to Evolutionary Economics," in *The Evolutionary Foundations of Economics*, ed. Kurt Dopfer, 391–430 (New York: Cambridge University Press, 2005): 420.
40. Blackmore, *The Meme*, 19–20.
41. Serge Moscovici, *Social Representations: Explorations in Social Psychology* (New York: NYU Press, 2001): 30.
42. Richard Pocklington and Michael L. Best, "Cultural Evolution and Units of Selection in Replicating Text," *Journal of Theoretical Biology* 188, no. 1 (1997): 81.
43. Nicolas Claidière and Jean-Baptiste André, "The Transmission of Genes and Culture: A Questionable Analogy," *Evolutionary Biology* 39, no. 1 (2012); Maria Kronfeldner, *Darwinian Creativity and Memetics* (Stocksfield, UK: Acumen, 2011); and Adam Kuper, "If Memes Are the Answer, What Is the Question," in *Darwinizing Culture: The Status of*

Memetics as a Science, ed. Robert Aunger (Oxford: Oxford University Press, 2000): 180–193.
44. Hodgson and Knudsen, *Darwin's Conjecture*, 38.
45. de Chardin, *The Phenomenon of Man*, 223.
46. Walter G. Runciman, "Culture Does Evolve," *History and Theory* 44, no. 1 (2005): 4–5.
47. Robert Aunger, *The Electric Meme: A New Theory of How We Think* (New York: Free Press, 2002); Hodgson and Knudsen, *Darwin's Conjecture*; Mo Jamshidi, "Tools for Intelligent Control: Fuzzy Controllers, Neural Networks and Genetic Algorithms," *Philosophical Transactions of the Royal Society of London A: Mathematical, Physical and Engineering Sciences* 361, no. 1809 (2003); and Mayfield, *The Engine*, 145–169.
48. Aunger, *The Electric Meme*, 94–113; Mayfield, *The Engine*, 181–191; Plotkin, *Darwin Machines*, 70–72.
49. Blute, *Darwinian Sociocultural*, 115–120.
50. Sonja J. Prohaska and Peter F. Stadler, "Genes," *Theory in Biosciences* 127, no. 3 (2008): 215.
51. James A. Shapiro, *Evolution: A View from the 21st Century* (London: FT Press Science, 2011): 2, 29.
52. Gilles Fauconnier and Mark Turner, *The Way We Think: Conceptual Blending and the Mind's Hidden Complexities* (New York: Basic Books, 2002).
53. Ibid., 384. For a wide array of inventions and their evolutionary histories, see Charles Panati, *Panati's Extraordinary Origins of Everyday Things* (New York: William Morrow, 1987).
54. Mayfield, *The Engine*, 255.
55. Dan Sperber, "An Objection to the Memetic Approach to Culture," in *Darwinizing Culture*.
56. Trey Hedden et al., "Cultural Influences on Neural Substrates of Attentional Control," *Psychological Science* 19, no. 1 (2008).
57. Shennan, *Genes, Memes*, 47.
58. Mayfield, *The Engine*, 272–273.
59. Aunger, *The Electric Meme*, 325.
60. Ibid., 197.
61. Aunger, *The Electric Meme*, 249.
62. Markus Kiefer and Friedemann Pulvermüller, "Conceptual Representations in Mind and Brain: Theoretical Developments, Current Evidence and Future Directions," *Cortex* 48, no. 7 (2012).
63. Ibid., 820.
64. John Durham Peters, *Speaking into the Air: A History of the Idea of Communication* (Chicago: University of Chicago Press, 2012): 4.
65. Adam McNamara, "Can We Measure Memes?" *Frontiers in Evolutionary Neuroscience* 3 (2011).

66. Gonçalo C. Cardoso and Jonathan W. Atwell, "Directional Cultural Change by Modification and Replacement of Memes," *Evolution* 65, no. 1 (2011).
67. Robert Aunger, "What's the Matter with Memes?" in *Richard Dawkins: How a Scientist Changed the Way We Think*, ed. Alan Grafen and Mark Ridley (Oxford: Oxford University Press, 2006); Bruce Edmonds, "The Revealed Poverty of the Gene-Meme Analogy—Why Memetics per se Has Failed to Produce Substantive Results," *Journal of Memetics-Evolutionary Models of Information Transmission* 9, no. 1 (2005). However, I could not replicate Edmonds' finding about the precipitous drop in papers on Google Scholar mentioning "memetics" but not "memetic algorithm." The search string [memetics—"memetic algorithm"] found around 200 results in the year 2000, and over 1000 results in 2010. This could be due to changes in Google's search algorithm or an increase in the body of material it covered since Edmond's paper was written.
68. For example, Lada A. Adamic et al., "Information Evolution in Social Networks," *arXiv preprint*, arXiv:1402.6792 (2014); Michele Coscia, "Average Is Boring: How Similarity Kills a Meme's Success," *Scientific Reports* 4 (2014); Chip Heath et al., "Emotional Selection in Memes: The Case of Urban Legends," *Journal of Personality and Social Psychology* 81, no. 6 (2001); Tobias Kuhn et al., "Inheritance Patterns in Citation Networks Reveal Scientific Memes," *Physical Review X* 4, no. 4 (2014); and Limor Shifman and Mike Thelwall, "Assessing Global Diffusion with Web Memetics: The Spread and Evolution of a Popular Joke," *Journal of the American Society for Information Science and Technology* 60, no. 12 (2009).
69. Harms, *Information & Meaning*, 67.
70. Kronfeldner, *Darwinian Creativity*, 12.
71. Russell, *A History*, 49–52, 121–122, 142; Plotkin, *Darwin Machines*, 14.
72. Simon Blackburn, *The Oxford Dictionary of Philosophy* (Oxford: Oxford University Press, 1996): 194, 289.
73. Owen Flanagan, *The Problem of the Soul* (New York: Basic Books, 2003): 2.
74. Runciman, *The Theory*, 214.
75. Liane Gabora, "Autocatalytic Closure in a Cognitive System: A Tentative Scenario for the Origin of Culture," *Psycoloquy* 9, no. 67 (1998).
76. Blackmore, *The Meme Machine*; Paul Higgs, "The Mimetic Transition: A Simulation Study of the Evolution of Learning by Imitation," *Proceedings of the Royal Society of London B: Biological Sciences* 267, no. 1450 (2000).
77. Robert A. Foley and M. Mirazón Lahr, "The Evolution of the Diversity of Cultures," *Philosophical Transactions of the Royal Society of London B: Biological Sciences* 366, no. 1567 (2011).
78. Kronfeldner, *Darwinian Creativity*, 138–139.

79. Susan T. Fiske and Patricia W. Linville, "What Does the Schema Concept Buy Us?" *Personality and Social Psychology Bulletin* 6, no. 4 (1980): 552.
80. Hiroko Nishida, "A Cognitive Approach to Intercultural Communication Based on Schema Theory," *International Journal of Intercultural Relations* 23, no. 5 (1999).
81. Susan T. Fiske and Shelley E. Taylor, *Social Cognition: From Brains to Culture* (New York: McGraw-Hill).
82. Klaus Fielder, "Causal Schemata: Review and Criticism of Research on a Popular Construct," *Journal of Personality and Social Psychology* 42, no. 6 (1982).
83. Fiske and Linville, "What Does."
84. George J. Spilich et al., "Text Processing of Domain-Related Information for Individuals with High and Low Domain Knowledge," *Journal of Verbal Learning and Verbal Behavior* 18, no. 3 (1979).
85. Asher Koriat et al., "Toward a Psychology of Memory Accuracy," *Annual Review of Psychology* 51, no. 1 (2000).
86. Fiske and Linville, "What Does," 544, 550.
87. Susan T. Fiske et al., "Category-Based and Attribute-Based Reactions to Others: Some Informational Conditions of Stereotyping and Individuating Processes," *Journal of Experimental Social Psychology* 23, no. 5 (1987); Nishida, "A Cognitive."
88. Elizabeth G. Rice, "On Cultural Schemata," *American Ethnologist* 7, no. 1 (1980).
89. Robert M. Entman, "How the Media Affect What People Think: An Information Processing Approach," *The Journal of Politics* 51, no. 2 (1989).
90. Milton Lodge and Ruth Hamill, "A Partisan Schema for Political Information Processing," *American Political Science Review* 80, no. 2 (1986).
91. Rice, "On Cultural," 155.
92. Gustav Jahoda, "Critical Notes and Reflections on 'Social Representations'," *European Journal of Social Psychology* 18, no. 3 (1988); Jonathan Potter and Ian Litton, "Some Problems Underlying the Theory of Social Representations," *British Journal of Social Psychology* 24, no. 2 (1985).
93. Martha Augoustinos and John Michael Innes, "Towards an Integration of Social Representations and Social Schema Theory," *British Journal of Social Psychology* 29, no. 3 (1990); Jorge Vala, "Representações Socias para uma Psicologia Social do Pensamento Social," in *Psicologia Social*, ed. Jorge Vala and Maria Benedicta Monteiro, 353–384 (Lisbon: Fundação Calouste Gulbenkian, 1993).

94. Martha Augoustinos, "The Openness and Closure of a Concept: Reply to Allansdottir, Jovelovitch and Stathopoulou," *Papers on Social Representations* 2, no. 1 (1993).
95. Martha Augoustinos et al., *Social Cognition: An Integrated Introduction* (New York: Sage, 2006).
96. Michael Billig, *Ideology and Opinions: Studies in Rhetorical Psychology* (New York: Sage, 1991).
97. Wolfgang Wagner and Nicky Hayes, *Everyday Discourse and Common Sense: The Theory of Social Representations* (New York: Palgrave Macmillan, 2005).
98. Augoustinos and Innes, "Towards an Integration," 227.
99. Augoustinos et al., *Social Cognition*, 99–101.
100. Caroline Howarth et al., "Editorial: 50 Years of Research on Social Representations: Central Debates and Challenging Questions," *Papers on Social Representations* 20 (2011); Wolfgang Wagner et al., "Theory and Method of Social Representations," *Asian Journal of Social Psychology* 2, no. 1 (1999).
101. Serge Moscovici, *Psychoanalysis: Its Image and Its Public* (New York: Polity, 2008): 32.
102. Serge Moscovici, "Attitudes and Opinions," *Annual Review of Psychology* 14, no. 1 (1963): 251.
103. Wagner and Hayes, *Everyday Discourse*, 120, 123.
104. Moscovici, *Psychoanalysis*, 32.
105. Guy Elcheroth et al., "On the Knowledge of Politics and the Politics of Knowledge: How a Social Representations Approach Helps Us Rethink the Subject of Political Psychology," *Political Psychology* 32, no. 5 (2011): 736.
106. Moscovici, *Social Representations*, 32–33.
107. Erich Kirchler and Erik Hoelzlde, "Social Representations and Economic Psychology," in *Social Representations in the "Social Arena"*, ed. Annamaria S. de Rosa, 223–232 (New York: Routledge, 2012).
108. Pierre Vergès and Raymond Rybade, "Social Representations of the Economy," in *Social Representations in the "Social Arena."*
109. Daniel Bar-Tal and Dikla Antebi, "Siege Mentality in Israel," *International Journal of Intercultural Relations* 16, no. 3 (1992).
110. James H. Liu and Denis J. Hilton, "How the Past Weighs on the Present: Social Representations of History and Their Role in Identity Politics," *British Journal of Social Psychology* 44, no. 4 (2005).
111. Elcheroth et al., "On the Knowledge."
112. Ibid., 752.
113. Caroline Howarth, "A Social Representation Is Not a Quiet Thing: Exploring the Critical Potential of Social Representations Theory," *British Journal of Social Psychology* 45, no. 1 (2006): 75.

114. Martin W. Bauer and George Gaskell, "Social Representations Theory: A Progressive Research Programme for Social Psychology," *Journal for the Theory of Social Behaviour* 38, no. 4 (2008); Elcheroth et al., "On the Knowledge."
115. Serge Moscovici, "Notes Towards a Description of Social Representations," *European Journal of Social Psychology* 18, no. 3 (1988): 215.
116. Wagner and Hayes, *Everyday Discourse*, 278, 281.
117. Moscovici, "Notes Towards," 214.
118. Moscovici, *Social Representations*.
119. Moscovici, *Psychoanalysis*, 7.
120. Kenneth Boulding, *The Image: Knowledge in Life and Society* (Ann Arbor: University of Michigan Press, 1961): 58.
121. Moscovici, *Psychoanalysis*, 11.
122. Dan Sperber, "Anthropology and Psychology: Towards an Epidemiology of Representations," *Man* (1985); Dan Sperber, "The Epidemiology of Beliefs," in *The Social Psychological Study of Widespread Beliefs*, ed. Colin Fraser and George E. Gaskell, 25–44 (Oxford: Oxford University Press, 1990).
123. Sperber, "Anthropology and Psychology," 76.
124. Sperber, "Anthropology and Psychology," 87.
125. Sperber, "The Epidemiology," 41.
126. Pléh, "Thoughts On," 40.
127. For example, Fouad Bou Zeineddine and Felicia Pratto, "The Need for Power and the Power of Need: An Ecological Approach for Political Psychology," *Political Psychology* 38 (2017): 3–35.
128. Roy Bhaskar, *A Realist Theory of Science* (London: Verso, 2008): 18.
129. Jonah Berger and Katherine L. Milkman, "What Makes Online Content Viral?" *Journal of Marketing Research* 49, no. 2 (2012).
130. Rael J. Dawtry et al., "Why Wealthier People Think People Are Wealthier, and Why It Matters from Social Sampling to Attitudes to Redistribution," *Psychological Science* 26, no. 9 (2015).
131. Wagner and Hayes, *Everyday Discourse*, 297–299; see also Michael Polyani, *The Tacit Dimension* (Chicago: University of Chicago Press, 2009): 35–36.
132. Hodgson and Knudsen, *Darwin's Conjecture*, 45.
133. Jessica C. Nelson et al., "The Marley Hypothesis: Denial of Racism Reflects Ignorance of History," *Psychological Science* 24, no. 2 (2013).
134. David Kowalewski, "Teaching War: Does It Pacify Students?" *Journal of Instructional Psychology* 21, no. 3 (1994).
135. Jeffrey Friedman, "Beyond Cues and Political Elites: The Forgotten Zaller," *Critical Review* 24, no. 4 (2012): 447.

136. Susan Blackmore, *Consciousness: A Very Short Introduction* (Oxford: Oxford University Press, 2005): 78–92.
137. Jeffrey Friedman, *Power Without Knowledge: A Critique of Technocracy* (Oxford University Press, forthcoming): 36.
138. Ibid., 31.
139. David Dunning, "The Dunning–Kruger Effect: On Being Ignorant of One's Own Ignorance," in *Advances in Experimental Social Psychology*, Vol. 44, ed. James M. Olson and Mark P. Zanna, 247–296 (San Diego: Elsevier, 2011): 248–251.
140. Steven Sloman and Philip Fernbach, *The Knowledge Illusion: Why We Never Think Alone* (New York: Riverhead Books, 2017): 174.
141. Kaidi Wu and David Dunning, "Hypocognition: Making Sense of the Landscape Beyond One's Conceptual Reach," *Review of General Psychology* 22, no. 1 (2018): 25–35.
142. Kathleen Taylor, *Brainwashing: The Science of Thought Control* (Oxford: Oxford University Press, 2006): 27.
143. Max Stirner, *The Ego and Its Own* (New York: Cambridge University Press, 1995): 72.
144. Scott L. Althaus et al., "Assumed Transmission in Political Science: A Call for Bringing Description Back In." *The Journal of Politics* 73, no. 4 (2011): 1065.
145. Sandra Braman, *Change of State: Information, Policy, and Power* (Cambridge, MA: MIT Press, 2006): 26.
146. Walter Lippmann, *Public Opinion* (Blacksburg, VA: Wilder, 2010).
147. Friedman, *Power Without Knowledge*, 61.
148. H.H. Gerth and C. Wright Mills, "Introduction: The Man and His Work," in *From Max Weber: Essays in Sociology*, trans. and ed. H.H. Gerth and C. Wright Mills, 3–76 (New York: Oxford University Press, 1947): 62–63.
149. George Orwell, *England Your England and Other Essays* (London: Secker & Warburg, 1953).
150. Harms, *Information & Meaning*, 72.

CHAPTER 3

Evolution: How We Got the Minds We Have Today

> "*Any change in men's views as to what is good and right in human life make[s] its way but tardily at the best. Especially is this true of any change in the direction of what is called progress; that is to say, in the direction of divergence from the archaic position – from the position which may be accounted the point of departure at any step in the social evolution of the community.*"
> —Thorstein Veblen, *The Theory of the Leisure Class*

Our brains are the product of a staggeringly long period of evolution: 60–70 million years since the ancestral primates first emerged.[1] As species appeared and branched off to develop independently, primate brains grew. Larger brains, while metabolically costly, bring benefits to the animals most like us. Primate species that appeared more recently, like apes, have relatively larger brains than New World monkeys. Our closest relative, the chimpanzee (also a relative newcomer), shares with us not only a sizeable brain, but also many of its most salient features. Our own brains are not massively different than those of chimps—much of the relevant evolution occurred before we branched off from our primate cousins.

One helpful feature of primates' increasingly large brains is that they allow for both individual and social learning. Across primate species, bigger brains are associated with greater use of tools, innovative behaviors, and social learning. Primate species with larger brains exhibit greater behavioral flexibility facilitated by longer periods of juvenile development.[2] Cognitive evolution proceeds from the inflexible specializations of small brains ("if you see a larger animal, run!"), to the self-regulated, intentional actions of large brains, which draw on mental representations, inferences, and self-monitoring ("if you see a larger animal, decide whether you know anything about it; then choose what to do depending on the danger it poses, its value as food, and your own ability to kill it").[3] Bigger brains take over some of the functions genes perform: The flexible behavior large brains allow helps animals adjust immediately, instead of having to wait for genetic evolution to provide a hard-wired adaptation.[4]

Three million years ago, our big-brained ancestors had developed an upright stance and were living in African forests. Two and a half million years ago, a change in climate brought drought to our home in East Africa, drying rivers and forests and expanding grasslands. While the forest was not the safest place, our ancestors were even more imperiled in the grassland, where lions and other predators could spot us from afar and outrun us for a kill. There was a strong selection pressure for adaptations that would help us survive in the novel environment of the African savanna.[5]

The climatic changes that forced our ancestors from the forest to the savanna were only to become more severe and variable.[6] The average global temperature was dropping, while fluctuations in temperature, rainfall, and atmospheric carbon dioxide became more drastic. During the past two and a half million years, life on earth was buffeted by rapid changes in climate. These were too fast for genetic evolution to produce appropriate adaptations—instead, behavioral flexibility was the best adaptation genes could provide. And as behavioral flexibility requires big brains, during the last 2.5 million years, brain size for mammals increased more than during the previous 20 million years. The primate lineage leading to humans witnessed the fastest rate of growth.

Concurrently, our ancestors were evolving a much smaller difference between the sizes of male and female bodies. Termed "sexual dimorphism," this phenomenon gives us clues about the social organization of a species: with high sexual dimorphism, males are much larger than females and likelier engage in violent competition over mates and resources. Lower sexual dimorphism indicates a less hierarchical social structure, more monogamous pair bonding, and a lower rate of violent competition. The fossil record indicates that our ancestors may have evolved a nonhierarchical, egalitarian social structure 1.9 million years ago.[7]

Interdependence in food provision and protection from predators created a selection pressure for the skills and temperament facilitating collaboration. Early humans likely had to choose their partners, which created a selection pressure against cheaters, laggards, and bullies. And that meant early humans had to develop a self-image, imagine what others thought of them, and work at improving their reputations.[8] Public relations had evolved.

By 350,000 years ago, the first signs of cumulative cultural evolution appear in the form of stone tool technology. Our ancestors produced a variety of stone blades using complex techniques, which varied by region as ideas spread and local improvements were made.[9] Big brains, with their high metabolic costs, paid dividends.

Language is harder to pin down in the archaeological record—words do not leave fossils. However, there is good reason to believe it developed early in our evolutionary history.[10] The radical environmental changes our ancestors faced 2.5 million years ago created a strong selection pressure for something to help us adapt, and a higher level of cooperation was likely the solution "favored" by natural selection. Cooperation requires effective communication; and advances in communication probably began with pointing, directing attention to features of the environment. Pantomiming is a natural adjunct to pointing, but requires the communicator to correctly imagine what others infer. This can only work between people who share understandings and goals—joint intentionality and a theory of mind. "What is she likely to think when I point to that watering hole?" "If I bare my teeth and make a scratching gesture, will she realize I'm warning her about lions drinking there?"

Ingenious experiments with our primate relatives have revealed that great apes have not evolved joint intentionality.[11] While they have social-cognitive skills to understand the intentional actions of others, they cannot understand that different individuals have different perspectives on the same thing. Unlike human children, they cannot engage in joint collaborative activity; they cannot imagine a "we" focused on achieving a joint goal. We alone can use inferences to share information with accuracy and coordinate our intentions and actions to achieve joint goals.

As point-and-pantomime language evolved, groups could conventionalize signs. As in the game of Charades, where touching the ear is understood to mean "sounds like," certain gestures became associated with meanings. These gestures would have been less vulnerable to misinterpretation and combined to convey ever more complex messages. As groups became bigger and competed, living in one became an overarching collaborative activity in its own right—and the traditions, practices, and technologies of the group became a culture. Standardized gestures could be replaced by vocal sounds, and language became part of culture. Evidence suggests that human language reached its current state of development between 150,000 and 50,000 years ago.[12]

When our species, *Homo sapiens*, emerged in Africa no further than a couple hundred thousand years ago, our hominid relatives had spread throughout much of the world. Ours was one of several hominid species enjoying success; the blind gambit evolution played with a highly intelligent, social, and cooperative simian had paid off. Around 100,000 years ago, the newest hominid—us—migrated from Africa. However, our Neanderthal cousins in the Levant region of West Asia likely stopped us and subsequently we nearly went extinct. From 90–60,000 years ago we evolved more complex and coherent social groups and more extensive trading networks, possibly developing the first religions.[13] This new and improved *Homo sapiens* made a second migration, and in relatively short time eliminated (or partially assimilated through interbreeding) all other hominids and colonized nearly the entire planet. From around 40–10,000 years ago, social evolution again picked up. Technology developed faster, long-distance alliances and trading networks formed, social diversification increased, group identities sharpened, and we began to symbolically record information.[14]

Starting around 12,500 years ago, the wildly oscillating global climate stabilized.[15] As average temperatures rose, ice withdrew and the climate became more predictable. As carbon dioxide increased in the atmosphere, farming became a viable subsistence strategy.[16] Prior to the dawn of agriculture, we had been "egalitarian anarchists"[17] living in small groups without any sort of domineering leader—or, we changed our social structures seasonally[18]—but the advent of sedentary agriculture changed that.[19] Not all farming societies embraced hierarchy (social stratification) and inequality, and some that did went back to traditional egalitarianism.[20] But agriculture relaxed the economic strictures and modified the social logic that led to our egalitarian (or seasonally variable) social structure.[21] The food surplus sedentary agriculture produced allowed the evolution of tiered systems of social organization; hierarchy, even slavery, seemed to have been a functional necessity for agricultural societies.[22] By around 9,000 years ago, "achievement-based" societies appear in the archaeological record. These allowed some members to gain and enjoy higher status than others on the basis of their skills in warfare or religious ritual. From achievement-based societies developed societies based on *hereditary* rank: the Lucky Sperm Club was born. Finally, hereditary rank societies were sometimes violently merged by an ambitious ruler to form a kingdom, the first of which appeared around 5,000 years ago.[23]

From this long perspective, human history and *recorded* history are discordant. For a large part of hominid history, including that of *Homo sapiens*, we lived in small, mobile, egalitarian bands. At the dawn of recorded history, however, we were split between traditional societies and newly hierarchical, sedentary mega-groups. The new groups—the rank societies and kingdoms—could not stray far from our evolved nature for long, however. By 2,500 years ago (or 500 BCE, the "Axial Age"), civilizations from China and India to Greece developed similar systems of ethics that reinstated, at least normatively if not in practice, traditional forms of equality, altruism, and cooperation.[24] Throughout recorded history—the fraction of human history beginning after sedentary agriculture—people struggled and fought against hierarchy.[25] What, then, is our evolved nature—or more accurately, our evolved psychology?

1 Evolutionary Psychology—What We Know About How Our Minds Came to Be

"All human activity that does not contribute, even indirectly, to testicular and ovarian arousal, to the meeting of sperm and egg, is contemptible... I see no other reason for our being here, spinning like slow tops in a gratuitous universe."
—Mario Vargas Llosa, *The Notebooks of Don Rigoberto*

Darwin's theory of evolution by natural selection made an indelible impact on scientists in several fields, including psychology.[26] Psychologists realized that if humans had been evolving for millions of years and had branched off the tree of life from a common chimpanzee ancestor, the key to understanding our minds could be found by studying our evolutionary history.

An evolutionary approach to psychology seeks *ultimate* explanations—"*why* do we tend to think or act this way"—as opposed to *proximate* explanations, "*what* is the immediate cause of our thinking or acting this way."[27] For instance, a proximate explanation for why we feel sexual jealousy might be the fear of losing companionship. An ultimate explanation, however, would be rooted in evolution: since natural selection promotes behaviors that tend to make organisms leave more offspring, jealousy must have evolved because it tends to help prevent the loss of mating opportunities leading to offspring.[28] Few if any of us think in terms of evolutionary ultimate explanations, but the reason why jealousy exists in the first place is evolutionary. (Darwin himself was one of the first to realize that evolution shaped and molded human sexuality.)[29]

Sexuality may be low-hanging fruit for evolutionary explanations; natural selection is fundamentally about survival and reproduction, and sex is no small part of the latter. Yet evolutionary psychology has successfully explained other, less obvious features of human cognition. Take anger. We feel anger for many reasons, but often when we want or expect something or treatment from another and we are not receiving it.[30] Evolutionary psychologists ran experiments to see what factors increased the occurrence of anger in conflicts. They hypothesized that anger would come more easily to those with greater bargaining power, to tip the scales. Since greater bargaining power can come in several forms, they chose two easily measurable characteristics: upper-body strength in men and attractiveness in women. They found that stronger men and more attractive women were more prone to anger, felt entitled to better treatment, and tended to prevail more than weaker men and less attractive women.

Or take "change blindness," how we often fail to notice changes in our visual scenes. For instance, if we look at two photographs, one doctored to add or remove some physical feature, we often fail to notice. Evolutionary psychologists hypothesized that we would demonstrate less change blindness to animals since ancestrally animals were food and threats. Experiments confirmed this: we notice changes involving animals to a higher degree than other elements of a scene, including cars (a much greater present danger).[31]

Because the environment in which our species evolved—the "environment of evolutionary adaptation" or EEA—was vastly different than ours, our psychology is better adapted to the EEA than the contemporary environment. The EEA is not a particular point in time and space, like Central Africa 1 million years ago or South Asia 40,000 years ago, but a statistical aggregate of environments and selection pressures that existed over millions of years of our ancestors' evolution. These produced the majority of our psychological *adaptations*. They also produced *exaptations*, features that evolved under one selection pressure and persisted to be co-opted for another purpose. An example of an exaptation would be birds' feathers, originally evolved to provide warmth and co-opted to aid flight; another would be the pleasure we feel beholding an attractive person, originally evolved under selective pressure to reproduce with healthy mates, but co-opted to help advertisers sell products. *Spandrels* are nonadaptive or even maladaptive by-products of an adaptation—most of human culture can be considered spandrels, by-products of selection pressure for larger brains capable of social learning, cooperation, and flexible behavior. While large brains are adaptive, many of their contents are nonadaptive (modern art) or even evolutionarily maladaptive (celibacy).[32]

Moral considerations play no role in the evolutionary logic that produced our minds, along with animals and plants. The only driving forces are reproduction and survival. Whether evolution will favor a new trait or psychological tendency depends only on the extent to which it tends to provide an organism more surviving offspring, who produce more surviving offspring of their own: "fitness." It is not as though evolution actively "selects" reproduction-and-survival promoting behavior; rather, reproduction-and-survival promoting behavior tends to outlast and crowd out behaviors that do not lead to as much reproduction and survival.

Hence certain behaviors, like altruism and homosexual sex, pose explanatory challenges for evolutionary theory. Altruism seems like it could not possibly arise from evolution—after all, selfish individuals could take advantage to increase their reproduction-and-survival fitness at the expense of altruists, driving them extinct. Homosexual sex has been documented in hundreds of species; but a mutation causing animals to engage in nonprocreative sex would be expected to be driven to extinction. Yet there are several theories as to how evolution may have produced homosexual behavior.[33] For one, if homosexual pair bonding tends to produce more resources for heterosexual siblings, genes for homosexuality could survive and spread. Although the homosexual couple would not pass on their genes, in this "kin selection" scenario they would be helping to pass on the 50% of genes they share with their siblings by providing them with resources, care, or protection. Homosexuality may also be an exaptation of high sexual responsiveness: genes that promote hypersexuality may spread due to their promotion of more procreative sex, even if they also promote nonprocreative sex. Another possibility is that same-sex intercourse acts as a social glue, forming bonds and alliances that increase members' fitness overall, as is seen in dolphins.

While altruism and homosexuality seem to pose a challenge to evolutionary theory, all sorts of morally abhorrent behavior are easily explainable. For instance, infanticide is understandable as a way for males to maximize their reproductive success by eliminating rivals' offspring and making females available for being impregnated with the killer's offspring. Violence of all sorts is a perfectly reasonable evolutionary adaptation, as it can help males in particular defeat rivals for sex or food.[34] Even war has been explained by the same evolutionary logic; human males may have an innate (if unconscious) psychological connection between sex and violence.[35] Rape, a phenomenon present in some nonhuman species, is likely another unfortunate product of amoral evolutionary logic.[36]

Yet the same amoral logic that produced infanticide, war, and rape also produced morality. Altruism (defined as an action that produces a benefit for another person while incurring a cost for the actor) is a challenge for evolutionary reasoning to explain, yet intense, extensive cooperation is the key trait that differentiates our species from our closest relatives. To evolve, such behaviors would have to benefit an organism's "inclusive fitness," that is, the organism's relatives. Through kin selection, a fitness-sacrificing individual would be increasing the fitness of relatives who share many of the individual's genes.

However, this is not the only way. Humans have an innate tendency to form groups, and altruism and cooperation can readily evolve so long as they emerge within a group context; that is, they benefit group members.[37] Then, given favorable conditions in terms of group size and competition, even evolutionary anomalies like altruism and cooperation can be favored by natural selection. Human morality—which has a universal core across cultures, including variations on the Golden Rule—is a set of adaptations that allows for altruism and cooperation to flourish. While evolution produces the most immoral behaviors, it has also produced the innate sense by which we now judge these behaviors immoral.[38]

2 What Evolutionary Psychology Is, and Is not

This brief overview of evolutionary psychology should be complemented with a discussion of its limitations. For instance, cultural features can confound evolutionary psychology, especially when spread widely. Evolutionary psychologists have found that men in dozens of cultures prefer women with a certain waist-to-hip ratio similar to that of attractive movie stars, presumably because this signals fertility. However, it is also possible that this is due to the equally widespread reach of Hollywood movies. When researchers tested the preferences of men in an isolated South American jungle tribe, they found that they preferred the body shape common among women of their tribe, not of Hollywood stars.[39] Likewise, evolutionary psychologists have found that women more than men across many societies prefer mates with money and status, which is hypothesized to arise from an evolutionary history in which high-status, resource-rich men are presumed to have been better caretakers of children. However, the majority of societies today exhibit stark wealth gaps between men and women; hence, this may be a rational decision to mitigate the effects of this gender wealth gap. Further experiments found that women enjoying prosperity do not exhibit any hard-wired preference for wealthy mates.[40]

Given the rapid climatic changes we experienced during the past few million years, our psychology would have evolved to be adaptable. Our decision-making tendencies substantiate this. Dozens of experimental studies in psychology and behavioral economics show that we are not the rational decision-makers imagined by liberal economists.[41] Instead, we display flexible decision-making strategies attuned to our environment. Children raised in unfavorable environments, whether exposed to malnutrition, head injuries, or poverty, tend to make riskier decisions; as do those low in "embodied capital" (qualities like intelligence, strength, or attractiveness that aid in competition for resources).[42] The general rule is that those in situations of greater need take greater risks. (Including when the "need" is to impress potential mates.)[43]

Evolutionary psychology has attracted considerable criticism, much of which has been constructive, engaging with experimental and other data to suggest alternate hypotheses.[44] Overall, however, evolutionary psychology is not a philosophy, still less a moral code. It is little more than a hypothesis-generating mechanism attached to arguably the most productive scientific theory in history. It uses evolutionary logic to propose and test hypotheses about how our minds work. Effectively critiquing evolutionary psychology is impossible without engaging with the empirical testing of evolutionary hypotheses. Evolutionary-psychological hypotheses are just that—hypotheses—but when these have generated empirical support, the only way to argue against them is to offer a more thorough and satisfying interpretation.

Although evolutionary psychology provokes negative reactions, oftentimes their targets are unjustified interpretations of the evidence. Just because something *is* a certain way, does not mean that it *ought* to be: that a capacity for violence is part of our evolved psychology does not mean that we *ought* to be violent. More generally, there is no reason to make the "goals" of mindless evolution—reproduction and survival—our goals. There is an important distinction between attaining the highest level of evolutionary fitness and maximizing human happiness and satisfaction.[45] The two may often be at odds. And perhaps they *should* be; as Thomas Huxley argued, "the ethical progress of society depends not on imitating the cosmic process, still less in running away from it, but in *combating* it."[46]

Additionally, evolutionary psychology is unlikely to easily explain many features of modern human life. Even leaving social evolution aside, recent improvements in our understanding of genetics and epigenetics have complicated the simple picture of genetic inheritance predominant only decades ago. Whereas we once thought genes rather directly coded for traits and features, we now know that most traits are polygenic (caused by a great variety of genes acting in combination) and most genes are pleiotropic (causing a variety of effects). Drawbacks to evolutionary explanations—fitness-reducing yet relatively common phenomena such as depression, autism, and schizophrenia—may be the product of genes that usually, individually or in combinations, produce adaptive effects. These large assortments of genes may only produce nonadaptive or maladaptive effects (spandrels) in some combinations and under the influence of certain environmental factors, leaving the majority of the population with these genes to exhibit fitness-enhancing adaptations.[47] This would be similar to the case of sickle-cell anemia, which is caused by an allele that when paired with other variants (as it commonly is) protects from malaria, but when paired with another copy of the same allele causes disease.

3 Human Cooperation: How Evolution Managed to Create and Sustain It

Given the selfish, amoral logic that characterizes evolution, widespread human cooperation is an anomaly that deserves attention. Edward O. Wilson explains:

Natural selection at the individual level, with strategies evolving that contribute maximum number of mature offspring, has prevailed throughout the history of life. It typically shapes the physiology and behavior of organisms to suit a solitary existence, or at most to membership in loosely organized groups. The origin of eusociality, in which organisms behave in the opposite manner, has been rare in the history of life because group selection must be exceptionally powerful to relax the grip of individual selection. Only then can it modify the conservative effect of individual selection and introduce highly cooperative behavior into the physiology and behavior of the group members.[48]

Wilson should know; he gained renown studying ants, a eusocial insect. Until recently the cooperativeness of ants was thought to be exclusively explainable by a higher degree of genetic relatedness between ants in a colony—as high as 75% under some circumstances, versus a genetic relatedness of 50% between parents and children in mammals, and even lower levels between parents and grandchildren, cousins, etc.[49] This high relatedness and the theory of kin selection were thought to explain how evolution could produce cooperation in ants and bees, without selfish freeloaders emerging to sap its foundations. Hence Wilson's pithy reaction to Marxism: "Good ideology. Wrong species."[50] In other words, the level of cooperation Marxism prescribes is a great idea, but it would only work in a species like ants with their higher degree of relatedness. Humans, presumably, would be too selfish and competitive for socialism to work. However, science has progressed, and Wilson with it.[51]

Today we know that cooperation is written into our DNA.[52] Cooperation, rather than competition, is our default, as revealed by experiments in which people put under time constraints or primed to think intuitively act more cooperatively.[53] But unlike competition, which we share with apes and other animals, cooperation is a relatively new addition to our nature. Over the past few million years of hominid history, we can see that it was a momentous addition: cooperation, and the intelligence it requires, drove us from a marginal ape in East Africa threatened with extinction to traveling to the moon and sending rockets to Mars. As has happened repeatedly during the overall course of evolution on earth over billions of years, a major new transition has occurred. The eight major transitions evolution has produced in the complexity of living things have commonly involved the emergence of new forms of cooperation and interdependence; and in most transitions, the new form of cooperation was made possible by a new method of information transmission.[54]

Cooperation is the first of the two key ingredients. Chimpanzees live in highly competitive societies, though they are capable of minor examples of cooperative behavior like group hunting of small monkeys. Even so, this may be only the barest form of cooperation, with individuals primarily trying to catch the prey for themselves, but preferring that another chimp capture it to it escaping.[55] Human infants, however, interact to achieve joint goals by fourteen to eighteen months. In one series of experiments, infants at this age were paired with an adult and given the use of a two-person apparatus to obtain a toy. When the adult stopped playing her role, the children reacted unhappily and tried to reengage their erstwhile partners. Human-raised chimps, however, ignored the quitting partner and tried to achieve the common goal alone.[56]

By the time human children reach three, they display commitment to achieving joint goals even in the face of temptations and distractions.[57] In another experiment, pairs of three-year-olds were given a joint task with a reward. For one of the children, the reward was given before the task was accomplished—yet the child persevered until the task was complete and the other child received her reward. Chimpanzees in the same experiment do not persevere once rewarded—they quit, and leave their partner to fend for themselves. This is likely because while chimps can make *competitive* inferences—inferring food under a bucket a researcher is desperately reaching for—they cannot make *cooperative* inferences.

When cooperation was emerging as a hominid trait, it was likely helped (or even "supercharged") by sexual selection. Just as sexual selection has produced the wasteful but beautiful peacock's tail, it may also have helped produce our penchant for cooperation. How? Because we find morality sexy. Indeed, researchers have found that humans consider the following virtues sexually attractive: kindness, responsiveness to the needs of others, empathy, agreeableness, honesty, and heroism.[58] This reads like a list of requirements for effective cooperation; and once we started finding these qualities sexy, sexual selection could have driven them to levels not strictly justified by the cold logic of natural selection. Genes for altruistic and cooperative behavior are easy to spot (if less so than genes for a peacock's tail), making them easy targets for sexual selection.[59]

Being a good cooperative altruist may bring more sex, but that is not the end of its relationship to pleasure. Neuropsychological experiments reveal that behaving altruistically activates the same reward centers of the brain activated when receiving a gift.[60] And unlike receiving gifts, altruism results in brain signals reaching regions where emotional-bonding hormones circulate, as if to start an emotional bond with the beneficiary of our good deed.

These may be the same bonds described by selective investment theory, which proposes that altruism and cooperation were able to evolve outside of close family relationships through the formation of close social bonds. This meant we could evolve a capacity for significant long-term investment in the well-being of others because we could be assured that our partners in these bonds (between married couples, lifelong friends, business partners, soldiers) would do the same for us. From an evolutionary perspective, the closeness of these bonds effectively makes the individual fitnesses of those involved into one, interdependent fitness.[61] There is always the threat that one of the partners will seek individual advantage—marriages end in divorce, friends become enemies, business partners cheat, and soldiers become traitors. Yet so long as the benefits exceed the risk of betrayal, this phenomenon could be selected for by evolution. Also, since evidence suggests that we act more altruistically to those with whom we share friends,[62] social networks may help reduce the risk of betrayal by raising its cost.

The difference in cooperative ability between humans and other primates is even written into our faces: of the more than 200 species of primate, ours is the only one with highly visible eye direction.[63] The whites of our eyes communicate which way we are looking, and children as young as twelve months follow the eye direction rather than the head direction of others; apes, instead, follow head direction only. Since we are always advertising the direction of our gaze, we must have experienced predominantly cooperative situations during the period of hominid evolution; otherwise, our visible eye direction would have been used competitively or exploitatively ("I see where he has spotted food, so I'll get there first!"), and would likely have been eliminated by selection. It is not, as the studies of human children and adult apes might suggest, that humans simply evolved a higher degree of overall intelligence than our relatives. When two-and-a-half-year-olds were compared with chimpanzees and orangutans on tests of general intelligence, the human children only excelled in social tasks.[64]

One of the most interesting features of human reasoning is that it seems to have evolved to support argumentation. In light of the vast research into human reasoning and its flaws, one of the best-supported hypotheses is that its primary function is to argue effectively; even the many serious defects in human reasoning are beneficial for making arguments.[65] This applies to moral reasoning too, in which we miss the actual reasons we came to a moral judgment (which are largely hidden from conscious view) and search for the best reasons someone else ought to agree with our judgment.[66] This form of argumentation likely arose in a cooperative context, like group hunting, in which it benefits everyone for each individual to make the strongest case for their opinion so that group decisions can be made on the strongest available evidence.[67] In experimental models of similar scenarios, the most common outcome of this kind of group argumentation is "truth wins"—that is, the group usually chooses the best option.[68] This result may depend on the group having a diversity of opinions and an egalitarian structure.[69]

4   Aggressive Egalitarians

"Nature has left this tincture in the blood
That all men wou'd be tyrants if they cou'd"
—Daniel Defoe, *The History of the Kentish Petition*

Cooperation, language, and reasoning laid the tracks for humanity's runaway success. But evolution does not often make 180-degree turns: we could not have gone from a fully competitive, individualistic species to a fully cooperative, group-oriented one overnight. Instead, even as evolution promoted cooperation and altruism, older tendencies toward competitiveness and exploitation remained. For cooperation and altruism to emerge and remain rooted, we had to find ways to ensure that our self-aggrandizing, selfish instincts were sidelined.

Enter the "aggressive egalitarians." Sounding like a PR firm's suggested name for Stalin's secret police, evolutionary anthropologist Christopher Boehm coined it to characterize hominid societies during our evolution; it is what allowed our ancestors to hunt cooperatively, especially for big game.[70] Members of early human groups were equals, and if any member attempted to become a boss or chief, he would be ridiculed. If that did not work and the would-be boss continued to try wielding power, he would be ostracized. If he persisted, he would either be expelled—a potentially life-threatening punishment—or executed outright, usually by a family member after group consultations. This is observed among all extant hunter-gatherer societies.

Ancestral chimpanzees, however, were just as hierarchical as today, with alphas bullying others to monopolize mates and food. Just as today, there would have been subordinate rebellions, when lower ranking chimps gathered allies to overthrow an alpha—even in chimpanzee psychology there is a strong dislike of being dominated.[71] As hominids branched off from the lineage we share with chimps, we retained the tendency for individuals to maximize power, but also a strong dislike of being dominated. At some point, however, our dislike of others dominating us became stronger than the individual desire to wield power. (This also extended to sex equality.)[72] This was the case by 250,000 years ago, when our ancestors first took on large-game hunting as a regular occupation. Large-game hunting requires considerable cooperation, making it vulnerable to free riders or exploitative bullies: if someone tries to shirk their responsibilities, or take the largest share and dole out leftovers according to whim, cooperation collapses.[73] If left unsuppressed by aggressive egalitarian social structures, such conflicts would have sapped the foundations of cooperative hunting, making it a functional impossibility and leaving rich sources of food untapped. Additionally, while there is a wealth of evidence from climate science, anthropology, evolutionary biology, and archaeology to support the egalitarian model of our ancestral social structure, there is little convincing evidence for the existence of human hierarchies until recently.[74]

Although the timing of the development of aggressive egalitarianism is uncertain, there are only three alternatives:

> One is that archaic humans had not progressed very far beyond ancestral behaviors in the matter of keeping down alphas and that large-game hunting led to radical political change and also to some severe initial conflict in putting down the poorly inhibited alphas. Another would be that before that, with earlier humans their coalitions would have partially reduced alpha power – in order to improve personal autonomy and probably also to increase the breeding opportunities of lower-ranking males – and that this would have made the transition to relying upon large game much easier. The third would be that decisive egalitarianism was already in place [possibly as early as 1.8 million years ago] when such hunting began and that in fact this might actually have been a prerequisite for large-game hunting to succeed.[75]

We evolved an "egalitarian syndrome," a universal part of human psychology defined as "the complex of cognitive perspectives, ethical principles, social norms, and individual and collective attitudes promoting equality."[76] This did not require a lucky mutation, but would have emerged from selfish tendencies that did not entail genetic relatedness on the part of cooperators.[77] Experiments in neuroscience have revealed that our concerns for equality are "implemented on a fundamental physiological level similar to breathing, heartbeat, hunger, and pain," and our ability to imagine the feelings of others drives the egalitarian syndrome.[78] Our brains even register signals of pleasure at punishing those who abuse trust.[79]

The "aggressive" part of our egalitarian social structure would not only have supported the cooperation required for big-game hunting, but left an impact on the gene pool: the most aggressive and domineering individuals—alphas in ancestral groups—would have been exiled or killed, eliminating their genes. Likewise, inveterate cheaters and thieves would have been selected against.[80] This sort of punishment is essential for cooperative behaviors to emerge and stabilize in the first place, and in modern societies, the willingness to punish unequal behavior is correlated with altruism in that society.[81] The underlying evolutionary solution to the problem of free riders or bullies came in the form of morality, the feelings or dispositions we share that promote altruism, act as a social glue, and prevent dangerously anti-social impulses from destroying the foundation of group cooperation.[82] Although the moralities of different cultures vary, they all condemn murder, abuse of authority, cheating, lying, theft, and disruptive behavior.[83]

Yet viewed from today's perspective, aggressive egalitarianism is alien. Since hierarchy was reestablished ten to twelve thousand years ago,[84] our species has seen a massive growth in inequality, such that seemingly every week a new statistic shows how a hundred, fifty, and maybe then just a handful of people own more wealth than the bottom half of the population. Since we are largely ignorant of our species' pre-written history, we view hierarchy as normal, even natural. But it is a recent anomaly for us.

5 THE OTHER EVOLUTION

Comparing the success of humans with other animals, one can forgive the hubris of the first person to propose that God made us in His image. We represent a quantum leap in evolution. "The human species is a spectacular evolutionary anomaly, so we ought to expect that the evolutionary system behind it is pretty anomalous as well."[85]

As in other major transitions in evolutionary history, the transition we represent was facilitated by greater cooperation and a new means of transmitting information: language. Before us, the only form of information to have evolved on earth was that encoded in DNA. Once we developed language, however, another form of information displayed the telltale signs of an evolutionary process: ideas.[86]

The history of technology demonstrates in clear fashion how ideas evolve. The wristwatch is a good example: incredibly complex devices, built step by step, over decades and centuries, with countless inventors adding one small improvement here, one clever innovation there. Even simple devices like forks or paper clips evolved in the same piecemeal fashion, with variations introduced during their development but only a few enduring.[87] This is not *analogous* with, or similar to, biological evolution, it is simply a separate instantiation of the same evolutionary algorithm.[88]

Unlike biological evolution, social evolution features random and intentional forces. On the random side, there is cultural mutation, in which an idea is misremembered or understood in a different way while being learned (similar to what happens in a game of telephone), and cultural drift, when certain ideas are lost at the death of the few people who know them (as when languages die or complex skills to produce older technologies are lost). Intentional or decision-making forces are those produced by acts of human choice, and come in several forms. Guided variation occurs when ideas are modified as they are received and passed on. The development of technology or science is an example; we do not simply pass on the same idea, we improve it. Another intentional force is biased transmission. There is content-based bias, whereby features of the idea make it likelier to spread or one version of it becomes more common because it is easier to remember. Frequency-based bias occurs when people copy ideas most common within their culture. Fashion trends, or the decision by millions of people globally to learn English as a second language, are examples. There is also model-based bias, in which the ideas held by successful or prestigious people are preferentially copied—the bias advertisers take advantage of when they pay celebrities to endorse products. Lastly, even old-fashioned natural selection can act as a force in social evolution whenever the content of ideas influences the survival and reproductive success of those holding the idea. For example, some religious ideas can spread through natural selection if they influence believers to have more children than people subscribing to another religion—or none.[89] This has been observed for conservative Christian denominations in the USA over the past century.[90] Social psychologists have studied these intentional forces of social evolution independently of evolutionary theory.[91]

Social evolution is powerfully affected by ecological and economic conditions. A study of rice-growing versus wheat-growing regions in China found that the choice of crop was a powerful predictor of whether the region was predominantly individualist or collectivist. Growing rice requires greater cooperation, and culture has evolved to adapt to this ecological and economic constraint.[92] Biological constraints, particularly disease-causing pathogens, have also been found to influence social evolution. Areas prone to pathogens tend to be conservative, ethnocentric, and collectivist (and so less able to spread or be infected by diseases), while regions with fewer pathogens tend to be inhabited by individualist cultures.[93]

Social evolution does not operate in isolation and since the emergence of culture, biological evolution has not operated alone either. Instead, these processes have engaged in a dance.[94] Biology influences culture so profoundly that it is often invisible. No culture can survive which prohibits its members from eating, tells them they can fly from cliffs, or enjoins them to marry bears. Biology, in other words, keeps culture leashed—and culture influences biology. The cultural practice of raising cattle has produced genetic mutations that allow adults to digest cow's milk (lactose intolerance was our species' default) and the cultural development of language has modified the genes that build our larynx and auditory system. Social evolution can even obviate the need for biological evolution, as when humans settled cold regions and instead of evolving fur, constructed clothing from the fur of animals who *had* biologically adapted to the climate.[95]

Gene-culture coevolution has even affected the biology of other species. Cultural products like pesticides have killed off some insects and helped propagate others, and antibiotics have killed some bacteria while cultivating deadlier bacteria.[96] The dance between social and biological evolution creates chaotic, fractal-like complexities, making predictions impossible. For instance, a cholera outbreak is usually understood only as

> the coming of cholera bacteria to lots of people. But cholera lives among the plankton along the coasts when it isn't in people. The plankton blooms when the seas get warm and when runoff from sewage and from agricultural

fertilizers feed the algae. The products of world trade are carried in freighters that use seawater as ballast that is discharged before coming to port, along with the beasts that live in that ballast water. The small crustaceans eat the algae, the fish eat the crustaceans, and the cholera bacterium meets the eaters of fish. Finally, if the public health system of a nation has already been gutted by structural adjustment of the economy, then the full explanation of the epidemic is, jointly, *Vibrio cholerae* and the World Bank.[97]

These social-biological complexities bedevil efforts to explain our social world and devise intelligent policies. For instance, knowing a pesticide kills a certain bug may lead us to believe that its use will control the pest (a complex, ecological claim), and will thereby increase food production to alleviate hunger (a political-economic claim).[98] Yet even if we knew that a new pesticide kills pests, we cannot be sure that increased food production will have any effect on hunger worldwide—there are too many social variables. Wars could break out that make delivery of the extra food impossible; religious leaders may forbid followers from eating it; or the spread of a new ideology may alter systems for distributing extant food, ending hunger with no help from the pesticide.

With family-strength bonds extended to members of one's tribe, the scope for cooperative gains increased. And since "tribe" is an arbitrary distinction, our hard-wired instincts have been repurposed—turned into exaptations—by social evolution over time.[99] From family, to tribe, to kingdom, to nation (and possibly beyond, to humanity), our social instincts have been used to support ever-larger groups and make them cohere. It seems as though the great gains to be had from cooperation are an evolutionary force pushing us toward unity as a species.[100] While there are differences across cultures,[101] experimental studies have found that as globalization increases, so too do individuals draw broader group boundaries, "eschewing parochial motivations in favor of cosmopolitan ones."[102]

However, since social evolution proceeds exponentially faster than biological evolution, our hard-wired instincts can hardly catch up.[103] As two pioneers in the field of gene-culture coevolution put it:

> Our social instincts do not prepare us to submit to command or tolerate inequality. As a result, our social institutions should resemble a well-broken-in pair of badly fitting boots. We can walk quite a ways in the institutions of complex societies, but at least some segments of society hurt for the effort.[104]

6 Recent Evolution—In Evolution, and Our Understanding of It

Evolutionary psychology broadly accepts that our psychology evolved during the period starting with the emergence of hominids, continuing through the emergence of *Homo sapiens*, and ending with the development of sedentary agricultural civilizations.[105] There is, however, evidence that our evolution may have sped up over the past 10–20,000 years.[106] The high population growth our species experienced would itself predict an acceleration, as the number of mutations overall would likewise increase. Moreover, high population growth makes it likelier that adaptive mutations would spread to saturation. Techniques for uncovering recently selected genes have found that the past 10–20,000 years have seen a significant increase in genetic evolution.

Some of this recent selection has domesticated us. The most aggressive have been weeded out especially fast during our most recent period of evolution.[107] Not only are aggressive individuals likelier to kill each other, but large civilizations reduce their numbers further by sending them to die in wars or executing them for crimes. Additionally, those who found it harder to conform to social norms and restrain aggressive impulses would be less likely to be chosen as mates, further reducing their numbers.[108] (This may help explain the historical trend away from violence— ancient sedentary societies experienced rates of violent deaths thirty times higher than those of the past century, even with its two world wars and countless smaller wars.)[109] As a result, our features softened— jaws reduced, faces flattened—changes like those seen in many of our favorite breeds of dog as we bred them to be friendlier. Less flatteringly, our brains have shrunk since the beginning of agriculture 10,000 years ago.[110]

One recently selected gene that plays a role in speech[111] may have contributed to the creative explosion of modern humans who spread from Africa.[112] Even genes for lighter skin, apparent in populations living in northerly climates with less sun, appear to have originated recently, after agriculture. Lighter skin allows for vitamin D to be produced by ultraviolet radiation acting on the skin, a strangely plantlike way of provisioning this vitamin. Fresh meat contains plenty of vitamin D, however, so our ancestors in darker climates did not need to lose melanin until agriculture changed our diets by replacing calories (and vitamins) from meat with calories from plants (without vitamin D).

Also, populations with a longer history of agriculture, with a longer exposure to a high-carbohydrate diet, are less susceptible to diabetes today.[113] Long-time farming populations have also been exposed to a greater variety of infectious diseases due to high population density, and therefore have recently evolved more effective immune-system defenses than hunter-gatherers.[114]

Studies have revealed that college students' genes differ significantly in the areas associated with mathematical abilities, motivation, executive functions, and adjustment-related behaviors involving alcohol use and emotions compared to those who do not go to college.[115] Here, culture may be acting as an agent of natural selection: *if* college graduates reproduce at a different average rate.

This brings up an important point: recent selective pressures can only exert an appreciable effect if those whose genes are better suited to the pressures had more children. It is not enough to identify a selection pressure, note that one group tended to have more children than other groups, and leap to the conclusion that the more successful group had *genes* that better equipped them to handle that selection pressure. For instance, one hypothesis is that recent evolution during the Industrial Revolution produced people more capable of excelling under capitalist forms of economic organization,[116] so that those whose genes facilitated a better business sense became rich and had more surviving children and grandchildren. Hence eventually, the entire population became better suited to capitalism and this explains why today some countries are more competitive in the global economy.

Leaving aside the obvious flaw that such a theory is innocent of economic, political, military, and cultural history, there is a fundamental defect in its *evolutionary* logic. The traits that tend toward greater success in capitalism, and the genes that presumably contribute to such traits, may have had nothing to do with the ancestral accumulation of wealth. For instance, those who had accumulated appreciable wealth a millennium ago in England may have done so thanks to a greater capacity for organized violence, rather than any greater-than-average mercantile skill.[117] As generations went by and property was inherited, the wealthy class would comprise those "selected" for ancestral predation (not mercantile skill) as well as those of lower classes whose political and mercantile skills (plus social network position, luck, and other historical factors) allowed them to accumulate fortunes. Exactly which traits were conducive to rising from poverty and accumulating a fortune is an open question, but given the central role of the slave trade in generating the capital for Europe's rise, a psychopathic disdain for other people may have been just as much a "selected" trait as mercantile skill.[118] Furthermore, it is unlikely that the traits (and family histories) helping to make fortunes in the feudal era are the same leading to success in business during the capitalist era.[119] Forces of social evolution, particularly economic and political institutions, could account entirely for patterns of wealth within and between nations.[120]

The most recently selected (5–10,000 years ago) areas of the human genome are associated with the immune system, the cell cycle, DNA and protein metabolism, reproduction, and the brain.[121] The recently selected genes affecting the brain are linked to better school-related skills, but worse performance in several social, emotional, and cognitive tasks. However, we do not know how these genes affect development and it is likely that the expression of such recently selected genes is heavily influenced by environmental factors. Hence a genetic cause (at least as a sole or primary cause) for today's national differences in wealth and power is implausible.

Although it is plausible to speculate that the rise of agricultural civilizations may have had something to do with group-level genetic differences, the historical record of such civilizations rising around the same time in far-flung locations (today's Egypt, India/Pakistan, China, Mexico, and Peru) tends to falsify such a hypothesis.[122] In addition, the genetic variability of modern humans is low in comparison with our numbers—less than chimpanzees, for instance, even though there are far more humans than chimps.[123] Genetic variability is also not restricted to that *between* human cultures; rather, "any small village typically contains about the same amount of genetic variation as another village located on any other continent. Each population is a microcosm that recapitulates the entire human macrocosm even if the precise genetic compositions vary slightly."[124] Therefore, while differences between groups *can* explain superficial features (skin tone, lactose intolerance, facial structure), they are highly unlikely to fully explain observed differences in social structures, economics, politics, or other emergent characteristics.

This is particularly likely given what we are currently learning about epigenetics, which describes how variations in traits and behavior arise that are not strictly attributable to genetic variation.[125] The most basic revelation is that how genes express themselves is highly dependent on environmental conditions: A gene "for" one trait in one environment may produce different effects in another. More revolutionary, epigenetic changes during the lifetime of an organism can be passed on. Smoking tobacco during pregnancy not only affects the exposed offspring, but nicotine-linked disruptions of the pulmonary system are transmitted to subsequent generations.[126] A study of the Dutch Hunger Winter during World War II found that six decades later, those who had suffered from malnutrition displayed persistent epigenetic effects on a gene regulating growth and development.[127] The children of Holocaust survivors also display epigenetic effects of their parents' trauma.[128] These changes are often compounded by political and economic pressures in the cases of Native and African-Americans in the USA.[129] (In a dark irony, *social* evolution begins to create small epigenetic, *biological* differences between "races" which did not exist when the "race" meme was created.)

Social traits and behaviors are also affected by epigenetic changes. The highly social cichlid fish has an elaborate dominance hierarchy, and when an alpha male is removed from a group, a formerly-subordinate male quickly adopts dominant behaviors—during this time, not only does the new alpha change his body's coloration, but genes involved in his brain express differently.[130] In humans, children born into low socioeconomic status experience epigenetic changes linked to a defensive, stress-reactant psychology, which may better prepare them for threatening conditions (while increasing their likelihood of physical and mental illnesses). These changes may even have a transgenerational impact, with affected children's epigenetic adaptations being passed on to their children as well.[131]

Therefore, theories of recent human evolution that rely on the older, simpler picture of genetic development and evolution are implausible or at least cannot be tested until significant progress is made in genetics and epigenetics. The 2,500-year-old view of Confucius is more likely accurate: "Men's natures are alike; it is their habits that carry them far apart."[132]

7 So What? How Evolution Matters to Today's Societies

Biological evolution is the source of our species and its characteristics, from cooperativeness to aggression, from skin color to bone structure. But it is harder to imagine how the evolution of genes could have any effects on something as purely cultural as politics. Yet there is considerable evidence that biological evolution has made significant contributions to our political nature.

Perhaps the easiest way to test for the effects of genes on human behaviors and dispositions arises from a natural experiment provided by identical and fraternal twins. Identical (monozygotic) twins come from the same fertilized egg and share roughly all of their genes,[133] while fraternal (dizygotic) twins come from two separate fertilized eggs and share roughly half of their genes, as do all siblings. Hence, the first place to look for genetic effects on any trait is in the differences and similarities between identical and fraternal twins. If a sample of identical twins correlate at a rate of 80% on a trait (e.g., if eight out of ten identical twins have the same favorite flavor of ice cream) and a paired sample of fraternal twins correlate at 40%, we can estimate that *on the level of population* (not at the individual level), ice cream preferences are 40% heritable. In other words, 40% of the population-level variation in ice cream preferences can be linked to genetic heritability. The remaining 60% of variation can be ascribed to shared environmental influences (like the ice cream flavors their parents brought home), unique environmental influences (like one's unique friends and the influence of their flavor preferences), and measurement error (like when a survey question is interpreted differently from how the questioner intended). To disentangle the effects of shared versus unique environments, measurements are taken of common variables in twins' home environment.

Twin studies of political attitudes along a Left-Right dimension have consistently found heritable genetic factors to play a significant role. Opinions on political issues like socialism or federal housing were found to have an average heritability of 32%.[134] Political ideology has been found to be 56% heritable, egalitarianism 50%, and right-wing authoritarianism 48%.[135] Forms of political participation have been found to be partly heritable, with estimates of 35% for attending protests, 41% for voting and contacting officials, 44% for financial contributions, and 52% for contacting government officials.[136] Even social trust has been found to be heritable at rates between 30–40%.[137]

Similar results have also been found in cross-cultural studies, with heritability estimates of political ideology varying across countries, with an average level of around 40%.[138] Broadening twin studies by including extended family members in heritability estimates has produced similar results.[139] Studies looking at the heritability of political attitudes over time have found that environmental influences play a stronger role during childhood, while genetic influences assert themselves more after children have left their parents' home.[140] A rare study investigating heritability differences between right-wing and left-wing ideologies found that genetic influences on the development of left-wing ideology were more affected by the home environment, while right-wing ideology was more affected by one's unique environment outside of the home.[141]

Overall, these studies seem to show that different sets of genes may create varying levels of susceptibility to particular political ideologies.[142] It is not as though these studies suggest a "socialism" gene that disposes people to be favorable to socialism, or a "federal housing" gene that makes people support the idea of the government providing low-cost housing for the poor. Rather, genes have broad effects on individual psychology and personality, which make us likelier to adopt one political position rather than another—for instance, genetic variations that affect one's sensitivity to fear may affect our reactions to unknown outsiders, shaping our stance on immigration policy.[143]

After twin studies confirm some genetic heritability underlying political attitudes, the next challenge is to locate genes that may produce these population-level effects.[144] The first step has been to analyze portions of many people's genomes, identifying genetic similarities that correlate with similarities in ideology. Many such regions have been identified in one study, but only one area with a reliably high correlation contained any gene known to be associated with human social behavior.[145] Another way to proceed is by choosing a gene known to be associated with social behavior, and testing a sample of people with and without it. This has been done for a gene associated with brain function, and another study found that those with a variant of the gene displayed more altruistic behavior than those without.[146] Such studies can also test for environmental influences on genes. For instance, a gene associated with novelty-seeking behavior was found to correlate with left-wing political ideology, and this increased as a function of the number of friends an individual had as a child.[147] Hence, this gene may predispose people to seek new experiences, and if a holder of this gene has friends during childhood who provide exposure to a variety of opinions, there is a greater likelihood they will develop a left-wing ideology.

However, the conclusions of these studies are not straightforward. A part of the problem is the complex way genes work. For instance, an animal as simple as a fruit fly, with only 100,000 neurons compared to our 100 billion, has at least 266 separate genes that code for proteins known to be involved in varying levels of aggression—yet the heritability of aggression in fruit flies is only about 10%.[148] Causation in biological systems runs in two directions, upward from the genome and epigenome and downward from the environment, organism, organs, tissues, and even cells, with feedback and feed-forward loops between levels.[149] Furthermore, since the genome is so large, finding correlations between genes and traits is highly likely due to chance, and extremely large sample sizes may be required.[150] Hence capturing individual genes' contributions to the heritability of political ideology remains a distant goal.

Twin studies require particularly conservative interpretation. For instance, one twin study found that empathy was about 30% heritable (an estimate roughly in line with prior research).[151] Yet a meta-analysis of studies measuring levels of empathy in US college students from 1979 to 2009 found that empathy had decreased by 34–48% in that time.[152] Could genes explain 30% of this drop—did empathic people stop having as many children during these three decades? Such an interpretation is highly unlikely.

The precise-seeming heritability estimates produced by twin studies warrant skepticism. First, heritability is confusing: it seems like a property of the trait, when it is a description of the population in which the trait appears.[153] "Political ideology is 40% heritable" does not mean 40% of one's ideology is passed on or that there is a 40% chance a child will develop the ideology of its parent, but that within the studied population 40% of the variance between parents and children was heritable. Also, a high degree of heritability *within* a group says nothing about variation *between* groups. Most of the variation in political attitudes among Trinidadians may be genetic, but that does not mean that their political attitudes are (mostly) genetically transmitted. It means Trinidadians exhibit genetic variation that affects political attitudes more than environmental and cultural differences in Trinidad. This tells us little about Jamaicans or any other group. In addition, heritability estimates can be strongly affected by environmental conditions.[154]

Apportioning variance in political ideology to *either* genetic *or* environmental factors is problematic. The conceptual opposition between nature and nurture arose in Anglo-American culture in the 1800s and has influenced science since—but if "nature versus nurture" *ever* made sense, it does not in light of contemporary genetics.[155] More specifically, twin studies can only offer trustworthy, precise estimates of genetic and environmental contributions to a trait when *all* causal factors have been demarcated and act *independently*.[156] However, everything we know about biology tells us that it is complex, non-linear, and nonadditive—making truly independent causal factors unlikely.[157]

Twin studies also rely on an assumption that the environments experienced by identical twins are no different on average from the environments experienced by fraternal twins. This is how an estimate of heredity can be plucked out of data about similarities between identical and fraternal twins: if the identical twins are more alike than fraternal twins, this extra similarity must be genetic, *providing* there is nothing about identical twins' environments that is more similar than those of fraternal twins. (Greater similarities between identical versus fraternal twins must come from their more-similar genes if the environments are essentially the same.) Estimates of heritability rely on this assumption, and they are inflated to the extent that the environment shared by identical twins is more similar than the environment shared by fraternal twins. This would occur, for instance, if family members, teachers, and friends tended to treat identical twins more similarly than fraternal twins. Studies of twins have found precisely that.[158] This may be the source of the "mystery of missing heritability" arising from high estimates of heritability from twin studies, but studies of the genome itself that have turned up relatively few genes associated with various traits, and which explain only a fraction of the estimated heritability. Twin studies may produce inflated estimates for heredity by confounding genetic effects with gene-culture, gene-environment, and a host of potential epigenetic interactions.[159]

Twin studies are useful for determining *whether* there are genetic effects on a trait, but less for determining *how much*.[160] They are valuable for demonstrating that some characteristics we would likely have assumed entirely environmentally determined—such as political views—are influenced by genes. Likewise, critiques of genome-wide association and gene-behavior linkage studies are correct in urging caution. The tools available can only make slow progress in understanding *how* genes and environment interact to produce political dispositions.[161] A great deal of future research is needed to tease apart the contributors to ideological development.[162]

8   What We Know About Our Evolved Political Psychology

While we may be decades from approaching a complete understanding of how genes interact with our environment to produce political dispositions, we can sketch an outline. Genetic evolution has produced minds with varying propensities and traits that pull us in the direction of one or another of the political ideologies we are exposed to. Even though we do not know exactly how individual genes function to produce this result, the result is clear. It is written into our brains.

Not many people would guess that the way our brains react to seeing disgusting pictures could predict political ideology. Yet that is what a study found using fMRI scans of participants' brain activity, which reliably predicted whether participants aligned with the Left or Right.[163] In another study, brain scans of people making judgments of risk were found to be better predictors of ideology (82.9% accurate) than knowing the political party a person's mother and father identifies with (69.5% accurate).[164] Even the size of certain brain structures can predict political orientation: those with greater volume of gray matter in the ACC (which processes conflicts between parts of the brain) tend toward the Left, while those with greater volume of gray matter in the right amygdala (which processes fear) and the left insula (which processes disgust) tend toward the Right.[165]

Sensitivity to disgust and fear is one of the fundamental neurological differences between people who identify with the Right or Left. While leftists are better at detecting (and overriding) conflicts between their intentions and automatic responses, rightists are constitutionally more vigilant at detecting threats.[166] In studies across several countries and using different research methods, rightists display greater attention to, and fixation on, negative, disturbing, and disgusting images.[167] Leftists exhibit stronger connections in the "human mirror-neuron system," which simulates the feelings of others and is linked to social and emotional cognition, including empathy.[168] In general, leftists are more attuned to "appetitive," or positive features of the environment, while rightists are more responsive to "aversive," negative stimuli.[169]

Beyond brain scanners, neurological differences appear in so-called implicit association tasks, where automatic reactions too fast for conscious deliberation are measured. Rightists display greater automatic preferences for order over chaos and conformity over rebelliousness, while leftists show preferences for flexibility over stability and progress over tradition.[170] Research has even found that people can judge politicians' ideologies—with better-than-chance accuracy—by viewing their photographs.[171]

Even between five and seven, children of right-wing versus left-wing parents display neurological differences, with children of right-wing parents showing greater neurological sensitivity to angry, threatening faces.[172] By 18, children of parents with authoritarian parenting attitudes are likelier to be right wing, while those of parents using more sensitive caregiving styles were closer to the Left.[173] By the first year of primary school, children already exhibit structured and consistent political orientations.[174] In one study, the personalities of preschool children were analyzed and then reexamined 20 years later.[175] Children that would later grow into conservative adults were described as fearful, rigid, vulnerable, inhibited, easily offended, and relatively over-controlled; children that would later grow into liberal adults were described as resilient, self-reliant, energetic, somewhat dominating, developing close relationships, and relatively under-controlled.

Neuroimaging research has revealed that thinking about politics taps into parts of our brain that evolved to facilitate social cognition, which involves coalitions, hierarchies, cooperation, and alliances.[176] Only people who are unknowledgeable about politics use the same parts of their brains to think about politics as they would technical subjects, such as plumbing or science.[177] If political cognition is simply the newest form of social cognition, these neurological results make sense. We do not have genes "for" conservatism or liberalism (in the U.S.); communism or capitalist democracy (in China); social democracy or neoliberalism (in Europe); we have genes that tend to produce psychological dispositions in social cognition that express themselves by making us likelier to adopt one or another ideology present in our information ecology. These dispositions are gut reactions: unthinking tendencies to respond a certain way to different ideas and situations. Most likely, they evolved alongside morality, the key psychological adaptation that allowed us to navigate life in highly cooperative societies. For the majority of evolutionary history they have been tuned to respond to pre-agricultural life, so that today we form opinions (Stirner's "spooks") on political issues involving millions, using psychological adaptations designed for smaller groups. So it is that political elites can manipulate judgments using individual stereotypes of inveterate criminals and dangerous foreigners.[178]

Just as some chemical compounds mix while others repel (like water and oil), we display "elective affinities" toward some ideas and aversions to others.[179] After a significant amount of political ideas have been learned, our brains display signs of pleasure or reward when we are exposed to other ideas that fit with our Left or Right disposition and background knowledge. This can produce a physiological feedback loop, causing our initial political disposition to snowball into an ever stronger, tightly organized, and knowledgeable ideological stance.[180]

The basic psychological dispositions that lead toward the adoption of one or another political ideology may be the same that produce differences in personality.[181] The strongest associations are between "openness to new experiences" and left-wing orientation, and between "conscientiousness" and right-wing orientation.[182] (More recent work has cast doubt on this link,[183] which may be better explained by needs for cognition and cognitive closure influencing ideology.)[184] Experiments in Italy and the Netherlands found that leftists tend to be more pro-social or other-oriented, while rightists tend to be more individualistic and competitive.[185] Studies of liberals and conservatives in the United States found that liberals were more novelty-seeking, open-minded, curious, and creative, and conservatives more organized, conventional, and orderly. These characteristics were consistently found using self-reported personality assessments, observed behavior in social interactions, and even personal possessions and the organization of living and working spaces.[186] (For instance, conservatives' bedrooms were neater, cleaner, and included more organizational items like calendars, while liberals' bedrooms included more cultural memorabilia, and books and music of greater variety.)

In meta-analyses of dozens of studies, left-wing orientation correlated moderately with cognitive ability, tolerance of ambiguity, and integrative complexity.[187] Independent of educational attainment, those on the Left tend to demonstrate greater intelligence. Individuals with lower intelligence are likelier to endorse right-wing ideologies and harbor prejudice against minorities, independent of education and socioeconomic status.[188] Right-wingers report greater certainty and stability in their opinions, exhibit more consistency between implicit and explicit attitudes, score higher on intuitive thinking and self-deception, and tend to process information heuristically rather than systematically; in general, right-wingers are less epistemically rigorous.[189] Related scientific results include relationships such as low-effort thinking promoting political conservatism, abstract thinking reducing conservative prejudices, and lower creativity and stronger illusory correlations among conservatives[190] (although these relationships may pertain only to social conservatives as opposed to economic conservatives).[191] These results may be partially explained by right-wingers' greater persistence in hewing to habit and lower levels of cognitive control and self-regulation.[192] In experiments involving attribution-making (deciding whether someone's actions were due to the person's intrinsic nature, or situational and environmental factors), left-wingers can be made to reason like right-wingers by imposing time constraints or distractions, suggesting that the cognitive style of the Right is simpler.[193] These differences in cognitive ability appear early, with children having greater difficulty attending to tasks at 54 months being likelier to align with the Right by 18.[194]

While genetic and neuroscientific research suggests a hard-wired, heritable component to political orientation, there is evidence that our environments can reshape our brains' structure.[195] For instance, while left-wing and right-wing people display differences in the sizes and activity levels of certain brain structures, involvement with partisan politics may drive those differences irrespective of heredity. Changes in cognitive functions of other types are also known to change brain structure, as when people studying a map of London for a taxi driver examination demonstrated growth in the brain region relating to memory formation.[196] Therefore, while genetic influences shape our brains and make some ideologies more attractive, so too ideologies may shape our psychological and physiological characteristics. People choose ideas and ideas choose people.[197]

Environmental influences also shape personality traits and shift political orientations. For instance, low socioeconomic status is a reliable predictor of obedience to authority, which correlates with right-wing political orientation.[198] Genes may influence media preferences, which affect the development of ideology.[199] Even writing an autobiography has been shown to temporarily increase conservatism, by focusing on how the status quo was arrived at by a series of free choices (and hence must be just).[200] Studies of experienced academics and Supreme Court nominees suggest that working in an occupation that requires understanding multiple, conflicting arguments and evidence increases the likelihood of a leftward shift in opinions.[201] A study of voting records and economic performance in the USA over nearly a century found that a threatening economic environment influences voting toward the Right, while a positive economic environment influences voting toward the Left.[202]

Though several parts of the world remain to be studied, our evolved psychology may include general dispositions that tend to lead us to support tradition and inequality (the psychological Right) or change and equality (the psychological Left). (An alternative conception depicts these dispositions as protection from threat or freedom from oppression—research in this area is ongoing.)[203] Genes and environment produce the biology of our minds, including the basic components of political orientation. During development, our minds form cognitive, emotional, and information-processing traits; these, along with early social environments, affect the development of our personality and values, which influence our selection of a political ideology from those to which we are exposed.[204] In some cases, the prevalent ideological packages fit our genetic predispositions and in other cases they conflict,[205] producing a kaleidoscopic pattern of ideological components.[206] Each of these factors exerts mutual influence on each other during one's lifetime.[207] One may have a genetic predisposition to right-wing ideas, but losing one's job or experiencing financial problems may incline one to adopt left-wing economic views.[208]

Some ideas or pieces of information are more "sticky," depending on the political orientation our genes and environments jointly produce. Other ideas are likelier to be adopted simply because they fit with the political discourse we are exposed to through the media.[209] For instance, we may strongly believe abortion is evil and have no strong opinions on free trade agreements. But if the political discourse we hear packages opposition to abortion with support for free trade agreements, we may also adopt the latter. Hence, gene-culture coevolution produces a variety of conflicting forces: biological predispositions, environmental influences on development, and the political ideologies and their informational content prevalent in various cultures at different times.

The political environment offers limited choices with which to match our evolved dispositions for tradition/change or equality/inequality (or protection/freedom). For instance, in Western Europe, with its history of a capitalist socioeconomic structure, acceptance of inequality correlates strongly with right-wing political orientation. However, in Eastern Europe, with its recent history of socialism, there is no such correlation.[210] This could be due to the fact that during the recent history of Eastern Europe, a desire for tradition over change would have meant preferring the relatively equal distribution of wealth characteristic of socialism. In Scandinavian countries, with a recent history of egalitarian economic and social policies, those on the psychological Left who are predisposed toward social change (and higher in cognitive ability) tend to support more *laissez faire* policies and reduced income redistribution—policies that in other countries with less egalitarian economic systems would tend to be supported by those on the psychological Right.[211] Worldwide, right-wing social views are more commonly correlated with left-wing economic views (supporting the protection/freedom depiction of the psychological Left/Right split).[212]

If our species can be broadly separated into having Left and Right psychological orientations, this may be because this separation provides a so-called evolutionarily stable strategy.[213] An evolutionarily stable strategy is a particular distribution of types within a population that cannot be improved upon by a different distribution or by uniformity. Examples of evolutionarily stable strategies abound in nature, with one of the most familiar being the 50/50 sex ratio in humans. The basic logic is that in many circumstances, it is better to have a certain variety of types rather than just one. Hammers are better than screwdrivers and saws for nailing, but if you are working on a complex project that requires more than one tool to accomplish, you are better off with a full toolkit than a dozen hammers.

Differences in Left-Right orientation may have provided evolutionarily stable variation that enabled humans to navigate the challenges of social evolution.[214] Just as evolutionarily stable variation in personality types allow us to adapt to a wide array of environments,[215] evolutionarily stable variation in political orientation may allow us to adapt our social structures to changing environments. The social change/tradition dimension concerns whether new ideas, practices, and social structures should be given a try (Left) or whether traditional ways should be followed (Right). The dimension of acceptance versus rejection of inequality may reflect the millions-of-years-old conflict between the propensity for hierarchy (Right) we inherited from our primate ancestors, and the aggressive egalitarian tendencies (Left) that evolved in hominids. In other words, "the polarization that afflicts many modern democracies may be a vestige of the mixes of the behaviorally relevant, biological predispositions that worked well in [our ancestral] small-scale societies."[216] Together, a population composed of some hewing to the Left and others hewing to the Right may provide careful steering of cultural evolution. The Right ensures that social evolution does not swerve too rapidly in unpredictable and potentially dangerous directions, while the Left provides the flexibility required to adapt to changing circumstances instead of driving straight ahead, unwaveringly, into a tree or off a cliff.

9 Evolution, Morality, and Politics

Morality differs between and within cultures. The vast array of standards of morality makes it difficult to summarize in a sentence, but from an evolutionary perspective, this definition suffices: "Morality is a set of psychological adaptations that allow otherwise selfish individuals to reap the benefits of cooperation."[217]

Recent studies of morality have arrived at five basic categories, or senses, that moral rules can be classified into: fairness, respect for authority, loyalty, sanctity, and care.[218] These are proposed as core components of a universal human psychology, but how they are expressed varies depending on ecological, institutional, economic, and ideational (e.g., religious) factors.[219] Violating the moral rules that cultures live by is likely to cause moral indignation, anger, and punishment—hence morality can be seen as a psychological adaptation to enforce certain kinds of behavior required for group cooperation.

Fairness probably arose to solve the evolutionary challenge of supporting cooperation against cheating and exploitation. A sense of fairness ensures that no one can make off with more than his or her own fair share, providing a key condition for large-scale cooperation to work. As with all moral senses, fairness is a broad feeling that can be used to support different moral rules and social arrangements. What is considered fair in Cuba or on a kibbutz is different from what is considered fair in Saudi Arabia or on Wall Street. The moral sense of fairness is more acute among those on the Left than those on the Right.[220]

Respect for authority is probably the oldest moral sense, as it ensures that hierarchies function smoothly. Although hominid evolution broke from the hierarchal social structures of our primate relatives, underlying genetic mechanisms persist. For instance, in vervet monkeys and us, having more power and being more aggressive is associated with higher levels of whole blood serotonin.[221] This is one of several biochemical mechanisms that produce the behaviors and feelings required for a social hierarchy. Those with power have to feel and act more domineeringly and those without have to feel (or at least act) submissively. Dominance hierarchies establish rules about who gets preferential access to resources or mates, saving animals the time, energy, and risks of constant fighting.[222] Respect for authority, then, ensures that those without power will be duly submissive. (If this can be considered a moral tenet, breaking it was the aggressive-egalitarian *Homo sapiens*' original sin.) During our ancestral period, the feelings underlying deference to authority may have been exapted to help groups cohere—if egalitarian groups are considered an authority, then submission to an alpha could have been repurposed to support submission to the group. The capacity for self-denial would then have gone from supporting dominance hierarchies to supporting group cohesion. The further one is to the political Right, the more authority matters.[223]

Loyalty as a moral sense likely evolved as the glue to hold social groups together. Our ease at creating groups would have gone nowhere without loyalty to make us stick with the group, and without stable groups our aggressive egalitarian social structure could never have arisen. Loyalty makes us care for our groups more than ourselves, and this is evident from studies of politics in which self-interest is a poorer predictor of political opinions than *group* interest.[224] Loyalty to the in-group may have helped reduce the risk of exposure to pathogens by minimizing contact with outsiders[225] and could even be responsible for the formation of "pseudospecies" within humanity by erecting artificial barriers to interbreeding.[226] Loyalty as a moral sense is more important the further one is to the Right.[227]

The dark side of loyalty is that it is often limited to a small in-group, leaving others not only outside its scope but out of moral consideration. For instance, those on the Right are more concerned by threats posed by criminals, pathogens, and foreigners, while ignoring threats posed by poverty or environmental destruction. This may be because the former threats affect the self and in-group, while the latter are large, systemic, and affect everyone.[228] The loyalty moral sense is also linked to the fact that as ethnic heterogeneity increases in a society, support for redistribution of income drops.[229] After all, if one's loyalty is to one's ethnic group, why share with outsiders? Ethnocentrism has been found to affect opinions on an array of seemingly unrelated issues.[230]

Sanctity is perhaps the most interesting moral sense: it is undergirded by the sense of disgust, and probably evolved to keep us from eating or interacting with poisonous or disease-causing elements in our environment. Today, this moral sense is an incredibly diverse exaptation, forbidding pork in some religions and beef in others, deeming menstruating women unclean here and homosexuality abhorrent there. Sanctity or purity is the third moral sense more important on the Right than the Left,[231] and it can have strange effects. For instance, in a simple experiment in which participants filled out surveys about their political attitudes, those told to stand near a hand sanitizer dispenser reported greater conservatism.[232] Violations of sanctity produce a strong feeling of disgust, as would be expected for an evolutionary adaption designed to protect us from poison or infections; only now, it has been exapted in highly diverse, often poorly suited or nonsensical ways.

The moral sense of care may be another extremely old exaptation, based on the emotional response we feel toward vulnerable children or needy family members, and repurposed for nonrelatives. The human mirror-neuron system may underlie this, allowing us to accurately imagine other people's suffering.[233] Interestingly, this may have evolved to track only simple actions and their consequences; it is less responsive to instances of passively caused harm and harm involving complex causal chains (as in the concept of "structural violence").[234] Care, along with fairness, is the second moral sense more acute among the Left.[235]

While all five moral senses are important to the Right (though care and fairness rank at the bottom), on the Left the importance of care and fairness tower over loyalty, authority, and sanctity. All five display an evolutionary legacy. The status of loyalty, authority, and sanctity as *morals* is, however, contestable.[236] (Interestingly, psychopaths evince a significant moral deficit in care and fairness, but no deficit in authority or sanctity, and *increased* endorsement of loyalty.)[237] To the extent respect for authority overlaps with authoritarianism, sanctity overlaps with irrational prejudice, and loyalty to the in-group overlaps with ethnocentrism or racism, many would consider them vices rather than virtues. Care and fairness, however, have no such obvious doppelgangers. Yet respect for authority, sanctity, and loyalty have good and bad instantiations; and with their less acute sense for these evolutionary morals, leftists may lose the good with the bad.

10 The Significance of Our Evolutionary Minds

Our species colonized the world with astounding rapidity, aided by the behavioral flexibility and technology produced by gene-culture coevolution. Yet despite such flexibility, evolution has left other marks on the design of our minds. They are foremost fashioned for reproduction and survival, and our current form of rationality is still skewed toward the achievement of these goals. They are furthermore designed for social intelligence: understanding others, forming coalitions, and designing and navigating social structures. In other words, politics—just on a much smaller scale than the politics of today.

Our political orientations are to some extent written into our nature in the language of DNA. We do not, however, share a uniform political nature. The evolutionary conflicts of the past—our history of proto-hominid hierarchical social structures alongside the more recent aggressive egalitarianism of *Homo sapiens*, the forces keeping us moored alongside those nudging us to try something new—live on. We pass some part of these propensities to our children, which exert a pull even as they develop their own political orientations in their unique environments. What commonly results from these interactions is a population split between those more comfortable with hierarchy and tradition (or protection from threat) and those more comfortable with equality and change (or freedom from oppression).

Where human social evolution will go is impossible to know. Evolution is intrinsically unpredictable, although evolutionary pressures can be identified and plausible directions imagined.[238] One of the key current pressures is the conflict between our young contemporary hierarchal social structure and our evolved egalitarian impulses. How social evolution will navigate this conflict is uncertain; but to keep any evolutionary system functioning, it is essential to balance change-generating and stability-maintaining mechanisms. The circulatory system of social evolution, the media, must provide the ingredients for stasis and change. Providing narratives that overwhelmingly support the status quo can only lead to social sclerosis, while providing narratives supportive only of continual and radical experimentation mimics the uncontrollable mutations of cancer. The media at the least must ensure diversity—to allow, in the best conservative tradition, our evolved minds to continue as they have for hundreds of thousands of years.

Notes

1. Eric J. Vallender et al., "Genetic Basis of Human Brain Evolution," *Trends in Neurosciences* 31, no. 12 (2008).
2. Peter J. Richerson and Robert Boyd, *Not by Genes Alone: How Culture Transformed Human Evolution* (Chicago: University of Chicago Press, 2008): 135–136.
3. Michael Tomasello, *A Natural History of Human Thinking* (Cambridge, MA: Harvard University Press, 2014): 26.
4. Henry Plotkin, *Darwin Machines and the Nature of Knowledge* (Cambridge, MA: Harvard University Press, 1994): 144–152, 243–244.
5. Stefan Klein, *Survival of the Nicest: How Altruism Made Us Human and Why It Pays to Get Along* (New York: Workman Publishing, 2014): 110–111.
6. Richerson and Boyd, *Not by Genes*, 133–134.

7. Doron Shultziner, "Genes and Politics: A New Explanation and Evaluation of Twin Study Results and Association Studies in Political Science," *Political Analysis* 21, no. 3 (2013): 331.
8. Tomasello, *Natural History*, 37.
9. Richerson and Boyd, *Not by Genes*, 143.
10. Tomasello, *Natural History*, 5.
11. Tomasello, *Natural History*.
12. Luigi L. Cavalli-Sforza, *Genes, Peoples, and Languages* (Berkeley, CA: University of California Press, 2001): 60.
13. Matt Rossano, "The African Interregnum: The 'Where,' 'When,' and 'Why' of the Evolution of Religion," in *The Biological Evolution of Religious Mind and Behavior*, ed. Eckart Voland and Wulf Schiefenhövel, 127–141 (Berlin: Springer, 2009): 127–128, 138.
14. Ofer Bar-Yosef, "The Upper Paleolithic Revolution," *Annual Review of Anthropology* (2002): 363–393.
15. Doron Shultziner et al., "The Causes and Scope of Political Egalitarianism During the Last Glacial: A Multi-disciplinary Perspective," *Biology & Philosophy* 25, no. 3 (2010): 323.
16. Kent Flannery and Joyce Marcus, *The Creation of Inequality: How Our Prehistoric Ancestors Set the Stage for Monarchy, Slavery, and Empire* (Cambridge, MA: Harvard University Press, 2012): 122–123.
17. Gregory Cochran and Henry Harpending, *The 10,000 Year Explosion: How Civilization Accelerated Human Evolution* (New York: Basic Books, 2009): 105.
18. David Wengrow and David Graeber, "Farewell to the 'Childhood of Man': Ritual, Seasonality, and the Origins of Inequality," *Journal of the Royal Anthropological Institute* 21, no. 3 (2015): 597–619.
19. Wengrow and Graeber, 2015, 605.
20. Ian Kuijt, "People and Space in Early Agricultural Villages: Exploring Daily Lives, Community Size, and Architecture in the Late Pre-pottery Neolithic," *Journal of Anthropological Archaeology* 19, no. 1 (2000).
21. Kim Sterelny, "Cooperation in a Complex World: The Role of Proximate Factors in Ultimate Explanations," *Biological Theory* 7, no. 4 (2013).
22. Morris, *Foragers, Farmers*, 57–67, 83–84.
23. Flannery and Marcus, *The Creation*, 551–556.
24. Klein, *Survival*, 180–182. The ideas of Confucius, Jesus, Buddha, and the like were, however, soon coopted by nearby states, blunting the force of their critiques (Morris 2015, 81–81).
25. Morris, *Foragers, Farmers*, 71–92, 198; James C. Scott, *The Art of Not Being Governed: An Anarchist History of Upland Southeast Asia* (New Haven, CT: Yale University Press, 2014).

26. Donald A. Dewsbury, "Charles Darwin and Psychology at the Bicentennial and Sesquicentennial: An Introduction," *American Psychologist* 64, no. 2 (2009).
27. Steven Pinker, *The Blank Slate: The Modern Denial of Human Nature* (New York: Penguin, 2003): 53–55.
28. Jaime C. Confer et al., "Evolutionary Psychology: Controversies, Questions, Prospects, and Limitations," *American Psychologist* 65, no. 2 (2010).
29. David M. Buss, "The Great Struggles of Life: Darwin and the Emergence of Evolutionary Psychology," *American Psychologist* 64, no. 2 (2009).
30. Leda Cosmides and John Tooby, "Evolutionary Psychology: New Perspectives on Cognition and Motivation," *Annual Review of Psychology* 64 (2013): 223–224; C. Daniel Batson et al., "Anger at Unfairness: Is It Moral Outrage?" *European Journal of Social Psychology* 37, no. 6 (2007).
31. Cosmides and Tooby, "Evolutionary Psychology," 206.
32. David M. Buss et al., "Adaptations, Exaptations, and Spandrels," *American Psychologist* 53, no. 5 (1998): 536.
33. Nathan W. Bailey and Marlene Zuk, "Same-Sex Sexual Behavior and Evolution," *Trends in Ecology & Evolution* 24, no. 8 (2009); see also Lukas and Huchard (2014).
34. James R. Liddle et al., "Why Can't We All Just Get Along? Evolutionary Perspectives on Violence, Homicide, and War," *Review of General Psychology* 16, no. 1 (2012); Christopher J. Ferguson and Kevin M. Beaver, "Natural Born Killers: The Genetic Origins of Extreme Violence," *Aggression and Violent Behavior* 14, no. 5 (2009).
35. David J. Anderson, "Optogenetics, Sex, and Violence in the Brain: Implications for Psychiatry," *Biological Psychiatry* 71, no. 12 (2012); Lei Chang et al., "The Face That Launched a Thousand Ships: The Mating-Warring Association in Men," *Personality and Social Psychology Bulletin* 37, no. 7 (2011).
36. William F. McKibbin et al., "Why Do Men Rape? An Evolutionary Psychological Perspective," *Review of General Psychology* 12, no. 1 (2008).
37. Richerson and Boyd (2008, 202–203).
38. Dennis L. Krebs, "Morality: An Evolutionary Account," *Perspectives on Psychological Science* 3, no. 3 (2008).
39. Jonathan Marks, *What it Means to Be 98% Chimpanzee: Apes, People, and Their Genes* (Berkeley, CA: University of California Press, 2003): 154–155.

40. Daniele Marzoli et al., "Environmental Influences on Mate Preferences as Assessed by a Scenario Manipulation Experiment," *PloS One* 8, no. 9 (2013): e74282.
41. For example, Herbert A. Simon, "Human Nature in Politics: The Dialogue of Psychology with Political Science," *American Political Science Review* 79, no. 02 (1985).
42. Sandeep Mishra, "Decision-Making Under Risk: Integrating Perspectives From Biology, Economics, and Psychology," *Personality and Social Psychology Review* (2014).
43. Richard Ronay and William von Hippel, "The Presence of an Attractive Woman Elevates Testosterone and Physical Risk Taking in Young Men," *Social Psychological and Personality Science* 1, no. 1 (2010): 57–64.
44. David J. Buller, *Adapting Minds: Evolutionary Psychology and the Persistent Quest for Human Nature* (Cambridge, MA: MIT Press, 2005). However, see also Edouard Machery and H. Clark Barrett, "Essay Review: Debunking Adapting Minds," *Philosophy of Science* 73, no. 2 (2006).
45. Keith E. Stanovich, *The Robot's Rebellion: Finding Meaning in the Age of Darwin* (Chicago: University of Chicago Press, 2005): 27.
46. Thomas H. Huxley, *Evolution and Ethics and Other Essays*, Vol. 9 (New York: D. Appleton, 1894): 83 (Emphasis added).
47. Carolyn L. Funk, "Genetic Foundations of Political Behavior," in *The Oxford Handbook of Political Psychology*, ed. Leonie Huddy et al., 237–261 (Oxford: Oxford University Press, 2013): 242–243.
48. Edward O. Wilson, *The Social Conquest of Earth* (New York: W.W. Norton & Company, 2012): 55.
49. Edward O. Wilson and Bert Hölldobler, "Eusociality: Origin and Consequences," *Proceedings of the National Academy of Sciences of the United States of America* 102, no. 38 (2005).
50. Josh Getlin, "Natural Wonder: At Heart, Edward Wilson's an Ant Man. But It's His Theories on Human Behavior that Stir Up Trouble," *Los Angeles Times* (October 21, 1994).
51. Compare Wilson's *Sociobiology* (1975), which brought him such anger from the contemporary Left, with his *The Social Conquest of Earth* (2012).
52. David Cesarini et al., "Heritability of Cooperative Behavior in the Trust Game," *Proceedings of the National Academy of Sciences* 105, no. 10 (2008).
53. David G. Rand et al., "Spontaneous Giving and Calculated Greed," *Nature* 489, no. 7416 (2012): 427–430.
54. Eörs Szathmáry and John Maynard Smith. "The Major Evolutionary Transitions," *Nature* 374, no. 6519 (1995): 227–232.

55. Tomasello, *Natural History*, 32.
56. Ibid., 39.
57. Ibid., 39–40, 52.
58. Geoffrey F. Miller, "Sexual Selection for Moral Virtues," *The Quarterly Review of Biology* 82, no. 2 (2007): 98, 109.
59. Aleksandr Kogan et al., "Thin-Slicing Study of the Oxytocin Receptor (OXTR) Gene and the Evaluation and Expression of the Prosocial Disposition," *Proceedings of the National Academy of Sciences* 108, no. 48 (2011).
60. Klein, *Survival*, 85–86. For a good discussion of the difficulty in interpreting neuroscientific findings, however, see Robert A. Burton, *A Skeptic's Guide to the Mind: What Neuroscience Can and Cannot Tell Us about Ourselves* (New York: Macmillan, 2013).
61. Stephanie L. Brown and R. Michael Brown, "Selective Investment Theory: Recasting the Functional Significance of Close Relationships," *Psychological Inquiry* 17, no. 1 (2006).
62. Nicholas A. Christakis and James H. Fowler, *Connected: The Surprising Power of Our Social Networks and How They Shape Our Lives* (New York: Little, Brown & Co., 2009): 299.
63. Ibid., 77.
64. Ibid., 125–126, 135–143.
65. Mercier and Sperber, "Why Do Humans Reason?"; Hugo Mercier and Dan Sperber, *The Enigma of Reason* (Cambridge, MA: Harvard University Press, 2017).
66. Jonathan Haidt, *The Righteous Mind: Why Good People Are Divided by Politics and Religion* (New York: Random House, 2013): 44, 75–76.
67. Tomasello, *Natural History*, 110–111.
68. Mercier and Sperber, "Why Do Humans," 72; Joaquin Navajas et al., "Aggregated Knowledge from a Small Number of Debates Outperforms the Wisdom of Large Crowds," *Nature Human Behaviour* 2, no. 2 (2018).
69. Julie A. Seaman, "Winning Arguments," *Law & Psychology Review* 41 (2016); Pentland, *Social Physics*, 28–29, 88.
70. Christopher Boehm, *Moral Origins: The Evolution of Virtue, Altruism, and Shame* (New York: Basic Books, 2012): 35, 195–199.
71. Sarah F. Brosnan et al., "Mechanisms Underlying Responses to Inequitable Outcomes in Chimpanzees, Pan troglodytes," *Animal Behaviour* 79, no. 6 (2010).
72. Mark Dyble et al., "Sex Equality Can Explain the Unique Social Structure of Hunter-Gatherer Bands," *Science* 348, no. 6236 (2015); Robert S. McElvaine, *Eve's Seed: Biology, the Sexes, and the Course of History* (New York: McGraw-Hill, 2001).

73. Boehm (2012, 151).
74. Shultziner et al., "The Causes."
75. Boehm, *Moral Origins*, 69–70, 155.
76. Sergey Gavrilets, "On the Evolutionary Origins of the Egalitarian Syndrome," *Proceedings of the National Academy of Sciences* 109, no. 35 (2012): 14069.
77. Ibid., 14072.
78. Christopher T. Dawes, "Neural Basis of Egalitarian Behavior," *Proceedings of the National Academy of Sciences* 109, no. 17 (2012): 6480.
79. Klein, *Survival*, 128–129.
80. Boehm, *Moral Origins*, 153–154.
81. Joseph Henrich, et al., "Costly Punishment Across Human Societies," *Science* 312, no. 5781 (2006).
82. Boehm, *Moral Origins*, 161.
83. Ibid., 34.
84. Vincent Falger, "Evolutionary World Politics Enriched: The Biological Foundations of International Relations," in *Evolutionary Interpretations of World Politics*, ed. William Thompson, 30–51. (New York: Routledge, 2001): 39.
85. Richerson and Boyd, *Not by Genes*, 15.
86. See, for instance, Blackmore, *The Meme Machine*; Blute, *Darwinian Sociocultural*; Mesoudi, *Cultural Evolution*; Runciman, *Theory of Cultural*; and Shennan, *Genes, Memes*.
87. Panati, *Panati's Extraordinary*; Richerson and Boyd, *Not by Genes*, 51.
88. Dennett, *Dangerous Idea*, 50–51.
89. Richerson and Boyd, *Not by Genes*, 69.
90. Thomas J. Bouchard Jr., "Authoritarianism, Religiousness, and Conservatism: Is 'Obedience to Authority' the Explanation for Their Clustering, Universality, and Evolution," in *The Biological Evolution of Religious Mind and Behavior*, ed. Eckart Voland and Wulf Schiefenhövel, 165–180 (Berlin: Springer, 2009): 173.
91. Alex Mesoudi, "How Cultural Evolutionary Theory Can Inform Social Psychology and Vice Versa," *Psychological Review* 116, no. 4 (2009).
92. Talhelm, Thomas, "Large-Scale Psychological Differences Within China Explained by Rice Versus Wheat Agriculture," *Science* 344, no. 6184 (2014).
93. Gordon Brown et al., "Personality, Parasites, Political Attitudes, and Cooperation: A Model of How Infection Prevalence Influences Openness and Social Group Formation," *Topics in Cognitive Science* (2015); Corey L. Fincher et al., "Pathogen Prevalence Predicts Human

Cross-Cultural Variability in Individualism/Collectivism," *Proceedings of the Royal Society B: Biological Sciences* 275, no. 1640 (2008).
94. See, for instance, Joan Y. Chiao and Katherine D. Blizinsky, "Culture–Gene Coevolution of Individualism–Collectivism and the Serotonin Transporter Gene," *Proceedings of the Royal Society B: Biological Sciences* (2009).
95. Kevin N. Laland, "How Culture Shaped the Human Genome: Bringing Genetics and the Human Sciences Together," *Nature Reviews Genetics* 11, no. 2 (2010): 141.
96. Lewontin and Levins, *Biology Under*, 89.
97. Ibid., 21.
98. Ibid., 204.
99. Richerson and Boyd, *Not by Genes*, 196–197.
100. Robert Wright, *Nonzero: The Logic of Human Destiny* (New York: Random House, 2001).
101. Shalom H. Schwartz, "Universalism Values and the Inclusiveness of Our Moral Universe," *Journal of Cross-Cultural Psychology* 38, no. 6 (2007).
102. Nancy R. Buchan, "Globalization and Human Cooperation," *Proceedings of the National Academy of Sciences* 106, no. 11 (2009): 4138.
103. Laland et al., "How Culture Shaped," 139.
104. Richerson and Boyd, *Not by Genes*, 230–231.
105. See, for instance, Cosmides and Tooby, "Evolutionary Psychology," 203.
106. John Hawks et al., "Recent Acceleration of Human Adaptive Evolution," *Proceedings of the National Academy of Sciences* 104, no. 52 (2007): 20755–20757.
107. Boehm, *Moral Origins*, 168.
108. Haidt, *Righteous Mind*, 211.
109. Steven Pinker, "Decline of Violence: Taming the Devil Within Us," *Nature* 478, no. 7369 (2011). However, Pinker's reading of the *pre*-historical evidence has been thoroughly criticized (Ferguson, 2013a, b; Fry, 2013, 15–20). Instead of a consistent downward trend, there is an *N*-shaped curve: low levels of violence in pre-history, a massive spike beginning with the agricultural revolution, and then a gradual decline continuing into the modern era.
110. Ann Gibbons, "How We Tamed Ourselves—and Became Modern," *Science* 346, no. 6208 (2014).
111. Sarah A. Graham and Simon E. Fisher, "Decoding the Genetics of Speech and Language," *Current Opinion in Neurobiology* 23, no. 1 (2013).
112. Gregory Cochran and Henry Harpending, *The 10,000 Year Explosion: How Civilization Accelerated Human Evolution* (New York: Basic Books, 2009): 63.
113. Ibid., 78–80.

114. Ibid., 87.
115. Chuansheng Chen et al., "Genotypes Over-Represented Among College Students Are Linked to Better Cognitive Abilities and Socioemotional Adjustment," *Culture and Brain* 1, no. 1 (2013).
116. Nicholas Wade, *A Troublesome Inheritance: Genes, Race and Human History* (New York: Penguin, 2014): 155–164.
117. See, generally, Thorstein Veblen, *The Theory of the Leisure Class* (Oxford: Oxford University Press, 2007).
118. Eric Williams, *Capitalism and Slavery* (Raleigh, NC: UNC Press Books, 1994).
119. Gregory Clark and Neil Cummins, "Surnames and Social Mobility in England, 1170–2012," *Human Nature* 25, no. 4 (2014).
120. Deniz Kellecioglu, "Why Some Countries Are Poor and Some Rich: A Non-Eurocentric View," *Real-World Economics Review* 52 (2010).
121. Chuansheng Chen, et al., "The 'Encultured' Genome: Molecular Evidence for Recent Divergent Evolution in Human Neurotransmitter Genes," in *The Oxford Handbook of Cultural Neuroscience*, ed. Joan Y. Chiao et al., 315–337 (Oxford: Oxford University Press, 2015).
122. Wilson, *Social Conquest*, 101–102.
123. Pinker, *Blank Slate*, 142–143.
124. Cavalli-Sforza, *Genes, Peoples*, 29.
125. Frances A. Champagne, "Epigenetic Influence of Social Experiences Across the Lifespan," *Developmental Psychobiology* 52, no. 4 (2010): 300.
126. John S. Torday and Virender K. Rehan, "An Epigenetic 'Smoking Gun' for Reproductive Inheritance," *Expert Review of Obstetrics & Gynecology* 8, no. 2 (2013).
127. Bastiaan T. Heijmans, et al., "Persistent Epigenetic Differences Associated with Prenatal Exposure to Famine in Humans," *Proceedings of the National Academy of Sciences* 105, no. 44 (2008).
128. Rachel Yehuda et al., "Holocaust Exposure Induced Intergenerational Effects on FKBP5 Methylation," *Biological Psychiatry* (2015).
129. Michelle Sotero, "A Conceptual Model of Historical Trauma: Implications for Public Health Practice and Research," *Journal of Health Disparities Research and Practice* 1, no. 1 (2006); Shannon Sullivan, "Inheriting Racist Disparities in Health: Epigenetics and the Transgenerational Effects of White Racism," *Critical Philosophy of Race* 1, no. 2 (2013).
130. Robinson et al., "Genes and Social Behavior," 897.
131. Champagne, "Epigenetic Influence," 303, 306.
132. Quoted in Pinker, *Blank Slate*, 142.
133. However, see Charney, "Behavioral Genetics," 12–14.

134. John R. Alford, et al., "Are Political Orientations Genetically Transmitted?" *American Political Science Review* 99, no. 02 (2005): 160.
135. Carolyn L. Funk et al., "Genetic and Environmental Transmission of Political Orientations," *Political Psychology* 34, no. 6 (2013): 813.
136. Christopher Dawes et al., "The Relationship Between Genes, Psychological Traits, and Political Participation," *American Journal of Political Science* 58, no. 4 (2014): 892.
137. Sven Oskarsson et al., "The Genetic Origins of the Relationship Between Psychological Traits and Social Trust," *Twin Research and Human Genetics* 15, no. 01 (2012).
138. Peter K. Hatemi, et al., "Genetic Influences on Political Ideologies: Twin Analyses of 19 Measures of Political Ideologies from Five Democracies and Genome-Wide Findings from Three Populations," *Behavior Genetics* 44, no. 3 (2014): 289.
139. Peter K. Hatemi et al., "Not by Twins Alone: Using the Extended Family Design to Investigate Genetic Influence on Political Beliefs," *American Journal of Political Science* 54, no. 3 (2010): 810.
140. Lindon Eaves et al. "Age Changes in the Causes of Individual Differences in Conservatism," *Behavior Genetics* 27, no. 2 (1997); Peter K. Hatemi et al., "Genetic and Environmental Transmission of Political Attitudes Over a Life Time," *The Journal of Politics* 71, no. 03 (2009).
141. Inga Schwabe et al., "Genes, Culture and Conservatism-A Psychometric-Genetic Approach," *Behavior Genetics* (2015).
142. Kevin Smith et al., "Biology, Ideology, and Epistemology: How Do We Know Political Attitudes Are Inherited and Why Should We Care?" *American Journal of Political Science* 56, no. 1 (2012): 28.
143. Peter K. Hatemi and Rose McDermott, "The Genetics of Politics: Discovery, Challenges, and Progress," *Trends in Genetics* 28, no. 10 (2012): 529; Smith et al., "Biology, Ideology," 18.
144. Zoltán Fazekas and Peter K. Hatemi, "Genetic and Environmental Approaches to Political Science," in *Emerging Trends in the Social and Behavioral Sciences*, ed. Robert A. Scott and Stephen M. Kosslyn (New York: Wiley, 2015), https://doi.org/10.1002/9781118900772. etrds0342; Nicholas Martin et al., "A Twin-Pronged Attack on Complex Traits," *Nature Genetics* 17 (1997).
145. Peter K. Hatemi, et al., "A Genome-Wide Analysis of Liberal and Conservative Political Attitudes," *The Journal of Politics* 73, no. 01 (2011): 276.
146. Martin Reuter et al., "Investigating the Genetic Basis of Altruism: The Role of the COMT Val158Met Polymorphism," *Social Cognitive and Affective Neuroscience* (2010): 5.

147. Jaime E. Settle et al., "Friendships Moderate an Association Between a Dopamine Gene Variant and Political Ideology," *The Journal of Politics* 72, no. 04 (2010).
148. Evan Charney and William English, "Genopolitics and the Science of Genetics," *American Political Science Review* 107, no. 02 (2013): 392.
149. Evan Charney and William English, "Candidate Genes and Political Behavior," *American Political Science Review* 106, no. 01 (2012): 30.
150. Daniel J. Benjamin et al., "The Genetic Architecture of Economic and Political Preferences," *Proceedings of the National Academy of Sciences* 109, no. 21 (2012).
151. Mark H. Davis et al., "The Heritability of Characteristics Associated with Dispositional Empathy," *Journal of Personality* 62, no. 3 (1994): 380.
152. Sara H. Konrath et al., "Changes in Dispositional Empathy in American College Students Over Time: A Meta-Analysis," *Personality and Social Psychology Review* (2010): 186.
153. Marks, *What It Means*, 146.
154. Jon Beckwith and Corey A. Morris, "Twin Studies of Political Behavior: Untenable Assumptions?" *Perspectives on Politics* 6, no. 04 (2008): 785–786; Shultziner, "Genes and Politics," 354.
155. For an excellent overview, see Evelyn Fox Keller, *The Mirage of a Space Between Nature and Nurture* (Durham, NC: Duke University Press, 2010).
156. Ibid., 39.
157. Shultziner, "Genes and Politics," 357.
158. Beckwith and Morris, "Twin Studies," 787; Allan V. Horwitz et al., "Double Vision: Reply to Freese and Powell," *Journal of Health and Social Behavior* (2003); Jay Joseph, "The Genetics of Political Attitudes and Behavior: Claims and Refutations," *Ethical Human Psychology and Psychiatry* 12, no. 3 (2010): 205–206. However, see Levente Littvay, "Do Heritability Estimates of Political Phenotypes Suffer from an Equal Environment Assumption Violation? Evidence from an Empirical Study," *Twin Research and Human Genetics* 15, no. 01 (2012).
159. Jordana T. Bell and Tim D. Spector, "A Twin Approach to Unraveling Epigenetics," *Trends in Genetics* 27, no. 3 (2011); Evan Charney, "Behavior Genetics and Postgenomics," *Behavioral and Brain Sciences* 35, no. 05 (2012): 26; and Or Zuk et al., "The Mystery of Missing Heritability: Genetic Interactions Create Phantom Heritability," *Proceedings of the National Academy of Sciences* 109, no. 4 (2012).
160. Wim E. Crusio, "Heritability Estimates in Behavior Genetics: Wasn't That Station Passed Long Ago?" *Behavioral and Brain Sciences* 35, no. 05 (2012): 362.

161. James H. Fowler and Christopher T. Dawes, "In Defense of Genopolitics," *American Political Science Review* 107, no. 02 (2013).
162. For example, Peter Beattie, "The 'Chicken-and-Egg' Development of Political Opinions: The Roles of Genes, Social Status, Ideology, and Information," *Politics and the Life Sciences* 36, no. 1 (2017).
163. Woo-Young Ahn et al., "Nonpolitical Images Evoke Neural Predictors of Political Ideology," *Current Biology* 24, no. 22 (2014).
164. Darren Schreiber et al., "Red Brain, Blue Brain: Evaluative Processes Differ in Democrats and Republicans," *PloS One* 8, no. 2 (2013): e52970.
165. John T. Jost and David M. Amodio, "Political Ideology as Motivated Social Cognition: Behavioral and Neuroscientific Evidence," *Motivation and Emotion* 36, no. 1 (2012): 61; John T. Jost et al., "Political Neuroscience: The Beginning of a Beautiful Friendship," *Political Psychology* 35, no. S1 (2014): 22–23; and Ryota Kanai et al., "Political Orientations are Correlated with Brain Structure in Young Adults," *Current Biology* 21, no. 8 (2011).
166. Douglas R. Oxley et al., "Political Attitudes Vary with Physiological Traits," *Science* 321, no. 5896 (2008).
167. John R. Hibbing et al., "Differences in Negativity Bias Underlie Variations in Political Ideology," *Behavioral and Brain Sciences* 37, no. 03 (2014): 301.
168. Jost et al., "Political Neuroscience," 24; Roger Newman-Norlund et al., "Human Mirror Neuron System (hMNS) Specific Differences in Resting-State Functional Connectivity in Self-Reported Democrats and Republicans: A Pilot Study," *Journal of Behavioral and Brain Science* 3, no. 4 (2013).
169. Michael D. Dodd et al., "The Political Left Rolls with the Good and the Political Right Confronts the Bad: Connecting Physiology and Cognition to Preferences," *Philosophical Transactions of the Royal Society B: Biological Sciences* 367, no. 1589 (2012).
170. John T. Jost et al., "Ideology: Its Resurgence in Social, Personality, and Political Psychology," *Perspectives on Psychological Science* 3, no. 2 (2008): 128–129.
171. Jakub Samochowiec et al., "Political Ideology at Face Value," *Social Psychological and Personality Science* 1, no. 3 (2010).
172. Jost et al., "Political Neuroscience," 19–20.
173. R. Chris Fraley et al., "Developmental Antecedents of Political Ideology a Longitudinal Investigation from Birth to Age 18 Years," *Psychological Science* 23, no. 11 (2012): 1427.
174. Jan W. van Deth et al., "Children and Politics: An Empirical Reassessment of Early Political Socialization," *Political Psychology* 32, no. 1 (2011).

175. Jack Block and Jeanne H. Block, "Nursery School Personality and Political Orientation Two Decades Later," *Journal of Research in Personality* 40, no. 5 (2006).
176. James H. Fowler and Darren Schreiber, "Biology, Politics, and the Emerging Science of Human Nature," *Science* 322, no. 5903 (2008).
177. Funk, "Genetic Foundations," 244.
178. Michael Bang Petersen, "Public Opinion and Evolved Heuristics: The Role of Category-Based Inference," *Journal of Cognition and Culture* 9, no. 3 (2009).
179. John T. Jost et al., "Political Ideology: Its Structure, Functions, and Elective Affinities," *Annual Review of Psychology* 60 (2009).
180. Jost et al., "Political Neuroscience," 14.
181. Brad Verhulst et al., "Correlation not Causation: The Relationship Between Personality Traits and Political Ideologies," *American Journal of Political Science* 56, no. 1 (2012): 47–48.
182. Jost et al., "Political Neuroscience," 18.
183. Peter K. Hatemi and Brad Verhulst, "Political Attitudes Develop Independently of Personality Traits," *PloS One* 10, no. 3 (2015).
184. Aleksander Ksiazkiewicz et al., "The Role of Cognitive Style in the Link Between Genes and Political Ideology," *Political Psychology* 38, no. 1 (2016).
185. Paul A.M. Van Lange et al., "Are Conservatives Less Likely to Be Prosocial than Liberals? From Games to Ideology, Political Preferences and Voting," *European Journal of Personality* 26, no. 5 (2012).
186. Dana R. Carney et al., "The Secret Lives of Liberals and Conservatives: Personality Profiles, Interaction Styles, and the Things They Leave Behind," *Political Psychology* 29, no. 6 (2008).
187. Emma Onraet et al., "The Association of Cognitive Ability with Right-Wing Ideological Attitudes and Prejudice: A Meta-analytic Review," *European Journal of Personality* 29, no. 6 (2015); Alain Van Hiel et al., "The Relationship Between Social-Cultural Attitudes and Behavioral Measures of Cognitive Style: A Meta-Analytic Integration of Studies," *Journal of Personality* 78, no. 6 (2010): 1790–1791.
188. Gordon Hodson and Michael A. Busseri. "Bright Minds and Dark Attitudes Lower Cognitive Ability Predicts Greater Prejudice Through Right-Wing Ideology and Low Intergroup Contact," *Psychological Science* 23, no. 2 (2012): 192.
189. John T. Jost and Margarita Krochik, "Ideological Differences in Epistemic Motivation: Implications for Attitude Structure, Depth of Information Processing, Susceptibility to Persuasion, and Stereotyping," in *Advances in Motivation Science*, ed. Andrew Elliot, 181–231 (San Diego: Elsevier, 2014); Andrea L. Miller et al., "Political Ideology

and Persuasion: Systematic and Heuristic Processing among Liberals and Conservatives," *The Yale Review of Undergraduate Research in Psychology* (2010).
190. Gordon Hodson, "Is It Impolite to Discuss Cognitive Differences Between Liberals and Conservatives?" *Behavioral and Brain Sciences* 37, no. 03 (2014): 313.
191. John R. Hibbing et al., "Negativity Bias and Political Preferences: A Response to Commentators," *The Behavioral and Brain Sciences* 37, no. 3 (2014): 339–341; Steven G. Ludeke and Colin G. DeYoung, "Differences in Negativity Bias Probably Underlie Variation in Attitudes toward Change Generally, not Political Ideology Specifically," *The Behavioral and Brain Sciences* 37, no. 3 (2014): 320; and Ariel Malka and Christopher J. Soto, "How Encompassing Is the Effect of Negativity Bias on Political Conservatism?" *The Behavioral and Brain Sciences* 37, no. 3 (2014).
192. David M. Amodio et al., "Neurocognitive Correlates of Liberalism and Conservatism," *Nature Neuroscience* 10, no. 10 (2007).
193. Linda J. Skitka et al., "Dispositions, Scripts, or Motivated Correction? Understanding Ideological Differences in Explanations for Social Problems," *Journal of Personality and Social Psychology* 83, no. 2 (2002): 484.
194. Fraley et al., "Developmental Antecedents," 1429.
195. John T. Jost et al., "The 'Chicken-and-Egg' Problem in Political Neuroscience," *The Behavioral and Brain Sciences* 37, no. 3 (2014); Jost et al., "Political Neuroscience," 29–30.
196. Schreiber et al., "Red Brain," e52970–e52971.
197. Jost et al., "Political Neuroscience," 29.
198. Jaime L. Napier and John T. Jost, "The 'Antidemocratic Personality' Revisited: A Cross-National Investigation of Working-Class Authoritarianism," *Journal of Social Issues* 64, no. 3 (2008): 607.
199. Xiaowen Xu and Jordan B. Peterson, "Differences in Media Preference Mediate the Link Between Personality and Political Orientation," *Political Psychology* 38, no. 1 (2015).
200. Joris Lammers and Travis Proulx, "Writing Autobiographical Narratives Increases Political Conservatism," *Journal of Experimental Social Psychology* 49, no. 4 (2013).
201. Jost et al., "Ideology: Its Resurgence," 133–134; Idan S. Solon, "Scholarly Elites Orient Left, Irrespective of Academic Affiliation," *Intelligence* 51 (2015).
202. Jan-Emmanuel De Neve, "Ideological Change and the Economics of Voting Behavior in the US, 1920–2008," *Electoral Studies* 34 (2014).

203. Ariel Malka, Yphtach Lelkes, and Christopher J. Soto. "Are Cultural and Economic Conservatism Positively Correlated? A Large-Scale Cross-National Test," *British Journal of Political Science* (2017): 1–25.
204. Beattie, "The 'Chicken-and-Egg'"; Kevin B. Smith et al., "Linking Genetics and Political Attitudes: Reconceptualizing Political Ideology," *Political Psychology* 32, no. 3 (2011).
205. Brad Verhulst et al., "Disentangling the Importance of Psychological Predispositions and Social Constructions in the Organization of American Political Ideology," *Political Psychology* 33, no. 3 (2012).
206. Peter K. Hatemi et al., "It's the End of Ideology as We Know It," *Journal of Theoretical Politics* 24, no. 3 (2012).
207. Zoltán Fazekas and Levente Littvay, "The Importance of Context in the Genetic Transmission of U.S. Party Identification," *Political Psychology* 36, no. 4 (2015); Christian Kandler et al., "Life Events as Environmental States and Genetic Traits and the Role of Personality: A Longitudinal Twin Study," *Behavior Genetics* 42, no. 1 (2012).
208. Peter K. Hatemi, "The Influence of Major Life Events on Economic Attitudes in a World of Gene-Environment Interplay," *American Journal of Political Science* 57, no. 4 (2013).
209. Brad Verhulst et al., "Disentangling," 388–389.
210. Hulda Thorisdottir et al., "Psychological Needs and Values Underlying Left-Right Political Orientation: Cross-National Evidence from Eastern and Western Europe," *Public Opinion Quarterly* 71, no. 2 (2007): 198.
211. Sven Oskarsson et al., "Linking Genes and Political Orientations: Testing the Cognitive Ability as Mediator Hypothesis," *Political Psychology* 36, no. 6 (2015).
212. Malka et al., "Are Cultural."
213. Dawkins, *The Selfish Gene*, 69–87.
214. Michael Bang Petersen and Lene Aarøe, "Individual Differences in Political Ideology are Effects of Adaptive Error Management," *The Behavioral and Brain Sciences* 37, no. 3 (2014): 325; Michael Bang Petersen and Lene Aarøe, "Evolutionary Theory and Political Behavior," in *Emerging Trends in the Social and Behavioral Sciences*, ed. Robert A. Scott and Stephen M. Kosslyn (New York: Wiley, 2015): 11. https://doi.org/10.1002/9781118900772.
215. Michael Gurven et al., "The Evolutionary Fitness of Personality Traits in a Small-Scale Subsistence Society," *Evolution and Human Behavior* 35, no. 1 (2014).
216. Hibbing et al., "Differences in Negativity," 306.
217. Joshua Greene, *Moral Tribes: Emotion, Reason, and the Gap Between Us and Them* (New York: Penguin, 2013): 23.
218. Haidt, *Righteous Mind*, 153–154.

219. Jesse Graham et al., "Cultural Differences in Moral Judgment and Behavior, Across and Within Societies," *Current Opinion in Psychology* 8 (2016).
220. Haidt, *Righteous Mind*, 161.
221. Douglas Madsen, "A Biochemical Property Relating to Power Seeking in Humans," *The American Political Science Review* (1985).
222. John H. Kaufmann, "On the Definitions and Functions of Dominance and Territoriality," *Biological Reviews* 58, no. 1 (1983).
223. Haidt, *Righteous Mind*, 161.
224. Ibid., 86. For a review of the evidence where self- and group-interest are indistinguishable, see Jason Weeden and Robert Kurzban, "Self-Interest Is Often a Major Determinant of Issue Attitudes," *Political Psychology* 38 (2017): 67–90.
225. Chiao and Blizinsky, "Culture-Gene Coevolution," 3.
226. Harold J. Morowitz, *The Emergence of Everything: How the World Became Complex* (Oxford: Oxford University Press, 2002): 149.
227. Haidt, *Righteous Mind*, 161.
228. Shalom H. Schwartz, "Negativity Bias and Basic Values," *The Behavioral and Brain Sciences* 37, no. 3 (2014): 328.
229. Petersen and Aarøe, "Evolutionary Theory," 4–5.
230. Donald R. Kinder and Cindy D. Kam, *Us Against Them: Ethnocentric Foundations of American Opinion* (Chicago: University of Chicago Press, 2010).
231. Haidt, *Righteous Mind*, 161.
232. Erik G. Helzer and David A. Pizarro, "Dirty Liberals! Reminders of Physical Cleanliness Influence Moral and Political Attitudes," *Psychological Science* 22, no. 4 (2011): 517–522.
233. Klein, *Survival*, 57–61.
234. Greene, *Moral Tribes*, 249.
235. Haidt, *Righteous Mind*, 161.
236. For example, Matthew Kugler, John T. Jost, and Sharareh Noorbaloochi, "Another Look at Moral Foundations Theory: Do Authoritarianism and Social Dominance Orientation Explain Liberal-Conservative Differences in 'Moral' Intuitions?" *Social Justice Research* 27, no. 4 (2014): 413–431.
237. Andrea L. Glenn et al., "Are All Types of Morality Compromised in Psychopathy?" *Journal of Personality Disorders* 23, no. 4 (2009).
238. Runciman, *Theory of Cultural*, 195–196.

CHAPTER 4

When Our Evolved Minds Go Wrong: Social Psychological Biases

The struggle between the first conservatives and liberals of the eighteenth and nineteenth centuries was definitively won by the liberals. Their victory was so thorough that even modern-day conservatives have adopted the liberal vision of the extent of human capacities and the ideal form of government. Today's conservatives do not argue that an aristocracy or monarchy is required for a flourishing human society; instead, they agree with the early liberals that democracy (if a representative democracy) is the best and only legitimate form of government. While the first conservatives worried that the fading of institutions like the aristocracy and monarchy would destroy vital social bonds, resulting in bloody struggles and societal disintegration, modern conservatives have adapted to the idea that democratic, market-based societies are not only healthy, but the ideal form of large-scale human organization. In a way, modern conservatives resemble early liberals more than modern (U.S.) liberals. The ideas characterizing modern liberalism have evolved beyond that which early liberals would have been prepared to contemplate: the equality of human "races" and sexes, the illegitimacy of imperialism, gay rights, etc. And while modern liberals in the United States support a government-provided social safety net, modern U.S. conservatives hold truer to the classical liberal position of limited government.

But what is the liberal vision of human capacities that informs the political worldview held by modern-day conservatives and liberals alike? In the liberal vision of human capacities, we are rational beings who have the right and ability to choose our pursuits and participate in self-government. (While early liberal writers acknowledged irrational features of our psychology, their observations were later jettisoned to provide surer foundations for liberal economics, which needed a strong form of human rationality to be coherent.)[1] No doubt influenced by the view of the soul as the seat of reason, separate and distinct from animal nature, liberals from the beginning believed that we are capable of reasoning to the truth. As more and more people jettisoned the idea of the soul as a reasoning machine, the mind seamlessly succeeded the soul as the seat of reason.[2] Whether due to a spiritual soul or a corporeal brain, the liberal vision retained a belief in human rationality. And as such, humanity should flourish where our capacity for self-directed reasoning was allowed free rein. No monarchy or aristocracy is needed to govern individuals who can decide what they want and how they can achieve it, and who can collectively create an effective government by voting in their own individual, well-informed interests.

It is this vision that informed John Stuart Mill in arguing for freedom of thought and expression. In Mill's view, humans need no paternalistic intervention from the state or church to regulate the contents of the mind. To the conservatives of his day, this was a recipe for disaster, as liberty of expression would allow harmful (possibly fatal) ideas to spread. But in Mill's liberal view, it was "important to give the freest scope possible to uncustomary things, in order that it may in time appear which of these are fit to be converted into customs."[3] Freedom of expression would subject ideas to the discretion of the human mind. In the words of Oliver Wendell Holmes, "the ultimate good desired is better reached by free trade in ideas ... the best test of truth is the power of the thought to get itself accepted in the competition of the market..."[4] This helped introduce the modern "marketplace of ideas" metaphor and forms the backbone of the liberal defense of freedom of expression.[5]

Marketplaces "work" because they are the aggregate of individuals pursuing their self-interest, and this is hypothesized to provide the best collective outcome.[6] A free market of ideas works to the extent to which information is shared, debated, and selected on the basis of its merit by intelligent, rational individuals. Take away any of these elements and you have a failed market, which does not select the best ideas but allows untruthful or outdated ideas to proliferate.[7] One of the ways a marketplace of ideas can fail to achieve an ideal outcome is what concerned Justice Holmes in his dissent in the *Abrams* case: censorship. By blocking ideas perceived as harmful or wrong, a distortion is introduced. At issue in *Abrams* were leaflets arguing against US military intervention in the Russian Revolution; even supposing the ideas contained in the leaflets to be wrong, censoring them might provide them a veneer of legitimacy that could propel them to spread at a greater rate than if they were open to withering criticism. While Holmes was in the minority when he wrote his dissenting opinion, by now his disdain for censorship and embrace of the marketplace of ideas is the majority opinion. Modern liberals and conservatives alike have embraced the marketplace of ideas and its promise to provide an ideal environment for the evolution of ideas.

But what of other possible market failures—for instance, a marketplace in which information is freely shared and debated on the basis of perceived merit, but selection is not performed by intelligent, rational individuals? What if the liberal vision of human capacities is wrong? As the liberal political philosopher John Rawls conceded, for liberalism to work, citizens must be "capable of revising and changing [their conception of the good] on reasonable and rational grounds..."[8] Furthermore, "[r]ational autonomy ... rests on persons' intellectual and moral powers. It is shown in their exercising their capacity to form, to revise, and to pursue a conception of the good, and to deliberate in accordance with it."[9] If political liberalism relies on a rational moral psychology, then an important question is: to what extent are we rational?

To answer this question, we turn to what social psychologists have discovered about the human mind. Far from approximating a rational soul created by God to enable human reason or the subsequent ideal of a purely material mind with the same capabilities, the human mind is deeply and systematically flawed. It is as unlikely to have been designed by a Creator for the purpose of best facilitating pure reason as to have *evolved* to that end. The evidence suggests that the human mind evolved for the same reason as every other product of evolution: for self-propagation in an at once competitive and cooperative natural environment. The picture of the human mind emerging from social psychological research contradicts the view taken for granted by liberal economists and political scientists.[10] And because they have informed so much of what are now uncontroversial, widely shared beliefs about politics and social organization, the reality of the human mind is disturbing to many today. Yet these weaknesses or alarming flaws from a liberal perspective could be overcome and superseded—*if*, and most likely *only if*, we evolve our institutions beyond the form in which they were shaped by the liberal view of human capacities.

1 How Psychology Explains the Brain's Contribution to Information Ecology

Psychology may be a late bloomer among the sciences. While major advances in mathematics occurred in antiquity and significant progress in physics is centuries old, the workings of the human mind remained mired in speculation until recently. As the great American philosopher George Santayana explained:

> The idea of the physical world is the first flower or thick cream of practical thinking. Being skimmed off first and proving so nutritious, it leaves the liquid below somewhat thin and unsavoury. Especially does this result appear when science is still unpruned and mythical, so that what passes into the idea of material nature is much more than the truly causal network of forces, and includes many spiritual and moral functions.[11]

Many consider Sigmund Freud, whose life's work ended less than a century ago, as merely a glorified armchair theorist.[12] While his theories have become widespread and popular, they were arrived at not by the scientific method of hypothesis creation and experimental testing, but by supposition and extrapolation from the patients he treated. Once subjected to scientific scrutiny, his theories have not fared well.[13]

Part of the reason for the slow progress of psychology has been the difficulty of applying the scientific method to studying the human mind. Nonetheless, social psychologists have made considerable recent progress in uncovering how our minds work in dealing with a shared social reality, creating artificial (often social) situations or thinking tasks, manipulating aspects of them, and measuring behavioral or cognitive changes in response to the manipulation. While multiple social processes operate concurrently and interdependently, experiments in social psychology isolate processes to better understand them. What emerges is a better idea of what is going on behind the scenes in human minds. Predictions about overall social outcomes (like whether the United States will evolve into a more or less egalitarian society) are hard to come by, since they comprise innumerable individual and societal-level processes operating simultaneously, but explanations of the processes involved in social evolution are possible to derive.

This strategy faces significant challenges, however. Due to the heterogeneity of people's cultures, beliefs, and memes, "generalizations from one locale to another may express nothing more than the parochialism of those who make the generalizations."[14] Since most research in social psychology has used US college students, the "locale" from which generalizations are made is Western, Educated, Industrialized, Rich, and Democratic—or WEIRD.[15] Hence, it is problematic to assume that the results of social psychological experiments on WEIRD populations are features of universal human psychology, as the hypothesis that such results are caused by one social environment cannot be disconfirmed.[16] A review of the differences between WEIRD populations and others globally concluded: "The sample of contemporary Western undergraduates that so overwhelms our database is not just an extraordinarily restricted sample of humanity; it is frequently a distinct outlier vis-à-vis other global samples. It may represent the worst population on which to base our understanding of *Homo sapiens*."[17] This has led many psychologists to reject an empiricist approach in favor of a more holistic, qualitative methodology focused on ideational and cultural influences from the social environment.[18]

However, this problem only affects attempts to confidently generalize from the population studied to humanity as a whole. *Tentative* generalizations, keeping in mind the limitations of available evidence, are immune. For instance, take the (ironically named) "fundamental attribution error": once thought to describe *humanity's* tendency to focus on intrinsic dispositions while ignoring situational influences, research on diverse populations has revealed it to be the product of cultural and ideational influences in Western societies.[19] Hence, any phenomenon uncovered by experiments on one population may be provisionally considered to be part of universal psychology, but this remains an untested hypothesis until a variety of populations are tested. Many of the phenomena discussed in this chapter have not yet been tested on a sufficiently diverse set of populations and, as such, their status as features of universal human psychology should be considered a hypothesis.

They can be considered features of human psychology in *Western* societies with a higher degree of confidence—as the product of universal psychology interacting with Western social environments. The results of social psychological research have been found to be about as consistent as the results of research in physics.[20] And although a recent large-scale attempt to replicate a random sample of social psychological findings succeeded only slightly over one-third of the time,[21] a later analysis found that context sensitivity was significantly correlated with replication success—that is, the more context-sensitive the original results, the less likely they would be successfully replicated.[22] This is another side of the generalization problem: not only are generalizations across cultures problematic, but generalizing beyond the unique contexts of social psychological experiments can also be problematic. Likewise, the solution here is additional replication.[23]

Another critique centers on the domination of social psychology by liberals, which makes conservative students less likely to enter the field or have research papers accepted.[24] As the authors' choice of terminology suggests (liberal/conservative), however, their argument applies only to the Anglosphere; a look at Eastern Europe suggests instead that social psychologists across cultures tend to set themselves in opposition to the ideology of the lower class in their society.[25] Likewise, scientists in a variety of sciences are more liberal—and drastically less religious—than the general population of the USA, a concomitant of the Enlightenment elevation of science over religion.[26] Unmentioned by the authors of the critique, but possibly more important and insidious, would be a bias toward the methodological status quo[27] and pressure to publish producing a bias toward positive results.[28] (Similar biases in economics have produced disastrous results.)[29] Nonetheless, such biases are rife in science—and institutional responses are needed to mute them. The philosopher of science, Miriam Solomon, argues that they should be called (the epistemically neutral) "decision vectors," since the history of science shows such biases to be variably conducive *and* harmful to scientific progress: "[t]hus the widespread practice of calling them 'biasing factors,' which suggests undesirable irrationality, is inappropriately judgmental.... [Their] influence *may or may not* be conducive to scientific success..."[30]

As Santayana implied, and Auguste Comte made explicit, psychology is intrinsically a more difficult subject to study scientifically than "simpler," or less complex fields like physics and chemistry.[31] If chemistry is an emergent phenomenon of physics, and biology emerges from chemistry, psychology emerges from biology, etc., then the social sciences are unavoidably more complex than the physical sciences.[32] At each succeeding level, the laws and regularities of the previous level remain, but are joined by emergent forces and tendencies. As such, we should not expect to identify scientific *laws* or certainties, but contingent probabilities.[33] The only other alternative is a retreat into radical skepticism, with all of its attendant problems.[34]

2   A Bias Tour of the Human Mind

Let us start with a look at an aspect of the human mind that makes humanity what it is: morality. In the liberal and popular view, morality is the product of moral reasoning. We learn a code as children, and modify and expand it through experience. When we are presented with a moral question, we ponder it, consider the factors involved, and arrive at a conclusion. Or, so it seems.

The reality, as uncovered by a number of experimental studies, is that when presented with a moral dilemma, we have an automatic, unconscious reaction: something feels morally right, or wrong. Then, after our minds have unconsciously arrived at a conclusion, reasoning kicks in. Not to determine whether our gut instinct was correct—rather, our conscious reasoning acts as a lawyer for our unconscious moral decision.[35] Instead of coolly subjecting a moral question to analysis, our brains quickly and unconsciously arrive at a moral decision and then our reasoning process is left with devising an explanation for why we arrived at it.[36] We are not judges when it comes to moral questions; we are lawyers, who are presented with a client and then tasked with creating an exculpatory argument.

This counterintuitive reality has been unveiled through experimental studies across countries. In one example, participants were hypnotized to feel disgust after seeing a certain neutral word, such as "take" or "often."[37] Then, they were presented with six short stories concerning moral violations. When the story contained the chosen neutral words, the moral violations in the stories were judged *more* morally disgusting. Revealingly, the seventh story did not contain any moral violation at all—it was about a thoughtful student council president who picked interesting topics for discussions. When the story contained the manipulated "disgust word," a third of the participants condemned the thoughtful student council president. All hypnotized participants had felt a mild wave of disgust when they saw "take" or "often" in the story—but most had overruled their initial gut reaction as their reasoning kicked into judge the student council president as good. For the rest, their reasoning process only created a tortured justification for their gut reaction, calling the student council president a "popularity-seeking snob" for trying to please others or voicing suspicions about his intentions.

Such experimental results powerfully suggest that when faced with a moral dilemma, we make an instinctual, unconscious decision about the morally correct response; then, we take a biased view of the evidence to make a case that our morally correct response would also lead to the best practical outcome as well.[38] Reading persuasive essays about the morality of capital punishment—which did not contain arguments regarding the deterrent effect of the death penalty or other practical consequences—was found to change participants' factual assessments of whether capital punishment deterred future crime (for the pro-death penalty essay) or led to miscarriages of justice (for the anti-death penalty essay). Even the ideally objective theories adopted by economists are "suspiciously correlated with their moral values."[39] Although it seems—and we like to think—we make rational, conscious deliberations on moral (and political) questions, the reality is the reverse. We unconsciously make moral determinations and then take a biased tour through the facts in order to contrive a justification for our moral determination.

Granted, it is unsettling and counterintuitive to see our reasoning as a mere lawyer hired to defend the conclusions arrived at by a part of our brains over which we do not have control. That is not how it *feels* to reason over moral questions. Yet even more unsettling are experimental studies of people who have undergone split-brain surgery. Some people with severe epileptic seizures have undergone surgery to sever the neural fibers that connect the left and right hemispheres of the brain. Since the left eye communicates with the right cerebral hemisphere, and the right eye with the left hemisphere, scientists can study split-brain patients to see how the hemispheres interact.[40] In a series of experiments, participants were presented with a written command seen only by the left eye, which is connected with the right cerebral hemisphere. Since the participants had undergone the surgery that severed the connection between their right and left hemispheres, the left hemisphere (where most verbal processing occurs) had no exposure to the displayed command. Then, participants were asked why they performed the command. In answering, they used their verbal-dominant left hemispheres, which had no knowledge of the command, only the knowledge that the participant had performed an action. Shockingly, whatever the participants had been commanded, the left side of their brains invented a plausible reason. The natural reaction was not to say "I don't know," but instead to generate a made-up, *ad hoc* rationalization. For instance, when one participant had been instructed to walk via a message to the right side of their brain, when asked why, their left side came up with the reason that they were fetching a soda.[41] Most importantly, these participants had no idea that they were making anything up.

Decades of split-brain research by Michael Gazzaniga led him to propose an "interpreter" mechanism in the verbal-dominant left hemisphere of our brain.[42] This interpreter monitors other areas of our brains and generates narrative explanations for what occurs there. In his view, the interpreter mechanism is what we feel to *be* human: our sense of being the person we are, with free will and the ability to make decisions. However, as the split-brain experiments suggest, the interpreter in our brains may simply be telling a story. And it is the feeling of the story we mistake for the liberal ideal of a rational control center in our minds.

But not all psychological research challenges our intuitions at such a profound level. Lots of psychological research challenges our intuitions about how our minds work at a mundane level too. For instance, the liberal view in economics has traditionally assumed that humans are epistemological gods and native number crunchers, capable of absorbing all relevant information from the environment and performing accurate calculations of utility and expected future utility. There is even a supposition in neoclassical economics that increases in national debt set off a wave of people making complicated calculations about future tax increases required to pay the debt (after interest rates for government bonds increase due to future investors' higher perceived risk of holding the debt due to its increased amount hence higher risk of default); then, these human supercomputers make cuts in current expenditures proportional (after time-discounting) to the expected increase in their future tax burden—and the economy suffers. We hardly need psychological research to realize why this is absurd, but it does reveal some interesting, unexpected, and stable patterns of irrationality in our most basic calculations.[43] These are heuristics, decision-making shortcuts, and we are perfectly unaware that we use them. Heuristics make calculations less taxing, but also less accurate. They are what we would expect to find in a mind produced by evolution, favoring economy over perfection.

For instance, our reasoning is biased by the "representativeness" and "availability" heuristics.[44] The representativeness heuristic biases our judgments of probability, by making membership in a category seem more probable on the basis of features we associate with that category. The availability heuristic also biases our judgments of probability, by basing our judgments about the likelihood of an event on how easily we recall examples of it. Therefore, we tend to judge the likelihood of something on the basis of how often we have experienced it and how well we remember and categorize the experiences. Thus, we might know that only 1% of a certain minority group has committed a crime. Yet, if we remember salient examples (from television or personal experiences) of a member of that minority group committing a crime, we will use those memories instead of the statistical fact to judge a newly encountered member of that group. So we may know that statistically only a fraction of one percent of Anglo-Saxons are financial criminals; but if we see a few salient examples of Anglo-Saxon financial crooks in the media, when we first encounter an unknown Anglo-Saxon, we may find ourselves feeling for our wallets.

Research into biases in simple reasoning and calculations is vast. It has uncovered a surprising number of biases, from anchoring (being influenced in one's numerical estimates by simple exposure to a random number), to framing effects (the same proposition presented in different ways will be responded to differently on the basis of the presentation), and the endowment effect (we value something we own more highly than that same thing if we do not own it). This research has revealed that we are "risk averse" for potential gains and "risk seeking" for potential losses. In other words, when we are in danger of losing we are likelier to gamble and either greatly deepen the loss or eliminate it, but when we stand to gain, we are unlikely to take a gamble that would greatly increase our gain or eliminate it.[45] Not only do these heuristics and biases violate the liberal view of human rationality, they prove that the models of human calculations used in liberal economics are describing something other than human actors.

Lest these seem like biases affecting only bean counting, loss aversion can affect even whether we support our country waging a war: when a war is sold as preventative and defensive, we are likelier to support it versus when it is sold as promoting gain.[46] When Daniel Kahneman and Jonathan Renshon reviewed 40 years of psychological research on biases, they were startled to find that *all* favored proponents of war: "These psychological impulses ... incline national leaders to exaggerate the evil intentions of adversaries, to misjudge how adversaries perceive them, to be overly sanguine when hostilities start, and overly reluctant to make necessary concessions in negotiations. In short, these biases have the effect of making war."[47]

This and other research has uncovered two distinct systems of thought at play in the human mind.[48] System 1 is fast and effortless thought, performed automatically and unconsciously, emotionally charged at times, and difficult to consciously control. System 2 is slower, effortful, flexible, conscious, and intentionally directed.[49] Heuristics and moral judgments are part of System 1, while the rationalizations or justifications for moral judgments are part of System 2. Many of the simpler decision biases of System 1 may be caused by systematic errors in the way we store and retrieve information, errors which make judgments predictably irrational.[50] System 2 is more complex and likely to be where Gazzaniga's "interpreter" resides. Therefore, in a manner reminiscent of split-brain patients, we are only conscious of one half of our mind. While System 1 is whirring away, making judgments and decisions on its own without our conscious awareness (we are aware only of the results), System 2 makes up what it *feels* like to think: conscious, deliberative, and rational. The liberal view, like our own subjective experience, sees only System 2.

This phenomenon of unconscious (System 1) and conscious (System 2) thought processes operating in tandem is demonstrated in research on persuasion. When we think about being persuaded, we imagine that we hear an argument, consider its merits and demerits, and decide whether it convinces us. In the research, this is referred to as the "central route" to persuasion or attitude change and involves conscious, effortful System 2 thought. Strangely, however, there is another route, the so-called peripheral route. This is a System 1 process and operates outside of conscious awareness, when our conscious attention is distracted. We think strong arguments tend to be convincing, while weak arguments rarely convince us—and this is what happens using System 2, central route processing. However, when we are distracted and using System 1, peripheral route processing, *weak* arguments can have a better chance of convincing us than strong arguments.[51] Peripheral route processing uses simple cues to determine whether a message is trustworthy: the attractiveness, likeability, or expert status of the speaker, the simplicity of the message, or whether the message is in a low-effort medium like radio or television as opposed to writing. Thankfully, personal investment and having a personality that enjoys thinking make System 2, central route processing likelier; yet, that still leaves System 1 to process countless messages.[52]

The confidence we have in our thoughts also affects the likelihood we will be convinced by a message when we are using System 2.[53] This is good, as it suggests we are unlikely to be convinced of an argument if we are not confident in our response to it. For instance, if we do not know much about a proposed trade agreement and the economic theory underlying it, when exposed to a strong argument in favor of it, we recognize our incompetence, are less confident about our reaction, and are less likely to be convinced. The problem is that we are terrible judges of our competence. As Thomas Jefferson wrote, "The wise know too well their weakness to assume infallibility; and he who knows most, knows best how little he knows."[54] By implication, the foolish may assume infallibility; he, who knows least, does not know how little he knows. In experiments testing this phenomenon, the most incompetent people were also likeliest to overestimate their competence.[55]

The view of the human mind provided by social psychology is different from the liberal view of human capacities, namely that the human mind naturally adopts the Golden Rule: do to others as you would want them to do to you. This is a succinct and complete statement of a moral code that all reasonable minds might assent to. Psychology suggests a different Golden Rule: whoever has the gold makes the rules. Our conception of justice is dependent on what is advantageous for the social system we are a part of.[56] And this is not the kind of justice liberal, rational minds would arrive at through a process of pure reason; rather, it is influenced by historical accidents such as the status quo one happens to be living in. Nor are the failings of the human mind a problem limited to the uneducated or unintelligent—most biases affect us all.[57] Intellectual elites cannot save us, as they have demonstrated a variety of cognitive biases in real-world situations: for instance, economists blinding themselves to ideologically-uncongenial evidence about the causes of recessions[58] and international relations practitioners making disastrous foreign policy decisions.[59]

The process of learning about the political realm through the media *should* go something like this. We select media sources, expose ourselves to the information and arguments made in them, make judgments about each bit of information or argument (and the source itself), store them in memory, and call upon our memory when asked to discuss a political topic with someone or to participate in the political process by voting or campaigning. If we had minds that fit the liberal ideal, each of these steps would be unproblematic almost no matter what sort of media system we had. However, we have human, not liberal, minds. And each step in this process of accumulating political knowledge from the media is fraught with dangers, difficulties, and problems arising from psychological biases. Hence, for democracy—the liberal ideal of government—to function in the absence of liberal minds, media systems must be suited to human minds.

3   Confirmation Bias

"Faced with the choice between changing one's mind and proving there is no need to do so, almost everyone gets busy on the proof."
—John Kenneth Galbraith, *Economics, Peace and Laughter*

In 2009, Google unveiled a personalized search feature that remembers one's previous searches and which results were subsequently visited, making inferences about what one was searching for. These are used in future searches to tailor results. So, if you searched for "sox," the results would be split between Web pages selling socks and those about the Chicago White Sox; if you clicked on a Web page about the baseball team, future "sox" results would be more limited to Web pages about the baseball team. This sparked worries that people may become more and more ideologically polarized: after all, once Google's algorithm determined that you were conservative based on past searches, during future searches about any given political issue, your results would be more limited to conservative sources of information.

It probably would not have soothed anyone to learn that this potential bias in Google searches is already hard-wired into our minds. It is confirmation bias, and it makes us seek or interpret evidence to confirm what we already believe or expect.[60] This pervasive bias has been fleshed out by modern psychological research, but philosophers have discussed it at least since Francis Bacon:

> The human understanding when it has once adopted an opinion (either as being the received opinion or as being agreeable to itself) draws all things else to support and agree with it. And though there be a greater number and weight of instances to be found on the other side, yet these it either neglects and despises, or else by some distinction sets aside and rejects; in order that by this great and pernicious predetermination the authority of its former conclusions may remain inviolate.[61]

Among cognitive biases, the confirmation bias might be considered supreme—it compounds the effects of other biases, strengthening the erroneous conclusions they draw, and protecting them from disconfirming evidence.

The confirmation bias works in a number of ways.[62] It restricts our attention to a favored hypothesis, even when there are competing hypotheses. For instance, if we hear of an attack against a ship by an enemy country and believe it ruled by power-mad despots, we will likely restrict our attention to the hypothesis that the attack was due to that country's dangerous leaders. Alternative hypotheses—the torpedo was fired by accident, the explosion caused by faulty equipment, or our ship fired first—are ignored. The confirmation bias also makes us preferentially treat evidence supporting our beliefs and dismiss contradictory evidence. We may give great weight to evidence of the enemy country's aggressive militaristic tendencies and dismiss equally relevant evidence that stormy conditions led to an accidental firing, a history of dangerous mechanical problems on our ship, or reports from nearby vessels that our ship fired first. The confirmation bias also leads us to look primarily for evidence that supports our beliefs (even when we do not care deeply about those beliefs). The confirmation bias makes us overweight incidents that confirm our beliefs and gives less weight to incidents that disconfirm our hypothesis. This can cause an illusion of consistency: a country believed to be peaceful will be misjudged to be *consistently* peaceful, and one believed to be belligerent misjudged as *consistently* belligerent. Not only does the confirmation bias infect our searches for new information, but it also affects the process of searching our memory.[63] Worse, this biased search of our memory is perceived to be objective and thorough, creating an illusion of objectivity—we have no conscious awareness that our memory search is biased in the direction of confirming our beliefs. Therefore, even if we have examined plenty of evidence supporting alternate explanations of the explosion, when we are discussing the issue and relying on memory, our recollection is also biased.

Far from being a problem that affects only the poorly educated, the confirmation bias is present even in science, where bias is most painstakingly avoided. In experiments testing whether the confirmation bias affects scientists' judgments of scientific studies, participants were given research articles to judge.[64] Some were in accord with the scientists' prior beliefs and others were contrary. As predicted, the scientists judged studies inconsistent with their beliefs more harshly than similarly designed studies consistent with their beliefs—and this was so even though the scientists were aware of the bias and tried to apply the normative value of impartiality. While the scientists' criticisms of the studies that challenged their views were ostensibly based on methodological grounds, the inconsistency with which they applied methodological standards made clear that it was the conclusions that made the scientists so critical. This cognitive bias may be *more* prevalent among those higher in cognitive reflection and numeracy.[65] However, there is evidence that forms of specialized training can reduce the effects of biased reasoning.[66]

Confirmation bias is linked to "belief persistence," the phenomenon that once a belief or opinion has taken root, it can demonstrate tough resistance to change—even when we are exposed to compelling evidence that it is wrong. And belief persistence can be seen throughout society, from politics to economics to science: "[o]ne can see a confirmation bias both in the difficulty with which new ideas break through opposing established points of view and in the uncritical allegiance they are often given once they have become part of the established view themselves."[67] Here is the root of the Planck Principle: when physicist Max Planck met resistance from older physicists against his (correct) theories, he proposed that scientific advances occur not by established scientists being convinced of superior, new theories, but older scientists dying and being replaced by younger adherents of new theories.

Confirmation bias, the core of "motivated reasoning," does not require conscious or subconscious motivation to warp information seeking and processing. (However, MRI scans of people engaging in reasoning about presidential candidates, compared to pop culture figures, reveal greater activity in brain regions associated with emotion and affect regulation.)[68] It can be explained in terms of System 1 and 2 processes and the selective quantity of thought we apply.[69] Put simply, when we encounter information consistent with our beliefs, our System 1 approves, we get a good feeling about it, and we do not subject it to much System 2 scrutiny (for instance, considering alternate explanations). However, for belief-inconsistent, disconfirming evidence, our System 1 raises a red flag, and System 2 kicks into scrutinize the evidence, running it through a fine-toothed comb. Therefore, the confirmation bias or motivated reasoning can persist without a conscious or subconscious desire to cherry-pick evidence or construct tortured justifications. It can persist in a simple process of subjecting belief-inconsistent evidence to a thorough, critical System 2 vetting, while evidence that confirms beliefs simply slips through.

This is consistent with a less "psychological," more subjective or commonsense view of the phenomenon:

> [A]n interpretation makes sense of part of the world's blooming, buzzing overabundance of information. But in so doing it tends to screen in a biased and self-confirming sample of information: information that

is consistent with the interpretation. Other information will tend to be screened out as irrelevant, incomprehensible, absurd, or suspect. Thus, the process of interpretation-based learning should, ceteris paribus, initiate a spiral of confirmation bias, i.e., a "spiral of conviction," that progressively strengthens the conviction that one's interpretation is correct.[70]

This is also consistent with network models of attitude change and formation, which picture ideas as embedded in networks of schemas in the brain.[71] These models explain phenomena like confirmation bias, cognitive dissonance reduction, and system justification tendency without positing subconscious motivations, but rather as the structural effect of neural networks operating under a consistency constraint: the links between ideas cannot be contradictory.

Thankfully, the confirmation bias is not all-powerful.[72] While we are motivated to argue against disconfirming evidence, as it builds up we become more anxious, leading to a tipping point.[73] The problem lies in the low likelihood that we will encounter such "knowledge constraints" if we tend to accumulate only knowledge that fits preexisting beliefs.

4   Cognitive Dissonance Reduction

"The lust for comfort; that stealthy thing that enters the house as a guest, and then becomes a host, and then a master."
—Kahlil Gibran, *The Prophet*, "On Houses"

Cognitive dissonance is a phenomenon uncovered over half a century ago.[74] It describes the unpleasant feeling experienced when we encounter evidence that conflicts with our beliefs, such as knowledge or opinions about the outside world, social environment, and one's self or behavior. When we feel cognitive dissonance, we are drawn to reduce it. This can be done by rejecting the veracity of the new evidence, ignoring or reinterpreting it; or, the least likely option, changing prior beliefs to make them consistent with the new evidence.

Doubtless cognitive dissonance struck the passers-by in the biblical parable on the road to Jericho. The priest and the Levite must have felt that their disregard of the wounded traveler was inconsistent with their view of themselves as good, caring people. Perhaps they explained away their cognitive dissonance, reminding themselves that they were late for something important and that someone else would help. Or, they might have imagined the wounded traveler a disguised robber, even feeling moral indignation at the Roman authorities for not solving the crime problem, forcing good people to face such uncomfortable dilemmas. Only the Good Samaritan reduced his cognitive dissonance by eliminating its source: helping the wounded traveler and bringing his actions in line with his view of himself.

We do not often select this option. In an experiment of students at Princeton Theological Seminary, a shabbily dressed confederate was positioned, slumped-over in apparent distress, along the path students had to take to deliver a talk.[75] The experimenters found that the only variable that made a difference in whether or not the students stopped to help the man was the amount of time pressure they were under—even when the student's talk was on the Good Samaritan story.

The interesting thing about cognitive dissonance and cognitive dissonance reduction is that it does not always flow from belief to behavior that is inconsistent with the belief. It can flow the opposite way too. In one study, participants were asked to read aloud a sheet of disparaging lawyer jokes.[76] Half were told that reading the jokes was optional and half that it was a requirement. Afterward, those who were given a choice reported a lower opinion of lawyers than those required to read the jokes. Cognitive dissonance reduction was set in motion by *choosing* to read the jokes. Participants who had been given a choice avoided cognitive dissonance by lowering their opinion of the profession. For the participants who were required to read the jokes, being obligated was not inconsistent with holding generally positive views of lawyers.

Cognitive dissonance reduction is so widespread due to the strength of our desire for cognitive consistency.[77] We want to believe our beliefs about the world and ourselves are consistent and that our behavior is in line with our beliefs. We do not want to be hypocrites. However, this does not mean cognitive dissonance reduction is the result of a consciously chosen strategy; we are blissfully ignorant of it. Cognitive dissonance reduction may be the accidental outcome of an unconscious epistemic process aimed at maintaining cognitive consistency. Overall, we want to believe that desired beliefs are true and undesired ones false; if we encounter inconsistent evidence, it creates cognitive dissonance over the apparent error in our belief system. The process of cognitive dissonance reduction kicks into smooth out the apparent error. We do not engage in this unconscious process when we receive a judgment in accord with our beliefs, negative or positive. This process has also been used to explain prejudice, our tendency to judge people on their intrinsic qualities while ignoring situational influences, and the strength of our first impressions of people.[78]

Cognitive dissonance reduction manifests in myriad ways, often strange. In one experiment, participants were instructed to deliver electric shocks to "victims," some of whom would be able to retaliate.[79] Participants were given the opportunity to insult and derogate the victims, and the amount of derogation was measured across retaliation and non-retaliation conditions. Researchers found that participants who did not expect their victims to retaliate derogated the victims more. In their minds, shocking a victim who could not retaliate created an inequity in their relationship. This caused uncomfortable cognitive dissonance and, to reduce it, they sought to justify their act by derogating the victim (as if they *must have* deserved it because they had some negative quality). Those who expected their victims to retaliate experienced no such cognitive dissonance, because they expected the inequity to be eliminated (by the victim delivering electric shocks to them in retaliation). These participants derogated their victims less. (Hence, the joke about the English soldier beating an Irish man, who asks why the English hate the Irish so; the soldier replies "we'll never forgive you for what we've done to you.")

Ironically, only psychopaths may be immune from cognitive dissonance reduction.[80] In cases where behavior toward another person is inconsistent with the norms of empathy and honesty, psychopaths demonstrate no unpleasant cognitive dissonance. For the rest of us, however, cognitive dissonance reduction is pervasive.

The problem with cognitive dissonance reduction for the liberal ideal of the human mind is not that cognitive dissonance is uncomfortable and avoided. Avoiding inconsistency is a good design feature for a rational mind. The problem lies in *how* cognitive dissonance is reduced: oftentimes, it is irrational. There can be no rational defense of derogating innocent victims. So too with the hypothetical ways in which the priest and Levite reduced their cognitive dissonance: instead of inventing specious rationalizations, they should have owned their hypocrisy or revised their self-images to include the fact that they are the type of person to pass by a wounded stranger. Or, ideally, made their behavior uphold their principles.

5 Meaning Maintenance—Accounting for a Bevy of Biases

A recent theory suggests that *all* experiences that violate expected relationships between people or things cause physiological, aversive arousal, which sets in motion compensatory efforts to eliminate the aversive arousal; most unexpectedly, these efforts may have nothing to do with the root experience.[81] "Expected relationships," in this theory, are at the core of what *meaning* means for us. The meaning of "snow" involves an expected relationship with cold; the meaning of "kindness" involves one between people that are friendly and helpful; the meaning of "enemy" involves one with danger, harm, potential violence, and so on. When an expected relationship is violated—say, by noticing that our behavior violates an expected relationship between ourselves and the ideal of a good person—an unconscious feeling of anxious arousal sets in. Although we do not consciously experience it, there is a release of epinephrine (adrenaline) and often cortisol (another stress hormone), followed by increased skin conductance, constriction of blood vessels, and variability in cardiac activity. This anxious arousal is described as a "physiological threat response," as if a violation of expected relationships is perceived as a physical threat. In one experiment on cognitive dissonance, some participants were given a placebo pill they were told would reduce anxiety—and it was these participants who displayed no cognitive dissonance reduction.[82] Cognitive dissonance reduction is only performed to reduce anxious arousal, which these participants believed a pill had resolved.

This anxious arousal may make sense for encountering information that profoundly challenges our worldviews. But just about any violation of expected relationships will do, even interacting with an Asian American with a southern US accent[83]; making facial expressions that conflict with the emotions being experienced[84]; or being a minority group member who expects others to be prejudiced, interacting with someone who is not prejudiced.[85] The "meaning maintenance" phenomenon could arise from "crossed wires" in our brains, with anxiety aroused by one piece of information being subdued by processing unrelated, soothing information.[86]

We have five possible strategies—performed outside of conscious awareness—to reduce this anxiety.[87] First, we can assimilate discordant evidence by modifying it to fit with our beliefs. Second, we can accommodate our beliefs to it. These two are fairly straightforward.

Third, we can use abstraction to compensate for a violation of expected relationships by *creating* a new relationship from our environment. For instance, when subliminally presented with nonsense word pairs, participants were better able to detect patterns in strings of letters[88]; when made to feel they lacked control, participants were likelier to see patterns in events, including by creating conspiracy theories.[89] Fourth, we can use assembly or meaning-making, creating a new framework to make sense of a violation. However, this does not need to be related to the meaning violation that gave rise to it, which might be why periods of cultural upheaval give rise to enhanced artistic output.[90] (This is related to the underlying rationale for art therapy: using creativity to soothe unrelated sources of personal distress.) A fifth way, affirmation, is absolutely irrational: we reduce anxious arousal by affirming familiar values and beliefs, *even when these have nothing to do with the violation*. For instance, being reminded of one's mortality led municipal court judges to affirm their moral beliefs by setting a significantly higher bond on women facing prostitution charges,[91] and hearing an absurd joke or being subliminally presented with nonsense word pairs made experimental participants express a desire to punish criminals more harshly.[92]

While this meaning maintenance framework helps explain why some people turn to religion during distress, or societies support conservative policies after a national trauma, it is in diametric opposition to the liberal ideal of a rational mind. The experiments that have been done in this area have largely concerned topics of minor interest to politics, but there is little reason to doubt that the same phenomenon is at work in our thinking about politics. As the late comedian Bill Hicks joked:

> People say to me, 'Hey, Bill, the [Gulf] war made us feel better about ourselves.' Really? What kind of people are these with such low self-esteem that they need a *war* to feel better about themselves? I saw them on the news, waving their flags. May I suggest, instead of a war to feel better about yourself, perhaps ... sit-ups?[93]

The answer to Hicks' "what kind of people" question may simply be: human people. If violations of expected relationships make us anxious, and we can soothe ourselves by punishing criminals more harshly, why might not even the organized mass murder of *war* function similarly?

6   Groupishness and Bias

"What should one write to ruin an adversary? The best thing is to prove that he is not one of us – the stranger, alien, foreigner. To this end we create the category of the true family. We here, you and I, the authorities, are a true family. We live in unity, among our own kind. We have the same roof over our heads, we sit at the same table, we know how to get along with each other, how to help each other out. Unfortunately, we are not alone."

—Ryszard Kapuscinski, Shah of Shahs

"Groupishness" is a neologism created by psychologists studying group dynamics. It refers to the ease with which we create and sort ourselves into often arbitrary groups, and discriminate against other groups.[94] Any distinction—from eye color to shirt color—can be used to form such groups. The mere use of words like "us" and "them" primes our groupish instincts and subtly influences how we judge unknown others.[95] Even using a noun instead of an adjective to describe someone's nationality (e.g., "Pole" vs. "Polish") makes a difference: in-group bias is more sensitive to nouns.[96] For better or worse, we are a deeply groupish species.

"Intergroup bias" describes our systematic tendency to judge fellow members of our group (an in-group) more favorably than members of groups of which we are not members (out-groups). This unconscious bias can include discriminatory behaviors, prejudicial attitudes, and stereotyping.[97] We even apply different standards of justice: more allowing for "us," more exacting for "them."[98] Negative out-group bias is generally weaker than positive in-group bias,[99] but once out-groups act, intergroup bias can initiate a bevy of negative reactions. Out-groups violating our in-group norms can make us disgusted; out-groups believed to be benefiting unjustly from a resource can elicit resentment and provoke actions to cut them off from that resource; and out-groups we view as threatening can make us feel afraid and prompt us even to violent action.[100]

The intergroup bias is so pervasive it extends to and biases even our language.[101] When describing positive in-group behaviors and negative out-group behaviors, we are likelier to use expressive verbs (interpretive action verbs) and highly abstract terms—linguistic devices that subtly suggest that good things done by our in-group and bad things done by an out-group are general and widespread. Alternatively, we are prone to use concrete terms (descriptive action verbs) to describe positive out-group and negative in-group behaviors. Thereby, subtly suggesting that bad things done by our in-group and good things by an out-group are exceptions and outliers, not generalizable to the group as a whole. These distinctions make a difference: reading articles with out-group linguistic bias subtly increases prejudice against the groups described.[102]

Intergroup bias can have positive effects too. It can enhance self-esteem, as the positive affect and pride can rub off on ourselves individually. Also, members of high-status groups may demonstrate magnanimity to lower-status out-groups when the gap separating them is wide—and they tend not to demonstrate bias on dimensions of their group that are irrelevant to their high status.[103] Members of a rich and powerful national in-group are unlikely to be biased against national out-groups that are better than them only in cricket or musical creativity.

Still, the dark side of intergroup bias looms larger. Once groups enter into perceived competition—as when immigrants are perceived to take citizens' jobs or an undue share of social welfare benefits—group enhancement turns to group defense and intergroup relations deteriorate.[104] Intergroup bias is attuned to situational variables. Believing in the superiority of one's national in-group is correlated with prejudice against ethnic minority out-groups.[105] Minority groups with high power display particularly strong discrimination against out-groups, while high-power and equal-power groups demonstrate greater bias than groups with little power.[106] High-power groups are more prone to underestimate commonalities and polarize the difference between themselves and low-power groups.[107] Within countries, economic problems and a high percentage of immigrant out-group members exacerbate intergroup bias, in particular prejudice on the part of the dominant in-group.[108] Intergroup bias can cause in-group favoritism when allocating benefits, and conditions such as inferior status and social instability can aggravate in-group bias.[109] When reading newspaper stories of violent acts committed by in-group members, we are likelier to attribute them to situational factors (poverty or political oppression); but when we read about violent acts committed by members of out-groups, we are likelier to attribute them to dispositional factors (an intrinsically violent character or culture).[110] This aspect of intergroup bias helps prop up an inequitable status quo: members of high-status in-groups will attribute the condition of low-status, low-power out-groups to their personal inadequacies, ignoring social, environmental, and situational constraints.[111]

Similarly disturbing, intergroup bias causes us to judge out-groups as more homogenous than in-groups—and this effect is found with real-world and experimental groups.[112] Compounding this problem, encounters with out-groups affect our judgments of the group overall; worse, encounters with *a single member* of an out-group can influence our impression of the entire group.[113] Furthermore, mere geographical distance makes a behavior appear due to a person's intrinsic disposition, rather than as the result of situational and environmental factors.[114] Therefore, if we have a bad experience while traveling in a foreign country, or see a news story about a threatening behavior by a foreign national, our perception of that entire country—comprising several, maybe hundreds of millions of people—can be powerfully and negatively influenced.

Stereotypes are an influential by-product of intergroup bias. Interestingly, stereotypes have a way of perpetuating themselves not only by biased processing on the part of the stereotype holders, but also by the behavior of the stereotyped.[115] Behavioral confirmation of stereotypes occurs when a powerful group has stereotyped a low-power group. To "get along" with the powerful group, members of the low-power group may unconsciously follow a strategy of not causing the powerful group any confusion, by displaying stereotypical behavior themselves. This behavioral confirmation effect has been noted in experimental studies organized around "getting acquainted" and cooperative task scenarios. When stigmatized and nonstigmatized groups are combined, nonstigmatized group members display dominant behaviors and stigmatized groups avoidant behaviors, which equally help to perpetuate the stereotypes purportedly describing the groups. For instance, if a stigmatized group member perceives prejudice, the person is likely to react with an avoidant style of interaction; this avoidance is interpreted to confirm negative stereotypes held by nonstigmatized group members ("this person is so hostile, just as I expected from a member of that group"). Mere anxiety caused by contact with out-group members can increase stereotyping, as anxiety inhibits our ability to concentrate on individuating information. Stereotypes thereby create their own justification and support by eliciting the very behaviors hypothesized by the stereotype itself. Even when behavioral confirmation does not occur, we are more likely to remember stereotype-consistent than stereotype-inconsistent behaviors.

Demagogues openly appeal to in-group membership to denigrate or attack out-group members. But this is an overt, conscious phenomenon. In particular among the U.S. college student population that makes up the majority of samples, overt and openly expressed biased attitudes are rare. Yet in experimental studies, the prevalence of intergroup bias suggests processes operating behind conscious awareness. While nationalist or racist demagogues openly and consciously express ideas that boost their in-group and derogate out-groups, the process by which they arrived at those ideas was powerfully influenced by *unconscious* intergroup bias.

It is tempting, to protect a rosy picture of our minds, to suppose that the experimental evidence demonstrating the existence of intergroup bias and behavioral confirmation is of limited applicability. After all, these experimental situations are simple and the world is complex. Yet the simplicity of the "minimal group paradigm" in intergroup bias research is its strength. If such tiny, irrelevant distinctions as t-shirt color are sufficient to activate intergroup bias, this proves their power.[116]

7   Beliefs Persist, Memories Less so

Psychologists who study memory have noted seven major classes of memory problems: transience, how information becomes less accessible over time; absentmindedness, the inattentive processing of information that weakens memories; blocking, or the tip-of-the-tongue phenomenon where information is temporarily inaccessible; misattribution, where we mistakenly link an idea to the wrong source; suggestibility, false memories created by leading questions and an attempt to recall distant experiences; bias, the distortion caused by unconscious influences that affect current knowledge and belief; and persistence, items in memory we wish we could forget, but cannot.[117]

Of greatest political interest are suggestibility and bias. Suggestibility has been the root of many false confessions, as well as false testimony by witnesses who believe themselves to be telling the truth. Bias in the context of memory can cause all sorts of political problems in a democracy. A population given to memory bias can be manipulated, as the people of the USA and Britain demonstrated with regard to the war against Iraq, its original rationale, and subsequent twists and turns in its justifications. Memory bias is painfully apparent in polls of the British and U.S. public, asking how many people in Iraq died as a result of the war: only a tiny fraction responded with anything approaching the scientific estimates or even the record of violent deaths that made it into news reports.[118] Instead, people in the United States and Britain drastically underestimated the number of innocent people killed by a war for which they were at least distally responsible.

Political memories may be particularly susceptible to error. Not only do few of us have experiences with politicians and government officials, but also political issues are abstract and emotionally charged. In one study, liberals and conservatives were shown doctored photographs of Barack Obama shaking hands with Iranian President Mahmoud Ahmadinejad and George W. Bush entertaining baseball star Roger Clemens at his home while New Orleans was underwater after Hurricane Katrina.[119] Short captions putting the photographs in context were included. Conservatives had a higher rate of false memory for the fabricated event putting Obama in a bad light, and liberals for the event negatively depicting Bush.

If the problem with memories is that they are unreliable and can fade too easily, the problem with some beliefs is that they persist. Beliefs that have been discredited or invalidated by evidence tend to remain believed: the phenomenon of belief persistence.[120] Belief persistence occurs first when we are exposed to evidence that suggests a causal explanation, but later our explanation becomes functionally independent of the evidence that supported it. So when that evidence is later discredited or invalidated, our causal explanation—our belief—remains. For instance, in one experiment participants were given two case studies suggesting either that risk-taking made one more or less successful as a firefighter.[121] Some were then asked to write about why this relationship exists. Then, participants were told that the case study evidence was fake—no known relationship existed between risk-taking and success as a firefighter. Nonetheless, the participants continued to believe in the relationship.

Key to belief persistence is the generation of a causal explanation that puts evidence into a narrative context. When we create a causal narrative, we are integrating it into a neural network, which persists after that evidence is discredited.[122] Only when we do not create explanations for later-discredited evidence is belief persistence unlikely.[123]

Part of the problem is that we initially accept as true any proposition.[124] At first glance, this seems farfetched. The philosopher

René Descartes would certainly have disagreed: according to him, we are at first neutral with regard to propositions and as we process them we determine their truth. Baruch Spinoza, however, believed that we initially consider propositions true; afterward, we may either examine them and decide they are false, or not examine them (for instance, if we are busy or distracted) and continue to believe. This philosophical debate was well summarized by Gilbert and colleagues: "For many centuries, philosophers have wondered whether the having and holding of ideas are psychologically separable operations, and for just as many centuries, ordinary folk have considered this a perfectly stupid question. Clearly, one experiences belief as though one were capable of entertaining ideas before endorsing them."[125]

Nonetheless, a solid body of experimental evidence supports the proposition that we accept information as true and only later may decide whether it is false. This ordering of our mental system may be evolutionarily adaptive: it is more economical to initially accept information and critically examine it (if we have the chance) later. The problem is that we do not always have the mental resources to subject new information to rigorous examination. When we are otherwise occupied, our System 1 process stamps "this is true" on new information, and our System 2 process never gets the chance to make a second, more elaborative determination. This is also how our visual system works.[126] We believe whatever we see and only sometimes does our System 2 process tell us we are witnessing an illusion. The way we process information seems to have evolved from the same functional lineage as our perceptual system.

This explanation receives support in experiments where participants are asked to process information and are later told whether it was true. When participants were not distracted and could process without hindrance the initial information and the subsequent message explaining whether it was true or false, they could remember which statements were true or false. However, when participants were given a distracting task, they misremembered false statements as true—yet did not misremember true statements as false.

Even when we know ahead that information we will be encountering is false, we continue to initially classify it as true. This is shown by an experiment where participants were sometimes told before and sometimes after being presented with information whether it was true or false—and no significant difference emerged.[127] We are incapable of adopting a true skeptic's mindset and evaluating information as false as we encounter it. Hence, this mental process of classifying new information is outside of voluntary, conscious control. Even if our conscious, System 2 process is warning us that the information we are about to be exposed to is false, our unconscious System 1 process still stamps it with the only stamp it has: "true!" Our System 2 process can kick in and reclassify the information, but the problem with this corrective process is that we are often too distracted.

Moreover, we treat beliefs similarly to how we treat possessions. For one, our beliefs may be subject to the endowment effect: we value more highly a thing we possess than that same thing if we do not possess it.[128] So too, we value our own beliefs more highly than ideas we do not believe. And we treat many of our beliefs as possessions, being as sensitive to criticism of them as we are careful in adopting only those new beliefs that do not conflict with the ones we cherish. Robert Abelson explains:

> If anyone is critical of [our beliefs], one feels attacked and responds defensively, as though one's appearance, taste, or judgment had been called into question. One occasionally adds new beliefs to one's collection, if they do not glaringly clash with those one already has. It is something like the accumulation of furniture. One is reluctant to change any of one's major beliefs. They are familiar and comfortable, and a big change would upset the whole collection.[129]

Hence, we are so difficult to persuade, even when our beliefs are premised on false information. If persuasion means giving up a belief, to be persuaded is to lose a cherished possession.

Our tenacity in holding on to beliefs is exacerbated with distal beliefs—Max Stirner's "spooks"—ideas concerning abstract concepts, objects that are only remotely experienced, or anything that cannot be verified by our senses.[130] Distal beliefs include almost all political beliefs: whether austerity policies are economically beneficial, a war is justified and necessary, social spending will lead to a healthier society or economic ruin, etc. Because these beliefs do not lend themselves to corrective falsification, they are notoriously difficult to change. Further calcifying distal beliefs about politics, beliefs tend to increase in perceived value when they are threatened.

8 If You Can't Beat 'Em, Join 'Em: System Justification Theory

"People are not so easily got out of their old forms, as some are apt to suggest. They are hardly to be prevailed with to amend the acknowledged faults in the frame they have been accustomed to. And if there be any original defects, or adventitious ones introduced by time, or corruption; it is not an easy thing to get them changed, even when all the world sees there is an opportunity for it."
—John Locke, *Second Treatise of Government*

Marx theorized that the ruling class determines which ideas become prevalent, leading to "false consciousness" among the oppressed as they adopt the system justification offered by their oppressors; Gramsci updated and elaborated this idea with his conception of "cultural hegemony," detailing the institutional and cultural means through which the ruling class created false consciousness among the masses.

Within psychology, system justification theory proposes another, related explanation which has accumulated significant evidentiary support. It explains that we are psychologically motivated to a greater or lesser extent to excuse the moral and practical failings of the social, economic, and political systems we live in and even to derogate and dismiss alternatives. This unconscious process drives us to exaggerate our systems' benefits, downplay negative aspects, and view the status quo as more just and desirable than it is.

Several aspects of our system justification tendency are well established by experiments: we are unconsciously motivated to defend and justify the status quo, including current social, economic, and political systems and institutions.[131] The degree to which we are so motivated depends on individual (including neurological)[132] differences and situations; this motivation is aroused when we feel dependent on or controlled by the system, when the status quo seems inevitable, inequality is salient, and the system is challenged or threatened. System justification soothes existential threats and insecurities, and helps us achieve certainty in shared worldviews that coordinate social relationships. Moreover, system justification enhances individual and collective self-esteem for those with high status and conflicts with self-esteem for those with low status, leading them to display out-group favoritism. Because confronting injustice and inequity is painful, system justification is palliative; while it leads us to resist social change in general, we are prone to embrace change perceived as inevitable, likely, or as permitting the preservation of the system and its ideals.

In one experiment, members of a disadvantaged group were given legitimate, illegitimate, or no explanations for a power differential between themselves and another group. Legitimate and illegitimate (legitimacy was based on independent, pre-test ratings) explanations served to make the disadvantaged group feel better and positively stereotype the more powerful out-group.[133] The system justification motive even led members of the disadvantaged group to misremember illegitimate explanations as legitimate (which more than 30% did, as opposed to only 3% who misremembered legitimate explanations as illegitimate).

The status quo holds a special attraction, regardless of what we would like the status quo to be. In studies of an *anticipated*, future status quo, participants judged *likely* eventualities to be more desirable than *unlikely* eventualities.[134] In particular, before the 2000 presidential election in the USA, Democrats and Republicans judged potential Bush and Gore presidencies more desirable as their likelihood increased and less desirable as their likelihood decreased. In other words, despite wanting Bush or Gore to win, that Bush or Gore was *likelier* to win (and thereby form part of the future status quo) made either presidency more desirable. This effect did not make Bush supporters view a Gore victory as desirable (or vice versa), but it made a probable victory by the opposing candidate more desirable than it would have been. In the same way, immediately *after* President George W. Bush's announcement of war plans against Iraq, Americans of all political leanings substantially increased their support for the war.[135]

Part of the reason this is counterintuitive is that the system justification motive occurs outside conscious awareness. For instance, few African-Americans would consciously accept that their unequal status on financial, professional, or educational measures is legitimate. But when intergroup bias is measured *implicitly*, low-status minority groups including African-Americans often do not display common in-group bias, instead showing preferences for high-status out-groups. Only in the System 2 realm, when African-American respondents were asked to explicitly and consciously describe their opinions, the results were the opposite: higher in-group favoritism. Due to the operation of the system justification tendency, European-Americans display higher implicit in-group favoritism and African-Americans higher implicit out-group favoritism.[136] This same pattern was uncovered in studies of young and old, gay and straight, and is accentuated by increasing political conservatism.

In another experiment, American participants were subliminally presented with the word "death," which led to greater accessibility of death-related thoughts and, oddly, a stronger preference for pro-American over anti-American authors.[137] This suggests that many uncomfortable thoughts can increase our support for the social, economic, and political system.

Interestingly, while it makes intuitive sense that low-power groups with few socioeconomic resources should follow self-interest in wanting to reform the system, the opposite is the case. Groups low on the socioeconomic ladder tend to score higher on measures of right-wing authoritarianism, political conservatism, and the belief that the world is just.[138] In one experiment, after being reminded how difficult it would be to leave a given system, participants became more accepting of that system's flaws *and* critical of dissident groups.[139] In another series of experiments, powerlessness—reported or primed—led to a greater sense of legitimacy and justification for one's superiors, the economic and social systems, and governmental authorities.[140] False consciousness, indeed: to escape the psychological pain inflicted by being at the bottom of an unjust or unequal social system, we unconsciously rationalize, justify, and support the source of that psychological pain, even to the point of criticizing would-be reformers.

Perhaps of greatest concern for liberal democracy is evidence that as complex political issues become more urgent, we tend to avoid them more.[141] That is, as an issue looms larger and more dangerous, we defend ourselves against the threat in the manner (falsely) imputed to ostriches, burying our heads in the sand. We feel greater dependence on government leading to increased trust in it, trust that can only be protected by intentionally avoiding the issue. A series of five experiments bears this theory out, as the experimenters explained:

> [R]ather than ensuring those in charge are maximally qualified to be in charge, and rather than remaining especially attuned to any limitations of the system, the psychological processes that are instigated when issues are seen as both severe and complex may limit any criticism of the current system and its decision-making process. And, perhaps even more critically, they may also prevent the types of behaviors, such as information gathering, that are necessary to efficacious social action…[142]

While the system justification tendency varies by context, its existence means that information suggesting a need to change the status quo—particularly if change is perceived to be difficult or "unrealistic"—is likelier to be ignored or denigrated in favor of specious arguments that deny the need for change. More disturbingly, we choose to remain ignorant of complex, urgent issues in proportion to their complexity and urgency.

9   But Wait, There's More: Attitude Inoculation and Counterintuitive Effects

"The most perfidious way of harming a cause consists of defending it deliberately with faulty arguments."
—Friedrich Nietzsche, *The Gay Science*

We are familiar with how vaccines and inoculation work: a weak form of a pathogen or antigen is injected, which allows our immune system to evolve a stronger defense. Strangely, psychological research has uncovered the same process operating in the realm of ideas. When confronted with a weak form of an argument, we are less likely to be persuaded later by a strong form of that argument.[143] While inoculation is uniformly beneficial in the medical context, in the intellectual context its effects are mixed: we are just as likely to become inoculated against a bad argument as a good one.

When we are first exposed to a weak form of an argument, we incorporate it into existing beliefs. Since this argument is weak, it is unlikely to fit among our existing network of beliefs. Instead, we consider it false and incorporate it into our beliefs by relating how it could not possibly be true given x, y, and z. Later, when presented with a strong version of that argument, we already have our network of beliefs organized negatively with respect to it. Whereas the strong argument *before* inoculation may have prompted us to reorganize our network of beliefs so as to accept it, the strong argument *after* inoculation meets with strong resistance from a network of beliefs prearranged to reject it. Even receiving a mere warning that we are about to hear an argument we will disagree with can significantly decrease our likelihood of being persuaded.[144]

Not only can weak arguments (or warnings) inoculate us from persuasion by a strong argument, but sometimes weak arguments can convince us in the contrary direction, strengthening our confidence in the antithesis.[145] This phenomenon can occur whenever we are presented with two sides: as jurors in a courtroom, as friends hearing a dispute from two perspectives, or as democratic citizens hearing arguments about a political issue in the media. We hear the argument of the first side, set down a reference point anchor related to that argument's strength; then, when we hear the counterargument, it must exceed that reference point to convince us. Otherwise, the counterargument *increases* our confidence in the initial argument. This poses dangers in how arguments are presented in the media. While it might seem acceptable to give plenty of airtime or column inches to official spokespeople, and less to independent analysts or pressure groups on the other side of an issue, this may not provide balance. It may serve to strengthen the argument made by the side given more opportunity to make their case and leave viewers and readers feeling more unfavorably toward the opposing side than even if they were given no opportunity to present their argument.

This danger is more acute in the realm of hot-button political issues, where we are already likely to assimilate arguments in a highly biased fashion.[146] Exposure to arguments against our preferred side causes a negative affective reaction: we emotionally recoil (and sometimes find them "offensive"). This affective reaction then results in biased assimilation, potentially leaving us even more convinced that our side of the argument is correct.

This counterintuitive prediction is borne out by experiments on news media exposure. In one, participants were exposed to two frames of an issue, one weak and one strong, at different times.[147] The experimenters expected that when exposed to a strong frame of an issue and later a weak frame of the same issue from a different perspective, participants would display little effect from the strong frame (as its effect might decay over time), and that the later weak frame would register insignificant effects; the net result being a reversion to the mean. Instead, they found that the strong frame shifted opinion in its direction and stayed there. The only effect of exposure to the weak frame was to increase accessibility of the strong frame to which participants had been exposed three weeks prior. Only equally strong frames cancel each other; hence, if media balance is not achieved by equally strong presentations of competing arguments, the only effect of presenting shorter or weaker forms of opposing arguments may be to strengthen opinions in the direction of the argument given a stronger presentation.

10   Moral Rationalization and Conflict

"It is forbidden to kill; therefore all murderers are punished unless they kill in large numbers and to the sound of trumpets."
—Voltaire, *Questions sur l'Encyclopédie*

Stanley Milgram's experiments on obedience are widely known—and if history were not already clear, they demonstrate how easily ordinary people can be made to commit evil acts. The psychological mechanisms that facilitate evil actions are of political interest beyond the actions themselves. In democracies, where the machinery of the state is at least normatively under the control of the citizenry, these mechanisms have a dual import: we are also interested in them insofar as they may influence us in giving democratic assent to evil actions committed by our governments. Democratic governments cannot survive without public support.

Even Milgram's classic experiments suggest ways in which democratic citizens can come to support evil state action.[148] When asked by the experimenter to apply potentially lethal electric shocks to the "learner," only a third of participants who were so remote from their "learner" victim that they could not hear or see him defied the experimenter. However, with each stage of further proximity, from those who could only hear the victim's shouts, to those required to hold the victim's hand on the shockplate, defiance increased. As Milgram observed, "it would appear that something akin to fields of force, diminishing in effectiveness with increasing psychological distance from their source, have a controlling effect on the subject's performance" in committing violence.[149] Being distant from our group's victim facilitates our participation in group violence: hear no evil, see no evil, allows us to commit evil. (Personality and ideological variables have also been found to influence compliance in a Milgram-like experiment.)[150]

The participants in Milgram's experiments often felt distress, whether complying with the experimenter in delivering shocks or defying him. This point may be the one anomaly separating this laboratory experiment from real-life: as two psychologists noted, Milgram's "obedience paradigm generates conflict-induced stress rarely seen in individuals in ongoing organizations" whose ends are destructive.[151] In real-world groups, evil actions are so fragmented by organizational structure that the moral content of actions is made irrelevant. Furthermore, in organizational structures information is distributed such that it is impossible for any given individual to know what others in the organization are doing. Compounding this, language is often policed to replace words that nakedly reveal ongoing evil with euphemisms. And while psychological distance is one way to reduce responsibility, it can be further reduced by other mechanisms, including a single-minded focus on following orders in lieu of any other motivation. When recruiting members of the *Einsatzgruppen*, the Nazis' mobile killing units, those who felt physical pleasure from murdering and torturing were weeded out in favor of those whose single-minded focus would be the mere following of orders. Subsequent research confirms the macabre wisdom of this recruitment policy: a focus on roles is an important facilitator of immoral behavior, as it distracts us from the realization that we are violating our moral code.[152] We are "just following orders." The same effect is produced by routinization, which distracts us from the meaning of a task. Lastly, self-affirmation provides us an escape valve if we come face to face with the intrinsic evil of our actions and role within a group. We need only to affirm another part of ourselves to paper over evil actions we commit.

In societies at war or other extended violent conflict, researchers have noted eight societal beliefs that sustain an "ethos of intractable conflict:" that the nature of group goals is just, of supreme importance, and failing to achieve them may threaten its existence; that the opponent is evil, wrong, aggressive, or dangerous; that the in-group is skilled, virtuous, moral, heroic, and has contributed positively to humanity; that the in-group has been victimized by an opponent; that security is under serious threat; a form of patriotism in which group members are asked to sacrifice for the group, and blind adherence to leaders is demanded; that unity is necessary for the accomplishment of the common cause; and that peace is the ultimate goal, but is imagined in utopian, general, and vague terms without concrete steps to achieve it.[153] Though psychological biases may be sufficient to support an ethos of intractable conflict, they can be reinforced and aided through media coverage either designed to assist in achieving military goals or simply being deferential to the government and the military.[154]

Whenever war, military aid to foreign countries, or even economic policies that threaten to decimate other countries' economies are involved, moral rationalization is a danger. Firstly, all three involve great distances, separating democratic citizens from the potential victims of government policies. Not only are military aid and predatory economic policies distant in geographical terms, but also rarely attract media coverage that might make them seem appreciably present. Even war itself, while potentially attracting more media coverage, rarely presents victims' perspectives. Bombers taking off from aircraft carriers can make it into media coverage, but the bloody, contorted bodies of bombing victims almost never enter citizens' living rooms. Moreover, the moral fragmentation of military organizations makes it into media coverage through embedded journalism: individual soldiers are presented as human-interest stories and in terms of individual tasks and roles. The sanitizing effect of euphemistic language also comes through media coverage of war, turning dismembered bodies of innocents into "collateral damage," an entirely affectless term. Topping off this dangerous mixture is the morally soothing effect of self-affirmation. Reminding media readers and viewers of the moral justification for a war and the moral virtue of their country overall provides self-affirmation. Lastly, fear of being demonized as "unpatriotic" or losing market share by being contrarian can push media outlets into reinforcing an ethos of intractable conflict, providing specious justifications for acts of violence while hiding or sanitizing them.

11   Self-Deception

"Nothing is so easy as to deceive one's self; for what we wish, we readily believe."
—Demosthenes, *Third Olynthiac*

If the biases discussed above carry a whiff of self-deception, there is a strong evolutionary reason: accumulated evidence from evolutionary biology, studies of our animal cousins, and experiments on our evolved psychology support the hypothesis that self-deception is adaptive.[155] Through deceiving ourselves we better deceive others, by avoiding the display of any cues of conscious deception that might give away our intent. Secondarily, by evolving the capacity to deceive ourselves we were able not only to avoid the cognitive costs of consciously mediated deception, but also reduce the retribution we would face if our deception were uncovered. The legal system and common person alike understand that *intent* matters; if we have not *intended* to deceive, we can expect people to be less retaliatory if they discover that they have been deceived.

Confidence is a major determinant of our influence: the more confident we seem, the likelier we are to be believed. As such, confidence is evolutionarily adaptive and we can expect mechanisms to have evolved to increase displays of confidence. This is what has been found in an array of experiments: we exaggerate our virtues and minimize shortcomings, to the point of interpreting or remembering events in the light most favorable to ourselves.[156] We do not consciously recognize this, but deceive ourselves. This enables us to increase our status in the eyes of our peers.[157]

Initially, self-deception seems contradictory: how can the same person believe one thing and its opposite, and how can one deceive oneself without letting oneself in on the deception?[158] However, once we discard the notion of a unitary self, self-deception makes sense. In light of advances in psychology and neuroscience, it is clear that different parts of the mind operate outside of conscious awareness, at cross-purposes.[159] *The* self does not deceive *the* self; parts of the self deceive other parts.

Self-deception is rife in our memories.[160] At its base is our dual-track memory: we are capable of storing information that we can consciously recollect and information for which we have no recollection. This may be because we tend to store and rehearse self-promoting (mis)information in consciously accessible memory, while information that would frustrate self-deception is relegated to inaccessible memory. Rehearsing misinformation makes memory more resilient and its origin more difficult to ascertain. Sharing a self-deceptive memory makes it stronger, and receiving social confirmation for a shared memory makes it stronger still. At the end of this winnowing and selection process, we retain false, self-enhancing memories in conscious memory and relegate accurate information to unconscious memory.

Another form of self-deception we have touched on centers around explicit and implicit attitudes. High-power groups tend to have modest conscious, explicitly expressed opinions of themselves, but less modest unconscious, implicit opinions; to the contrary, low-power groups have higher explicit opinions of themselves, but unconsciously tend to have higher implicit opinions of high-power out-groups. So it is that people who are asked whether they are prejudiced against a minority ethnic group say that they are not; yet when their implicit, unconscious responses to minority ethnic group members are measured, their hidden prejudice is revealed. This does not occur due to conscious lying. Rather, it is self-deception: we are unaware of our prejudice. This dissociation between implicit and explicit attitudes facilitates self-deception by enabling us to express socially desirable attitudes, while *acting on* hidden, socially undesirable attitudes such as ethnic prejudice. Through self-deception, we confer plausible deniability on ourselves.[161]

Just as attitudes and memory have separate conscious and unconscious components, so too do our goals and efforts in achieving them. We are capable of maintaining conscious and unconscious goals. Behavior aimed at achieving our goals can take place outside of conscious awareness.[162] For instance, we may have a conscious goal of continuing a romantic relationship because we love another person for who they are; yet we may have an unconscious goal to continue a romantic relationship for sexual or material benefits. When asked why we are in the relationship, we can honestly say, without mental effort, that we love the other person for who they are. Remember the split-brain experiments by Michael Gazzaniga: the "interpreter" in our minds is adept at creating convincing yet false explanations to ourselves, without any awareness that these are essentially lies or half-truths.

Unconscious self-deception can work on several levels: by selectively searching for evidence that supports our conscious goals or desires or by selectively devoting attention to such information; through biased interpretation of evidence or information; misremembering evidence that weighs against our unconsciously desired self-image; rationalizing the motives of a behavior to make it more socially acceptable; or convincing ourselves a lie is true. These powerful mechanisms may explain how the system justification tendency works. Since we unconsciously avoid the psychologically painful realization of the injustice and inequity we face, through these mechanisms of self-deception we convince ourselves that the system is fair and those groups who dominate or exploit our own deserve their status.

12 Styles of Thought

At least since the work of developmental psychologists like Jean Piaget and Lawrence Kohlberg, there has been great interest in the development of moral and other reasoning. By analyzing the moral reasoning of young boys across several countries, Kohlberg and Gilligan proposed six discrete stages of development divided into three major levels: the preconventional, conventional, and postconventional or autonomous.[163] Like Piaget's stages of cognitive development, these developed in sequence, though not everyone within a population achieved the highest level. Intelligence quotient (IQ) test scores do not correlate closely with such development in reasoning sophistication, and perhaps surprisingly, a large percentage of adult Americans were found to have failed to develop to the highest stage of reasoning and displayed serious difficulty with abstract moral thought.

As cognitive and evolutionary psychology developed, Piaget's and Kohlberg's theories of development in reasoning were questioned. Evidence accumulated that our minds are compartmentalized to handle different sorts of thinking, and that development across these modules proceeds unevenly.[164] More recent work, which builds on Piaget and Kohlberg, has proposed three discrete styles of reasoning that can characterize individuals' thought.[165]

The simplest is sequential, which is dominated by immediate circumstances and feelings; its focus is constantly shifting and depends on appearances while evading abstract concepts, categories, and complex causal relations. One could imagine the process of sequential reasoning as consisting of innumerable unconnected line segments, joining perceptions to separate evaluations, without being organized into any complex, overarching relationships. The most common form of reasoning is linear thinking, which is comfortable with abstracting actors and actions from the observed environment and judging them across situational contexts. Linear thinkers tend toward the all-or-nothing in evaluating individuals and groups: if a person is judged positively, then all of his or her attributes are also likely to be judged positively, and likewise for a group or category. When linear thinkers are confronted with new observations that conflict with their categorizations, they explain away or diminish the inconsistencies (as in cognitive dissonance reduction). Linear reasoning could be imagined as a series of connected line segments in two dimensions, but without many interconnections. Linear thinkers might reason "Baptists are good people → Joe is a Baptist → therefore Joe must be a good person"—and if confronted with evidence that Joe often commits morally wrong actions, explain away the evidence or decide that Joe must not be a true Baptist. Systematic reasoning, the most complex form, can be imagined as a complex network diagram in three dimensions, with nodes connected to each other with several separate lines. A systematic thinker in the same example above would be unlikely to consider "Baptists are good people" in the first place—rather, systematic thinkers would conceive of Baptists as a heterogeneous group, a majority of which are good people, but including those who act in morally reprehensible ways. Systematic thinkers most closely approximate the liberal ideal of human reasoning, yet they are unlikely to comprise more than a small fraction of an overall population.

While research has yet to determine whether, or to what extent, sequential, linear, and systematic thinkers are differentially vulnerable to the psychological biases discussed above, the question is ripe for speculation and experimental testing. The three types have been shown to exhibit significant differences in conceptualizing national identity and opinions on immigration.[166] In particular, the worrying results of much media effects research—for instance, the power of framing to influence public opinion—may be a by-product of linear reasoning and could be limited to those who primarily think in a linear fashion.[167] One study examining media effects in light of these styles of thinking found precisely that: linear thinkers are most vulnerable to persuasion by how information is presented in television news.[168]

13   Conclusion

The rational ideal of the human mind promoted by liberal theorists is inaccurate. As Christopher Achen and Larry Bartels conclude:

> *All* the conventional defenses of [liberal] democratic government are at odds with demonstrable, centrally important facts of political life. One has to believe six impossible things before breakfast to take real comfort in any of them. Some of the standard defenses romanticize human nature, some mathematize it, and others bowdlerize it, but they all have one thing in common: They do not portray human beings realistically, nor take honest account of our human limitations.[169]

If we are to reap the benefits of a properly functioning marketplace of ideas, our media systems must be geared to our psychology and not a liberal idealization.

Overall, however, it is hard to argue that the liberal ideal is not *ideal*. If not the actual practice, the liberal democratic *ideal* has spread throughout the world[170]; one force operating within the global information ecology that facilitated it surely was the egalitarian syndrome we evolved along with eusociality. Just because this ideal is a natural fit for a part of our psychology, however, does not mean that it can be implemented. Our evolved biases and heuristics, along with the innate complexity of the human social system, pose a significant challenge to liberal democracy and its ability to produce successful policies.[171] Yet human history is a record of surmounting seemingly impossible challenges, starting with the emergence of eusociality in a species so different from eusocial insects. The younger, optimistic Walter Lippmann had it right:

> Man is no Aristotelian god contemplating all existence at one glance. He is the creature of an evolution who can just about span a sufficient portion of reality to manage his survival, and snatch what on the scale of time are but a few moments of insight and happiness. Yet this same creature has invented ways of seeing what no naked eye could see, of hearing what no ear could hear, of weighing immense masses and infinitesimal ones, of counting and separating more items than he can individually remember. He is learning to see with his mind vast portions of the world that he could never see, touch, smell, hear, or remember. Gradually he makes for himself a trustworthy picture inside his head of the world beyond his reach.[172]

If we are to attempt to achieve the liberal ideal, we must design a functioning marketplace of ideas.

Notes

1. Sheldon S. Wolin, *Politics and Vision: Continuity and Innovation in Western Political Thought* (Princeton: Princeton University Press, 2004): 297–307.
2. "The distinction between the 'natural' and the 'preternatural' could now be resolved by simply absorbing within the first whatever of the second retained its credibility" (Runciman 2009, 214).
3. Mill, *On Liberty*, 39.
4. Abrams v. United States, 250 U.S. 616. (1919): 630.
5. John Durham Peters, "'The Marketplace of Ideas': A History of the Concept," in *Toward a Political Economy of Culture: Capitalism and Communication in the Twenty-First Century*, ed. Andrew Calabrese and Colin Sparks, 65–82 (New York: Rowman and Littlefield, 2004): 71–72.
6. F.A. Hayek, *The Road to Serfdom* (Chicago: University of Chicago Press, 2007).
7. Mill, however, acknowledged impediments that have fallen out of view of today's "marketplace" proponents (Peters 2004, 71).
8. John Rawls, *Political Liberalism* (New York: Columbia University Press, 2005): 30.
9. Ibid., 72.

10. Rosenberg, "Against."
11. George Santayana, *The Life of Reason* (Amherst: Prometheus Books, 1998): 29.
12. For withering criticism, see Frederick C. Crews and his critics, *The Memory Wars: Freud's Legacy in Dispute* (New York: New York Review of Books, 1995).
13. Edward Erwin, *A Final Accounting: Philosophical and Empirical Issues in Freudian Psychology* (Cambridge, MA: The MIT Press, 1996).
14. Friedman, *Power Without Knowledge*, 189.
15. Joseph Henrich et al., "The Weirdest People in the World?" *Behavioral and Brain Sciences* 33, no. 2–3 (2010): 61.
16. Yehuda Amir and Irit Sharon, "Are Social Psychological Laws Cross-Culturally Valid?" *Journal of Cross-Cultural Psychology* 18, no. 4 (1987).
17. Ibid., 82.
18. Michael Cole, *Cultural Psychology: A Once and Future Discipline* (Cambridge, MA: Harvard University Press, 1996).
19. Henrich et al., "The Weirdest," 72.
20. Larry V. Hedges, "How Hard Is Hard Science, How Soft Is Soft Science? The Empirical Cumulativeness of Research," *American Psychologist* 42, no. 5 (1987).
21. Open Science Collaboration, "Estimating the Reproducibility of Psychological Science," *Science* 349, no. 6251 (2015).
22. Jay J. Van Bavel et al., "Contextual Sensitivity in Scientific Reproducibility," *Proceedings of the National Academy of Sciences* (2016).
23. Scott E. Maxwell et al., "Is Psychology Suffering from a Replication Crisis? What Does 'Failure to Replicate' Really Mean?" *American Psychologist* 70, no. 6 (2015).
24. José L. Duarte et al., "Political Diversity Will Improve Social Psychological Science," *Behavioral and Brain Sciences* 38 (2015).
25. Michal Bilewicz et al., "Is Liberal Bias Universal? An International Perspective on Social Psychologists," *Behavioral and Brain Sciences* 38 (2015).
26. Benjamin Beit-Hallahmi, "Method and Matter in the Social Sciences: Umbilically Tied to the Enlightenment," *Behavioral and Brain Sciences* 38 (2015).
27. Albert Pepitone, "Lessons from the History of Social Psychology," *American Psychologist* 36, no. 9 (1981).
28. Daniele Fanelli, "Do Pressures to Publish Increase Scientists' Bias? An Empirical Support from US States Data," *PloS One* 5, no. 4 (2010).
29. Tony Lawson, "Contemporary Economics and the Crisis," *Real-World Economics Review* 50 (2009).

30. Miriam Solomon, *Social Empiricism* (Cambridge, MA: MIT Press, 2001): 53, emphasis added.
31. Dean Keith Simonton, "Psychology as a Science Within Comte's Hypothesized Hierarchy: Empirical Investigations and Conceptual Implications," *Review of General Psychology* 19, no. 3 (2015).
32. For example, Morowitz, *The Emergence*; Edward O. Wilson, *Consilience: The Unity of Knowledge* (New York: Vintage Books, 1999).
33. Hayek 1967, 41–42.
34. For example, Peter Dews, *Logics of Disintegration: Post-structuralist Thought and the Claims of Critical Theory* (London: Verso, 2007); David Couzens Hoy, *Critical Resistance: From Poststructuralism to Postcritique* (Cambridge, MA: MIT Press, 2005).
35. Jonathan Haidt, "The Emotional Dog and Its Rational Tail: A Social Intuitionist Approach to Moral Judgment," *Psychological Review* 108, no. 4 (2001); Haidt, *The Righteous Mind*.
36. Peter H. Ditto and Brittany S. Liu, "Moral Coherence and Political Conflict," in *Social Psychology of Political Polarization*, ed. Piercarlo Valdesolo and Jesse Graham, 102–122 (New York: Routledge, 2016).
37. Thalia Wheatley and Jonathan Haidt, "Hypnotic Disgust Makes Moral Judgments More Severe," *Psychological Science* 16, no. 10 (2005).
38. Brittany S. Liu and Peter H. Ditto, "What Dilemma? Moral Evaluation Shapes Factual Belief," *Social Psychological and Personality Science* 4, no. 3 (2013).
39. Anthony Randazzo and Jonathan Haidt, "The Moral Narratives of Economists," *Econ Journal Watch* 12, no. 1 (2015): 53; see also Mark Horowitz and Robert Hughes, "Political Identity and Economists' Perceptions of Capitalist Crises," *Review of Radical Political Economics* 50, no. 1 (2018): 173–193.
40. Michael S. Gazzaniga, "Forty-Five Years of Split-Brain Research and Still Going Strong," *Nature Reviews Neuroscience* 6, no. 8 (2005).
41. Michael S. Gazzaniga, *Nature's Mind: The Biological Roots of Thinking, Emotions, Sexuality, Language, and Intelligence* (New York: Basic Books, 1992): 122–129.
42. Ibid., 129–137; Michael S. Gazzaniga, *The Mind's Past* (Berkeley, CA: University of California Press, 2000): 1–27.
43. For a discussion of critiques of this approach, see Peter B.M. Vranas, "Gigerenzer's Normative Critique of Kahneman and Tversky," *Cognition* 72 (2000).
44. Daniel Kahneman, "A Perspective on Judgment and Choice: Mapping Bounded Rationality," *American Psychologist* 58, no. 9 (2003).
45. Ibid., 703–705.

46. Miroslav Nincic, "Loss Aversion and the Domestic Context of Military Intervention," *Political Research Quarterly* 50, no. 1 (1997).
47. Daniel Kahneman and Jonathan Renshon, "Why Hawks Win," *Foreign Policy*, no. 158 (January/February 2007): 36.
48. Jonathan St. B.T. Evans and Keith E. Stanovich, "Dual-Process Theories of Higher Cognition: Advancing the Debate," *Perspectives on Psychological Science* 8, no. 3 (2013): 223–241.
49. Kahneman, "A Perspective," 698–699.
50. Martin Hilbert, "Toward a Synthesis of Cognitive Biases: How Noisy Information Processing Can Bias Human Decision Making," *Psychological Bulletin* 138, no. 2 (2012).
51. Richard E. Petty and John T. Cacioppo, "The Elaboration Likelihood Model of Persuasion," in *Advances in Experimental Social Psychology*, Vol. 19, ed. Leonard Berkowitz, 1–24 (New York: Springer, 1986).
52. Richard E. Petty et al., "Conceptual and Methodological Issues in the Elaboration Likelihood Model of Persuasion: A Reply to the Michigan State Critics," *Communication Theory* 3, no. 4 (1993).
53. Richard E. Petty et al., "Thought Confidence as a Determinant of Persuasion: The Self-Validation Hypothesis," *Journal of Personality and Social Psychology* 82, no. 5 (2002).
54. Benjamin S. Catchings, ed., *Master Thoughts of Thomas Jefferson* (New York: The Nation Press, 1907): 31.
55. Dunning, "The Dunning–Kruger Effect"; Justin Kruger and David Dunning, "Unskilled and Unaware of It: How Difficulties in Recognizing One's Own Incompetence Lead to Inflated Self-Assessments," *Journal of Personality and Social Psychology* 77, no. 6 (1999).
56. John T. Jost et al., "A Decade of System Justification Theory: Accumulated Evidence of Conscious and Unconscious Bolstering of the Status Quo," *Political Psychology* 25, no. 6 (2004).
57. Keith E. Stanovich and Richard F. West, "On the Relative Independence of Thinking Biases and Cognitive Ability," *Journal of Personality and Social Psychology* 94, no. 4 (2008).
58. Adam Kessler, "Cognitive Dissonance, the Global Financial Crisis and the Discipline of Economics," *Real-World Economics Review*, no. 54 (2010).
59. Steve A. Yetiv, *National Security Through a Cockeyed Lens: How Cognitive Bias Impacts US Foreign Policy* (Baltimore: JHU Press, 2013).
60. Raymond S. Nickerson, "Confirmation Bias: A Ubiquitous Phenomenon in Many Guises," *Review of General Psychology* 2, no. 2 (1998).
61. Francis Bacon, "Novum Organum," in *The English Philosophers from Bacon to Mill*, ed. Edwin A. Burtt, 24–123 (New York: Random House, 1939): 36.

62. Nickerson, "Confirmation Bias."
63. Ziva Kunda, "The Case for Motivated Reasoning," *Psychological Bulletin* 108, no. 3 (1990): 483.
64. Jonathan J. Koehler, "The Influence of Prior Beliefs on Scientific Judgments of Evidence Quality," *Organizational Behavior and Human Decision Processes* 56, no. 1 (1993). Non-scientists reviewing scientific studies evince the same bias (Kunda 1990, 489–490).
65. Dan M. Kahan, "Ideology, Motivated Reasoning, and Cognitive Reflection: An Experimental Study," *Judgment and Decision Making* 8 (2012); Dan M. Kahan et al., "Motivated Numeracy and Enlightened Self-Government," Yale Law School, Public Law Working Paper 307 (2013).
66. Dan M. Kahan et al., "'Ideology' or 'Situation Sense'? An Experimental Investigation of Motivated Reasoning and Professional Judgment," *University of Pennsylvania Law Review* 164, no. 2 (2016). However, judges have been found susceptible to in-group bias in free speech cases (Epstein et al., 2013), and statistical experts have been found to commit the conjunction fallacy (Tversky and Kahneman 1983, 297–298).
67. Nickerson, "Confirmation Bias," 197.
68. Drew Westen et al., "Neural Bases of Motivated Reasoning: An fMRI Study of Emotional Constraints on Partisan Political Judgment in the 2004 US Presidential Election," *Journal of Cognitive Neuroscience* 18, no. 11 (2006): 1947–1958.
69. Peter H. Ditto, "Passion, Reason, and Necessity: A Quantity-of-Processing View of Motivated Reasoning," in *Delusion and Self-Deception: Affective and Motivational Influences on Belief Formation*, ed. Tim Bayne and Jordi Fernández, 23–54 (New York: Psychology Press, 2008).
70. Friedman, *Power Without Knowledge*, 234.
71. Brian M. Monroe and Stephen J. Read, "A General Connectionist Model of Attitude Structure and Change: The ACS (Attitudes as Constraint Satisfaction) Model," *Psychological Review* 115, no. 3 (2008).
72. Kunda, "The Case," 493.
73. David P. Redlawsk et al., "The Affective Tipping Point: Do Motivated Reasoners Ever 'Get It'?" *Political Psychology* 31, no. 4 (2010).
74. Leon Festinger, *A Theory of Cognitive Dissonance* (Evanston, IL: Row Peterson, 1957).
75. John M. Darley and C. Daniel Batson, "'From Jerusalem to Jericho': A Study of Situational and Dispositional Variables in Helping Behavior," *Journal of Personality and Social Psychology* 27, no. 1 (1973).

76. Karen L. Hobden and James M. Olson, "From Jest to Antipathy: Disparagement Humor as a Source of Dissonance-Motivated Attitude Change," *Basic and Applied Social Psychology* 15, no. 3 (1994).
77. Bertram Gawronski, "Back to the Future of Dissonance Theory: Cognitive Consistency as a Core Motive," *Social Cognition* 30, no. 6 (2012).
78. Gawronski, "Back to the Future," 662–663.
79. Ellen Berscheid et al., "Retaliation as a Means of Restoring Equity," *Journal of Personality and Social Psychology* 10, no. 4 (1968).
80. Ashley A. Murray et al., "Psychopathic Personality Traits and Cognitive Dissonance: Individual Differences in Attitude Change," *Journal of Research in Personality* 46, no. 5 (2012).
81. Travis Proulx and Steven J. Heine, "Death and Black Diamonds: Meaning, Mortality, and the Meaning Maintenance Model," *Psychological Inquiry* 17, no. 4 (2006); Travis Proulx and Michael Inzlicht, "The Five 'A's of Meaning Maintenance: Finding Meaning in the Theories of Sense-Making," *Psychological Inquiry* 23, no. 4 (2012).
82. Mark P. Zanna and Joel Cooper, "Dissonance and the Pill: An Attribution Approach to Studying the Arousal Properties of Dissonance," *Journal of Personality and Social Psychology* 29, no. 5 (1974).
83. Wendy Berry Mendes et al., "Threatened by the Unexpected: Physiological Responses During Social Interactions with Expectancy-Violating Partners," *Journal of Personality and Social Psychology* 92, no. 4 (2007).
84. Jennifer L. Robinson and Heath A. Demaree, "Physiological and Cognitive Effects of Expressive Dissonance," *Brain and Cognition* 63, no. 1 (2007).
85. Sarah S.M. Townsend et al., "Can the Absence of Prejudice Be More Threatening Than Its Presence? It Depends on One's Worldview," *Journal of Personality and Social Psychology* 99, no. 6 (2010).
86. Colin Holbrook, "Branches of a Twisting Tree: Domain-Specific Threat Psychologies Derive from Shared Mechanisms," *Current Opinion in Psychology* 7 (2016).
87. Proulx and Inzlicht, "The Five."
88. Daniel Randles et al., "Turn-Frogs and Careful-Sweaters: Non-conscious Perception of Incongruous Word Pairings Provokes Fluid Compensation," *Journal of Experimental Social Psychology* 47, no. 1 (2011).
89. Jennifer A. Whitson and Adam D. Galinsky, "Lacking Control Increases Illusory Pattern Perception," *Science* 322, no. 5898 (2008).
90. Proulx and Inzlicht, "The Five," 328–329.

91. Abram Rosenblatt et al., "Evidence for Terror Management Theory: I. The Effects of Mortality Salience on Reactions to Those Who Violate or Uphold Cultural Values," *Journal of Personality and Social Psychology* 57, no. 4 (1989): 682–683.
92. Travis Proulx et al., "When Is the Unfamiliar the Uncanny? Meaning Affirmation After Exposure to Absurdist Literature, Humor, and Art," *Personality and Social Psychology Bulletin* (2010).
93. Bill Hicks, "Chicago (1991) [Bootleg]," YouTube Video, 21:10, from an untelevised performance, posted by AMP3183 (November 29, 2014).
94. Henri Tajfel, "Experiments in Intergroup Discrimination," *Scientific American* 223, no. 5 (1970).
95. Charles W. Perdue et al., "Us and Them: Social Categorization and the Process of Intergroup Bias," *Journal of Personality and Social Psychology* 59, no. 3 (1990): 482; John F. Dovidio and Samuel L. Gaertner, "Stereotypes and Evaluative Intergroup Bias," in *Affect, Cognition and Stereotyping: Interactive Processes in Group Perception*, ed. Diane M. Mackie and David L. Hamilton, 167–193 (San Diego: Academic Press, 1993): 176–179.
96. Sylvie Graf et al., "Nouns Cut Slices: Effects of Linguistic Forms on Intergroup Bias," *Journal of Language and Social Psychology* 32, no. 1 (2012).
97. Miles Hewstone et al., "Intergroup Bias," *Annual Review of Psychology* 53, no. 1 (2002).
98. Anca M. Miron et al., "Motivated Shifting of Justice Standards," *Personality and Social Psychology Bulletin* 36, no. 6 (2010).
99. Diane M. Mackie and Eliot R. Smith, "Intergroup Relations: Insights from a Theoretically Integrative Approach," *Psychological Review* 105, no. 3 (1998).
100. Hewstone et al., "Intergroup Bias," 585–587.
101. Luigi Anolli et al., "Linguistic Intergroup Bias in Political Communication," *The Journal of General Psychology* 133, no. 3 (2006).
102. Daniel Geschke et al., "Effects of Linguistic Abstractness in the Mass Media," *Journal of Media Psychology* 22, no. 3 (2010).
103. Hewstone et al., "Intergroup Bias," 585.
104. Mackie and Smith, "Intergroup Relations," 509–510.
105. Ibid., 511; Rui J.P. De Figueiredo and Zachary Elkins, "Are Patriots Bigots? An Inquiry into the Vices of In-Group Pride," *American Journal of Political Science* 47, no. 1 (2003).
106. Hewstone et al., "Intergroup Bias," 585.
107. Dacher Keltner and Robert J. Robinson, "Defending the Status Quo: Power and Bias in Social Conflict," *Personality and Social Psychology Bulletin* 23, no. 10 (1997).

108. Lincoln Quillian, "Prejudice as a Response to Perceived Group Threat: Population Composition and Anti-immigrant and Racial Prejudice in Europe," *American Sociological Review* (1995).
109. Hewstone et al., "Intergroup Bias," 587.
110. Amarina Ariyanto et al., "Intergroup Attribution Bias in the Context of Extreme Intergroup Conflict," *Asian Journal of Social Psychology* 12, no. 4 (2009); Pamela Johnston Conover, "The Role of Social Groups in Political Thinking," *British Journal of Political Science* 18, no. 1 (1988).
111. Patricia Gurin et al., "Stratum Identification and Consciousness," *Social Psychology Quarterly* (1980): 46.
112. Olivier Klein and Mark Snyder, "Stereotypes and Behavioral Confirmation: From Interpersonal to Intergroup Perspectives," *Advances in Experimental Social Psychology* 35 (2003); David M. Messick and Diane M. Mackie, "Intergroup Relations," *Annual Review of Psychology* 40 (1989): 55–57.
113. Eaaron I. Henderson-King and Richard E. Nisbett, "Anti-black Prejudice as a Function of Exposure to the Negative Behavior of a Single Black Person," *Journal of Personality and Social Psychology* 71, no. 4 (1996).
114. Yaacov Trope and Nira Liberman, "Construal-Level Theory of Psychological Distance," *Psychological Review* 117, no. 2 (2010): 448.
115. Klein and Snyder, "Stereotypes," 163–172.
116. Klein and Snyder, "Stereotypes," 218–219.
117. Daniel L. Schacter, "The Seven Sins of Memory: Insights from Psychology and Cognitive Neuroscience," *American Psychologist* 54, no. 3 (1999).
118. Joe Emersberger, "Poll Shows That UK Public Drastically Underestimates Iraqi War Deaths," *Spinwatch* (June 4, 2013).
119. Steven J. Frenda et al., "False Memories of Fabricated Political Events," *Journal of Experimental Social Psychology* 49, no. 2 (2013).
120. Martin F. Davies, "Belief Persistence after Evidential Discrediting: The Impact of Generated Versus Provided Explanations on the Likelihood of Discredited Outcomes," *Journal of Experimental Social Psychology* 33, no. 6 (1997).
121. Craig A. Anderson et al., "Perseverance of Social Theories: The Role of Explanation in the Persistence of Discredited Information," *Journal of Personality and Social Psychology* 39, no. 6 (1980).
122. Davies, "Belief Persistence," 575.
123. Ibid., 574–576.
124. Daniel T. Gilbert, "How Mental Systems Believe," *American Psychologist* 46, no. 2 (1991); Daniel T. Gilbert et al., "Unbelieving the Unbelievable: Some Problems in the Rejection of False Information," *Journal of Personality and Social Psychology* 59, no. 4 (1990).

125. Gilbert et al., "Unbelieving the Unbelievable," 610.
126. Gilbert, "How Mental Systems," 116–117.
127. Gilbert et al., "Unbelieving the Unbelievable," 606–607.
128. Kahneman, "A Perspective," 705.
129. Robert P. Abelson, "Beliefs Are Like Possessions," *Journal for the Theory of Social Behaviour* 16, no. 3 (1986): 231.
130. Ibid., 229.
131. Jost et al., "A Decade"; John T. Jost et al., "'The World Isn't Fair': A System Justification Perspective on Social Stratification and Inequality," in *APA Handbook of Personality and Social Psychology*, Vol. 2, ed. Jeffry A. Simpson and John F. Dovidio, 317–340 (Washington, DC: American Psychological Association, 2015).
132. Hannah H. Nam et al., "Amygdala Structure and the Tendency to Regard the Social System as Legitimate and Desirable," *Nature Human Behaviour* 2, no. 2 (2018).
133. Elizabeth L. Haines and John T. Jost, "Placating the Powerless: Effects of Legitimate and Illegitimate Explanation on Affect, Memory, and Stereotyping," *Social Justice Research* 13, no. 3 (2000).
134. Aaron C. Kay, "Sour Grapes, Sweet Lemons, and the Anticipatory Rationalization of the Status Quo," *Personality and Social Psychology Bulletin* 28, no. 9 (2002).
135. Jost et al., "A Decade," 889.
136. Ibid., 894–906.
137. Tom Pyszczynski et al., "A Dual-Process Model of Defense against Conscious and Unconscious Death-Related Thoughts: An Extension of Terror Management Theory," *Psychological Review* 106, no. 4 (1999).
138. Jost et al., "A Decade," 910.
139. Kristin Laurin et al., "Restricted Emigration, System Inescapability, and Defense of the Status Quo: System-Justifying Consequences of Restricted Exit Opportunities," *Psychological Science* 21, no. 8 (2010).
140. Jojanneke van der Toorn et al., "A Sense of Powerlessness Fosters System Justification: Implications for the Legitimation of Authority, Hierarchy, and Government," *Political Psychology* 36, no. 1 (2015).
141. Steven Shepherd and Aaron C. Kay, "On the Perpetuation of Ignorance: System Dependence, System Justification, and the Motivated Avoidance of Sociopolitical Information," *Journal of Personality and Social Psychology* 102, no. 2 (2012).
142. Ibid., 275–276.
143. Michael Pfau et al., "Attitude Accessibility as an Alternative Explanation for How Inoculation Confers Resistance," *Communication Monographs* 70, no. 1 (2003).

144. Jonathan L. Freedman and David O. Sears, "Warning, Distraction, and Resistance to Influence," *Journal of Personality and Social Psychology* 1, no. 3 (1965).
145. Craig R.M. McKenzie et al., "When Negative Evidence Increases Confidence: Change in Belief after Hearing Two Sides of a Dispute," *Journal of Behavioral Decision Making* 15, no. 1 (2002).
146. Geoffrey D. Munro and Peter H. Ditto, "Biased Assimilation, Attitude Polarization, and Affect in Reactions to Stereotype-Relevant Scientific Information," *Personality and Social Psychology Bulletin* 23, no. 6 (1997).
147. Dennis Chong and James N. Druckman, "Dynamic Public Opinion: Communication Effects Over Time," *American Political Science Review* 104, no. 4 (2010).
148. Stanley Milgram, "Some Conditions of Obedience and Disobedience to Authority," *Human Relations* 18, no. 1 (1965).
149. Ibid., 66.
150. Laurent Bègue et al., "Personality Predicts Obedience in a Milgram Paradigm," *Journal of Personality* 83, no. 3 (2015).
151. Maury Silver and Daniel Geller, "On the Irrelevance of Evil: The Organization and Individual Action," *Journal of Social Issues* 34, no. 4 (1978): 128.
152. Jo-Ann Tsang, "Moral Rationalization and the Integration of Situational Factors and Psychological Processes in Immoral Behavior," *Review of General Psychology* 6, no. 1 (2002).
153. Ervin Staub and Daniel Bar-Tal, "Genocide, Mass Killing and Intractable Conflict: Roots, Evolution, Prevention and Reconciliation," in *The Oxford Handbook of Political Psychology*, ed. David O. Sears et al., 710–743 (Oxford: Oxford University Press, 2003).
154. Yoram Peri, "Intractable Conflict and the Media," *Israel Studies* 12, no. 1 (2007).
155. Robert Trivers, *The Folly of Fools: The Logic of Deceit and Self-Deception in Human Life* (New York: Basic Books, 2011); William Von Hippel and Robert Trivers, "The Evolution and Psychology of Self-Deception," *Behavioral and Brain Sciences* 34, no. 1 (2011).
156. Mark D. Alicke and Constantine Sedikides, "Self-Enhancement and Self-Protection: What They Are and What They Do," *European Review of Social Psychology* 20, no. 1 (2009).
157. Von Hippel and Trivers, "The Evolution," 5.
158. Stanley Cohen, *States of Denial: Knowing About Atrocities and Suffering* (Cambridge: Polity Press, 2001): 38–39.
159. Tatiana Bachkirova, "A New Perspective on Self-Deception for Applied Purposes," *New Ideas in Psychology* 43 (2016): 1–5.

160. Von Hippel and Trivers, "The Evolution," 6–10.
161. Ibid., 5–6.
162. Ibid., 7–9.
163. Lawrence Kohlberg and Carol Gilligan, "The Adolescent as a Philosopher: The Discovery of the Self in a Postconventional World," *Daedalus* (1971).
164. For example, Cosmides and Tooby, "Evolutionary Psychology."
165. Shawn W. Rosenberg, *The Not So Common Sense: Differences in How People Judge Social and Political Life* (New Haven: Yale University Press, 2002).
166. Shawn Rosenberg and Peter Beattie, "The Cognitive Structuring of National Identity: Individual Differences in Identifying as American," *Nations and Nationalism* (2018); Rosenberg et al., "Migration: The Political Psychology of the Host Nation" (unpublished manuscript, May 30, 2016) Microsoft Word file.
167. Rosenberg, *The Not So Common*, 182–183.
168. Joseph J. Braunwarth, "The Cognitive Conceptualization of Television News and the Practice of Politics" (PhD diss., University of California, Irvine, 1999).
169. Christopher H. Achen and Larry M. Bartels, *Democracy for Realists: Why Elections Do Not Produce Responsive Government* (Princeton: Princeton University Press, 2016): 306.
170. Ronald Inglehart, "How Solid Is Mass Support for Democracy—And How Can We Measure It?" *Political Science and Politics* 36, no. 1 (2003).
171. For example, Friedman, *Power Without Knowledge*.
172. Lippmann, *Public Opinion*, 21.

CHAPTER 5

The Transition: Information from Media to Mind

"*Nothing appears more surprising to those, who consider human affairs with a philosophical eye, than the easiness with which the many are governed by the few; and the implicit submission, with which men resign their own sentiments and passions to those of their rulers. When we enquire by what means this wonder is effected, we shall find, that, as FORCE is always on the side of the governed, the governors have nothing to support them but opinion. It is therefore, on opinion only that government is founded; and this maxim extends to the most despotic and most military governments, as well as to the most free and most popular.*"
—David Hume, *Of the First Principles of Government*

In the United States, the media has been called the fourth branch of government. This implies not only coequal status with Congress, the Executive, and Judiciary, but calls attention to the contrast: the media is not part of the government, but exerts power *at least* coequal with the other branches.[1] This is not supposed to be problematic. The media's role is to provide an unbiased source of information about public affairs, sharing facts and partisan arguments. The media's audience—the rational citizen—can make up its mind about political questions, weighing arguments, and assessing information to arrive at voting decisions. In this ideal conception, the media provides a marketplace of ideas to enrich the public sphere: everyone is free to offer and select whatever ideas they want. It is not supposed to shape public opinion so much as to inform it and allow public opinion to shape itself. The ideal media system acts like a stock exchange: not favoring any company over another, merely creating a market and enforcing rules to ensure its smooth functioning.

This ideal conception describes reality only insofar as its starting assumptions hold. Problems—fundamental, worrying problems—begin at the moment these assumptions unravel. They include: that the media provides an unbiased selection of political information; that it does not pick winners or favorites from among political perspectives; that its presentation of information does not make any particular conclusion that could be drawn from it likelier; and that citizens using the media process information as close to the liberal ideal of rationality as possible. The last assumption has been discussed, and the first two will be covered later; we will focus on the third. To what extent does the media influence public opinion, making some conclusions likelier than others?

1 What the Media Does

"It ain't what you don't know that gets you into trouble. It's what you know for sure that just ain't so."
—Attributed to Mark Twain and Josh Billings

Walter Lippmann began his 1922 classic *Public Opinion* with a story about an island in 1914 inhabited by a few English, French, and German citizens.[2] The island was so remote, news of the outside world came only every 60 days, when a British mail steamer delivered newspapers. In September, the residents of this island were anticipating the arrival of the ship. They were eager to learn juicy details about the Prime Minister of France and his wife, accused of murdering a reporter who had threatened to release details of their sex life. Instead, when the ship delivered the mail, the island's residents learned that for the previous six weeks—while the English, French, and German citizens of the island had been enjoying their lives as friends—their countries had begun a vicious and bloody war. For six weeks, in blissful ignorance, the island's Germans had officially been enemies of the island's English and French residents.

Lippmann's story illustrates a fact of life that has not changed: in the main, we learn about the realm of politics from the media. Since information is physical, it has to be delivered, whether by mail steamer, pony express, telegraph, radio, television, the internet, etc. While few of us have personal connections to political leaders, a great many have a picture-in-our-heads about what is going on in the world far outside direct experience.

And while the media may have minor assistants who add flourishes—commentary and interpretation from acquaintances—it is without doubt the mass media that paints our picture of the political world. We may have friends or family who communicate about the situation in their home country or a foreign land they visited, but the majority of communication we receive about the far-flung world comes from the media. A Portuguese term for the media, *meios de communicação*, is illustrative: the mass media is merely another *means of communication*. What separates the media from other means of communication is its use of technologies (newsprint, radio, television, internet) and the institutions that comprise it.[3]

These pictures-in-our-heads Lippmann described are more pencil sketches than paintings. Public opinion is notoriously unstable, and the pictures-in-our-heads of the political world are constantly having bits erased and redrawn by incoming communications from the media.[4] Not only that, but the scope of the political world is so broad that the sketches the media provides can only ever be tiny pieces of the totality. And in selecting what to sketch, the media has the power not only to educate and inform, but also persuade and propagandize.[5]

The distinction between information and propaganda (in its pejorative sense) may seem relative, but distinctions can be drawn. Communication that manipulates a target through prejudice and emotion to adopt the communicator's perspective is *propaganda*; communication that seeks to provide information for critical thinking leading to conclusions that may differ from the communicator's is *education*.[6] The philosopher Jason Stanley defines propaganda as political rhetoric, the attempt to sway others through emotion; as such, it can be beneficial or harmful.[7] More commonly, "propaganda" carries a negative connotation, as in what Stanley calls the classical sense—the "manipulation of the rational will to close off debate"—or propaganda as biased speech, which hides or omits options we should consider.[8]

The stunning success of propaganda—whether the campaign to drum up support for the United States' entry into World War I, or World War II-era fascist propaganda in Germany, Italy, and Japan—spurred a lasting interest in studying how the media affects our minds. While propaganda in some form has existed since sedentary human civilization,[9] it has come into its own only with technologies of mass communication and institutions to utilize them: the media. Jacques Ellul noted that mass-mediated *news* is congenitally weaker at providing education than at providing a ceaseless stream of events divorced from synthesizing, explanatory narratives, making the "current-events man" a ready target for propaganda. Indeed, such a man is highly sensitive to the influence of present-day currents; lacking landmarks, he follows all currents. He is unstable because he runs after what happened today; he related to the event, and therefore cannot resist any impulse coming from the event. Because he is immersed in current affairs, this man has a psychological weakness that puts him at the mercy of the propagandist.[10]

Ellul broadened his focus beyond the news media proper to include what he called "sociological propaganda": advertising, movies, magazines, education, and other social technologies and institutions that spread ideas.[11] In sociological propaganda, the direction of an intentional propagandist is unnecessary. Yet its effects are so similar to political propaganda as to make the rough equivalence apparent. Though subtler, sociological propaganda can shape attitudes and behavior, generate support and legitimacy for institutions, or cement gender roles. Examples of sociological propaganda are easy to recall: role models for proper male behavior on television, ideal body types for women in advertisements, public relations campaigns on behalf of corporations, and an educational system that explains the system of social organization as basically just.

An example of combined sociological and political propaganda is the campaign in 1936 by the National Association of Manufacturers (NAM) to engineer public consent to a particular view of the capitalist economic system in the United States.[12] NAM sought to soften negative views of capitalism inspired by the Great Depression and undermine positive views of government intervention in the economy inspired by the New Deal. Its campaign of sociological and political propaganda (comprising newspaper advertising, press releases, targeted publication, and speeches to civic organizations) was stunningly successful in turning US opinion against the Office of Price Administration (OPA). Before NAM's targeted campaign against the OPA and price controls in 1946, 85% of the country believed it vital. After the campaign, during that same year, only 26% thought so.

The power of the mass media looms larger the longer a society's experience with democratic, liberal, and parliamentary institutions. While more authoritarian societies use the media as a blunt cudgel, in countries with longer democratic traditions the media needs to be wielded more dexterously to guide public opinion in directions favored by the powerful. The United States, with its long history of democratic government, has arguably the most sophisticated political and sociological propaganda in the world.[13] If public opinion is shaped and guided by an elite, U.S. democracy is merely oligarchy with an extra step: oligarchs having to plug their preferred opinions into the masses. Or worse; as Robert Dahl observed, "[i]f one assumes that political preferences are simply plugged into the system by leaders (business or other) in order to extract what they want from the system, then the model of plebiscitary democracy is substantially equivalent to the model of totalitarian rule."[14]

This threatening prospect has provoked many to deny the ability of the media to "plug in" ideas and preferences. Frank Biocca explained that "[s]ince much of the underpinnings of our social system lie anchored in Enlightenment notions of reason ... it is no wonder that potential threats to this philosophy, and the claims to self-determination that it upholds, have been met with desperate resistance."[15] Brooke Gladstone and Josh Neufeld's book of graphic non-fiction is exemplary of this defensive reaction.[16] Gladstone argues that the view in which the media powerfully influences public opinion is just the latest in a history of paranoid beliefs about a magical "influencing machine" capable of brainwashing people. In her view, the media is no more than a reflection of ourselves: a market-driven institution seeking to attract consumers by offering to reinforce their previously held, endogenously formed beliefs. Yet, even if we select media congenial to our beliefs, and the media attempts to attract us by offering viewpoints in accord with our own, does that mean that the media does not influence us? "[I]f in the shopping isles of media fare our active citizen chooses his or her banalities in pink, blue or red boxes, should we pronounce them free, active, and 'impervious to influence?'"[17]

Similar views were put forward in reaction to what was later described as the "magic bullet" or "hypodermic needle" theory of media effects: the idea that the media could, without difficulty, insert information and opinions into the public mind. This arose from the terrifying success of WWII propaganda, but it ran into initial disconfirmation when propaganda films made for US soldiers did not work as expected.[18] Subsequently, efforts to use psychoanalytic insights as "magic bullets" for use in advertising and CIA programs also resulted in failure.[19] Studies pioneered by Paul Lazarsfeld and others at Columbia University instituted the "minimal effects" paradigm in the 1940s and '50s, which was believed to have replaced the "magic bullet" theory with the idea that the media does little more than reinforce views.

Nonetheless, so-called "minimal effects" research did not support the hypothesis that the media has *no* effects. Rather, it focused on factors that mediate, channel, or limit media effects (which are implicitly assumed to be present). One example is the concept of opinion leaders: highly politically interested individuals who spread information within their social networks. While opinion leaders are sometimes assumed to lessen the power of the media—after all, instead of getting all of our political information from the media, many of us get such information from opinion-leading friends and family—they amplify it by spreading messages to those who do not receive them from the media.[20] Having conversations about information presented by the news media not only helps spread the information, but has been found to be as effective in promoting news comprehension as media exposure.[21] Hence, not only pure information or disembodied "facts" are spread through conversations about the news, but also the interpretation of those facts as originally presented.

The minimal effects paradigm introduced qualifications to any view of the media as an all-powerful influencing machine. Experiments in this tradition revealed that mere exposure could predict little by way of outcomes. Exposure is surely a *sine qua non*, but in addition, a series of variable conditions affect the outcome a given media message will have. These conditions include differences in message structure, medium, form, and content; plus differences between individuals receiving the message, the social context in which it is received, and individual selectivity in choosing and interpreting it.[22]

Another important observation is that media effects may *seem* minimal, but only because media messages are heterogeneous, and can cancel each other out. Also, strong opinions are less susceptible to media influence.[23] From this, we may be misled into thinking the media is capable of only minimal effects. As John Zaller argues, the minimal effects "consensus sees the media as relatively incapable of pushing citizens around, as if people are either too savvy, or too insulated from mass communication, to let that happen. I see the media as extremely capable of pushing citizens around, and [their effects] are hard to see only because the media often push in opposite directions."[24] Confirming Zaller's hypothesis, a study of viewers who primarily watched partisan channels (Fox and MSNBC)—rather than more balanced media sources that "push in opposite directions"—during the 2008 US presidential election found significant media effects on their attitudes toward the opposition candidate.[25] A study of exposure to partisan channels' coverage of the 2004 US Democratic and Republican Party conventions found similar effects.[26] Even more noticeable effects on opinions and attitudes were found by focusing on *opinion* shows on partisan channels.[27] Watching partisan opinion shows produces *direct* persuasion effects—even for liberals watching conservative shows and conservatives watching liberal shows.[28] Listening to partisan talk radio also produces persuasion effects; as an audience increases exposure to messages in partisan talk radio programs, their agreement with the positions advocated in the programs increases.[29]

Research on media effects rarely if ever seeks to predict whether any particular individual is likely to be influenced by a media source. The media effects uncovered are population-level, that is, changes in averages. This research is more akin to cancer epidemiology than chemistry. Instead of generating near-certainties, they generate population-level predictions.

Recent experimental research on the partisan media in the United States helps flesh out what effects this programming has and on whom.[30] In a series of experimental studies, watching partisan opinion shows produced direct effects on political attitudes—but only for those forced to watch them. For experimental participants given the choice between opinion shows and entertainment programming—an experimental condition more closely mimicking reality—only those with high interest in politics chose to watch opinion shows, and they did not significantly *change* their views, but reinforced them. These experiments confirm the truism that "the direct effects of partisan news talk shows are limited to the people who actually tune into them."[31] That is, an audience of only a few million in a country of over 300 million. However, another series of experiments elaborates these results. While partisan television reaches only a small audience comprising that minority of the US population with a good deal of political knowledge and relatively extreme partisan beliefs, when this audience is exposed to partisan programming, it makes their beliefs *more* extreme, certain and partisan. On issues for which viewers already have firm opinions, partisan news reinforces such opinions—but for emerging issues, partisan media is polarizing.[32] Furthermore, the partisan media influences the mainstream media agenda, which reaches more people, and helps polarize political elites, frustrating compromise.[33]

The minimal effects tradition has little to say on these and related questions, as it focused primarily on whether the broadcast media had short-term, persuasive effects during election campaigns.[34] Furthermore, the minimal effects paradigm emerged from research in the 1940s and '50s, when the USA enjoyed a stronger civil society with higher overall social cohesion, was far less of a "mass-mediated" society, and broadcast television had not been challenged by a proliferation of cable and satellite channels.[35]

Related to how media messages counteract one another is the problem of "imaginability," part of the availability heuristic. Imaginability is a tendency to base judgments and choices on what alternatives we can imagine.[36] If we lack knowledge of, or the ability to imagine, an alternative, our choices will be biased in the direction of what we *do* know or imagine. Robert Entman argues that this means the media's power is not only in presenting persuasive messages, but in omitting others: "[w]hile mass audiences can ignore any conclusion that bothers them and stick to their existing beliefs, it is harder for them to come up with an interpretation on their own, one for which the media do not make relevant information readily available."[37] Furthermore, rationalizations for economic and political policies are more persuasive when they are not accompanied by any analyses that refute them.[38] This power of omission is all too apparent in the age of television-dominated media systems:

> Not just the mere organization of a new party is becoming increasingly difficult – so is expression of a new political idea or doctrine. Ideas no longer exist except through the media of information. When the latter are in the hands of the existing parties, no truly revolutionary or new doctrine has any chance of expressing itself, *i.e.*, of existing. Yet innovation was one of the principal characteristics of democracy.[39]

2   Other Media Effects

Advertising had a humble role in the nineteenth century, providing simple price and product information to consumers (in the way that neoclassical economics still assumes obtains). But by the early twentieth century, advertising more resembled propaganda and its effectiveness became widely acknowledged; total advertising spending ballooned to 2% of GDP by 1920. From then, total annual advertising expenditure has averaged 2.2% of GDP, with current annual spending hovering around $300 billion,[40] which is quite a price tag for a "minimal" effect.

A recent meta-analysis of studies of advertising on children and adolescents reveals that exposure to advertising results in more positive associations with the advertised brands, increased brand comprehension, and selection of the advertised products.[41] The effects were small, but this is what would be expected in a market saturated with advertising. (Also, 70% of consumers report skepticism about advertising, further reducing its effect.) A review of research on advertising to adults found mixed results, with similarly small effects.[42] These results might lead to questions about the viability of the $300-billion-a-year advertising industry, but such doubts are answered in the same way as doubts about the effects of media in the political realm: commercial messages, like political messages, often cancel each other out. But try to sell a new product without advertising—or a new political idea without media exposure—and media power is clear.

Media violence and its link with aggression is another area of inquiry demonstrating more-than-minimal effects. In one provocative study, homicide rates were found to rise significantly on the third and fourth days after the nationally televised broadcast of heavyweight championship boxing matches.[43] Homicides increased along with publicity for the fight; chillingly, even the race of the fight's loser correlated with the race of murder victims. A meta-analysis of studies on media violence and aggression found a small effect size that was nonetheless larger than that of the effects of condoms on HIV transmission, lead exposure on children's intelligence, and calcium intake on bone mass.[44] (A meta-meta-analysis found similar results.)[45] As a predictor of aggression, exposure to media violence was of a comparable magnitude to factors such as alcohol use, corporal punishment on children, and the median sex difference between males and females.

Watching television news about traumatic events can cause effects similar to those from experiencing the traumatic events in person. Exposure to media coverage of the Iraq War and 9/11 attacks was found to predict symptoms of posttraumatic stress; in other words, the physical and psychological effects associated with *direct* exposure to trauma can also be caused by exposure to media coverage of traumatic events.[46] A study of exposure to media coverage of the Boston Marathon bombings found that watching six or more hours daily one week after the event was associated with *higher* acute stress symptoms than having direct exposure to the bombings.[47]

The media has also been found to have significant effects in promoting positive, pro-social behavior. Meta-analyses have found significant effects of watching pro-social television content on children's behavior and attitudes,[48] and of media health campaigns on health-related behavior.[49] In post-genocide Rwanda, a radio drama promoting inter-ethnic reconciliation was found to change perceptions of social norms, including more positive views of intergroup marriage, trust between ethnic groups, and open dissent on sensitive topics.[50] In Senegal, a local media campaign against female genital cutting reduced the practice.[51] One meta-analysis even found that media coverage of Magic Johnson's 1991 announcement of his HIV-positive status had positive effects: increasing knowledge of HIV/AIDS, improving attitudes toward the HIV-positive, encouraging safer behaviors, and getting people tested.[52] Although many pro-social media campaigns have failed to achieve the effects they were (poorly) designed for, media campaigns to reduce crime, stop smoking, and convince drinkers to use a designated driver have been successful.[53]

While the media does not act as a "hypodermic needle" painlessly injecting ideas and behaviors into the public, the hypothesis that the media has "minimal" effects is unsupportable. As the editors of a collection of meta-analyses of media effects concluded: "the argument that the impact of media on various social issues is miniscule is without foundation. The meta-analytic results indicate that the various forms of media demonstrate a consistent pattern of effect across a variety of domains…"[54] While the belief that the media exerts minimal effects is comforting to our democratic ideals, the accumulated evidence no longer allows the theory any claim on viability.[55]

3   Broad Effects: Cultivation Theory

"You're beginning to believe the illusions we're spinning here, you're beginning to believe that the tube is reality and your own lives are unreal! You do! Why, whatever the tube tells you: you dress like the tube, you eat like the tube, you raise your children like the tube, you even think like the tube! This is mass madness, you maniacs! … Television is not the truth! Television is a goddamned amusement park!"
—"Howard Beale" in *Network*, by Paddy Chayefsky

Long before there were so many nails in the coffin of the "minimal effects" paradigm, many researchers found it unsatisfying. One of the first alternatives was cultivation theory, which proposes that the media has powerful effects on society, but they are exerted over the long term.[56] Cultivation theory proposes that the media affects political ideas not merely through journalism, but television programs, movies, books—in other words, stories. Even though cultivation theory proposes a long-term, indirect form of media influence—propaganda without propagandists, exerting a constant gravitational pull—it is nonetheless powerful.[57] As the Scottish patriot Andrew Fletcher wrote, "If a man were permitted to make all the ballads, he need not care who should make the laws of a nation."[58]

Reminiscent of Walter Lippmann's anecdote about the Europeans living on a distant island, cultivation theory starts with a thought experiment:

> Imagine a person living all alone on a tiny deserted isle ... with no contact with anyone or anything in the outside world besides what he or she sees on television. Everything this hypothetical hermit knows about 'reality' is derived from the television world – a world that differs sharply from the 'real' world in terms of demography, violence, occupations and so on, and a world in which motivations, outcomes, and many normally invisible forces of life and society are made clear. How would our recluse see the world? To what extent do heavy viewers see the world that way?[59]

This thought experiment prefigures the results of cultivation research: heavy viewers of television have beliefs about the world that match the world portrayed on television. A meta-analysis of cultivation studies reveals a small but significant effect of television exposure on opinions ranging from the prevalence of crime to sex and racial stereotypes.[60] The average "cultivation differential"—or the difference between how heavy and light television viewers perceive an aspect of the world—was nearly 10%. That is significant, especially considering that the two groups do not live in hermetically sealed domes; light viewers interact daily with heavy viewers, sharing ideas and influence.

This result makes sense from the perspective of narrative research, which reveals that the human mind does not have a "toggle switch" to interpret fiction and non-fiction narratives differently.[61] If, as some psychologists believe, our minds have evolved to think in narrative form, the many fictional stories we see on television will likely (and unconsciously) affect our worldviews.[62] Experiments measuring reaction time to questions about the prevalence of crime show that heavy viewers respond faster—indicating that memories of fictional crimes on TV were highly accessible in memory and were used to make judgments about the world.[63] This was found for heavy viewers of soap operas: they were able to more quickly access instances of (dramatized) crime in memory, leading them to estimate an unrealistically high prevalence of crime.[64]

As a result, heavy viewers are likelier to believe people cannot be trusted and that everyone is primarily looking out for themselves.[65] The likelier one is to confuse fact with fiction, the more one is prone to view the world as portrayed on television: mean and violent.[66] An alternative hypothesis is that people who view the world as mean and violent choose to watch more television; however, this explanation has been tested and rejected through experiments.[67]

Heavy viewers exhibit many more interesting differences from light viewers. Exposure to television is positively correlated with the development of materialistic values in children[68] and adults[69]—particularly for adults with a high need for cognition, who pay close attention to what they view. (Materialism, incidentally, has been shown to lead to unhappiness in countries around the world.)[70] Watching wealth-celebrating reality TV shows like *The Apprentice* has been linked to the development of materialistic attitudes and opposition to welfare programs.[71] Exposure to gender stereotyping on television increases sex-stereotypical behavior and attitudes[72]; young girls who watch a lot of television tend to have more sexist attitudes when they are older.[73] Albert Bandura expands this list, arguing that "many of the shared misconceptions about occupational pursuits, ethnic groups, minorities, the elderly, social and sex roles, and other aspects of life are at least partly cultivated through symbolic modeling of stereotypes" on television.[74] Such stereotypes can have direct political effects, like when television portrayals of successful ethnic minority characters lead to the conclusion that racism is no longer a problem and that poor members of ethnic minorities are responsible for their circumstances.[75]

Cultivation research has revealed a fascinating phenomenon about television's effect on key political opinions and beliefs. Called "mainstreaming," it refers to how heavy viewers of television tend to hold homogenized political views. Compared to light viewers, heavy viewers in higher and lower income brackets are likelier to consider themselves middle class and moderate in their politics.[76] On issues such as communism, busing, interracial relations, rights for women and sexual minorities, among others, heavy viewing generates a mainstreaming effect, pushing people closer to conservatism. Heavy television viewing even reduces regional differences in ideology in the USA, with heavy viewers' outlooks converging on the conservative views of the South.[77] The mainstreaming effects of television are pervasive: "With political self-designation used as a control, one pattern emerged over and over: the attitudes of self-styled 'moderates' and 'conservatives' were barely distinguishable from each other, and from the 'liberals' who were heavy viewers. The only group 'out' of the mainstream was the light-viewing liberals."[78] The mainstreaming phenomenon draws outliers toward the mass media-defined cultural and political center and is more noticeable in groups further from the mainstream. This mainstream is mostly conservative, although mainstreaming can operate in a leftward direction for groups far to the right of center.[79]

The effects of cultivation can be uncovered in many ways, including outside of the cultivation research paradigm. In a series of experiments, participants were presented with a subliminal flash of the U.S. flag or a control image, prior to filling in word fragments with letters.[80] In the first study, the word fragments could be filled into form words related or unrelated to power. Those subliminally presented with the U.S. flag created more power-related words, *but only for those who followed U.S. political news* (and regardless of political ideology). A second experiment presented participants with the same subliminal stimulus, but asked them to rate the desirability of high-power and low-power roles. Those subliminally presented with the U.S. flag rated powerful roles as more desirable, but again, only if they followed U.S. political news. A third experiment found the same pattern for materialistic attitudes (subliminal exposure to the flag and U.S. political news exposure was linked to higher materialism), as did a fourth using word fragments that could be filled into create aggression-related words. In a fifth experiment, exposure to U.S. political news and the subliminal flag prime made participants likelier to interpret ambiguous behavior as aggressive. Lastly, in a sixth experiment, subjects were asked to look at a computer screen and answer whether the number of dots appearing was odd or even. After 80 trials, an error message was displayed, and the participants were informed that all data had been lost and they would have to start over. Although participants were consciously unaware of changes in mood, independent judges rated the reactions of those with high exposure to U.S. political news and exposure to the subliminal presentation of the flag as more hostile than the other participants.

The conclusions of cultivation research dovetail nicely with the conclusions of Brazilian media researcher Venício de Lima, who warns of

> the long-term power of the media to construct reality by means of its representations of different aspects of human life. The majority of contemporary societies can be considered media-centered, which is to say, they are societies that depend on the media – more than the family, school, churches, unions, political parties, etc. – for constructing the public understanding that conditions the possibilities for everyday decisions by each of society's members.[81]

De Lima draws on Antonio Gramsci's concept of hegemony to elaborate his "Setting of Political Representation" (*Cenário de Representação da Política*, CR-P). He defines the CR-P as "the specific space of political representations in contemporary 'representative democracies', constituted and constitutor, location and object of the articulation of total hegemony, constructed by long-term processes, in and by the media, overwhelmingly in and by television."[82] Television exerts this power by creating a virtual proximity to events and experiences that viscerally *feels* real, weakening the power of the written or spoken word through the power of the image (turning *homo sapiens* into *homo ocular*), blurring the distinction between fiction and reality, and exercising disproportionate control over the construction of culture. Although audiences retain the power to freely interpret media messages, the power of the media to design messages for particular interpretations is far greater. Media representations come to constitute reality.

Many of de Lima's observations on the media in Brazil apply to all contemporary media-centered societies: (1) the media occupies a central position in society, permeating human activity, in particular the political sphere; (2) there is no such thing as a "national politics" without the media; (3) the media have taken over many of the social roles traditionally played by political parties, from channeling public demands to constructing the public agenda; (4) the media has radically altered electoral campaigns; and (5) the media has transformed into an important political actor. Nonetheless, de Lima notes, "it is a common error to believe in the eternal omnipotence of the media."[83] The power of the media is considerable and pervasive, but it is not an all-powerful "influencing machine." As the example of Brazil's Lula demonstrates, even politicians despised by the media can win elections; civic organizations and the new electronic media can create a counter-hegemonic bloc.[84]

If the "representations" of the media are constitutors of reality (besides being constituted by it), the test of the power/effects of the media will have to be made on individuals' cognitive maps, which is to say, the manner by which people perceive and organize their immediate environment, their understanding of the world, and their orientation on certain topics; in other words, the test will have to be on the manner in which individuals construct their reality.[85]

4 Informing the Mind: The Micro Level

To draw our cognitive maps, we need ink; to construct reality, we need material; and to organize our political environment, we need something to organize. In politics, this something is the information provided by the media. A 1934 experiment demonstrated this simply: college students were given two versions of the same college newspaper, one with a positive and the other with a negative editorial about a foreign politician few were likely to have any information about.[86] When asked their opinions about the foreign politician, 98% of those who had read the favorable editorial thought positively about him, and 86% of those who read the unfavorable editorial thought negatively about him. This experiment illustrates a truism: if the media is our only source of information about something, the media will powerfully influence our opinions of that something.

Even as children, when we are developing political orientations, the news media is an influential source of political information; children exposed to more news media have more awareness of politics and political issues.[87] The direction of causality is clear: those with more political knowledge do not simply discuss politics more often and consume more news media; instead, those who discuss politics more often and consume more news media thereby gain more political knowledge.[88] No matter our values, to translate them into political positions—support for a policy or candidate—we need contextual information from the media for the translation.[89]

Media dependency theory points out that the size and scope of media effects depend on our needs for information and how we use the media to satisfy them.[90] For those who avoid politics, the news media is unlikely to exert any noticeable effects. For those interested in politics, or feel it is a democratic citizen's duty to be informed about politics, media effects are significant.[91] While we may attempt to evade the fact of our deep reliance on the media, Kathleen Taylor reminds us that "[u]ncritical reliance on media sources is a necessity. We simply do not have the resources to check every statement for ourselves, and so we either trust or, if trust is challenged, react with a blanket cynicism which is often no more than skin deep (in practice, disbelieving *everything* would simply incapacitate us)."[92]

To explain how information is organized on a micro level, media researchers have turned to the schema concept in psychology.[93] The emotional response attached to a schema can affect future information searches: if we read news that provokes anxiety, for instance, we are likelier to search for additional information on it to quell the anxiety.[94] Information from the media is organized into schemas and individual schemas (like the amount of national debt) are themselves organized into larger structures (like a narrative explaining how government spending is believed to affect the economy); and these structures of organized information affect how we comprehend new information.[95] Political experts, with many highly organized schemas, can store information in larger chunks. As new information is absorbed, they are better able to incorporate it into existing schemas, helping them to better remember it.[96] For instance, one experiment demonstrated that learning about political candidates' scandals did not *displace* policy-related information; rather, the scandal information was assimilated into overall schemas about the candidate, *strengthening* overall memory about the candidate.[97] This helps explain the knowledge-gap phenomena, whereby the knowledge-rich get richer and the knowledge-poor stay poor: well-developed schemas are better able to accommodate information, until they reach a saturation point where there is little to add.[98]

Influential media frames may produce their effects by activating widely shared and developed schemas.[99] Doris Graber explains that "[s]ince schemas become guides to information selection, the dimensions that they exclude are apt to be ignored in subsequent information processing. Hence, the odds favor schema maintenance over schema growth or creation of new schemas."[100] It is easier to modify incoming information to make it fit previously held ideas and beliefs, rather than to modify our previously held ideas and beliefs to fit incoming information. Experimental results show that, for instance, stories about economic *failures* in poor countries were processed more readily than stories about economic *successes*.[101] For a person with strong schemas connecting fraud with the poor rather than the rich, a news story about Medicaid fraud by *providers* is easily misremembered as about Medicaid fraud by *recipients*.[102]

Schemas based on personal experience or from trusted sources are particularly difficult to change. Likewise, schemas highly interrelated with other schemas are resistant to change, as a change in one would require a change in related schemas. Also, the less education one has, and the closer a given schema is related to our self-esteem (e.g., a belief that our nation is intrinsically good), the harder it is to modify or replace.[103] "Society, therefore, may depend for timely changes on people who take idiosyncratic views of reality and who are willing to form and propound schemas that diverge widely from cultural norms"[104]—assuming that such nonconformists can get their views into the media.

Even basic evolutionary psychological features of our minds can affect schema change. Our aversive ("tiger – run!") and appetitive ("ripe figs – mmm!") systems can influence our reception of information.[105] When media messages do not arouse our aversive system (they do not warn us of dangers), we tend to pay more attention to positive information than negative—we are led by our appetitive system to focus on good news. Nonetheless, when messages weakly arouse our aversive system, we tend to pay more attention to negative information. The problem is that when bad news strongly arouses our aversive system—when we are informed of a dangerous development—we kick into "flight" mode, which reduces our ability to process the bad news. Meanwhile, our appetitive system remains in operation, looking for silver linings. As our minds are impeded from accepting important information about serious problems, they are spurred into searching for an "out," good news to allay our concerns. News about the threats posed by global warming, for instance, may be subject to this maladaptive psychological tendency.

Another factor influencing the likelihood of fundamental change at the level of schemas is personality. Personality variables including need for cognition, self-monitoring, and dogmatism also powerfully influence whether information is accepted or rejected.[106] Those with a high need for cognition are likelier to entertain new information; high self-monitors are more susceptible to social pressure and to accepting popular versus unpopular ideas; and dogmatic personalities are unlikely to change their minds despite disconfirming evidence. Other differences exist at the gender level: sociopolitical attitudes of men tend to be more "hierarchy-enhancing," while those of women "hierarchy-attenuating." Studies of mean differences between the sexes show that males tend to be more militaristic, ethnocentric, xenophobic, anti-egalitarian, punitive, and in favor of the predatory exploitation of out-groups.[107]

5 THE BIGGER PICTURE: HOW DOES THE MEDIA CHANGE MINDS?

Knowing that the media provides the only path to political information for most people is one thing, but whether people take that path is another story. As Bandura put it, "[a]lthough structural interconnectedness provides potential diffusion paths, psycho-social factors largely determine the fate of what diffuses through those paths."[108] What are the psycho-social factors that determine the fate of the information flowing from the media? One would be bedrock ideas, or basic beliefs, shared by nearly all members of a given society:

> Such beliefs have the quality of political religion, learned early in childhood and never questioned. New information is processed so that it accords with these beliefs and contrary evidence is not generally permitted to undermine their strengths. Because these beliefs are so widely shared and constantly reinforced, they "may account for the mysterious processes in which large numbers of individuals seem to think and act in similar ways."[109]

Similar to basic beliefs, strongly held opinions are notoriously difficult to change and can only be argued around rather than against.[110] Such opinions are usually susceptible to change when a persuasive message presents a position close to the original opinion; only when our opinions are moderate and not strongly held do persuasive but considerably divergent messages show any strong success.[111]

Many strongly held opinions may be transmitted from parents to children, a common and durable means of information transmission.[112] And while the opinions of others in our social network beyond our families exert influence on our opinions, when we perceive an issue to be *moral*, our resistance to persuasion is heightened.[113] Importantly, media coverage can affect whether we think about an issue in moral terms.[114]

In the presence of basic beliefs and strongly held opinions, potentially conflicting information can only be accepted by one of a few maneuvers. We can deny the inconsistency; bolster one of the inconsistent ideas to make it consistent with our opinion; differentiate inconsistent ideas by splitting one into consistent and inconsistent parts; or transcend the conflict by embedding the inconsistent ideas within a larger explanatory structure that accommodates and resolves the conflict.[115] Development over the life cycle may also cause variation in openness to ideas, with the young, old, and migrants to a location with a different attitudinal environment likelier to adopt new ideas.[116]

The most well-developed theory of persuasion describing the psycho-social factors determining acceptance of media messages is the elaboration likelihood model of persuasion (ELM). As mentioned previously, the ELM proposes that there are two routes to persuasion: the central and peripheral routes.[117] Persuasion that occurs through the central route is incorporated into one's schematic structures, stable over time, and resistant to change; persuasion through the peripheral route is less stable and more likely to be changed by future arguments. As the personal relevance of a message increases, so too does the likelihood of using central route processes to evaluate it. Greater personal relevance, hence careful, central-route processing, can be activated when speakers evoke values shared by an audience.[118] When personally relevant messages are processed centrally, only strong arguments result in persuasion; but when messages of low personal relevance are processed peripherally, even weak arguments can result in persuasion. Need for cognition, a personality variable, and knowledge on the topic of the incoming message are other factors that increase the likelihood that we will use the central route.[119] Distraction is another key determinant: if we are distracted during a message, this reduces the amount of elaboration we can apply, making peripheral processing more likely. The graphics-heavy and soundbite-focused nature of much television news broadcasting suggests that peripheral route processing is applied to much of the information it transmits.[120] Richard Perloff explains that when people are processing information peripherally,

> they are susceptible to slick persuaders—and can be thus characterized by the saying attributed to P. T. Barnum: "There's a sucker born every minute!" In other circumstances (when processing centrally), individuals are akin to Plato's ideal students—seeking truth and dutifully considering logical arguments—or to Aristotelian thinkers, persuaded only by cogent arguments (logos). The model says people are neither suckers nor deep thinkers. Complex creatures that we are, we are both peripheral and central, heuristic and systematic, processors.[121]

The danger is that political messages from the media may be processed peripherally, making us accept arguments that we never would have had we processed them via the central route—thereby making us, for a moment at least, one of Barnum's suckers. The peripheral route is low-hanging fruit for persuaders, propagandists, advertisers, and other flim-flam men; it makes us vulnerable to craftily packaged messages preying on our distracted, busy minds. This is particularly worrisome for politics; and there is evidence, for instance, that candidate evaluations are often based on peripheral processing, using ideological cues that are largely symbolic rather than issue-oriented.[122]

Another factor increasing the likelihood of elaboration, hence central-route processing, is a perceived intent to persuade on the part of a communicator. Since a norm of journalism is attempted objectivity, this is one factor lessening the likelihood of elaboration, making peripheral route processing more likely. Attractive news anchors and seemingly expert guests on television news are other factors pushing toward peripheral route processing. Plus, decreasing levels of interest in politics means less motivation to learn, decreasing the likelihood of elaboration, and again making peripheral processing more likely—a proposition for which there is evidence.[123] Finally, as news broadcasts face stiff competition from entertainment programming and the internet, media companies have attempted to make the news more entertaining to increase viewership; and the evidence strongly suggests that more dramatic presentations actually do a poorer job of informing the audience.[124] The peripheral route has its perils.

6 Models of Media Influence: Priming

A common refrain about the results of media effects research is that while the media may not be good at telling people *what to think*, it is successful at telling them *what to think about*. A review of priming, agenda setting, and framing research demonstrates how thin this distinction is.

Priming is the ability of the media to call attention to some matters while ignoring others, thereby influencing the standards by which political matters and actors are judged.[125] Priming in this context differs from priming in the sense used by cognitive and social psychologists; in the latter sense, priming is a reminder that temporarily increases the accessibility of a concept in memory and dissipates quickly. In the media context, priming is a phenomenon that lasts longer (up to several weeks) by increasing *chronic* accessibility of concepts—much like in cultivation theory. A meta-analysis of 48 priming experiments and surveys involving 21,087 participants found a small but significant effect of media primes (with a larger effect for experimental than survey research).[126]

Media priming occurs when news stories focus on an issue and tie it to another issue or politician, leading viewers or readers to judge the politician or second issue on the basis of the primed issue. For instance, television news coverage of a president's handling of foreign affairs will prime viewers to judge the president's overall performance on the basis of foreign affairs. Priming is unlikely to determine the *only* issue or issues to be used in making such determinations, but it will introduce covered issues into the mix. Iyengar and Kinder's experiments revealed two sides to priming effects: they lead television viewers to be more certain about a politician's performance on an issue, and to attach greater importance to that performance in evaluating the politician overall.[127] Unlike other media effects, priming effects are pervasive among political junkies and the apathetic alike.[128] Its power lies not in directly manipulating beliefs, but manipulating the bases of political judgments, leading to changes in beliefs on the issues or politicians being judged.[129] (However, when we lack strong beliefs or much knowledge about an issue, media messages have little to prime—and may exert direct influence on opinions.)[130]

Priming is the key component of what is called "attribute agenda setting." Like priming, attribute agenda setting influences how and what people think about topics by focusing on some attributes while ignoring others. By priming or focusing attention on negative or positive aspects of a policy or politician, the media can powerfully influence people to reject or support that policy or politician. This effect has been found in operation in countries as diverse as the USA, Spain, and South Korea.[131] Priming in the "attribute agenda setting" context can be especially pernicious, narrowing the range of solutions to political problems, making *the* solution seem to be only that which has been offered in the media.[132]

7 Models of Media Influence: Framing

Media framing is the process by which facts are packaged into a narrative. For instance, a news story may contain facts such as "house prices have fallen by 25%," "subprime mortgages are defaulting at an unprecedented rate," "subprime-mortgage backed securities have lost nearly all of their value," and "GDP has shrunk by one percent over the past year." Framing is the process of tying these together into a comprehensible narrative: "A frenzy of housing speculation has gone into reverse, forcing house prices to fall by 25% and subprime mortgages to default at an unprecedented rate; this has caused trillions of dollars of financial derivatives tied to the housing market to crash, sending shockwaves throughout the financial system and the broader economy, causing a recession." As narratives, media frames include standard literary devices. The frame referenced above might include villains (irresponsible home buyers or greedy Wall Street banks), victims (Main Street, investors, the taxpayer), heroes (the president, activists, the Fed), conflicts (should banks or homeowners be bailed out), challenges (how to prevent a destructive contagion from spreading throughout the global economy), and, at the right time, endings (economic recovery, stagnation).

The influence of a frame can inhere in the *information* it presents, how that information is *framed*, or both. Therefore, framing effects can occur by the presentation of new information, the way new information is packaged into a narrative or, most commonly, a combination. For instance, a news story on a war can be framed positively or negatively, even if it transmits the same facts; however, including different pieces of information can add to the negative (number of innocent civilians killed) or positive (interviews with supporters of the war) slant. Framing effects have been found for "pure" frames and frames presenting different, supporting sets of information.[133]

One experiment illustrates how the subtlest difference in information can produce framing effects in the absence of differences in narrative.[134] Participants read a *New York Times* article describing partial-birth abortion. In one, only the word "fetus" appeared; in the other, the word "baby" was used exclusively. The results showed that those who read the story that used "fetus" were less supportive of a ban on partial-birth abortions than those who had read the same story using "baby."

Framing is most powerful when the news story deals with unfamiliar issues or events, or creates linkages between familiar issues and existing beliefs, attitudes, and values.[135] Framing can also work by inspiring emotional reactions, and frames that effectively use cognitive and affective appeals may prove most effective.[136] Particularly influential frames tap into deep-seated cultural narratives, convincing viewers or readers to interpret something according to a widely held belief, like "government is inefficient and bungling," or "my country always seeks to do good."[137] The power of framing relies on packaging information into a narrative familiar to the audience, drawing on their shared social norms.[138] As such, frames are especially powerful when they are designed and sponsored by one's favored political party, tapping into one's political beliefs and initiating the process of motivated reasoning.[139]

Additionally, preexisting knowledge moderates framing effects.[140] Unless we know nothing about a subject, our minds are not free to be shaped by media frames. Rather, frames interact with schemas; if we have well-developed, elaborate schemas, we are less likely to be influenced by a media frame that contradicts them. For instance, those with political beliefs emphasizing humanitarianism are likelier to be affected by media frames suggesting the need to help the unfortunate through welfare; while those with political beliefs emphasizing individualism are unlikely to be affected by the latter frame and likelier to be affected by frames emphasizing the need for a work requirement in welfare programs.[141] Media frames have also been shown to interact with political opinions in affecting the likelihood of taking expressive political action, such as discussing an issue with others or writing letters to newspapers.[142]

Climate change provides an illustration of framing effects in a real-world political context. In 1992, 92% of Democrats and 86% of Republicans supported stricter laws and regulations to protect the environment.[143] In the 1990s, right-leaning think tanks began a public opinion campaign to promote "environmental skepticism,"[144] bolstered by corporate funding.[145] This was remarkably successful—but consonant with framing research, only for conservatives. In 1974, conservatives expressed greater trust in science than liberals and moderates; but by 2010, conservatives—particularly *educated* conservatives—expressed considerably lower trust in science than liberals and moderates.[146] The better the understanding of climate change conservatives report having, the *less* concerned they are about it.[147] A study of shifts in public opinion on climate change from 2003 to 2010 found that the biggest influences were media coverage and elite cues (in the media), not extreme weather or scientific advances in understanding the issue.[148] This massive, polarizing shift occurred primarily through media influence.

Framing makes a direct impact on democratic functioning, not only through how issues are framed, but also how other issues are *not* framed. In other words, media framing has the potential to manipulate public opinion by commission (influencing interpretations) *and* omission. It is through omission that media framing sets the ideological boundaries for public discourse.[149] It is particularly dangerous when the media presents as equal a serious distortion of an issue alongside a careful consideration, creating an illusion of equality and cuing the audience to consider the egregious distortion as worthy of consideration.[150]

Framing can, however, be muted. Offering multiple, competing frames of an issue reduces framing effects and allows citizens to develop opinions more in line with their values.[151] This can have effects on elections. For instance, during the 2002 Brazilian presidential election, legally mandated free television time afforded to the candidates provided new frames of the issues that conflicted with the dominant frames in the media—swaying the election in favor of a candidate disliked by the economic elite and disfavored by the media.[152] Having conversations with people who have been exposed to conflicting frames also mutes framing effects—though conversations with people exposed to largely similar frames does not.[153] Those who get their news primarily from the internet may be less susceptible to framing effects simply by being exposed to a greater number of frames.[154]

8   Models of Media Influence: Agenda Setting

When one thinks of what should or could be on a democracy's political agenda, the possibilities are vast: taxes, public safety, environmental protection, immigration, constitutional amendments, welfare, unemployment, the military, foreign affairs with one or several countries—the list is nearly endless. Yet at any time, politicians and the public are concerned with only a small subset. The media's power to set the political agenda is a substantial reason: by focusing airtime and newspaper columns on some issues, the media not only sets *its* agenda, but to a disconcerting extent, *ours*.[155]

While there is no one-to-one correspondence between issues highlighted in the media and those considered important by the public, the correspondence is significant. (Even the way the media presents relationships among issues has been found to influence how citizens organize those issues).[156] In a meta-analysis of 90 studies spanning several decades and countries, the overall average correlation was found to be over 50%.[157] Over 400 studies have been conducted on agenda setting, including in North and South America, Europe, and Asia.[158] While agenda-setting research in Africa has been sparse, a study found strong agenda-setting effects in Kenya's 2007 presidential election.[159] Countries with more open governments and media systems tend to display stronger agenda-setting effects.

In Iyengar and Kinder's experiments, participants were shown news broadcasts that had been professionally edited to manipulate content.[160] They found that after watching edited newscasts highlighting the perils of the arms race, the percentage who viewed it as one of the country's three most important problems shot from 35% to 65%; for unemployment, from 50% to 85%. As would be expected from research on schemas and their rigidity, viewers with relatively less education, Independents, and the politically uninvolved were most influenced by agenda setting.[161] An analysis of trends in network news coverage and public opinion corroborated these findings.

Other investigators have found the same trend: public opinion tracks news media coverage.[162] In several countries, during different decades, examining a variety of issues and media sources, research has converged on the link between what the media covers and what the public considers important.[163] Increased exposure to the news media also powerfully predicts the degree of consensus on issue agendas between groups: men and women who read newspapers infrequently share a 55% correspondence, rising to 80% for those who read newspapers occasionally, up to a 100% correspondence for daily readers.

But could these results be explained in the reverse causal direction? Could real-world developments cause public shifts in opinion on the political agenda, which is merely reflected by the media? This has been investigated for several topics, in the USA and Germany, and the answer is no.[164] The public agenda strongly tracks the media agenda, disconnected from real-world trends. This occurred for the Vietnam War, campus protests, and urban riots; the German energy crisis of '73–'74; drug use in the USA during the '80s; crime in the '90s; environmental pollution during 1970–1990; and even shark attacks. While trends in the real world spiked or dipped—increases or decreases in drug use, crime, pollution, etc.—the public agenda did not track them. Instead, it tracked the media agenda, which also did not closely follow real-world trends. "In effect, these were natural experiments in a real-world setting that yield especially compelling causal evidence of the agenda-setting influence of the news media on the public."[165]

One important limitation to the media's agenda-setting power is in the realm of so-called obtrusive issues, those with which we have everyday experience.[166] The economy and crime, for instance, obtrude into our lives in many ways. Unobtrusive issues, like foreign affairs, are those with which we have little to no direct experience. In general, the media displays a greatly reduced agenda-setting power over obtrusive issues. In one study, not only did participants demonstrate agenda-setting effects only for unobtrusive issues, they were also likelier to say that the media was wrong about obtrusive issues, and express contrary opinions.[167] Interestingly, Graber found that over the course of a primary campaign, issues that had been unobtrusive were treated as obtrusive after repeat exposure, reducing the media's agenda-setting power. One exception is any issue of great personal importance: for example, unemployment for the unemployed or discrimination for ethnic minorities. For these issues, appearing at the top of the media's agenda validates the national importance of what someone may have thought to be merely personal—and agenda-setting effects are strong.[168] The media's agenda-setting power may also be linked to the ability of news items to provoke negative emotional reactions: prominent news stories that worry us or communicate a pressing need for solutions are likelier to make the move from the news agenda to ours.[169]

The reduced power of the media to set the public agenda for obtrusive issues may come as a relief to those worried about media influence. (Also, the internet has blunted the mass media's agenda-setting power.)[170] Yet, it puts into stark relief the power the media has to set the foreign affairs agenda.[171] Memories of the media's role in securing public approval for the war on Iraq are fresh enough to add a visceral bite to such concerns.

Another welcome exception to the media's agenda-setting power concerns trust. For instance, a study of the 1994 Taipei mayoral election revealed no agenda-setting effects for television news.[172] All three television stations in Taipei were controlled by the government, making them untrustworthy to the public. However, an agenda-setting effect was found for the two dominant—and independent—newspapers in Taipei. Reassuringly, a media source's lack of trustworthiness reduces not only its agenda-setting power, but its ability to influence by framing and priming.[173] This relationship between trust and media effects is not ironclad, however. For instance, in Chile under Pinochet's dictatorial regime, the government-controlled, right-wing press—hardly trustworthy—exerted influence on political opinions, even among leftists.[174] When citizens have few alternative sources of information, even untrustworthy media outlets can exert significant influence.

9 FROM WHAT TO THINK ABOUT, TO WHAT TO THINK

"The power of the press in America is a primordial one. It sets the agenda of public discussion; and this sweeping political power is unrestrained by any law. It determines what people will talk and think about – an authority that in other nations is reserved for tyrants, priest, parties and mandarins."
—Theodore H. White, *The Making of the American President 1972*

The priming, framing, and agenda-setting models of media influence suggest an uncomfortable truth. There is significant evidence that the media exerts substantial power over what the population thinks, not just what we think about. As Robert Entman pointed out:

> Although the distinction between "what to think" and "what to think about" is not entirely clear, the former seems to mean what people decide, favor, or accept, whereas the latter refers to the considerations they "think about" in coming to such conclusions. The distinction misleads because, short of physical coercion, all influence over "what people think" derives from telling them "what to think about." If the media really are stunningly successful in telling people what to think about, they must also exert significant influence over what they think.[175]

John Zaller's study of US public opinion provided considerable support for the view that public opinion surveys reveal only immediately accessible "considerations"—and these considerations are determined by the flow of information from the news media.[176] While the minority of the country knowledgeable about politics is resistant to media influence, the inattentive majority is largely uncritical about ideas to which they are exposed and then internalize from the media. This effect is particularly strong in U.S. elections for the House of Representatives, where even the relatively politically knowledgeable often lack information. Television coverage typically favors incumbents (via political advertising and coverage of the incumbent's actions in Congress) and as a result, exposure to television increases voters' familiarity with incumbents but does little for challengers.[177]

A study of the impact of Fox News' introduction into media markets in the USA between 1996 and 2000 estimated that mere exposure to this channel was effective in persuading 3–28% of non-Republican viewers to switch their votes.[178] Another study used Fox's varied channel positions (channels closer to 1 get more viewers) in cable markets to estimate its influence: pushing over 6% of the vote rightward in the 2008 presidential election, and accounting for two-thirds of the increase in political polarization in the USA.[179] Media *interpretations* of presidential debates can affect public opinion concerning who won the debate more powerfully than the debate itself: for instance, a poll taken immediately after a debate between Gerald Ford and Jimmy Carter found that viewers judged Ford to be the winner by 44 to 31%—but after one day of media coverage interpreting the debate as a Carter victory, public opinion shifted 61% to 19% in Carter's favor.[180] In Britain, several prominent conservative newspapers unexpectedly switched their endorsements for the Labour Party in 1997, allowing for a natural experiment to measure the effect this had on readers: a 10–25% shift in readers' votes.[181] In Italy, heavy watchers of television have been found to be likelier to vote for Silvio Berlusconi, who owns a majority of the Italian media.[182] In Russia, the only government-independent TV channel shifted votes in the 1999 presidential election by considerable margins—in those areas of the country where it was available—toward the opposition parties the channel supported.[183] Another study revealed that news anchors, reporters, special commentators, and guest experts exerted a striking effect on public opinion on 80 political issues over 15 years; single commentaries were associated with more than four points of opinion change.[184] Likewise, the tone of media coverage of politicians and candidates is strongly correlated with public support over time and in several countries.[185]

How public opinion tracks news media coverage is particularly striking evidence for the power of the media. Using a coding system to identify individual pieces of information in Associated Press dispatches and the opinions they supported, David Fan was able to design a model that accurately predicted shifts in public opinion for six issues over time.[186] This is a massive media effect: "when all AP messages were considered for these [six issues] studied, the accumulated power of mass media messages was found to determine opinion so strongly that accurate opinion time trends could be calculated from mass media [memes] alone."[187]

The news media's coverage of the economy has been found to influence our views of where the economy is headed; potentially, creating self-fulfilling prophesies by boosting or depressing consumer sentiment.[188] Media coverage of firms before their initial public offering (IPO) is linked to demand for their shares; a greater volume and more positive tenor of coverage correlates with greater demand and higher share prices.[189] Another analysis found that only five stories per month on inflation, and eleven per month on unemployment, were required to boost public concern about these issues by one percentage point.[190] More troubling is the financial media's propensity to support *laissez faire* policies and oppose economic theories advocating a greater role for government in the economy, stifling an area of potentially vibrant public debate.[191]

Perhaps most worrisome is the media's demonstrated power to persuade us to support wars.[192] As an unobtrusive issue, the media's influence (and the influence of political elites, on whom journalists rely) is unambiguous.[193] For instance, one study found that those who watched more television news were more supportive of a military rather than a diplomatic solution to the Gulf Crisis in the early '90s.[194] A similar pattern was found during the second war on Iraq, with false perceptions about Iraq linked to support for the war and exposure to television news (especially Fox News; the opposite was found for PBS/NPR).[195] Even earlier, in the '70s and '80s, public opinion on military spending followed the news media's lead—first supporting greater spending, then cuts.[196] The war on Vietnam reveals some interesting dynamics among generally pro-war conservative "hawks" and anti-war liberal "doves":

> First of all, the least informed within each camp behave similarly. Owing to their habitual inattentiveness to politics, they are late to support the war and also late to respond to antiwar information. Moderately aware hawks and doves also behave fairly similarly: They fail to support the war in its initial stage because they have not been sufficiently propagandized; as the prowar message heats up, they become more supportive of the war, but then just as quickly begin to abandon the war when the antiwar message becomes loud enough to reach them. The most politically aware ideologues, meanwhile, behave very differently. Highly aware doves begin turning against the war as early as 1966; highly aware hawks, by contrast, largely hold their ground, so that they are almost as likely to support the war in 1970 as they were at the start of the conflict. The explanation, of course, is that hawks were sustained by a steady flow of ideologically congenial prowar messages and were, at the same time, highly resistant to the ideologically inconsistent antiwar message.[197]

A different sort of media phenomenon is called the third-person effect: the belief that the media influences others more strongly than us.[198] While little more than an oddity alone, the third-person effect has downstream consequences. For instance, it can affect our views of *other's* opinions—making them seem more like what we see in the media—thereby creating "media-altered" social pressure to conform to beliefs and ideas propounded by the media or buy products viewed as widely desirable.[199] This can compound other media effects, by adding the pressure of social conformity.[200]

Political participation is another area in which the media has strong effects.[201] Exposure to local media, in interaction with the level of community integration, is linked to greater political participation.[202] During electoral campaigns, exposure to partisan news favoring the *opposing* party tends to sway partisans to defect and vote for the opposing candidate.[203] Exposure to like-minded partisan news significantly increases campaign activity over time and encourages an earlier decision time; while exposure to partisan news from the opposition has the opposite effects, depressing campaign activity and delaying voting decisions.[204] This research suggests that in future elections, the role of moderate voters with low levels of political knowledge will decrease as the role of partisan, knowledgeable voters increases. This trend is in evidence.[205]

Moreover, the media exerts influence on voting turnout. A field experiment in which some participants were given a brief, free subscription to one of two local newspapers found that those who received a subscription were likelier to vote than a control group.[206] A study of the nationwide expansion of *The New York Times* in the late '90s found that in markets with small, local papers losing subscribers to the *Times*, voting declined in local elections, but not in presidential elections.[207] This national newspaper did not actively promote apathy toward local elections; it simply did not disseminate information about them, leaving voters with little knowledge or reason to vote. Another study found that living farther from a state capital decreased knowledge of state politics, as the result of local papers providing less coverage.[208] The closure of local newspapers has been linked to deterioration in the quality of local governance.[209] Overall, two meta-analyses of studies on the relationship between news media exposure and voting found a strong relationship between newspaper reading and voting,[210] but a more complex, less generalizable relationship for television news.[211]

10   The Silent Death Rattle of Media-Centered Democracies

Spiral of silence theory explains how people first observe, then react to, what other people think about political and social topics.[212] Since people are afraid of social rejection and isolation, we are continually scanning our social environment to understand which opinions are common. When we perceive that our opinions are in the minority, or losing public support, we become less likely to express them—making these views seem even less popular to those looking to us to gauge their social acceptability. Over time, this positive feedback loop—the spiral of silence—results in minority views becoming less prevalent, until only a small group of hardcore adherents remain. And since opinion leaders get their political information almost exclusively from the media, it is the predominant arbiter of the climate of social opinion.[213]

These predictions about group behavior dovetail with Doris Graber's observations of her research participants who "obviously strove to adjust their expressed views, and possibly their actual views, to what they perceived to be the shared norms… [silent members] indicated that they had abstained from participation because they perceived their own views to be substantially out of line with those already articulated by the group."[214] They also evinced interest in public opinion polls to assess the merits of political policies and institutions, equating "failure to win substantial public endorsement with weakness and lack of merit."[215]

As a theory proposing a broad social phenomenon caused by interlinking processes, the spiral of silence has been difficult to prove through empirical research.[216] Nevertheless, research has upheld the core tenet of the theory, showing a correlation between the perceived climate of opinion and one's willingness to express a contrary opinion. One meta-analysis of 17 studies, corroborated by a later meta-analysis with 12 additional studies, found a small but statistically significant correlation.[217] Cultures valuing interdependence over individuality—conformity over independence—are more prone to its effects.[218] The appearance of internet-based media may tend to mute the spiral of silence, reducing the fear of social isolation (one can always find like-minded others on the internet), and providing an opportunity to bias perceptions of the climate of opinion in society.[219] (Already, there is evidence that the internet has helped the minority of atheists and agnostics in the United States to grow.)[220] Nor are opinions held by a majority predicted to be *invincibly* dominant by spiral of silence theory: dedicated and enthusiastic groups in the minority of public opinion can, by expressing their views with a force and exposure out of proportion with their size, initiate a spiral of increasing acceptance.[221] The successes of the civil rights and LGBT movements are positive examples of this counter-spiral.

11 Ideological Self-Segregation

Recent developments in the US media system have raised concern over the danger of ideological self-segregation: citizens choosing media sources that reinforce and never challenge their beliefs. As Jacques Ellul described the danger of ideological self-segregation:

> [T]he more propaganda there is, the more partitioning there is. For propaganda suppresses conversation; the man opposite is no longer an interlocutor but an enemy. And to the extent that he rejects that role, the other becomes an unknown whose words can no longer be understood. Thus, we see before our eyes how a world of closed minds establishes itself, a world in which everybody talks to himself, everybody constantly reviews his own certainty about himself and the wrongs done him by the Others.[222]

There is evidence that people naturally tend toward ideological self-segregation, seeking out information consonant with their beliefs.[223] This makes sense, as exposure to ideologically dissonant news has been linked to a spike in cortisol, a stress hormone.[224] When we are exposed to news that conflicts with our ideology, we increase our skepticism and actively argue against it.[225] This tendency is greater for those with higher levels of political knowledge.[226]

Furthermore, even if we do not *actively* seek ideologically congenial sources of information, we may be *passively* exposed to it and excluded from information that would challenge our beliefs. Studies of social networks have revealed that they tend toward homophily and homogeneity; that is, we naturally associate with those similar to ourselves. As we continue to get more news from social networking sites—the news that our (mostly like-minded) friends share—our risk of *passive* ideological self-segregation increases.[227] One study of social networks found that the more ideologically segregated our social network, the lower the quality and complexity of our political thinking.[228] An ideologically uniform social network creates a "social bubble" where we are rarely exposed to challenging information, causing our reasoning skills to atrophy.

There is evidence of *active* selective exposure too. A meta-analysis of 22 studies of selective exposure supported the conclusion that we tend to avoid cognitive dissonance by selecting ideologically congenial media, though the overall effect is small.[229] An experiment presenting participants with the option of reading news stories from conservative or liberal sources found that conservatives overwhelmingly chose a conservative source and liberals a liberal source—even for "soft" news about crime or travel.[230] A study of nationwide survey results found that 64% of conservatives select at least one conservative media source, compared to only 26% of liberals; while 76% of liberals select at least one liberal media source, compared to 43% of conservatives.[231]

However, most do not simply refuse to hear the other side. In the United States, most self-identified Republicans and Democrats have largely indistinguishable news diets, watching mostly non-partisan local TV news while ignoring the partisan media altogether. Only a small subset of the most politically engaged choose information on the basis of their preferred ideology.[232] Even on the internet, there is little evidence of extreme, symmetric ideological segregation.[233] While people tend to select ideologically congruent sources to a greater degree online than with TV news, magazines, and local newspapers, there is less ideological segregation on the internet than with national newspapers, and far less than in families, neighborhoods, voluntary associations, workplaces, and even zip codes. As other research has found, frequent users of social media are particularly likely to be exposed to ideological diversity,[234] and while ideologues tend to cluster together on the internet, they also debate with opponents.[235] An experimental study revealed that when we think we may have to participate in a conversation or debate, we are likelier to expose ourselves to a balance of ideological views online.[236] And among the nonideological majority, a balance of ideological views may lead to the formation of moderate opinions.[237] So far, research has contradicted the most extreme fears that the internet would lead to runaway group polarization and ideological segregation.[238] Yet the danger of ideological self-segregation on the internet remains, facilitated by social network homophily, social media algorithms, and potentially, personalized or manipulated search results which can exert powerful effects.[239] The asymmetric polarization currently in evidence on the internet in the U.S., with a right-wing bubble largely disconnected from a centrist core (and no significant left-wing presence), is less a product of the internet and more a consequence of pre-existing trends in the media ecosystem. As the authors of a comprehensive study of the recent U.S. media ecosystem explain, "[t]he American online public sphere is a shambles because it was grafted onto a television and radio public sphere that was already deeply broken".[240]

12   Mo' Media, Mo' Problems: And Less Knowledge

Alongside the danger of ideological segregation among the most politically involved, there is the problem posed by the rest: namely, apathy. Starting in the 1950s, television ownership in the United States went from a rarity to a fixture. By the middle of the decade, over 80% of households had a TV. Depending on one's location, the channels available were limited to three major broadcast networks and a smattering of local offerings. And on each of the networks, at the same time every evening, a nightly news program would be broadcast. Most had little interest in politics, but if they wanted to watch television after a day of work, they would nonetheless be presented with a non-partisan, middle-of-the-road presentation of the day's news from a major network.[241]

The effects of nightly news broadcasts on the public's political knowledge were extensive, particularly for the least educated. The steady increase in television channels and the geographical area they covered allowed for precise estimates of television's contribution to political interest and knowledge. The net difference between areas with no VHF station coverage and areas with at least three stations, for those in the 25th percentile of educational attainment, was a 12% increase in political knowledge.[242] Exposure to television increased voter turnout, particularly for those with below-average education. Television news can be an equalizing force, reducing the gap in political knowledge between the low and highly educated.[243]

In the 1980s, cable television took off, offering additional channels with entertainment options. Concurrently, the number of people tuning into the nightly network newscasts plummeted from the 1980s through the 2000s. As a result, those with less education lost the gains in political interest and knowledge they had made in the past through "incidental" exposure to nightly newscasts, and voter turnout dropped in turn.

Today's proliferation of entertainment and news options on television and the internet has caused greater stratification in political knowledge. A small minority are "news junkies" with easy access to far more information than in the past. Meanwhile, a much larger share of the population is choosing to avoid the news.[244] The end result is that "[s]trongly partisan minorities continue to roil national politics, but the largest segment of the public seems to have selected itself out of the game."[245] This stratification of political knowledge is unhealthy for a democracy: "[i]ncreasing inequality in news exposure, political knowledge, and turnout exacerbates concerns about the quality of public opinion and voting decisions."[246]

Decades of surveys of the U.S. public have revealed an exceptional lack of knowledge about even the most basic political facts.[247] From not understanding the differences between competing political philosophies to not knowing the essential functions of different governmental entities or names of powerful politicians, political ignorance is rampant in the USA.[248] (Most tellingly, for over half a century only one in five have been able to *define* conservatism and liberalism.) Although opinion polls on a variety of political issues typically report only a small percentage of people who "don't know," on the rare occasions pollsters ascertain how much their respondents *do* know, they find it to be little.[249] As James Stimson describes the reaction of early public opinion researchers to the astounding levels of political ignorance in the United States:

> Thus it seemed obvious that citizens were completely inept, totally unprepared to play their expected role in a democracy. It is hard to overstate the evidence of public ignorance, hard to express the analyst's initial despair at finding out what *isn't* known by people on the street. Everyone who has looked at survey data on public knowledge and preference has experienced it. The gap between what democracy seems to demand of voters and what voters supply is just immense.[250]

Given the real and opportunity costs of collecting information in a media system that does not provide it abundantly, such ignorance should not surprise. "[A] focus on information costs leads to the expectation that only some voters—those who must gather the information in the course of their daily lives or who have a particularly direct stake in the issue—will develop a detailed understanding of any issues. Most voters will only learn enough to form a very generalized notion of the position of a particular candidate or party on some issues, and many voters will be ignorant about most issues."[251]

As Scott Althaus put it, "[i]f ignorance is bliss, then the pursuit of happiness seems alive and well in American society."[252] Except, ignorance is not a *pursuit*, it is our default state, one that can only be left if information is provided "cheaply," easily, accessibly. Tom Ferguson writes that

> it is not necessary to assume or argue that the voting population is stupid or malevolent to explain why it often will not stir at even gross affronts to its own interests and values. Mere political awareness is costly; and, like

most of what are now recognized as 'collective goods,' absent individual possibilities of realization, it will not be supplied or often even demanded unless some sort of subsidy ... is supplied by someone.[253]

One problem with an ignorant populace is that it is more susceptible to Gresham's Law of political information: bad information drives out good.[254] Like the corresponding principle in economics ("bad money drives out good") from which its name derives, exposure to bad (false, misleading, irrelevant) information mutes the effects of accurate information. In an experimental study, less knowledgeable participants made worse decisions when they received both trustworthy and untrustworthy information.[255] Instead of disregarding the untrustworthy information, as the more knowledgeable did, the less knowledgeable participants took it into account and made poorer choices. As might be expected, the politically ignorant population of the United States is targeted with misinformation and dirty tricks, most effectively perhaps by manipulating the perceived political options on offer.[256]

An ignorant electorate is incapable of making voting decisions in accord with their values or even self-interest.[257] And a knowledgeable elite in the midst of a majority of ignoramuses can lead to the frustration, if not betrayal, of democratic ideals. When political knowledge and participation are concentrated among the relatively wealthy—as they are in the United States[258]—democracy veers closer to oligarchy.

In-depth, qualitative studies of the poor in the U.S. reveal that they live in "an impoverished information world.... in which mass media exposure does not yield new information to assist them and one in which interpersonal channels are closed."[259] Since the news media contains little information of practical relevance, the poor tend to use media to escape from the pressures of daily life through entertainment. While more advantaged people use the news media to learn about politics, the poor tend to use informal channels, like family members.[260] However, these informal channels are mainly used to gain information relevant to localized concerns, not the distant—and seemingly irrelevant—realm of politics.[261] (The internet may reduce the knowledge gap, providing a greater diversity of news sources—some of which, unlike mainstream outlets, may provide perspectives the poor find relevant and useful.)[262]

These dynamics, and their counterpart—the tendency of the wealthier to acquire and use information to enact their political preferences—create a knowledge gap separating those of low and high socioeconomic status.[263] This matters because ignorance of specific, policy-relevant facts is what separates actual preferences from "revealed preferences," that is, voting decisions.[264] Ignorance makes it possible for people to vote against their interests and values—or not to vote, again to the detriment of their interests and values. Since the poorer and less knowledgeable are worse at enacting their preferences, the richer and more knowledgeable exert disproportionate power by default. As Philip Converse observed, due to knowledge gaps, "upper social strata across history have much more predictably supported conservative or rightist parties and movements than lower strata have supported leftist parties and movements."[265] Ignorant lower strata (or an ignorant majority) lack the knowledge required to link their values and self-interest to a political party or program, biasing political power in favor of those few who do know how to link their values and self-interest to political action.

Not only is an ignorant population incapable of fully rational political decisions, but the little the public does know is unlikely to be used effectively—and may even cause serious errors.[266] "A little knowledge is a dangerous thing"—and in the political realm, the dangerous thing is a mass of largely ignorant citizens who use partisan shortcuts to make political decisions. While much has been made of voters' use of heuristics and shortcuts[267]—which are hoped to make up for ignorance—they are only as useful as the (limited) information with which they operate.[268] They may work well for the politically knowledgeable (who do not need them), but for the ignorant (who need them), they are worse than useless.[269]

In addition to garden-variety political ignorance, there is the phenomenon of "pluralistic ignorance": not knowing, or being wrong, about what the rest of the population thinks about political issues. Pluralistic ignorance tends to run in a conservative direction; that is, we tend to think the majority is more hawkish, conservative, and resistant to change than it is.[270] This tendency can inhibit the growth of movements for social change, as the inaccurate belief that the majority does not want change can sap would-be reformers' enthusiasm and make proposals for change "unrealistic."

Whether caused by the structure of the media, educational, or economic systems—or a combination—widespread political ignorance and the knowledge gap spells trouble for democracy. Ignorance makes people unlikely to vote or otherwise participate in politics, while making it more difficult to translate preferences into voting decisions. Ignorance also makes people vulnerable to false and misleading information. The knowledge gap only adds to the power of economic elites, putting restraints on the potential power of have-nots. Lastly, pluralistic ignorance and forms of cognitive conservatism damper social change, even—perhaps especially—when it is most needed.

At the core of the greatest problems we collectively face lies information; or, more accurately, a lack of it. There is no shortage of proposed solutions to the monumental problems humanity faces, yet they remain outside public debate because they are not widely known—as they are not extensively featured, discussed, and debated in the media. Simultaneously, technological developments have exponentially added to the power of the media—the *means of communication*—to disseminate information. Yet the commercial media, constrained by many of the political-economic factors that govern and limit politicians, staggeringly fails to disseminate the needed information.

Notes

1. See, for instance, George C. Edwards and B. Dan Wood, "Who Influences Whom? The President, Congress, and the Media," *American Political Science Review* 93, no. 2 (1999).
2. Lippmann, *Public Opinion*, 6.
3. de Lima, *Mídia: Teoria*, 27.
4. Michael A. Milburn, *Persuasion and Politics: The Social Psychology of Public Opinion* (Pacific Grove, CA: Thomson Brooks/Cole, 1991): 14–16.
5. Anthony R. Pratkanis and Elliot Aronson, *Age of Propaganda: The Everyday Use and Abuse of Persuasion* (New York: Macmillan, 2001): 268–270.
6. Ibid., 266.
7. Jason Stanley, *How Propaganda Works* (Princeton: Princeton University Press, 2015): 4.
8. Ibid., 48–49.
9. Pratkanis and Aronson, *Age of Propaganda*, 11–12.
10. Jacques Ellul, *Propaganda: The Formation of Men's Attitudes* (New York: Vintage Books, 1973): 47.
11. Ibid., 64–66.
12. Alex Carey, *Taking the Risk Out of Democracy: Corporate Propaganda Versus Freedom and Liberty* (Chicago: University of Illinois Press, 1997): 24–35.

13. Ibid., 12–16.
14. Robert A. Dahl, "Business and Politics: A Critical Appraisal of Political Science," *American Political Science Review* 53, no. 1 (1959): 29.
15. Frank A. Biocca, "Opposing Conceptions of the Audience: The Active and Passive Hemispheres of Mass Communication Theory," *Communication Yearbook* 11, no. 648 (1988): 60.
16. Brooke Gladstone and Josh Neufeld. *The Influencing Machine: Brooke Gladstone on the Media* (New York: W. W. Norton & Company, 2011).
17. Biocca, "Opposing Conceptions," 75.
18. Carl I. Hovland et al., *Experiments on Mass Communication*, Vol. 3 (New York: Wiley and Sons, 1949).
19. Pratkanis and Aronson, *Age of Propaganda*, 23–28.
20. Rüdiger Schmitt-Beck, "Mass Communication, Personal Communication and Vote Choice: The Filter Hypothesis of Media Influence in Comparative Perspective," *British Journal of Political Science* 33, no. 2 (2003); Gabriel Weimann, "Opinion Leadership and Public Opinion: Where Weak/Strong Media Paradigms Converge," in *The Spiral of Silence: New Perspectives on Communication and Public Opinion*, ed. Wolfgang Donsbach et al., 161–168 (New York: Routledge, 2014).
21. John P. Robinson and Mark R. Levy, "Interpersonal Communication and News Comprehension," *Public Opinion Quarterly* 50, no. 2 (1986).
22. Denis McQuail, "Paradigm Shifts in the Study of Media Effects," in *The Spiral of Silence*.
23. Larry M. Bartels, "Messages Received: The Political Impact of Media Exposure," *American Political Science Review* 87, no. 2 (1993): 275.
24. John Zaller, "The Myth of Massive Media Impact Revived: New Support For a Discredited Idea," in *Political Persuasion and Attitude Change*, ed. Diana C. Mutz et al., 17–78 (Ann Arbor, MI: University of Michigan Press, 1996): 37–38.
25. Glen Smith and Kathleen Searles, "Who Let the (Attack) Dogs Out? New Evidence for Partisan Media Effects," *Public Opinion Quarterly* 78, no. 1 (2014).
26. Jonathan S. Morris and Peter L. Francia, "Cable News, Public Opinion, and the 2004 Party Conventions," *Political Research Quarterly* 63, no. 4 (2009).
27. Glen Smith and Kathleen Searles, "Fair and Balanced News or a Difference of Opinion? Why Opinion Shows Matter for Media Effects," *Political Research Quarterly* 66, no. 3 (2013).
28. Lauren Feldman, "The Opinion Factor: The Effects of Opinionated News on Information Processing and Attitude Change," *Political Communication* 28, no. 2 (2011).

29. Gangheong Lee and Joseph N. Cappella, "The Effects of Political Talk Radio on Political Attitude Formation: Exposure versus Knowledge," *Political Communication* 18, no. 4 (2001).
30. Kevin Arceneaux and Martin Johnson, *Changing Minds or Changing Channels? Partisan News in an Age of Choice* (Chicago: University of Chicago Press, 2013); Matthew Levendusky, *How Partisan Media Polarize America* (Chicago: University of Chicago Press, 2013).
31. Arceneaux and Johnson, *Changing Minds*, 148.
32. Levendusky, *How Partisan*, 139.
33. Ibid., 148–156.
34. Elihu Katz, "Communications Research Since Lazarsfeld," *The Public Opinion Quarterly* 51 (1987).
35. W. Lance Bennett and Shanto Iyengar, "A New Era of Minimal Effects? The Changing Foundations of Political Communication," *Journal of Communication* 58, no. 4 (2008): 707–708.
36. Martha L. Cottam et al., *Introduction to Political Psychology*, 2nd ed. (New York: Psychology Press, 2010): 39–40.
37. Robert M. Entman, "How the Media Affect What People Think: An Information Processing Approach," *The Journal of Politics* 51, no. 2 (1989): 367.
38. Murray Edelman, *The Politics of Misinformation* (New York: Cambridge University Press, 2001): 65–66.
39. Ellul, *Propaganda*, 218.
40. Robert W. McChesney et al., "Advertising and the Genius of Commercial Propaganda," in *The Propaganda Society: Promotional Culture and Politics in Global Context*, ed. Gerald Sussman, 27–44 (New York: Peter Lang, 2011).
41. Roger Desmond and Rod Carveth, "Advertising on Children and Adolescents: A Meta-Analysis," in *Mass Media Effects Research: Advances through Meta-Analysis*, ed. Raymond W. Preiss et al., 169–179 (Mahwah, NJ: Lawrence Erlbaum Associates, 2007).
42. Stefano DellaVigna and Matthew Gentzkow, "Persuasion: Empirical Evidence," *Annual Review of Economics* 2, no. 1 (2010): 645–650.
43. David P. Phillips, "Natural Experiments on the Effects of Mass Media Violence on Fatal Aggression: Strengths and Weaknesses of a New Approach," in *Advances in Experimental Social Psychology*, Vol. 19, ed. Leonard Berkowitz, 207–250 (New York: Academic Press, 1986).
44. P. Niels Christensen and Wendy Wood, "Effects of Media Violence on Viewers' Aggression in Unconstrained Social Interaction," in *Mass Media Effects Research*. However, see Christopher J. Ferguson and John Kilburn, "The Public Health Risks of Media Violence: A Meta-Analytic Review," *The Journal of Pediatrics* 154, no. 5 (2009).

45. Media Violence Commission, and International Society for Research on Aggression (ISRA), "Report of the Media Violence Commission," *Aggressive Behavior* 38, no. 5 (2012).
46. Roxane Cohen Silver et al., "Mental- and Physical-Health Effects of Acute Exposure to Media Images of the September 11, 2001, Attacks and the Iraq War," *Psychological Science* 24, no. 9 (2013).
47. E. Alison Holman et al., "Media's Role in Broadcasting Acute Stress Following the Boston Marathon Bombings," *Proceedings of the National Academy of Sciences* 111, no. 1 (2014).
48. Marie-Louise Mares and Emory H. Woodard, "Positive Effects of Television on Children's Social Interaction: A Meta-Analysis," in *Mass Media Effects Research*.
49. Leslie B. Snyder, "Meta-Analyses of Mediated Health Campaigns," in *Mass Media Effects Research*.
50. Elizabeth Levy Paluck, "Reducing Intergroup Prejudice and Conflict Using the Media: A Field Experiment in Rwanda," *Journal of Personality and Social Psychology* 96, no. 3 (2009).
51. Armoudian, *Kill the Messenger*, 237–249.
52. Mary K. Casey et al., "The Impact of Earvin 'Magic' Johnson's HIV-Positive Announcement," in *Mass Media Effects Research*.
53. Richard M. Perloff, *The Dynamics of Persuasion: Communication and Attitudes in the Twenty-First Century* (New York: Routledge, 2010): 336–354.
54. Mike Allen and Raymond W. Preiss, "Media, Messages, and Meta-Analysis," in *Mass Media Effects Research*. 28.
55. Elisabeth Perse, "Meta-Analysis: Demonstrating the Power of Mass Communication," in *Mass Media Effects Research*.
56. Tae-Seop Lim and Sang Yeon Kim, "Many Faces of Media Effects," in *Mass Media Effects Research*.
57. George Gerbner, "Cultivation Analysis: An Overview," *Mass Communication and Society* 1, no. 3–4 (1998).
58. Quoted in James Shanahan and Michael Morgan, *Television and Its Viewers: Cultivation Theory and Research* (New York: Cambridge University Press, 1999): 13.
59. Ibid., 23.
60. Ibid., 110–136.
61. Richard J. Gerrig, *Experiencing Narrative Worlds: On the Psychological Activities of Reading* (New Haven, CT: Yale University Press, 1993): 196–242.
62. Michael Morgan et al., "Growing Up with Television: Cultivation Processes," in *Media Effects: Advances in Theory and Research*, ed. Jennings Bryant and Mary Beth Oliver, 34–49 (New York: Lawrence Erlbaum Associates, 2009): 40–41; Shanahan and Morgan, *Television*, 193.

63. L.J. Shrum, "Media Consumption and Perceptions of Social Reality: Effects and Underlying Processes," in *Media Effects*: 59.
64. L.J. Shrum, "Psychological Processes Underlying Cultivation Effects: Further Tests of Construct Accessibility," *Human Communication Research* 22, no. 4 (1996).
65. Morgan et al., "Growing Up," 39.
66. Shanahan and Morgan, *Television*, 186–188.
67. L.J. Shrum et al., "The Effects of Television Consumption on Social Perceptions: The Use of Priming Procedures to Investigate Psychological Processes," *Journal of Consumer Research* 24, no. 4 (1998).
68. Dale Kunkel et al., "Report of the APA Task Force on Advertising and Children" (Washington, DC: American Psychological Association, 2004): 30, 60; George P. Moschis and Roy L. Moore, "A Longitudinal Study of Television Advertising Effects," *Journal of Consumer Research* (1982).
69. Shrum, "Media Consumption," 68.
70. Tim Kasser, *The High Price of Materialism* (Cambridge, MA: MIT Press, 2003).
71. Rodolfo Leyva, "Experimental Insights into the Socio-cognitive Effects of Viewing Materialistic Media Messages on Welfare Support," *Media Psychology* (2018): 1–25.
72. Patricia A. Oppliger, "Effects of Gender Stereotyping on Socialization," in *Mass Media Effects Research*.
73. Shanahan and Morgan, *Television*, 96.
74. Bandura, "Social Cognitive," 107–108.
75. Shanahan and Morgan, *Television*, 95–96.
76. George Gerbner et al., "Charting the Mainstream: Television's Contributions to Political Orientations," *Journal of Communication* 32, no. 2 (1982).
77. Shanahan and Morgan, *Television*, 90–99.
78. Ibid., 91.
79. Ibid., 132, 158.
80. Melissa J. Ferguson et al., "On the Automaticity of Nationalist Ideology: The Case of the USA," in *Social and Psychological Bases of Ideology and System Justification*, ed. John T. Jost et al., 53–83 (Oxford: Oxford University Press, 2009).
81. de Lima, *Mídia: Teoria*, 117, my translation.
82. Ibid., 186, my translation.
83. Venício A. de Lima, *Mídia: Crise Política e Poder no Brasil* (São Paulo: Editora Fundação Perseu Abramo, 2006): 62, translation mine.
84. Castells, 2011, 374–375.

85. de Lima, *Mídia: Teoria*, 190–191, translation mine.
86. Albert D. Annis and Norman C. Meier, "The Induction of Opinion through Suggestion by Means of 'Planted Content'," *The Journal of Social Psychology* 5, no. 1 (1934).
87. Jan W. van Deth et al., "Children and Politics: An Empirical Reassessment of Early Political Socialization," *Political Psychology* 32, no. 1 (2011).
88. William P. Eveland Jr., et al., "Understanding the Relationship between Communication and Political Knowledge: A Model Comparison Approach Using Panel Data," *Political Communication* 22, no. 4 (2005).
89. John Zaller, *The Nature and Origins of Mass Opinion* (New York: Cambridge University Press, 1992): 25.
90. Sandra J. Ball-Rokeach and Melvin L. DeFleur, "A Dependency Model of Mass-Media Effects," *Communication Research* 3, no. 1 (1976).
91. Debra Merskin, "Media Dependency Theory: Origins and Directions," in *Mass Media, Social Control and Social Change: A Macrosocial Perspective*, ed. David Demers and Kasisomayajula Viswanath, 77–98 (Iowa City: Iowa State University Press, 1999).
92. Taylor, *Brainwashing*, 227.
93. Maxwell McCombs et al., *The News and Public Opinion: Media Effects on Civic Life* (New York: Polity, 2011): 96.
94. Michael B. MacKuen et al., "Affective Signatures and Attention: The Persistent Impact of Emotional Responses to the News" (paper presented at the annual meeting for the Midwest Political Science Association, Chicago, Illinois, April 11–14, 2013).
95. David R. Roskos-Ewoldsen et al., "Media Priming: An Updated Synthesis," in *Media Effects*: 84–87.
96. Michael R. DeWitt et al., "The Effects of Prior Knowledge on the Encoding of Episodic Contextual Details," *Psychonomic Bulletin & Review* 19, no. 2 (2012); Milburn, *Persuasion*, 79–80.
97. Beth Miller, "The Effects of Scandalous Information on Recall of Policy-Related Information," *Political Psychology* 31, no. 6 (2010).
98. Graber, *Processing the News*, 116–117.
99. Baldwin Van Gorp, "The Constructionist Approach to Framing: Bringing Culture Back in," *Journal of Communication* 57, no. 1 (2007).
100. Graber, *Processing the News*, 149.
101. Ibid., 130.
102. Ibid., 133.
103. Ibid., 142–143.
104. Ibid., 150.

105. Annie Lang et al., "Where Psychophysiology Meets the Media: Taking the Effects Out of Mass Media Research," in *Media Effects*: 199.
106. Perloff, *The Dynamics*, 224–234.
107. Jim Sidanius and Robert Kurzban, "Evolutionary Approaches to Political Psychology," in *Oxford Handbook of Political Psychology*, ed. David O. Sears et al., 146–181 (Oxford: Oxford University Press, 2003): 166–167.
108. Bandura, "Social Cognitive," 119.
109. Graber, *Processing the News*, 55 (quoting Bennett, 1981, 131).
110. Perloff, "The Dynamics," 146.
111. James O. Whittaker, "Cognitive Dissonance and the Effectiveness of Persuasive Communications," *Public Opinion Quarterly* 28, no. 4 (1964).
112. David O. Sears and Sheri Levy, "Childhood and Adult Political Development," in *Oxford Handbook of Political Psychology*, ed. David O. Sears et al., 60–109 (Oxford: Oxford University Press, 2003): 77.
113. Pazit Ben-Nun Bloom and Lindsey Clark Levitan, "We're Closer than I Thought: Social Network Heterogeneity, Morality, and Political Persuasion," *Political Psychology* 32, no. 4 (2011).
114. David Domke et al., "Rights and Morals, Issues, and Candidate Integrity: Insights into the Role of the News Media," *Political Psychology* 21, no. 4 (2000).
115. Milburn, *Persuasion*, 96–97.
116. Sears and Levy, "Childhood and Adult," 84, 88.
117. Richard E. Petty et al., "Mass Media Attitude Change: Implications of the Elaboration Likelihood Model of Persuasion," in *Media Effects*.
118. Thomas E. Nelson and Jennifer Garst, "Values-Based Political Messages and Persuasion: Relationships among Speaker, Recipient, and Evoked Values," *Political Psychology* 26, no. 4 (2005).
119. Perloff, *The Dynamics*, 140–141.
120. Pratkanis and Aronson, *Age of Propaganda*, 187.
121. Perloff, *The Dynamics*, 135.
122. Pamela Johnston Conover and Stanley Feldman, "The Origins and Meaning of Liberal/Conservative Self-Identifications," in *Political Psychology: Key Readings*, ed. John T. Jost and Jim Sidanius, 200–216 (New York: Psychology Press, 2004): 213–214.
123. Milburn, *Persuasion*, 129.
124. Ibid., 148–150.
125. Iyengar and Kinder, *News That Matters*, 63.
126. Roskos-Ewoldsen et al., "Media Priming."
127. Iyengar and Kinder, *News That Matters*, 87–89.
128. Ibid., 94.

129. Ibid., 114.
130. Michael Tesler, "Priming Predispositions and Changing Policy Positions: An Account of When Mass Opinion Is Primed or Changed," *American Journal of Political Science* 59, no. 4 (2015).
131. Sei-Hill Kim et al., "Attribute Agenda Setting, Priming and the Media's Influence on How to Think about a Controversial Issue," *International Communication Gazette* 74, no. 1 (2012); McCombs et al., *The News*, 86.
132. McCombs, *Setting the Agenda*, 79–80.
133. Emily K. Vraga et al., "Precision vs. Realism on the Framing Continuum: Understanding the Underpinnings of Message Effects," *Political Communication* 27, no. 1 (2010).
134. Adam F. Simon and Jennifer Jerit, "Toward a Theory Relating Political Discourse, Media, and Public Opinion," *Journal of Communication* 57, no. 2 (2007).
135. Dhavan V. Shah et al., "'To Thine Own Self Be True' Values, Framing, and Voter Decision-Making Strategies," *Communication Research* 23, no. 5 (1996); Tewksbury and Scheufele, "News Framing," 25.
136. Kimberly Gross, "Framing Persuasive Appeals: Episodic and Thematic Framing, Emotional Response, and Policy Opinion," *Political Psychology* 29, no. 2 (2008).
137. George Lakoff, "Changing Brains: Lessons from The Living Wage Campaign," in *Manipulating Democracy: Democratic Theory, Political Psychology, and Mass Media*, ed. Wayne Le Cheminant and John M. Parrish, 93–112 (New York: Routledge, 2011).
138. Timothy K.F. Fung and Dietram A. Scheufele, "Social Norms, Spirals of Silence and Framing Theory: An Argument for Considering Cross-Cultural Differences in Media Effects Research," in *The Spiral of Silence*.
139. Rune Slothuus and Claes H. De Vreese, "Political Parties, Motivated Reasoning, and Issue Framing Effects," *The Journal of Politics* 72, no. 3 (2010).
140. Fuyuan Shen, "Effects of News Frames and Schemas on Individuals' Issue Interpretations and Attitudes," *Journalism & Mass Communication Quarterly* 81, no. 2 (2004).
141. Fuyuan Shen and Heidi Hatfield Edwards, "Economic Individualism, Humanitarianism, and Welfare Reform: A Value-Based Account of Framing Effects," *Journal of Communication* 55, no. 4 (2005).
142. Michael P. Boyle et al., "Expressive Responses to News Stories about Extremist Groups: A Framing Experiment," *Journal of Communication* 56, no. 2 (2006).
143. Pew Research Center, "Trends in Political Values and Core Attitudes: 1987–2007" (March 22, 2007): 62.

144. Peter J. Jacques et al., "The Organisation of Denial: Conservative Think Tanks and Environmental Scepticism," *Environmental Politics* 17, no. 3 (2008).
145. Justin Farrell, "Corporate Funding and Ideological Polarization about Climate Change," *Proceedings of the National Academy of Sciences* 113, no. 1 (2016).
146. Gordon Gauchat, "Politicization of Science in the Public Sphere: A Study of Public Trust in the United States, 1974 to 2010," *American Sociological Review* 77, no. 2 (2012).
147. Deborah Lynn Guber, "A Cooling Climate for Change? Party Polarization and the Politics of Global Warming," *American Behavioral Scientist* 57, no. 1 (2013).
148. Robert J. Brulle et al., "Shifting Public Opinion on Climate Change: An Empirical Assessment of Factors Influencing Concern over Climate Change in The US, 2002–2010," *Climatic Change* 114, no. 2 (2012).
149. Robert M. Entman, "Framing Bias: Media in the Distribution of Power," *Journal of Communication* 57, no. 1 (2007).
150. Edelman, *The Politics*, 94.
151. Beattie and Milojevich, "A Test"; Mauro P. Porto, "Frame Diversity and Citizen Competence: Towards a Critical Approach to News Quality," *Critical Studies in Media Communication* 24, no. 4 (2007).
152. Mauro P. Porto, "Framing Controversies: Television and the 2002 Presidential Election in Brazil," *Political Communication* 24, no. 1 (2007).
153. James N. Druckman and Kjersten R. Nelson, "Framing and Deliberation: How Citizens' Conversations Limit Elite Influence," *American Journal of Political Science* 47, no. 4 (2003).
154. Yung-Ho Im et al., "The Emerging Mediascape, Same Old Theories? A Case Study of Online News Diffusion in Korea," *New Media & Society* 13, no. 4 (2011).
155. McCombs, *Setting the Agenda*, 5.
156. Hong Tien Vu et al., "Exploring 'The World Outside and the Pictures in Our Heads': A Network Agenda-Setting Study," *Journalism & Mass Communication Quarterly* 91, no. 4 (2014).
157. Wayne Wanta and Salma Ghanem, "Effects of Agenda Setting," in *Mass Media Effects Research*.
158. McCombs et al., *The News*.
159. Uche Onyebadi, "Towards an Examination and Expansion of the Agenda Setting Theory: Did the Media Matter in Kenya's Presidential Election, 2007?" (PhD diss., University of Missouri, Columbia, 2008).
160. Iyengar and Kinder, *News That Matters*.
161. Ibid., 59–60.

162. David P. Fan and Albert R. Tims, "The Impact of the News Media on Public Opinion: American Presidential Election 1987–1988," *International Journal of Public Opinion Research* 1, no. 2 (1989); McCombs et al., *The News*.
163. Maxwell McCombs and Amy Reynolds, "How the News Shapes Our Civic Agenda," in *Media Effects*: 2–5.
164. McCombs, *Setting the Agenda*, 22–30; Elisabeth Noelle-Neumann, "The Effect of the Mass Media on Opinion Formation," in *Mass Media, Social Control and Social Change*: 67–68.
165. McCombs, *Setting the Agenda*, 29.
166. Ibid., 60.
167. Graber, *Processing the News*, 106–107.
168. Iyengar and Kinder, *News That Matters*, 53.
169. Joanne M. Miller, "Examining the Mediators of Agenda Setting: A New Experimental Paradigm Reveals the Role of Emotions," *Political Psychology* 28, no. 6 (2007).
170. Renita Coleman and Maxwell McCombs, "The Young and Agenda-Less? Exploring Age-Related Differences in Agenda Setting on the Youngest Generation, Baby Boomers, and the Civic Generation," *Journalism & Mass Communication Quarterly* 84, no. 3 (2007); Sharon Meraz, "Is There an Elite Hold? Traditional Media to Social Media Agenda Setting Influence in Blog Networks," *Journal of Computer-Mediated Communication* 14, no. 3 (2009).
171. McCombs et al., *The News*, 81; Stuart N. Soroka, "Media, Public Opinion, and Foreign Policy," *The International Journal of Press/Politics* 8, no. 1 (2003).
172. McCombs, *Setting the Agenda*, 37.
173. James N. Druckman, "On the Limits of Framing Effects: Who Can Frame?" *Journal of Politics* 63, no. 4 (2001); Kinder, "Communication," 377; Joanne M. Miller and Jon A. Krosnick, "News Media Impact on the Ingredients of Presidential Evaluations: Politically Knowledgeable Citizens Are Guided by a Trusted Source," *American Journal of Political Science* (2000).
174. Pablo Halpern, "Media Dependency and Political Perceptions in an Authoritarian Political System," *Journal of Communication* 44, no. 4 (1994).
175. Entman, "How the Media," 165.
176. Zaller, *The Nature*.
177. Prior, *Post-Broadcast Democracy*, 187–190. See also Michael Schudson, *The Power of News* (Cambridge, MA: Harvard University Press, 1982): 214–215.

178. Stefano DellaVigna and Ethan Kaplan, "The Fox News Effect: Media Bias and Voting," *The Quarterly Journal of Economics* 122, no. 3 (2007).
179. Gregory J. Martin and Ali Yurukoglu, "Bias in Cable News: Persuasion and Polarization," *American Economic Review* 107, no. 9 (2017): 2565–2599.
180. Schudson, *The Power of News*, 121–122.
181. Jonathan McDonald Ladd and Gabriel S. Lenz, "Exploiting a Rare Communication Shift to Document the Persuasive Power of the News Media," *American Journal of Political Science* 53, no. 2 (2009). See also Chiang and Knight, 2011.
182. Massimo Ragnedda and Glenn W. Muschert, "The Regime of Propaganda in a Neoliberal State: Berlusconi and the Italian Media," in *The Propaganda Society*.
183. Ruben Enikolopov, et al., "Media and Political Persuasion: Evidence from Russia," *The American Economic Review* 101, no. 7 (2011).
184. Benjamin I. Page et al., "What Moves Public Opinion?" *American Political Science Review* 81, no. 1 (1987).
185. McCombs et al., *The News*, 114–115.
186. David. P. Fan, *Predictions of Public Opinion from the Mass Media: Computer Content Analysis and Mathematical Modeling* (Westport, CT: Greenwood Publishing Group, 1988).
187. Ibid., 133.
188. Joe Bob Hester and Rhonda Gibson, "The Economy and Second-Level Agenda Setting: A Time-Series Analysis of Economic News and Public Opinion about the Economy," *Journalism & Mass Communication Quarterly* 80, no. 1 (2003).
189. Timothy G. Pollock and Violina P. Rindova, "Media Legitimation Effects in the Market for Initial Public Offerings," *Academy of Management Journal* 46, no. 5 (2003).
190. Iyengar and Kinder, *News That Matters*, 28–32.
191. Aeron Davis, "Promotion, Propaganda, and High Finance," in *The Propaganda Society*.
192. Matthew A. Baum, *Soft News Goes to War: Public Opinion and American Foreign Policy in the New Media Age* (Princeton: Princeton University Press, 2003): 212–223.
193. Adam J. Berinsky, "Assuming the Costs of War: Events, Elites, and American Public Support for Military Conflict," *Journal of Politics* 69, no. 4 (2007); Friedman, "Beyond Cues."
194. Shanto Iyengar and Adam Simon, "News Coverage of the Gulf Crisis and Public Opinion A Study of Agenda-Setting, Priming, and Framing," *Communication Research* 20, no. 3 (1993).

195. Steven Kull et al., "Misperceptions, the Media, and the Iraq War," *Political Science Quarterly* 118, no. 4 (2003).
196. Zaller, *The Nature*, 15.
197. Ibid., 204–205.
198. Leo W. Jeffres et al., "Integrating Theoretical Traditions in Media Effects: Using Third-Person Effects to Link Agenda-Setting and Cultivation," *Mass Communication and Society* 11, no. 4 (2008).
199. Perloff, *The Dynamics*, 263.
200. Albert C. Gunther, "The Intersection of Third-Person Effect and Spiral of Silence," in *The Spiral of Silence*.
201. Barry A. Hollander, "Media Use and Political Involvement," in *Mass Media Effects Research*.
202. Hye-Jin Paek et al., "Local News, Social Integration, and Community Participation: Hierarchical Linear Modeling of Contextual and Cross-Level Effects," *Journalism & Mass Communication Quarterly* 82, no. 3 (2005); Jack M. McLeod et al., "Community, Communication, and Participation: The Role of Mass Media and Interpersonal Discussion in Local Political Participation," *Political Communication* 16, no. 3 (1999).
203. Susanna Dilliplane, "Activation, Conversion, or Reinforcement? The Impact of Partisan News Exposure on Vote Choice," *American Journal of Political Science* 58, no. 1 (2014).
204. Susanna Dilliplane, "All the News You Want to Hear: The Impact of Partisan News Exposure on Political Participation," *Public Opinion Quarterly* 75, no. 2 (2011): 304.
205. Markus Prior, "Media and Political Polarization," *Annual Review of Political Science* 16 (2013); Robert Y. Shapiro and Yaeli Bloch-Elkon, "Do the Facts Speak for Themselves? Partisan Disagreement as a Challenge to Democratic Competence," *Critical Review* 20, no. 1–2 (2008).
206. Alan S. Gerber et al., "Does the Media Matter? A Field Experiment Measuring the Effect of Newspapers on Voting Behavior and Political Opinions," *American Economic Journal: Applied Economics* (2009).
207. Lisa George and Joel Waldfogel, "Does the New York Times Spread Ignorance and Apathy?" (working paper, Wharton School of Business, University of Pennsylvania, Philadelphia, PA, 2002).
208. Michael X. Delli Carpini et al., "Effects of the News Media Environment on Citizen Knowledge of State Politics and Government," *Journalism & Mass Communication Quarterly* 71, no. 2 (1994).
209. Pengjie Gao, Chang Lee, and Dermot Murphy, "Financing Dies in Darkness? The Impact of Newspaper Closures on Public Finance" (August 10, 2018). Available at http://dx.doi.org/10.2139/ssrn.3175555.

210. Barry A. Hollander, "Media Use and Political Involvement," in *Mass Media Effects Research*.
211. Dorina Miron and Jennings Bryant, "Mass Media and Voter Turnout," in *Mass Media Effects Research*.
212. Jörg Matthes and Andrew F. Hayes, "Methodological Conundrums in Spiral of Silence Research," in *The Spiral of Silence*.
213. Hans Mathias Kepplinger, "Three Contexts of the Spiral of Silence Theory," in *The Spiral of Silence: New Perspectives on Communication and Public Opinion*, ed. Wolfgang Donsbach et al., 44–56 (New York: Routledge, 2014).
214. Graber, *Processing the News*, 35.
215. Ibid., 167.
216. Matthes and Hayes, "Methodological Conundrums."
217. Carroll J. Glynn and Michael E. Huge. "Speaking in Spirals: An Updated Meta-Analysis of the Spiral of Silence," in *The Spiral of Silence*; James Shanahan et al., "The Spiral of Silence: A Meta-Analysis and Its Impact," in *Mass Media Effects Research*.
218. Fung and Scheufele, "Social Norms"; Sonny Rosenthal and Benjamin Hill Detenber, "Cultural Orientation and the Spiral of Silence," in *The Spiral of Silence*.
219. Patricia Moy and Muzammil M. Hussain, "Media and Public Opinion in a Fragmented Society," in *The Spiral of Silence*; Patrick Rössler and Anne Schulz, "Public Opinion Expression in Online Environments," in *The Spiral of Silence*.
220. Allen B. Downey, "Religious Affiliation, Education and Internet Use," *arXiv preprint* arXiv:1403.5534 (2014).
221. Jacob Shamir, "Pluralistic Ignorance and the Spiral of Silence Meet: Mutual Lessons," in *The Spiral of Silence*.
222. Ellul, *Propaganda*, 213–214.
223. Matthew Gentzkow and Jesse M. Shapiro, "Ideological Segregation Online and Offline," *The Quarterly Journal of Economics* 126, no. 4 (2011); Sunstein, "The Law."
224. Hart Blanton et al., "Partisan Identification as a Predictor of Cortisol Response to Election News," *Political Communication* 29, no. 4 (2012).
225. Charles S. Taber, "Political Cognition and Public Opinion," in *The Oxford Handbook of American Public Opinion and the Media*, ed. Robert Y. Shapiro and Lawrence R. Jacobs, 368–383 (Oxford: Oxford University Press, 2013): 375; Charles S. Taber and Milton Lodge, "Motivated Skepticism in the Evaluation of Political Beliefs," *American Journal of Political Science* 50, no. 3 (2006).

226. Charles S. Taber et al., "The Motivated Processing of Political Arguments," *Political Behavior* 31, no. 2 (2009).
227. Mutz and Young, "Communication," 1038.
228. Elif Erisen and Cengiz Erisen, "The Effect of Social Networks on the Quality of Political Thinking," *Political Psychology* 33, no. 6 (2012).
229. Dave D'Alessio and Mike Allen, "The Selective Exposure Hypothesis and Media Choice Processes," in *Mass Media Effects Research*.
230. Shanto Iyengar and Kyu S. Hahn, "Red Media, Blue Media: Evidence of Ideological Selectivity in Media Use," *Journal of Communication* 59, no. 1 (2009).
231. Natalie Jomini Stroud, "Media Use and Political Predispositions: Revisiting the Concept of Selective Exposure," *Political Behavior* 30, no. 3 (2008).
232. Michael J. LaCour, "A Balanced News Diet, Not Selective Exposure: Evidence from a Direct Measure of Media Exposure," APSA 2012 Annual Meeting Paper (September 25, 2015). Available at SSRN: http://ssrn.com/abstract=2110621.
233. Gentzkow and Shapiro, "Ideological Segregation."
234. Jihyang Choi and Jae Kook Lee, "Investigating the Effects of News Sharing and Political Interest on Social Media Network Heterogeneity," *Computers in Human Behavior* 44 (2015).
235. Henry Farrell, "The Consequences of the Internet for Politics," *Annual Review of Political Science* 15 (2012): 41–42.
236. Nicholas A. Valentino et al., "Selective Exposure in the Internet Age: The Interaction Between Anxiety and Information Utility," *Political Psychology* 30, no. 4 (2009).
237. Jeffrey Conroy-Krutz and Devra C. Moehler, "Moderation from Bias: A Field Experiment on Partisan Media in a New Democracy," *The Journal of Politics* 77, no. 2 (2015).
238. Levi Boxell, Matthew Gentzkow, and Jesse M. Shapiro. "Is the Internet Causing Political Polarization? Evidence from Demographics." No. w23258. National Bureau of Economic Research, 2017.
239. Robert Epstein and Ronald E. Robertson, "The Search Engine Manipulation Effect (SEME) and Its Possible Impact on the Outcomes of Elections," *Proceedings of the National Academy of Sciences* 112, no. 33 (2015).
240. Yochai Benkler, Robert Faris, and Hal Roberts, *Network Propaganda: Manipulation, Disinformation, and Radicalization in American Politics* (New York: Oxford University Press, 2018): 386.
241. Prior, *Post-Broadcast Democracy*.
242. Ibid., 80–82.

243. Jennifer Jerit et al., "Citizens, Knowledge, and the Information Environment," *American Journal of Political Science* 50, no. 2 (2006).
244. Richard L. Fox and Amy Gangl. "'News You Can't Use': Politics and Democracy in the New Media Environment," in *Manipulating Democracy*.
245. Bennett and Iyengar, "A New Era," 722.
246. Prior, *Post-Broadcast Democracy*, 160.
247. For example, Scott L. Althaus, *Collective Preferences in Democratic Politics: Opinion Surveys and the Will of the People* (New York: Cambridge University Press, 2003): 10–12; Cottam et al., *Introduction*, 134–135; Friedman, *Power without Knowledge*, 249–251; Taber, "Information Processing," 455–456.
248. Donald R. Kinder and Nathan P. Kalmoe. *Neither Liberal nor Conservative: Ideological Innocence in the American Public* (Chicago: University of Chicago Press, 2017).
249. David William Moore, *The Opinion Makers: An Insider Exposes the Truth Behind the Polls* (Boston: Beacon Press, 2008).
250. James A. Stimson, *Tides of Consent: How Public Opinion Shapes American Politics* (New York: Cambridge University Press, 2015): 14, emphasis added.
251. Samuel Popkin et al., "Comment: What Have You Done for Me Lately? Toward an Investment Theory of Voting," *American Political Science Review* 70, no. 3 (1976): 787.
252. Althaus, *Collective Preferences*, 12.
253. Thomas Ferguson, *Golden Rule: The Investment Theory of Party Competition and the Logic of Money-Driven Political Systems* (Chicago: University of Chicago Press, 1995): 26.
254. Popkin, *The Reasoning Voter*, 78–81.
255. Cheryl Boudreau, "Gresham's Law of Political Communication: How Citizens Respond to Conflicting Information," *Political Communication* 30, no. 2 (2013).
256. Andrew Sabl, "Exploiting the Clueless: Heresthetic, Overload, and Rational Ignorance," in *Manipulating Democracy*.
257. Michael X. Delli Carpini and Scott Keeter, *What Americans Know About Politics and Why It Matters* (New Haven, CT: Yale University Press, 1997).
258. Kay Lehman Schlozman and Henry E. Brady, *The Unheavenly Chorus: Unequal Political Voice and the Broken Promise of American Democracy* (Princeton: Princeton University Press, 2012).
259. Elfreda A. Chatman and Victoria EM Pendleton, "Knowledge Gap, Information-Seeking and the Poor," *The Reference Librarian* 23, no. 49–50 (1995): 139.

260. Amanda Spink and Charles Cole, "Information and Poverty: Information-Seeking Channels Used by African American Low-Income Households," *Library & Information Science Research* 23, no. 1 (2001).
261. Elfreda A. Chatman, "The Impoverished Life-World of Outsiders," *Journal of the American Society for Information Science* 47, no. 3 (1996).
262. Goh, Debbie. "Narrowing the Knowledge Gap: The Role of Alternative Online Media in an Authoritarian Press System," *Journalism & Mass Communication Quarterly* 92, no. 4 (2015).
263. Emanuel Gaziano and Cecilie Gaziano, "Social Control, Social Change and the Knowledge Gap Hypothesis," in *Mass Media, Social Control and Social Change*.
264. Martin Gilens, "Political Ignorance and Collective Policy Preferences," *American Political Science Review* 95, no. 2 (2001).
265. Philip E. Converse, "The Nature of Belief Systems in Mass Publics," in *Political Psychology: Key Readings*, ed. John T. Jost and Jim Sidanius, 181–200 (New York: Psychology Press, 2004): 196.
266. Ilya Somin, "Knowledge about Ignorance: New Directions in the Study of Political Information," *Critical Review* 18, no. 1–3 (2006).
267. For example, Paul M. Sniderman et al., *Reasoning and Choice: Explorations in Political Psychology* (New York: Cambridge University Press, 1993): 14–27.
268. Bartels, "Uninformed Votes"; Friedman, forthcoming, 261, 263.
269. Richard R. Lau and David P. Redlawsk, "Advantages and Disadvantages of Cognitive Heuristics in Political Decision Making," *American Journal of Political Science* (2001).
270. Shamir, "Pluralistic Ignorance," 157–158.

CHAPTER 6

The Supply Side: What Affects the Supply of Information Provided by the Media

"Thus the environment with which our public opinions deal is refracted in many ways, by censorship and privacy at the source, by physical and social barriers at the other end, by scanty attention, by the poverty of language, by distraction, by unconscious constellations of feeling, by wear and tear, violence, monotony. These limitations upon our access to that environment combine with the obscurity and complexity of the facts themselves to thwart clearness and justice of perception, to substitute misleading fictions for workable ideas, and to deprive us of adequate checks upon those who consciously strive to mislead."
—Walter Lippmann, *Public Opinion*

We have discussed biases that operate within the human mind, which influence how we process information and develop beliefs and opinions. We have seen that the media influences public opinion by selecting and presenting information. But what information does the media present? A broad, pluralistic sample of the political ideas and ideologies in circulation, and the facts supporting and sustaining them? Or, are there pressures acting on the media that constrain it, making it likelier that only some ideas will be widespread, through selective presentation of arguments, facts, and frames?

According to the democratic ideal, political decisions are ultimately made by *the* people, although proximately through the people's representatives.[1] These representatives, although they have the authority to exercise political power, are constrained by the will of the people: if they displease the people in their exercise of authority, they should lose their authority and be replaced by a more obedient representative. The "will of the people," however, is tricky. The people rarely speak with one voice; more commonly, there will be disagreements and conflict over what "the people" want. These disagreements, alongside consensus and agreements, comprise the public sphere: the imaginary realm where citizens learn about, discuss, and debate public issues. The hope, central to democratic theory, is that through open debate in the public sphere, the best ideas will carry the day.[2] This debate will (hopefully) produce an informed public opinion, which will influence democratic representatives to govern wisely, in accordance with the winning ideas produced by and within the public sphere.

The public sphere consists of all communication that deals with political issues, and the biggest, most influential component of the public sphere in modern societies is the media. The media, then, is the cornerstone of modern democracy: without the media (or a *properly functioning* media), there is no public sphere; and without a public sphere, there can be no self-government. Hence legal scholar Edwin Baker's forceful conclusion that "a country is democratic only to the extent that the media, as well as elections, are structurally egalitarian and politically salient."[3]

For the media to play its ideal role as the infrastructure of the public sphere, it must at least provide unbiased information and space to all those who have an argument to set before the public.[4] It must produce an ecology of information neutral to particular ideas, memes, or ideologies. Scholars of the political economy of the media research the extent to which the media achieves this goal.[5] They have found several political-economic pressures powerfully influence the media, distorting the information ecology of the public sphere in complex but broadly predictable ways.

1 A Brief History of the Press

"If newspapers are useful in overthrowing tyrants, it is only to establish a tyranny of their own."
—James Fenimore Cooper, *The American Democrat*

For the majority of human history, the only way for information to spread was speech. To learn what was happening among a distant tribe dozens of kilometers away, one would have to visit them or listen to the report of an emissary. With the development of written language, this limitation was only barely surmounted: language barriers and widespread illiteracy remained powerful impediments to information flows between groups, and scrolls still needed delivering. The first Christians, for instance, were limited to handwritten texts and speech. They were evangelists because they had to be; there was no other way for them to spread the information their faith comprised but by preaching to whomever would listen.

After handwritten letters and books, the next major developments in communication occurred in China with the invention of printing in the seventh century,[6] and later in Africa with the development of the "talking drum." By encoding spoken messages into a drumbeat, which could be heard kilometers away and retransmitted by another drummer, messages could be communicated over a hundred kilometers in the space of an hour.[7] Meanwhile, in Europe the only way to communicate significant amounts of information was letters; and only by the fourteenth century were mail routes organized between major trading cities, while it took until the end of the seventeenth century for the mail to be accessible to the general public.[8]

While the first printing press with movable metal type was invented in Korea in the early fifteenth century, soon thereafter Gutenberg introduced the technology to Europe.[9] Its impact was inestimable. By reducing the human labor required to reproduce books, the printing press allowed for more copies and kinds of books to be produced. Having more copies of books stabilized and preserved existing knowledge (which had been subject to greater change over time in the age of oral and manuscript transmission), and having more kinds of books resulted in more widespread critiques of authority. The printing press was necessary for Martin Luther to spread his critique of the Catholic Church, and once his message had convinced many, the printing press allowed for the development of the first political propaganda, inspiring and fueling the massive bloodletting of Europe's religious wars.

With the rise of newspapers in the sixteenth century, the threat to authority represented by the printing press only increased. Governments censored newspapers and used them to secure their power.[10] Punishments for printing objectionable material were harsh, including breaking limbs and using an awl to bore through the tongue.[11] Nonetheless, seditious material continued to be printed and distributed. While governments could exercise control over printers within their borders, Europe's political diversity allowed for critical works to be published elsewhere for importation into the target country. Thanks to the ineffectiveness of state censorship, the small coterie of educated people in Europe had access to ideas that challenged the legitimacy of their political and religious leaders. This educated elite developed a political consciousness that rejected the absolute sovereignty of kings and demanded to be ruled by general laws approved by public opinion.[12]

The printing press created the conditions necessary for the emergence of a public sphere, where the seeds of the Enlightenment, and the American and French revolutions, were nurtured. Recognizing the power of the printing press and public opinion, Napoleon warned that "four hostile newspapers are more to be feared than 100,000 bayonets"[13] and Edmund Burke noted that "there were Three Estates in Parliament; but, in the Reporters' Gallery yonder, there sat a Fourth Estate more important far than they all."[14] From its beginnings, the media was a revolutionary force, as was recognized in a poem circulating through Germany at the time of the French revolution:

> The magic word before whose power
> Even the people's masters cower.
> Flapping their wigs officiously –
> Prick up your ears; the word – it is publicity.[15]

That the media was considered such a powerful force is surprising considering how few people read the political press: only 5% of the British population at the end of the eighteenth century.[16] A truly *mass* media was still in embryo. And this was exactly how the conservative elite in Europe wished it to be: it would not do to have the working masses educated, reading about politics, increasing their expectations, and making them discontent with their toil and drudgery.[17] In the southern American colonies, the knowledge gap between rulers and ruled was the same or worse—Virginia and Maryland outlawed printers. A royal governor of Virginia wrote to London in 1671, "I thank God, there are no free-schools, nor printing... for learning has brought disobedience, and heresy, and sects into the world, and printing has divulged them, and libels against the best government. God keep us from both!"[18] God, however, did not keep Virginia from learning and printing for long.

In 1735, a printer named John Peter Zenger published articles attacking a royal governor's abuses of power. Although there was no contest that by the letter of the law Zenger was guilty of seditious libel, his lawyer successfully used a jury nullification strategy, convincing the jurors to disregard the law and rule according to conscience and reason.[19] News of the verdict spread throughout the colonies, solidifying the idea that the proper role of the press was to protect popular liberty by scrutinizing government: it was to be the public's watchdog.[20] Royal officials soon gave up suppressing seditious libel, allowing the colonial press to criticize the royal administration.

Another key pre-revolutionary development was the British Parliament's 1765 imposition of a heavy tax on newspapers, pamphlets, and other printed material. This radicalized the American press, leading many newspapers to join in a campaign against British rule.[21] During the revolutionary war, the press was associated with the cause of freedom; and after winning independence, the American revolutionaries were quick to enshrine freedom of the press in the Constitution. This freedom was conceived less as journalistic independence from government interference and more as the freedom of individuals to access a printing press to disseminate their views[22]—and it was a legally-guaranteed freedom for which Europeans and others would have to wait over a century to enjoy.[23]

The American Revolution ushered in radical changes, foremost among them the free-school, the printing press, and the Post Office. While European nations taxed publications as a means of revenue and control, the revolutionary U.S. provided *subsidies* to newspapers in the form of artificially cheap postal rates, tax breaks, and government advertising.[24] A more indirect subsidy to the press was the network of locally financed and controlled schools, which provided a bigger market of the literate for newspapers. These forms of state intervention overcame the problems earlier political theorists believed would make a large republic impossible: by providing common schools and tying together a lightly populated, widespread territory through the political press and post office, the United States created a coherent, unified public sphere that was the envy of the contemporary world. Not only was the (free) population the best educated in the world, but the U.S. had more newspapers per capita than any other country.[25] European visitors to the U.S. in the early 1800s were amazed by the number of newspapers in circulation, even in the boondocks. Alexis de Tocqueville, traveling in frontier Michigan in 1831, wrote about his visit to a crude cabin on a back road: "You think that you have finally reached the home of the American peasant.

Mistake."[26] The resident of the cabin turned out to be literate and even offered de Tocqueville advice on French economic policy.

The early American press was rabidly partisan, and the first political parties grew out of the organizational base provided by newspapers.[27] Federalist newspapers railed against the Democratic-Republicans (including Thomas Jefferson), and Democratic-Republican newspapers pilloried the Federalists (including Alexander Hamilton).[28] The rancor and vitriol characteristic of the partisan press was enough to sour George Washington and Thomas Jefferson on newspapers; Jefferson lamented in 1807 that "[n]othing can now be believed which is seen in a newspaper. Truth itself becomes suspicious by being put into that polluted vehicle."[29] As the party system developed, newspapers remained key parts of established political parties and the *sine qua non* of upstart parties seeking a foothold in the political realm. Editors were more activists than journalists and often served as party committee members and convention organizers. As late as 1850, some 80–90% of newspapers in the USA had a party affiliation.[30]

Meanwhile in Britain, the 1800s witnessed the growth of combative, radical newspapers advancing the cause of the working class.[31] At first, the British government responded by levying heavy stamp taxes (as they had in the American colonies) on newspapers, such that only those marketed to the wealthy could survive. However, the radical press developed an underground network, surviving thousands of prosecutions and property seizures, until by 1836 the radical, unstamped press enjoyed a larger circulation than legal newspapers. In that year, the British authorities changed strategies; stamp taxes were reduced and coercive powers were increased to, in the words of the Chancellor of the Exchequer, "protect the capitalist" and "put down the unstamped papers."[32] These measures forced the radical press to increase their prices, but the papers' audience found creative ways to continue reading—and the radical press continued to grow. What finally destroyed the radical press in England was not government coercion, but free-market forces: specifically, the advertising market. When the government lifted taxes on advertising, newspapers came to rely more on advertising for revenue. This favored newspapers catering to a wealthier clientele, for which advertisers would pay more to gain access. As printing technology advanced, more expensive printing machines became necessary to survive in the market. The newer machines could produce more copies, which could be sold at an initial loss that was more than made up for through higher advertising revenue. The radical press found itself at a severe competitive disadvantage:

advertisers did not prize its working-class readership, so it could never match the "respectable" press in advertising revenue and so could not afford to keep up with costly technological advances. Eventually, at the hands of market forces, it met the fate that decades of government repression had failed to seal.

This same development in the newspaper market occurred in the U.S.[33] The traditional republican conception of the newspaper as a means of engaging citizens in the realm of politics faded and a new conception took hold: that of the newspaper as a means of attracting consumers whose attention could be sold to advertisers. Although ushered in by market forces, Paul Manning points out that these changes were "not the consequence of the preferences of particular individuals; rather it is the *structure* of the advertising market which produces a tendency to disadvantage the subordinate and to privilege the powerful."[34] In more anodyne language, James Hamilton explains that "[t]he shift from a party press to independence is a story of brand location, market segmentation [more accurately: conglomeration], economies of scale, technological change, and advertising incentives."[35] These changes were not merely the result of aggregate "revealed" consumer preferences: newsreaders did not simply *prefer* the cheaper, wider circulation, advertising-heavy papers.[36]

This development had contradictory effects on the independence of the press. As newspapers broke free of their strong links with political parties, they found themselves under another powerful influence: advertisers. As Jürgen Habermas argues, "[t]he history of the big daily papers in the second half of the 19th century proves that the press itself became manipulable to the extent that it became commercialized … it became the gate through which privileged private interests invaded the public sphere."[37] However, the increased revenues made possible by advertising also allowed for the development of (expensive) investigative reporting, or muckraking.[38]

From the mid-nineteenth to mid-twentieth century, the process of "professionalization" gradually changed the intensely partisan press into the neutral, "objective" press of today. The percentage of articles containing verifiable data rather than opinions increased, along with the share of articles relying on official sources.[39] Simultaneously, there developed centralized systems of supplying and distributing news: the Associated Press in the U.S., the Canadian Press in Canada, Agence France-Presse in France, and Reuters in Britain.[40] Alongside the professionalization of newspapers, centralized systems of news provision tended to produce a more uniform, homogenous style of reporting characterized by a focus not on the world itself, but on what is "new" about the world—very recent events, preferably dramatic—without providing much political analysis or historical context.[41]

Joseph Cannon, a former Speaker of the House in the early twentieth century, complained that the newly nonpartisan, professionalized, and commercialized press failed to present political arguments as effectively as the partisan press; further, "[t]he cut of a Congressman's whiskers of his clothes is [considered] a better subject for a human interest story than what he says in debate."[42] The British sociologist Leonard Hobhouse criticized the turn-of-the-century press as "more and more the monopoly of a few rich men," which instead of being "the organ of democracy" had become "the sounding board for whatever ideas commend themselves to the great material interests."[43] Journalists were critical of the professional turn too; Upton Sinclair decried the need of professional journalists to adapt their opinions to the "pocketbook of a new owner,"[44] and John Swinton, editor of the *New York Sun*, confessed of his profession that:

> There is no such thing as an independent press in America. I am paid for keeping my honest opinions out of the paper I am connected with. Any of you who would be so foolish as to write honest opinions would be out on the street looking for another job. ... We are the tools and vassals of the rich men behind the scenes. We are the jumping jacks; they pull the strings and we dance. Our talents, our possibilities and our lives are all the property of other men. We are intellectual prostitutes.[45]

2 A Brief History of Broadcast Media

In the 1910s, when radio was emerging as a technology accessible to hobbyists in the USA, before radio programming in its current form existed, it was primarily a tool for communication and education. For those of us who experienced the internet in the early-to-mid 1990s, this description of pre-broadcast radio in 1920 by Lee de Forest (considered "the father of radio")[46] is strangely familiar:

> It offers the widest limits, the keenest fascination, either for intense competition with others, near and far, or for quiet study and pure enjoyment in the still night hours as you welcome friendly visitors from the whole wide world.[47]

From the whole wide world to the World Wide Web. Just as many in the early days of the internet felt it would always be a tool for international communication and education, early radio enthusiasts felt that their medium would powerfully and exclusively serve the public good. In the early 1920s, airwaves were filled with nonprofit stations mainly affiliated with colleges and universities. Commercial stations were largely appendages to bricks-and-mortar businesses (newspapers, department stores, and power companies) so that, by 1929, few were earning profits of their own.[48] The business model of radio advertising had not been developed. In the early '20s, Herbert Hoover opined that it was "inconceivable that we should allow so great a possibility for service and for news and for entertainment and education to be drowned in advertising chatter,"[49] and the head of publicity for radio manufacturer Westinghouse advocated for the prohibition of radio advertising, claiming it "would ruin the radio business, for nobody would stand for it."[50] Even *Printer's Ink*, an advertising trade paper, considered radio an "objectionable advertising medium," and stated that "the family circle is not a public place, and advertising has no business intruding there unless it is invited."[51]

It was not long before commercial stations discovered not only that people *would* stand for radio advertising, but that through advertising, a radio license could become a veritable license to print money. AT&T, realizing it could leverage its monopoly over telephone lines to create the nation's first broadcasting network, became the leader in radio advertising. When radio revenues came primarily from the sale of equipment, it made business sense to allow as many broadcasters as possible (universities, churches, and other nonprofit entities): the more programming variety available, the more reason to buy a radio, and the more revenue for radio manufacturers. However, just as the rise of advertising in newspapers changed that industry's business model, so did advertising change the logic of the radio business. AT&T could spend more money on each radio program to maximize quality, transmit them via telephone lines to stations over the country, and recoup its expenses by selling nationwide advertising. As soon as this approach demonstrated success, competitors emerged. They were not only competing with AT&T for market share, but with the nation's nonprofit, noncommercial stations for radio bandwidth.[52]

In the fight against nonprofit radio stations, the commercial broadcasters united to lobby the Federal Radio Commission for control of the radio spectrum. By 1928, they won: the Commission set aside a majority of radio frequencies for commercial channels and the market for radio advertising boomed, leaping from barely existing before 1928 to $172 million annually by 1934.[53] Radio advertising had gone from an insignificant pariah to the dominant force in radio programming in less than a decade,[54] while nonprofit broadcasters, starved of the radio spectrum, declined. Between 1921 and 1936, 240 educational stations were established—but by the end of the period 80% had lost or sold their licenses.[55] The director of the University of Arkansas station lamented: "The Commission may boast that it has never cut an educational station off the air. It merely cuts off our head, our arms, and our legs, and then allows us to die a natural death."[56]

In Britain, commercial broadcasters were unable to secure a foothold before the government decided in 1922 to entrust the future of the medium to a British Broadcasting Company (BBC) monopoly. John Reith, the first general manager of the BBC, decided to use the airwaves to uplift the population, abjuring cheap entertainment in favor of high culture and educational programming. He was skeptical of commercial broadcasting's populist sensibilities, arguing that "[h]e who prides himself on giving what he thinks the public wants is often creating a fictitious demand for lower standards which he will then satisfy."[57] By 1934, *The Times of London* looked back and called it wise "to entrust broadcasting in this country to a single organization with an independent monopoly and with public service as its primary motive."[58] The British model was followed in Europe and Japan, while the U.S. model was copied throughout Latin America; in Canada and the Caribbean, a hybrid model was chosen.[59]

The U.S. government, instead of imagining what the future of broadcasting *should* be, merely accommodated the evolution of the radio business model and used its regulatory power to do the radio industry's bidding.[60] Because the key decisions over radio policy were made in the late 1920s, when business interests were at the height of their power, advertisers decided the future of the medium for decades.[61] Furthermore, the two main U.S. political parties went into debt to the commercial broadcasters for ads run during the 1928 and 1932 elections, leaving them in a delicate position when it came to regulating the airwaves.[62]

While the U.S. public largely ignored the battle between commercial and nonprofit broadcasters, the losing nonprofits were acutely aware of what was at stake. As a spokesman for an association of educational broadcasters warned in the early 1930s:

[C]ommercialized broadcasting as it is now regulated in America may threaten the very life of civilization by subjecting the human mind to all sorts of new pressures and selfish exploitations. ... There has never been in the entire history of the United States an example of mismanagement and lack of vision so colossal and far-reaching in its consequences as our turning of the radio channels almost exclusively into commercial hands. ... I believe we are dealing here with one of the most crucial issues that was ever presented to civilization at any time in its entire history.[63]

This may strike some as unduly alarmist, but in light of what we now know about media effects, it is hardly unwarranted.

A decade later, the same "father of radio" Lee de Forest wrote in an open letter to the National Association of Broadcasters: "What have you gentlemen done with my child? He was conceived as a potent instrumentality for culture, fine music, the uplifting of America's mass intelligence. You have debased the child...."[64] De Forest's complaint was widely shared. Major print publications from *Harpers*, *Time*, *Reader's Digest*, *Fortune*, and *Business Week* were strident in their criticism of the commercialization of radio.[65]

In response to such criticism, the National Association of Broadcasters hired Paul Lazarsfeld to perform a study of public opinion on radio published in 1946. The study revealed that a large majority of the population either did not mind or actively favored radio advertising. While this pleased the study's industry sponsors, Lazarsfeld acknowledged a significant caveat:

> It must be admitted, however, that a direct inquiry into people's dissatisfactions may not yield the most valid results. It is widely recognized in many fields of social research that, psychologically speaking, supply creates demand. ... Within certain limits, it is a recognized fact that people like what they get. ... A survey like the present one cannot tell what people would like if they had the opportunity to listen to different radio fare.[66]

Much like the commercialization of newspapers, the commercialization of radio proceeded according to a market logic that was other than the aggregate of true consumer preferences.

By the 1950s, a powerful competitor to radio had emerged in the USA: television. The US television market reached saturation in the mid-50s, and by the mid-60s television had exploded globally.[67] In 1949, on the eve of television's rise, a British journalist asked:

Thousands of people, and then people in millions, are going to become subject, to some degree, to their household screen. What will it mean to them? Good or ill? With this new power there are likely to be no half-measures; it will choose its way, and then do what it cannot stop itself from doing.[68]

However, even then, the future of television was not so open-ended; in the United States, the already-powerful radio broadcast networks determined television's future. They would apply the same business model, providing predominantly light, inoffensive entertainment to attract the largest (and most well-heeled) audience to sell to advertisers.

As a consequence, television evolved into a medium like radio, with critics raising the same concerns. In 1980, the United Nations' Educational, Scientific, and Cultural Organization (UNESCO) published a report warning that the media, and the economic pressures operating on it, could lead to greater inequalities, hierarchies, and increased social control. The report's author wrote that given the centrality of the media to all social, economic, and political activity worldwide, "human history becomes more and more a race between communication and catastrophe. Full use of communication in all its varied forms is vital to assure that humanity has more than a history … that our children are assured a future."[69]

3 The Fourth Branch of Government and the Marketplace of Ideas

While Edmund Burke had referred to the media centuries ago as the "Fourth Estate" for its role as a counterweight to authoritarian government,[70] the conception of the media as the fourth *branch* of government is tied to the U.S. context.[71] As in Burke's formulation, calling the media the fourth branch of government draws attention to its considerable power. Winning a political election is effectively impossible without the support of the media, or at least its attention. (Ask Jerry White, Virgil Goode, Rocky Anderson, or James Harris; all four ran in the 2012 U.S. presidential election and received negligible media coverage, remaining effectively unknown to the U.S. population.) Conceptualizing the media as the fourth branch of government also calls attention to the fact that it is the only branch without a counterweight; it is not subject to any constitutional system of checks and balances.[72] Instead, it is subject only to private, economic power, of owners and advertisers.

While the legislature is meant to write laws, the executive to apply them, and the judiciary to enforce and interpret them, the media is meant to maintain the public sphere where laws are first proposed and debated. In Habermas' conception, "[p]ublic debate was supposed to transform *voluntas* [will] into a *ratio* [reason] that in the public competition of private arguments came into being as the consensus about what was practically necessary in the interest of all."[73]

To nurture the public sphere, the media must provide a marketplace of ideas. Although this catchphrase has developed a liberal economic gloss from some commentators—suggesting the prescription that media companies be unregulated to provide a "free market" of media products—its original conception was limited to democratic, not economic, values.[74] That is, the marketplace of ideas metaphor originally referred to a public sphere in which all ideas could be propounded, discussed, and debated—not a *laissez faire* media market in which media companies could do as they pleased with no governmental oversight. The metaphor is commonly traced to John Milton and John Stuart Mill, although neither explicitly used it.[75] Both authors would likely have been hostile to the interpretation of the "marketplace of ideas" as an unregulated commercial media market; instead, their point was that the best hope for a self-governing society is to allow speakers of all political and ideological persuasions into the public sphere.[76]

This conception of a marketplace of ideas may have accurately described a bygone era, in which anyone who wanted to start a competitive newspaper or magazine could do so with little difficulty, but this is not the case today.[77] For one, the economics of media prevent all but the wealthiest or best financed from participating effectively in the modern public sphere.[78] Second, technological developments have changed the playing field. As former FCC commissioner Clifford Durr observed, the "soundest idea uttered on a street corner, or even in a public auditorium, can't hold its own against the most frivolous or vicious idea whispered into the microphone of a national network."[79] Before the question of free speech comes the question of "who controls the master switch,"[80] as former CBS News president Fred Friendly put it—and the marketplace of ideas is not supposed to come with a master switch. Legal scholar Stanley Ingber argues:

> [T]he marketplace of ideas is as flawed as the economic market. Due to developed legal doctrine and the inevitable effects of socialization

processes, mass communication technology, and unequal allocations of resources, ideas that support an entrenched power structure or ideology are most likely to gain acceptance within our current market. Conversely, those ideas that threaten such structures or ideologies are largely ignored in the marketplace.[81]

By excluding social groups and political perspectives from the mass media, the current marketplace of ideas looks less like store-studded 5th Avenue in New York and more like Pyongyang. While those with conventional and popular views are unlikely to notice distortions or barriers, dissidents and radicals shut out from the mass media are more perceptive.[82] Although many countries guarantee freedom of speech, Ingber points out that assuring an unpopular speaker that "he will incur no criminal penalty for his expression is of little value if he has no effective means of disseminating his views. A right that cannot be meaningfully exercised is, after all, no right at all."[83] While state censorship may be largely gone, limits on effective speech "are still present and still dangerous when the control is financial rather than political and administrative, when the bank and the chain shop have taken over from the Star Chamber and the censor."[84] Herbert Marcuse offers the same indictment: "[d]ifferent opinions and 'philosophies' can no longer compete peacefully for adherence and persuasion on rational grounds: the 'marketplace of ideas' is organized and delimited by those who determine the national and the individual interest."[85]

4 THE MEDIA OLIGOPOLY

A marketplace with one seller, or one landlord who owns all of the storefronts, is enough of a problem when the goods are mere consumer items. The problem is compounded in a marketplace of *ideas*, where the marketplace constitutes the public sphere. As early as 1945, the co-founder of the American Civil Liberties Union and legal counsel for the Newspaper Guild, Morris Ernst, wrote:

> The pipelines of thought to the minds of the nation are being contracted and squeezed. About thirty men realistically dominate the conduits of thought through the ether, the printing presses, and the silver screen. Without wide diversity of thought, freedom of speech and press become idle bits of a worn-out shibboleth. The cartelization of the mind of America is well on the way.[86]

Fears of this sort, and the complementary fear on the part of some media owners that popular concern would attract federal regulation, led to the formation of the Commission on the Freedom of the Press in 1944. The Commission was to spend two years investigating the state of the media in the United States, researching and hearing testimony from journalists, media critics, advertisers, and newspaper readers.[87] The Commission's report, issued in 1947, identified media concentration as one of three factors threatening press freedom.[88] Robert Hutchins, who was the final author, explained that the press had become a large-scale enterprise intertwined with finance and industry, subject to bias emanating from its economic structure. Increased concentration in the news media reduced competition and diversity of opinion, effectively silencing those who do not own a media company.[89] The Commission proposed that the press should become "common carriers" for the diversity of political opinion, subject to a new, independent agency to enforce an industry code of practice.[90]

This proposal was not implemented.[91] Although the Commission had been inspired and paid for by Henry Luce of *Time* magazine, its final report was distasteful to media owners. The industry counterattacked with charges of—what else?—communism and within a year the Report faded from public discussion. Its impact was blunted, but not eliminated: it did help codify the social responsibility model of the press, which had an impact on the norms of journalistic professionalism.

What was neither blunted nor eliminated, however, was the trend toward media concentration. This may have been slowed somewhat by the FCC, antitrust actions, and mid-century Supreme Court cases, but toward the end of the twentieth century the ideological and regulatory climate was of the let-the-market-work-its-magic sort.[92] Media mergers were thought to improve "efficiency," and the "free market" to unproblematically translate individual desires into optimal social outcomes.

The problem with such an economistic interpretation is that it confuses a *process* value for a *commodity* value.[93] Media mergers may reduce costs while providing the same *commodities* to consumers; greater consolidation may or may not reduce viewpoint diversity, depending on a variety of factors[94]; but this is beside the point. What is valued in the marketplace of ideas is the *process* by which some ideas gain more adherents than others: the process by which adherents have the ability to present their ideas for discussion and debate. Having this process intact provides a democratic safeguard. Even if a highly concentrated media market *did* provide a great deal of viewpoint diversity despite the inherent danger that fewer owners *could* restrict the number of viewpoints, an unconcentrated media market is superior for being intrinsically less vulnerable to this danger. (This is similar to the considerations underlying the "appearance of impropriety" standard for judicial ethics; here, the *potential* for impropriety is the evil to be avoided.)[95] Value considerations such as these are easy to lose in the weeds of empirical data.[96] However, the relevant evidence points to the negative effects of concentrated ownership.[97] For instance, an analysis of a large number of television stations, their owners, and the quality of their news programs found that as ownership size increased, news quality decreased.[98]

How concentrated, then, is the U.S. media? Surprisingly, answers vary. On one end is Ben Bagdikian, who finds that only five media conglomerates control most of the important media outlets[99]; on the other is Benjamin Compaine, contending that the media and information technology industries are unconcentrated compared to other sectors of the economy.[100] The overall level of concentration is probably somewhere in between,[101] but it depends on how one approaches the question.

According to one measure—the combined market share of a given media sector's four biggest companies—the US music (98%), television (84%), film (78%), and cable (61%) markets are highly concentrated, while the newspaper (48%) market seems unconcentrated; this in a country 98% of whose cities have only one daily newspaper.[102] The apparent discrepancy owes to the level of analysis: if concentration is measured nationwide, the newspaper industry is laudably unconcentrated; but if measured at the municipal level, the industry is terribly concentrated. Residents in the 98% of US cities with only one daily newspaper care little that they have the option of choosing another daily paper *if* they move to another city. Another point of confusion inheres in how an industry is defined: studies finding low levels of media industry concentration combine different media-related businesses (telephone companies, newspapers, computer hardware manufacturers, television networks, film studios, etc.) into "the media industry" for analysis.[103] Likewise, if instead of measuring concentration among car manufacturers, for instance, one combined car companies with bicycle, skateboard, and motorcycle manufacturers and train and bus companies into a "wheeled transport" industry, one would similarly expect low levels of concentration in this synthetic industry—even if car manufacturing proper were concentrated.[104]

A more sensible approach breaks down the media into its constituent industries and by locale. This was the approach taken by Eli Noam, whose impressive analysis found high levels of concentration in local radio, TV, cable, satellite, newspaper, magazine, and national broadcast television as well as internet portal markets.[105] Globally, the top ten media firms account for 80% of all media revenue.[106]

Media concentration is a traditional concern of the Left, but it is also a problem for the Right: as Milton Friedman and his mentor Henry Simons argued, capitalism is superior to socialism because it separates political from economic power.[107] But large, monopolistic firms vitiate this distinction, producing the same concentration of political and economic power conservatives fear. Nowhere is this concentration more concerning than in the mass media, with its unparalleled influence over political and cultural realms.[108] As Pedrinho Guareschi writes, "if a purely economic monopoly is already a social ill, then how much worse is a monopoly of values, beliefs, and symbols; the media cannot, for this reason, remain in the hands of only a few."[109]

The tendency toward monopoly is detrimental in other ways. Larger media firms can exert greater market power to manage demand, limit competition, and increase entry costs for would-be entrants.[110] Horizontally-integrated media conglomerates—corporations with holdings in multiple industries including media—are likelier to chip away at the old firewalls between news and advertising and are tempted (at the least) to tailor their news coverage to further the interests of their other business holdings.[111] Even the benefits of mergers (synergies, cost savings) in other industries are detrimental in the media context. A media merger that allows the newly formed company to reduce duplicative costs—primarily, journalists, and their salaries—reduces the positive externalities the redundant journalists would have produced, like reports exposing malfeasance in government or business.[112]

5 Journalism's Economic Crisis

Long before the internet threatened the business model of traditional journalism, the news media was cutting back on reporters, investigative resources, and foreign bureaus. In the 1970s and picking up steam in the '80s and '90s, television news in particular refocused from providing a public good and increasing the prestige of their parent company, to becoming as profitable as possible.[113] This involved firing journalists, increasing ad time, and reducing coverage of hard news. The cost-cutting process occurred while the news media was flush with cash, simply because media companies found it profitable in the short term.[114] The situation today, with sites like newspaperdeathwatch.com chronicling the impending demise of print journalism, has been a long time coming. While the number of employed journalists per capita has crashed since 2007, it had been in a long decline for the past two decades.[115]

In its attempt to attract the widest audience, the commercial news media has long devoted enormous attention to soft news like sports, entertainment, and lifestyle content. This strategy is failing in the internet age since soft news can be found for free on website devoted exclusively to these topics.[116] Newspaper circulation per capita has fallen by 50% over the half century and since 1980 the viewership of the nightly network news has nearly halved.[117] The number of journalists per capita in the United States has dropped by half since 1970, and the absolute number of staffers working in television news has halved since 1980.[118] From 2006 to 2013, total revenue supporting journalism in the U.S. fell by a third.[119] The revenue declines for newspapers have been starker: from their peak in 2005, *half* of advertising revenue had evaporated by 2012, and 17,000 newspaper jobs were lost.[120] Free online classified advertising and targeted advertising offered by internet portals have been major contributors to the drop in newspaper ad revenue, forcing many papers to become online-only and others into bankruptcy.[121] Overly optimistic mergers and acquisitions have piled debt on many newspapers, worsening their financial position.[122] Internet advertising, far from making up for lost print ad revenue, amounts to no more than 2% of all news ad revenue in the U.S.[123]

The crisis in journalism's bottom line is translating into a crisis in the quality of journalism. With fewer journalists to manage an increasing workload cranked up by the 24-hour news cycle, professional routines have been adversely affected. Journalists tend to be more desk-bound, dependent on sources, formulaic, and reliant on public relations material.[124] By 2009, for every journalist in the USA, there were four public relations specialists or managers.[125] And their sway is significant: Estimates range from 25 to 80% of US news is influenced by public relations specialists.[126] Compared to television news coverage in the 1970s, today's news spends less time covering Congress and more time covering celebrities.[127]

Unsurprisingly, the shift from a news media with a public service mission to a more profit-driven media correlates with the decline in public trust in the press. In 1973, 85% of those surveyed in the USA had either "a great deal" or "only some" confidence in the press; by 2008, 45% said they had "hardly any" confidence.[128] (A 2004 poll found only 10% of Americans have a great deal of confidence in the national news media—compared to 9% for lawyers.)[129] A recent survey of journalists found that the vast majority believes that the greatest problem facing the press is reduced quality due to commercial pressures.[130] Debra Clarke's in-depth study of news consumers in Canada found that the primary reason for dissatisfaction is the media's profit-driven nature, which pushes it toward a focus on soft news and away from investigative reporting and the provision of background and context for news stories.[131] This is as ironic as it is unfortunate: media companies' attempts to make the news more palatable and attractive have driven that audience to lose respect for it.[132] Sophia Kaitatzi-Whitlock explains that the "clash is between an anticipated, responsible 'civic trustee' role of the media, as political agency, versus the harshly economic role of the media as the 'pimp' of viewers."[133] As the news media becomes more a mere pimp selling its audience to advertisers, trust and use of the news media will likely continue to decline. Already, use of newspapers, news magazines, and television news in the U.S. is at a 50-year low.[134]

Given such a dire situation, many have understandably placed their hope in the internet that somehow, it will save and reinvigorate journalism. The available evidence suggests such hope is ill-founded.[135] Current studies of online journalism find it largely replicates the content and practices of print journalism (as well as its concentrated ownership structure).[136] The majority of the most-viewed internet sites are associated with traditional news companies and are owned by the top twenty largest media conglomerates.[137] Two of the most popular internet news sites, Google and Yahoo, merely reproduce material from the Associated Press and Reuters 85% of the time.[138] Advertising revenue for journalism on the internet looks similarly unpromising, with the lions' share of revenue going to ad networks and data handlers.[139]

6   Analyzing the Political Economy of Media—The Neoclassical Way

The news media provides a product different from most goods and services: while it would be irrational for an individual to choose to forgo food or clothing, it may be economically rational to choose not to "consume" information about politics.[140] After all, what chance does one person have to influence a government, even if that person used the news media to become informed? However, if a significant portion of the population remains ignorant, the entire society pays an enormous cost: in economic terms, the "externality" of being governed by ignoramuses or those who have tricked ignoramuses into voting for them. The news media can produce significant *positive* externalities too.[141] If only a few people pay for journalism that exposes corruption or malfeasance— yet word of this exposé spreads even to people who did not pay for it— everyone benefits. Whether democratic citizens are lamentably ignorant or laudably well-informed, the costs of bad or good government are shared, regardless of how many people paid for information from the media. The market, therefore, does not do what it should: apportion costs to those who receive a benefit and benefits to those who incurred a cost.

Why this is so can be answered within neoclassical economics. The news media produces a product with a marginal cost of zero, information, that is "nonrivalrous" (my consumption does not affect yours) and "nonexcludable" (it is difficult to exclude those who do not pay for news from receiving it—as media companies have learned through painful experience online).[142] As such, what the news media produces are "public goods," like military defense or public safety, which are traditionally viewed within neoclassical economics as best provided not by the market, but by the government.[143]

Instead of the interplay between supply and demand producing the optimal output and price for political information, the market fails to supply those willing to pay the *marginal* cost of news (which is next to nothing) but not the market price, and fails to reward producers of news for the social benefit they provide.[144] Since the social benefit the news media provides is enormous, a market failure in this sphere can produce a failed democracy. For these reasons, journalism has always been subsidized, whether by advertising, below-cost postal rates, and intellectual property law (by enforcing copyrights and trademarks, the government allows media companies monopoly-level profits on their brands and products).[145]

The preferred methodology of neoclassical economics is to create a mathematical model of the phenomenon—often complex and ingeniously devised—and draw conclusions on the basis of the model. (Here, the devil is less in the *details* of the models and more in drawing real-world conclusions from them[146] or picking the right one.)[147] Neoclassical economics can be useful in drawing out various economic forces and pressures operating in different kinds of markets and suggesting ways to make them run more efficiently or produce more positive social outcomes.

One such analysis modeled the effects of political "capture" of the media: when governments are able to exert undue influence on what the news media disseminates.[148] The study found that having a large number of independent media companies might make it more difficult for a government to control the news. It also found that government capture of the media is likely to lead to corruption and malfeasance, leaving voters unable to identify and remove corrupt or incompetent officials. Finally, the study's authors looked at a large sample of real-world countries and their media systems, finding a correlation between corruption, a high concentration of newspaper ownership, and high state ownership of newspapers.

In a similar vein, other economists modeled the effects of independent media sources on elections.[149] Their model suggested that having a maximum number of independent media outlets increases the likelihood that electoral competition will result in more balanced, less polarized, centrist policies. This result obtained even when the different media outlets were biased in favor of different political persuasions; however, this result was premised on the (psychologically dubious) assumption that voters interpret biased media "strategically," effectively de-biasing media reports as they are received.

Another study modeled the incentives of the media to provide news of relevance to different groups.[150] The model suggested that economic pressures induce the mass media to provide less news of relevance to small groups and the poor, and more news to large groups and segments of the population more valuable to advertisers (the young and rich). This translates into political policies biased toward the young and wealthy, as other groups will be unlikely to hear about policy proposals benefitting them. As a result, politicians planning to benefit the poor or minority groups are likely to receive less support at the ballot box.

Some of the most important such studies investigate the effects of concentrated media ownership and wealth inequality on democracies. In one, a model of voting decisions, inequality, and media ownership suggested that societies with more unequal distributions of wealth and more concentrated media ownership run a greater risk of the news media being captured by wealthy interests.[151] It suggested that concentrated wealth is likely to lead to concentrated media ownership, as those with disproportionate wealth will have interests that diverge sharply from the rest of the population, and are willing to pay a high price for control of the media since they have more to gain by manipulating the electorate. This capture of the media by those at the top of a highly unequal society is likely to lead to serious efficiency losses, as a misled electorate chooses inefficient policies that disproportionately benefit a small elite.

Using a different model, another study came to the same conclusions: the greater the inequality in a country, the higher the likelihood that the rich will spend money influencing the media to support policies in their interests at the expense of the non-wealthy.[152] Then, looking at real-world examples and a large, diverse sample of countries, the study found that income inequality is associated with lower levels of media freedom, particularly in democracies. The extent of media freedom, in turn, has a positive effect on the level of public spending on education and health—policies that benefit the entire society. In other words, societies that are more polarized between rich and poor are at greater risk of having their media captured by wealthy interests who will use it to convince the rest of the population to vote against their own interests.

Tom Ferguson goes further, arguing that "the public's prospects in a free market for information peopled only by profit-maximizing producers and totally self-interested consumers are even bleaker than indicated by existing discussions of 'imperfect markets' for information. In strict, neo-classical logic, for political information [useful to the non-wealthy], a market is unlikely to exist at all."[153] He provides a comparison between a media outlet providing accurate predictions of the stock market and one providing information about the political activities of businesses and their relationships with government officials. The former outlet will have an eager, willing audience of investors turning its information into profits. The latter may initially attract an audience, but one which will "face massive collective-action problems plus, commonly, direct repression and formidable transaction costs. While the social value of the information may be enormous, there is, from a purely self-interested individual economic standpoint, no reason to purchase the magazine at all. All one gets is a headache, accompanied perhaps by long-term demoralization."[154]

7   Media Bias

"You cannot hope to bribe or twist
(thank God!) the British journalist.
But, seeing what the man will do

unbribed, there's no occasion to."
—Humbert Wolfe, "Epigram"

While neoclassical studies are useful to arrive at a fuller understanding of the political economy of media, they need to be supplemented by analyses using a broader methodological toolkit. As one scientist put it, there are some truths that cannot be reached from the comfort of one's armchair.[155] To begin, there are a great variety of studies investigating the controversial topic of media bias: is the U.S. media biased in favor of the Right or Left, or is the issue of bias more complicated than this binary choice? And if the media does provide a biased supply of information and political analysis, what is the cause?

The results of a five-country survey of journalists working in the U.S., the U.K., Sweden, Italy, and Germany found that journalists place themselves on average a bit to the left of center on their respective national political spectrums.[156] Only in Italy did a significant minority place themselves significantly to the left of center; in all five countries, a substantial majority placed themselves at, or near, the midpoint of the political scale. When asked to place the news organization for which they worked on a political scale, however, journalists in a majority of countries placed them slightly to the *right* of center; in Italy, the average was slightly to the left, and in the U.S., the average was almost exactly in the center. The U.S. was also an outlier in the correlation between journalists' political beliefs and those of the news organizations they worked for: in the U.S., there was no correlation, while in Britain, Germany, Italy, and Sweden, left-of-center journalists tend to work for left-of-center news organizations and right-of-center journalists for right-of-center outlets.

The same study involved an experiment. The journalist participants were given a hypothetical scenario and asked to choose how to frame it for a newspaper article. The choices they were given reflected left-wing or right-wing biases, or a neutral tone. The result was that in all of the countries studied, journalists' political preferences "tend to shade the news rather than coloring it deeply."[157] (This dovetails with a similar, earlier experiment of elite US journalists, which found that when they "confront new information, they usually mange to process it without interjecting their own viewpoints.")[158] The U.S. and British news systems displayed the least partisan bias. In all five countries, journalists tended to be only slightly left of center and this exerted only a minimal effect on their reporting. However, several surveys of journalists in the U.S. have found that the vast majority tend to vote for Democratic over Republican candidates.[159]

Many of those who watch or read the news *perceive* political bias: a quarter of one survey's "very liberal" respondents, and nearly one half of "very conservative" respondents, perceived a great deal of political bias in television news.[160] Scores of books have been written to feed both perceptions, although those arguing a left-wing bias tend to focus on coverage of social issues, while those arguing a right-wing bias tend to focus on coverage of foreign policy issues.[161] Playing referee, Michael Schudson judges that "[r]ight-critics cannot point to media *structures* as biased against their views; the left-critics win hands down on this point. But the right-critics argue that reporters and editors at leading national news institutions have a predominantly liberal outlook. ... If corporate organization tilts unmistakably rightward, patterns of occupational recruitment veer just as sharply the other way."[162]

However, this applies only to the "Washington and New York-based news elite," and only to their views on social issues; on economics, they are centrist (from a U.S. perspective) or center-right (from a European perspective).[163] A more recent survey revealed Washington-based journalists to be significantly more conservative on economic issues (including health care) than the general population.[164] A snapshot of this news elite from 1980 found that its members

> grew up at a distance from the social and cultural traditions of small-town middle America. Instead, they came from big cities in the northeast and north central states. Their parents were mostly well off, highly educated members of the upper middle class, especially the educated professions. In short, they are a highly cosmopolitan group, with differentially eastern, urban, ethnic, upper-status, and secular roots.[165]

Those journalists with left-wing economic and political views are conspicuous by their rarity and have to work hard to hide their opinions from editors, fellow journalists, and readers.[166]

Left-wing and right-wing social scientists have measured political bias in the US media. Left-wing researchers Edward Herman and Noam Chomsky found a pronounced right-wing bias in foreign policy coverage using four detailed case studies.[167] In an examination using six case studies of media coverage of racial and sexual issues, right-wing researcher Jim Kuypers found a clear bias reflecting "liberal, upper-middle class, white baby-boomer activist politics."[168] He concluded that the U.S. media creates an environment in which those to the right of center, along with those to the left of a narrow band of mainstream liberal politics, will feel ignored, ostracized, or demonized—a conclusion Herman and Chomsky would likely agree with.

Another social scientist, Tim Groseclose, used an original method to measure media bias: first, members of the U.S. Congress were given a numerical score corresponding to their voting record on proposed laws, receiving points for every bill approved by a leading liberal interest group. (A higher score indicated a position on the Left; a lower score a position on the Right.) Then, all the transcribed speeches of these Congress members over a period of time were analyzed to measure the number of references to right-wing and left-wing think tanks, and media outlets were measured for their references to the same think tanks over the same period. By comparing media outlets' references to those of Congress members, media outlets were given a numerical score of political bias corresponding to the measure tracking the ideological pattern of Congress members' voting records. Using this measure, the majority of media outlets in the U.S. were found to have a left-of-center bias.[169] However, this measure only tracks right-wing or left-wing bias within the limited spectrum of political ideology in the U.S. Congress, which is significantly narrower than the global spectrum of political ideology.[170]

What this means is unclear: citing left-leaning think tanks more frequently than right-leaning think tanks suggests a leftward bias, but without detailed investigations into instances of reporting, it is hard to tell exactly how such a bias is manifested or whether something other than political bias is at work. The example Groseclose uses for bias in media coverage of social issues (partial birth abortion)[171] is apposite and telling, but his example of bias in media coverage of economic issues (George W. Bush's tax cuts)[172] is an awkward match for his thesis. Nonetheless, the accumulated evidence strongly suggests a left-of-center media bias for social issues.

Those who argue that the U.S. media is primarily biased toward the Right tend to reason that the left-of-center opinions of journalists carry less weight than the right-of-center opinions of the *owners* of media companies. In this view, claiming that liberal journalists bias the content of the news is like claiming that the preferences of cooks at McDonald's affect the menu.[173] This was the dominant view during the 1930s and

'40s, and right-wing bias in the media was particularly pronounced during the Red Scare in the late '40s.[174] A 1936 survey of journalists found a majority subject to ideological control from editors or owners; but surveys in 1960 and 1980 found a drastic reduction in such control.[175] More recent surveys have revealed that media owners have reasserted ideological control. In a survey of U.S. journalists in 2000, 41% of journalists said that they had avoided reporting stories—or had softened them—to benefit the owners of their media company.[176] A 2018 survey of television reporters found pressure from owners and executives to be the strongest influence on news content and coverage.[177]

One rough indication of contemporary right-wing bias is the amount of media coverage devoted to issues most voters consider Republicans to handle better (crime and national security) versus those considered to be handled better by Democrats (civil rights, labor, and social welfare). In an analysis of over 15,000 nightly news stories, Republican-owned issues appeared at a rate of 5 to 1 compared to Democrat-owned issues.[178] A right-wing bias appears particularly pronounced for foreign policy, where even left-leaning media outlets demonstrate bias in favor of military interventions.[179] And as foreign policy is a distant realm about which most citizens have no direct experience, the media exerts a stronger influence than over other issues.[180] The combination of right-wing bias and powerful media effects means that media coverage of foreign policy tends to push the population into supporting military intervention.[181] (And by omission—by *not* covering a military or covert intervention abroad, as occurs when political elites are in agreement on the policy—the media leaves the public in the dark, giving intervention *de facto* support.)[182]

Bias in coverage of economic policy is subtler and more mixed according to one study, with newspapers displaying partisan bias in the direction of their editors' (or owners') ideology for some issues and bias in the direction of their readership's ideology for others.[183] However, here as in foreign policy, it is safe to agree with Ralph Miliband that the media provides far more "to confirm conservative-minded viewers in *their* attitudes than is the case for 'radical' ones; as far as the latter are concerned, television, in any serious meaning of the word 'radical,' is a permanent exercise in dissuasion."[184] Michael Shudson agrees, writing that the "American media do not have a wide-screen view of the range of possible political positions. Compared to the press in most liberal democracies, they foreshorten the representation of views on the left...."[185] The spectrum of political bias in the media is in a fairly narrow center-right range for economic and foreign policy issues and excludes advocacy or even discussion of views considered "radical" on either the Left (significant wealth redistribution, pacifism) or Right (pure *laissez faire*, isolationism).

Additionally, media bias has arguably shifted over time within the U.S. During the first half of the twentieth century, the influence of conservative media owners dominated over that of liberal and socialist journalists.[186] In the second half, as ownership grew more concentrated in corporate form (but dispersed in terms of individual owners), the influence of socially-liberal journalists may have reached parity or even overwhelmed owner bias, at least until the '80s when the pendulum swung back to the Right.[187]

Ownership influence on the media does not overwhelm other influences on media content. Even one of the more ideological media owners, the right-wing Rupert Murdoch, for instance, once hired left-wing Thomas Frank to write an op-ed column. Furthermore, just as facts do not have wings, ideas do not emerge magically from interests (as Frank's *What's the Matter with Kansas* famously bemoaned). Walter Lippmann opined, "[t]he ordinary doctrine of self-interest usually omits altogether the cognitive function. So insistent is it on the fact that human beings finally refer all things to themselves, that it does not stop to notice that men's ideas of all things and of themselves are not instinctive. They are acquired."[188] In light of this, Jeffrey Friedman asks: "How, after all, would the putative corporate manipulators of cultural media figure out the direction in which they should skew the messages broadcast by their companies, if not by means of stereotypes about the world that come to them from the cultural media to which they themselves have been exposed—such as the television they have watched or the newspapers they have read (or the education they have received)?"[189] There is a reflexive, interpenetrating relationship inherent in ownership bias. Media owners are not the first movers, an uncaused cause of ideological bias in the outlets they own; their ideology does not spring from their material interests; rather, it too is influenced by cultural media of various forms and among other factors.

This is where ecological thinking brings clarity: ownership bias is merely one force among many, and whatever ideological bias owners have is itself the product of an ecology of information in which it developed. (Furthermore, whether and how that ideological bias is exerted on a media outlet involves its own complexities: hiring ideologically congenial editors and journalists is relatively simple, but issuing ideological directives that journalists follow obediently, without provoking attempts at subversion, or leaking out to the general public and hurting the outlet's credibility, is another matter.) Yet, despite the fact that our ideas are acquired rather than instinctive, and the process of acquisition is the chaotic, unpredictable result of countless interactions in the ecology of information, nonetheless we observe a strong correlation between having wealth and holding political and economic ideas serving (or purporting to serve) to protect and increase one's wealth.[190] Likewise, there is a correlation between *not* having wealth and having ideas serving (or purporting to serve) to redistribute wealth to the poor.[191]

8   Explanations for Media Bias: Market Determination

"Power corrupts, but lack of power corrupts absolutely."
—Adlai E. Stevenson, misquoting Lord Acton

Beyond the partisan claims (and counterclaims) about media bias, a different explanation proposes that media bias is best explained by economic factors: bias is profitable. Profitability helps explain not only political bias, but the bias against good journalism in favor of entertainment-focused news. This is not necessarily a story of greed—which implies free choice and will—but market pressures: the capitalist imperative articulated by Marx's "Accumulate, accumulate! That is Moses and the prophets!" Here, a *lack* of power corrupts; a lack of power in the face of market pressures that, if not accommodated, may lead to being weeded out of the market.

In James Hamilton's analysis of television news in the United States, he finds systematic bias in content and political ideology matching the ideological disposition of audience segments most desired by advertisers: women and young people.[192] Women are a desirable demographic because they make most purchasing decisions for households, and young people because they are viewed by advertisers as easier to influence to develop brand loyalties. Hence news programs that attract more women and young people command higher advertising rates. Although young people make up only about one-fifth of regular viewers of network news, they constitute nearly half of so-called marginal viewers—people who report that they only sometimes watch the news. News programmers often take regular viewers for granted and make programming decisions to attract marginal viewers; and since women and young people are more liberal than the US average, the news media displays a liberal bias on social issues to attract them.

Hamilton's analysis found that newspapers' coverage of crime did not correspond to crime trends but to audience demographics. Newspapers in cities with more elderly people focused less on violent crime, while newspapers in cities with more young males provided more salacious coverage of violence, regardless of changes in the occurrence of violent crime.[193] This pattern of audience-driven news coverage applies to several other issues, with the media giving more attention to issues favored by audiences.[194] And since audiences generally disfavor public affairs information, the commercial media receives little economic benefit from providing it, producing a downward spiral of public ignorance.[195] Only in local markets with a high demand for hard news does the media generously provide it; soft news (human interest stories, health tips) is more widely prevalent in markets with higher proportions of advertiser-desired young women.[196] "The market" does not ensure that media companies focus on what the population as a whole is interested in; only those residents who are desired by advertisers drive coverage. For instance, the incidence of poverty and food assistance in a city is *negatively* correlated with stories about food assistance programs or poverty.[197] Newspaper readers are unlikely to be poor or using food stamps and those who are poor are unattractive targets for advertisers.

The oft-lamented tendency of the news media to focus on negative stories is also driven by commercial pressures. Since the 1940s, studies of newspapers have found that readers are drawn to negative headlines.[198] This is in line with dozens of findings in experimental social psychology that the human mind is more powerfully affected by, and observant of, negative than positive phenomena.[199]

That market forces and commercial concerns determine the content of the news media is a powerful, *structural* hypothesis about the marketplace. It requires no conscious conspiracy on the part of media owners. In the end, however, the market determination hypothesis has problems.[200] Primary among them is the fact that even if media companies are at the mercy of the market, if some companies are relatively better than others at implementing profitmaking strategies then they also have the option of "subsidizing" other goals, like promoting their owners' ideology or business interests. Besides, the market determination hypothesis is a claim about the *long term*, but in the short term—years or decades—media companies can engage in ideological pursuits for long enough (before they are weeded out through market competition) to distort the public sphere, with lasting effects.

9   CENSORSHIP WITH AMERICAN CHARACTERISTICS: THE "PROPAGANDA MODEL"

"During the Cold War, a group of Russian journalists toured the United States. On the final day of their visit, they were asked by their hosts for their impressions. 'I have to tell you,' said their spokesman, 'that we were astonished to find, after reading all the newspapers and watching TV, that all the opinions on all the vital issues were, by and large, the same. To get that result in our country, we imprison people, we tear out their fingernails. Here, you don't have that. What's the secret?'"
—John Pilger, talk at Columbia University, April 4, 2006

Another structural model of media bias similar to the market determination hypothesis includes commercial pressures but adds several other factors influencing the supply of information provided by the media. While the market determination model of media bias explains why the news media tends toward liberal views on social issues, sensationalism, soft news, and a lack of investigative reporting or the provision of significant context for current events, the so-called propaganda model attempts to explain why the media covers international affairs the way it does.

Many Americans are still reeling from how the U.S. media covered the run-up to the invasion of Iraq, which was too deferential to the Bush administration's justifications for war and selective provision of evidence. This kind of deficient coverage is hardly new. In 1920, two of the era's leading journalists wrote a scathing review of the *New York Times*' coverage of the Russian Revolution, condemning it for an overreliance on official sources, a lack of independent investigation and fact-checking, and ideological bias. "[T]he news about Russia is a case of seeing not what was, but what men wished to see."[201] The propaganda model is an attempt to explain why the media covers foreign policy in a manner scarcely distinguishable from outright propaganda, without suggesting the existence of a conspiracy. (A conspiracy is highly unlikely to even be *possible* in a media system like that of the United States; the number of people required to execute a conspiracy would make its exposure a mathematical near-certainty in a just few years.)[202] Instead, like the market determination hypothesis, the propaganda model is purely *structural*; it explains propaganda-like results as emerging from structural features of the media, not any conscious intent on the part of journalists or conspiratorial directives from government official or media owners.

The propaganda model, as elaborated by Edward Herman and Noam Chomsky in the late 1980s, proposes that five structural forces or influences act as filters on the supply of information provided by the media, making some information likelier and other information less likely to appear in the news.[203] These are the size, ownership, and profit orientation of the mass media; the influence exerted by advertisers owing to the media's financial dependence on advertising revenue; source bias, or reliance on official sources for information; "flak," or organized pressure on the media through boycott, criticism, lawsuits, and other means to influence coverage; and the ideology of journalists and media owners (originally described as anticommunism in the '80s and today could be described as neoliberalism or adherence to the "war on terror" framework).[204] A sixth filter has since been proposed: occasional government influence over news content, by selectively providing misinformation to individual journalists (infamously, Judith Miller of the *New York Times*).[205]

Cumulatively, these filters tend to result in journalism with striking similarities to that of the Soviet Union. Many Soviet journalists felt that they were independent of state censorship because they never experienced it, but this resulted from their ideological affinity with the Soviet government.[206] Ironically, many Soviets argued that journalists in the U.S. were more constrained, due to the pressure of business interests on the press.[207] The Polish journalist Ryszard Kapuściński, who experienced his country's news media under communism and capitalism, argued there has been little improvement, only different mechanisms by which the common citizen is misinformed.[208]

The filters proposed by the propaganda model influence the ecology of information provided by the media without manipulation of journalists. This is an important feature not only of the propaganda model but of other non-conspiratorial explanations for media bias. Over a century ago, Karl Marx and Friedrich Engels argued that the wealthy control not only factories, but the means of producing ideas; they "rule also as thinkers, as producers of ideas, and regulate the production and distribution of ideas of their age: thus their ideas are the ruling ideas of the epoch."[209] Or as Ralph Miliband wrote of journalists in 1969:

[T]hey mostly "say what they like"; but this is mainly because their employers mostly like what they say, or at least find little in what they say which is objectionable. These "cultural workmen" are unlikely to be greatly troubled by the limitations and constriction imposed upon the mass media by the prevailing economic and political system, because their ideological and political makeup does not normally bring them up against these limitations. The leash they wear is sufficiently long to allow them as much freedom of movement as they themselves wish to have....[210]

More recently, a former producer at CBS explained that "everyone plays by the rules of the game if they want to stay in the game."[211] Pressures influencing journalists are built into the rules, as when overly critical journalists lose access to top sources in government.[212] Structural explanations of media bias like the propaganda model seek to provide a picture of the ecology of information in the media; they describe the structural factors explaining why some perspectives, ideas, memes, or information are more likely to appear than others. These structural explanations describe influences or filters operating on the media, not *determinants* as would be found in totalitarian societies.[213] The filters of the propaganda model are hardly omnipotent, and information often does evade or flow past them despite their being in effect,[214] like a net catching large fish but allowing minnows through.

Because they do not rely on conspiring agents, structural explanations such as the propaganda model can be criticized as "conspiratorial" only through misreading. Nevertheless, such sloppy criticism has been made.[215] Other critiques are merely weak[216] or argue that the propaganda model restates what other media researchers have pointed out before.[217] Besides inaccurate or underwhelming criticisms, the propaganda model has been largely ignored—even by researchers proposing similar structural models of media bias.[218]

However, cogent criticisms of the propaganda model have been made, focusing on its questionable applicability outside of the U.S. and the extent to which it downplays counteracting forces.[219] For instance, while there have been no empirical falsifications of the propaganda model's hypotheses since its introduction, this is only to be expected in the narrow political culture and uncompetitive media market of the United States.[220] Countries with a broader spectrum of political ideology and with a stronger public media are less likely to be accurately described by the propaganda model. As to whether the propaganda model downplays counteracting forces like journalists' autonomy, Herman and Chomsky wrote that "dissent and inconvenient information are kept within bounds and at the margins, so that while their presence shows that the system is not monolithic, they are not large enough to interfere unduly with the domination of the official agenda."[221] Whether their assessment is overly pessimistic is a matter for debate, and more importantly, empirical research.

So far, dozens of studies in Europe and North America (and one in Australia) have reinforced, refined, and extended the propaganda model of the media.[222] Other empirical investigations, while not explicitly using the propaganda model framework, have arrived at comparable conclusions.[223] As Edward Herman concluded his retrospective of the propaganda model a decade after its introduction: "[w]e are still waiting for our critics to provide a better model."[224]

10 The Ecology of Information in the Media: Key Influences

The market determination hypothesis of media bias may be incomplete, and the propaganda model may be given to an overly deterministic reading, but together they provide a solid foundation for understanding the ecology of information in the news media. The commercial pressure to sell audiences to advertisers at the highest possible rate, incorporated with the five (or six) filters of the propaganda model, powerfully explain what makes some information, facts, memes, or perspectives more likely to appear in the news.

Perhaps the most direct influence on journalists is the code of journalistic professionalism: the expectation that journalists should strive for objectivity and balance and avoid promoting their own political opinions or preferences. In practice, this form of professionalism leads to several negative outcomes. A strength of the partisan journalism of the nineteenth century was that it provided context for current events by framing them within a larger political ideology; modern professional journalism, however, tends to avoid context to evade ideological influence.[225] Journalists focus on providing a balance of views from official sources, making the news seem like little more than a concentrated stream of facts and official statements, often about personalized conflicts between politicians. This fragments the social world into disconnected and decontextualized events, ignoring social divisions in the attempt to attract an artificially unified, as-large-as-possible audience.[226] To the extent that they internalize the code of professionalism, journalists put on uniquely pernicious ideological blinders, of the invisible, "nonideological" variety. "An aversion to abstractions and philosophical issues may leave only unquestioned assumptions that are experienced as instinct. Many journalists who fancy themselves tough-minded pragmatists are instead captives of conventional wisdom, carriers of intellectual currents whose validity is taken for granted."[227]

The problems with contemporary journalistic professionalism are linked to the broader problem of source bias.[228] Not only is reliance on official sources (government and business spokespeople) part of the code of journalistic professionalism, but it is also half of a symbiosis between journalists and politicians: both need each other for professional survival and success.[229] This produces strong pressures on politicians to focus their efforts on issues the media will want to cover, and strong pressures on journalists to develop friendly relationships with politicians to gain access to fresh information. (This *quid pro quo* between journalists and their sources is also evident in business journalism, with company insiders trading private information in exchange for positive media coverage.)[230]

Source bias favors government officials in several ways.[231] The number of journalists and other media resources devoted to covering the government vastly exceeds that of any other sector. The amount and type of coverage of government officials is also exceptional: they receive more airtime and get to communicate their messages via pre-planned speeches, interviews, and press conferences. The way the media covers the government and its reliance on official sources leaves it open to manipulation by political operatives, who can create "newsworthy" events and manufacture conflicts—worst, they can cynically leverage journalistic norms of objectivity and balance to ensure that the media disseminates the most baseless of allegations and distortions.[232] Critics of the government rarely get such desirable media access, let alone the same media attention.[233]

Source bias does not exclusively favor government; rather, it operates to give an advantage in media access to any powerful social group whether in government or business, while further marginalizing groups without political or financial power. Those groups with power are more newsworthy by virtue of their greater influence and capacity to influence decision-making in other organizations; they have higher credibility stemming from their greater authority; they possess more information of value to journalists; they can better control information flows emerging from their organizations; they have more material and other resources; and they enjoy greater bargaining power with journalists.[234] Powerfully illustrating this analysis, a study of U.S. network news in 2001 by German research firm Media Tenor found that political and business elites were the predominant sources used.[235] 75% were Republicans, 25% were Democrats, and a mere 1% were Independents or members of other political parties; women made up only 15% of sources, and Whites made up 92% of the total; business representatives were over 35 times more prevalent as sources than representatives of labor unions. And as media companies cut ever more jobs for journalists, those who remain are less able to engage in investigative journalism, and more dependent on powerful sources in government and business.[236]

Perhaps nowhere else is source bias more dangerous than in coverage of international conflict. Here, the media's reliance on official sources tends toward a faithful adherence to the government's narrative. The U.S. media played this role during the majority of the Vietnam War, after the Truman and Eisenhower administrations had strengthened the government's ability to control information.[237] More recently, the media acted as a *de facto* propaganda arm of the government in the buildup to the invasion of Iraq, uncritically communicating hundreds of misleading or untruthful assertions by members of the Bush administration.[238] In times of *sudden* war or violent conflict, the media's dependence on official sources can be particularly damaging, as journalists are especially likely to retransmit the narrative provided by government officials without time to critically investigate.[239]

Source bias forms one of the propaganda model's filters, and one of its manifestations has been studied under the name of "indexing."[240] This occurs when journalists "index" the range of views expressed within government debate about an issue, instead of the range of views expressed among the population. Indexing tends to fill the public sphere with only the range of views expressed in public government debate, effectively silencing positions and perspectives that are not publicly propounded by officials. The indexing hypothesis was powerfully confirmed in a study of four years of *New York Times*' coverage of funding for the Nicaraguan *contras*: the ratio of opposition to support in the paper's editorial pages closely followed changes in the ratio of opposition to support in Congress.[241] A later test of the indexing hypothesis in a different foreign policy scenario found that the President rather than Congress controlled the terms of debate in the *Times*, and a lack of opposition in Congress forced the paper to index foreign elites to provide some weak balance.[242] The same pattern of indexing foreign elites when Congressional opposition is lacking was found in the run-up to the invasion of Iraq.[243]

Since the end of the Cold War, evidence suggests that the nature of indexing (and of the propaganda model's ideology filter) has changed. Instead of indexing only the range of debate in Congress, the media may be likelier to index a wider range of elite sources. A study comparing media coverage of conflicts with communist versus non-communist countries found significantly greater reliance on the range of debate in Congress when communism was involved.[244] Another study of media coverage of the early "war on terror" found that the media was again indexing foreign elites since opposition in Congress was lacking—however, these foreign voices of opposition tended to be marginalized in coverage.[245] While some argue that the commercial media is becoming more independent of government influence,[246] a study of newspaper coverage of the Abu Ghraib torture scandal found that the mainstream press closely followed the traditional pattern of indexing, providing attention only to the views of government elites even in the absence of meaningful debate; only the alternative press provided serious coverage of dissenting voices.[247]

Another key facet of the media's ecology of information arises from social psychology. "Pack journalism," a phenomenon wherein a large number of journalists cluster around a news site, copy and share information, and fail to confirm data using independent sources, has been proposed as a form of groupthink.[248] Social groups help reduce individual uncertainty by allowing for the creation of a consensus, which makes one's (shared) beliefs and opinions seem reliable.[249] In the context of journalism, social pressure produces a snowball effect: an emerging consensus among journalists becomes harder and harder to challenge, not only because it is more psychologically satisfying to go with the group, but copying the consensus is easier and cheaper, and challenging it may negatively impact a journalist's reputation.[250] (The internet likely adds speed and strength to this snowball effect.) In a survey of journalists in five Western countries, a majority in each said that wire services, other journalists in their own newsrooms, and journalists at leading national media outlets were important sources of guidance in making their news decisions.[251] (Editors too can be subject to similar social-psychological pressures.)[252] As one respected journalist explains,

[W]hen you hang around with other journalists, be it in Washington, D.C., or Shanghai, China, you all recirculate the same information. After a while that body of information becomes the common wisdom, which clouds your ability to process what you are seeing for yourself. Worse, when everyone is writing the same thing, a laziness sets in, and there's a tendency to accept what has been written as fact.[253]

This phenomenon was in effect during 2002, when journalists uniformly reported that weapons inspectors had been *thrown out* of Iraq in 1998 by Saddam's regime; whereas four years earlier, journalists had consistently reported instead that the inspectors had been *withdrawn* in anticipation of a US bombing offensive.[254]

Social pressures toward conformity among journalists are strengthened by their demographic similarities.[255] Scattered studies of demographic characteristics of journalists in Africa, Europe, and North America reveal that journalists are disproportionately male and come from middle-class families. Journalism is a demanding profession with irregular and long working hours; what little leisure time journalists have is often spent with other journalists. This further restricts journalists' exposure to the experiences of members of other social groups and strengthens the in-group bond shared by journalists.

Journalists can also be influenced by social pressure emanating from the groups they are covering. For instance, financial journalists have widely adopted the pro-market ideology of the financial market participants they cover,[256] and the business media has largely adopted the perspectives of central bank elites.[257] The existence of such influence on those whose job it is to critically monitor the economy has kept the public uninformed about, and unprepared for, developing economic crises. Doubtless reporters embedded with military units are also influenced by social pressures to adopt the views of the soldiers they live and work with, and who protect them.[258]

The core of the economic determination hypothesis is that the pressure for profits influences how the media covers issues; this is a "retail" influence. The propaganda model, however, points toward a wholesale influence emanating from media owners themselves, and the need to avoid displeasing companies that pay for advertisements. Both influences bring to the fore the fundamental conflict between the requirements of democracy and the demands of capitalism: the news media is forced to choose between coverage that attracts audiences and pleases advertisers while contributing little to good citizenship, and coverage that serves the public good but draws a smaller audience and displeases advertisers.[259] As one newspaper editor noted in the 1940s, the framers of the constitution could not foresee that the press would become so reliant on advertising, hence more dependent on "commercial interests than upon the people."[260] As a result, the United States and other liberal democracies have developed checks and balances to ensure that the *government* cannot unduly influence or control the media, but no measures to protect the media from private influence and control.[261]

Ownership of media outlets confers side benefits of power and influence not granted by owning companies in other industries, which is likely why private control of media firms is highly concentrated, and dispersed ownership is rarer in the news media than other businesses. In one study of 97 countries, only 4% of media enterprises were found to be widely held, a result the economist authors found "extreme" and indicative that "both the governments and the controlling private shareholders get the same benefit from controlling media outlets: the ability to influence public opinion and the political process."[262]

Dependence on ad revenue and the need to avoid displeasing advertisers also leaves a number of noticeable effects on media coverage.[263] News reports and editorials will tend to treat the products and business interests of advertisers with kid gloves, and media formats will be designed to create a "buying mood" among viewers and readers. (That is, providing "content the advertiser believes will leave [the] audience emotionally and intellectually most vulnerable to commercial messages.")[264] Moreover, partisanship (in nonpartisan outlets) and controversial topics will be avoided to maximize the audience by, for example, not offending advertisers' potential customers and avoiding boycotts.[265] Together, the result is a form of legal corruption: while a political representative or a judge would go to jail for taking money in exchange for influence, every day media companies receive advertising money from businesses looking to exert influence over the public sphere.[266] And while Panglossian economists engage in rhetorical and mathematical gymnastics to argue that the advertising model produces the best of all possible worlds, where consumers,' media companies,' and advertisers' interests meet in a happy equilibrium, their argument relies on patently unrealistic assumptions about information.[267]

Businesses are also a primary source of "flak," another of the propaganda model's filters, in the form of criticism, threatening lawsuits and boycotts, and other pressure tactics. For instance, the threat of a tobacco company lawsuit convinced CBS to kill a *60 Minutes* story on corporate malfeasance in the industry.[268] A former CEO of CNN stated in an interview that after the station presented reports of the killing of Afghan civilians during the US invasion, "big people in corporations were calling up and saying, 'You're being anti-American here.'"[269] This influenced him to instruct CNN journalists to reduce its coverage of civilian casualties. Additionally, the conglomerate structure of many media companies increases their vulnerability to flak from other companies. For example, book publishing subsidiaries of *Reader's Digest* and *Time* canceled publication of books critical of the advertising industry and Dupont, respectively, after their parent companies were threatened with advertising boycotts.[270]

The problem of business influence over the news media is possibly at its most dangerous in the realm of foreign policy. In an empirical analysis comparing the sources of influence on U.S. government officials' foreign policy decisions, business leaders were found to exert the greatest control, while public opinion produced no statistically measurable effect.[271] Part of the reason for this finding may be that media effects on public opinion are greatest for issues like foreign policy; so it is plausible that business influence over media content may be exerted to ensure that public opinion on international affairs is never sufficiently informed and aroused to jeopardize business leaders' control over foreign policy. This influence need not be direct; advertiser pressure to create a "buying mood" and avoid controversy may produce the same effect without intentional control.[272]

There is significant evidence that the U.S. government has been directly influencing news content. During the Cold War, the list of US media outlets that cooperated with the CIA reads like nothing less than a description of the core of the U.S. media system: CBS, ABC, NBC, *Time*, *Newsweek*, the *New York Times*, the Associated Press, United Press International, Reuters, Hearst Newspapers, Scripps-Howard, and others.[273] The details of such cooperation have remained largely undisclosed; but as a leading intelligence analyst put it, "one fact was incontrovertible: the CIA-media relationship had evolved by the late 1950s into a complicated matrix of people, activities and bonds of association."[274] For instance, in the 1950s CBS founder William Paley allowed the CIA to screen newsreels, eavesdrop on conversations between journalists, and permitted CIA agents to operate as CBS correspondents.[275] A 1976 Senate investigation into the CIA revealed the outlines of these extensive ties with the media (and academia, though the CIA refused to reveal details about these relationships during the investigation).[276] One key disclosure was the CIA's planting of anti-Allende propaganda in Chile, some of which later resurfaced as objective fact in the *New York Times* and the *Washington Post*.[277] Another aspect of the relationship was the high level at which the CIA exercised influence; as one former CIA official testified, "[y]ou don't need to manipulate *Time* magazine, for example, because there are Agency people at the management level."[278] Similar means of influencing the media have been used by intelligence agencies in Germany and Israel.[279]

Although the CIA promised to scale back their media operations under pressure from the Senate investigation, they have continued in some (undisclosed) fashion. Today, there is a high likelihood that intelligence agencies continue to work closely with the media, particularly since the U.S. military and political establishment has developed an approach toward information as a form of weaponry. The Pentagon considers information to be one domain, along with land, air, sea, and space, in which the US should exercise "full spectrum dominance."[280] Part of the military's strategy is the practice of selectively providing information to media outlets and embedding reporters in military units.[281] Embedded journalists have been shown to produce reports more favorable to the military, focusing on specific events to the exclusion of broad themes.[282] The U.S. and British military have programs to intervene on internet forums and social media to influence online debate.[283] The military has also taken to public relations as part of its "information operations" strategy, recently spending nearly $5 billion on PR in one year.[284] This adds a more overt filter to the propaganda model: instead of passive filters straining *out* pieces of information, this suggests the active *insertion* of information favorable to the government into the media ecology.

11   Conclusion

"Our wretched species is so made that those who walk on the well-trodden path always throw stones at those who are opening a new road. ... Compose some odes in praise of My Lord Superbus Fadus, some madrigals for his mistress;

dedicate a book on geography to his doorkeeper, and you will be well received; enlighten mankind, and you will be exterminated."
—Voltaire, *Philosophical Dictionary*, "Men of Letters"

The early United States was the envy of the enlightened world for its democratic government and media system. Over time, its news media has lost ground; as technology developed and political and economic ideologies evolved, the U.S. media has become too reliant on business and government. The marketplace of ideas it offers is one in which providers of ideas supporting the status quo enjoy a near monopoly, crowding out those offering critical perspectives.

Edwin Baker's warning deserves heeding:

> I share the sense of many keen observers in this country and around the world that American democracy is in trouble. America's strikingly inegalitarian domestic policy is surely unjust; policy choices systematically favoring private consumptive over public use of resources are incredibly unwise; and much of our foreign policy is not only immoral and illegal but entirely counterproductive from the perspective of any rational conception of domestic self-interest. Whether these policies reflect, as the democratic faith demands, views dominant within the public sphere is unclear. However, if that public sphere is itself uninformed or misinformed, if it is not robust in its debate of values and policies, any democratic faith is short-changed.[285]

The news media is the primary force shaping the ecology of information in modern societies. As it stands in the United States, the ideas, memes, and perspectives favored are those that benefit or are attractive to groups with power in society. Demographic groups with more disposable income tend to influence the supply of information because the media caters to their desires and prejudices to increase ad revenue. Large businesses pressure the media to offer a supply of information favorable to their interests, making information about corporate malfeasance or unsustainable economic trends less available in the public sphere. The government controls the supply of publicly available information about its own workings by controlling the media's access, unduly influencing the public's judgment about its policies and their alternatives.

The cumulative result of these political-economic pressures on the ecology of information in society is to keep the public sphere tethered to the status quo. Anyone seeking to change that status quo—geniuses or crackpots, prophets or charlatans—are without an effective voice.

In this ecology of information, ideas pushing in the direction of social evolution rather than stasis find poor soil and an inhospitable climate. This is a worrying state for an evolutionary system.

Notes

1. Hanna Fenichel Pitkin, *The Concept of Representation* (Berkeley, CA: University of California Press, 1967).
2. C. Edwin Baker, *Media Concentration and Democracy: Why Ownership Matters* (New York: Cambridge University Press, 2006): 11.
3. Ibid., 7.
4. Schudson, *The Power of News*, 28–29.
5. For example, Vincent Mosco, *The Political Economy of Communication* (New York: Sage, 2009).
6. Asa Briggs and Peter Burke, *Social History of the Media: From Gutenberg to the Internet* (New York: Polity, 2010): 13.
7. James Gleick, *The Information* (New York: Pantheon Books, 2011): 13–27.
8. Jürgen Habermas, *The Structural Transformation of the Public Sphere* (Cambridge, MA: MIT Press, 1991): 16.
9. Briggs and Burke, *A Social History*, 13–18, 69–73.
10. Habermas, *The Structural Transformation*, 22.
11. Jonathan M. Ladd, *Why Americans Hate the Media and How It Matters* (Princeton: Princeton University Press, 2011): 17.
12. Habermas, *The Structural Transformation*, 54.
13. Quoted in Briggs and Burke, *A Social History*, 88.
14. Quoted in Baker, *Media Concentration*, 5.
15. Quoted in Habermas, *Structural Transformation*, 70.
16. Paul Starr, *The Creation of the Media: Political Origins of Modern Communications* (New York: Basic Books, 2004): 41.
17. Habermas, *The Structural Transformation*, 102; Starr, *The Creation*, 40–41.
18. Quoted in Starr, *The Creation*, 53.
19. Clay S. Conrad, *Jury Nullification: The Evolution of a Doctrine* (Durham, NC: Carolina Academic Press, 1998): 32–38.
20. Starr, *The Creation*, 59.
21. Ibid., 65–68.
22. Ladd, *Why Americans Hate*, 21–22.
23. Briggs and Burke, *A Social History*, 182–183.
24. Geoffrey Cowan and David Westphal, "The Washington–Madison Solution," in *Will the Last Reporter Please Turn Out the Lights: The Collapse*

of Journalism and What Can Be Done to Fix It, ed. Robert W. McChesney and Victor Pickard, 133–137 (New York: The New Press, 2011): 133.
25. Robert W. McChesney, *Blowing the Roof off the Twenty-First Century: Media, Politics, and the Struggle for Post-capitalist Democracy* (New York: NYU Press, 2014): 232.
26. Quoted in Starr, *The Creation*, 48.
27. Ibid., 85.
28. Ladd, *Why Americans Hate*, 21.
29. Quoted in Ladd, *Why Americans Hate*, 27.
30. Ibid., 26.
31. James Curran, *Media and Power* (New York: Routledge, 2002): 79–103; Jonathan Hardy, *Critical Political Economy of the Media: An Introduction* (New York: Routledge, 2014): xiii–xiv.
32. Quoted in Curran, *Media and Power*, 83.
33. Starr, *The Creation*, 146.
34. Paul Manning, *News and News Sources: A Critical Introduction* (New York: Sage, 2001): 100.
35. James Hamilton, *All the News That's Fit to Sell: How the Market Transforms Information into News* (Princeton: Princeton University Press, 2004): 70.
36. C. Edwin Baker, "Advertising and a Democratic Press," *University of Pennsylvania Law Review* 140, no. 6 (1992): 2107–2119.
37. Habermas, *The Structural Transformation*, 185.
38. Starr, *The Creation*, 262.
39. Ladd, *Why Americans Hate*, 49.
40. Debra M. Clarke, *Journalism and Political Exclusion: Social Conditions of News Production and Reception* (Montreal: McGill-Queen's Press, 2014): 65.
41. Ibid., 144.
42. Quoted in Ladd, *Why Americans Hate*, 56.
43. Quoted in Briggs and Burke, *A Social History*, 191.
44. Quoted in Robert W. McChesney, *The Political Economy of Media: Enduring Issues, Emerging Dilemmas* (New York: Monthly Review Press, 2008): 74–75.
45. Seldes, *The Great Thoughts*, 405.
46. Victor Pickard, *America's Battle for Media Democracy: The Triumph of Corporate Libertarianism and the Future of Media Reform* (New York: Cambridge University Press, 2014): 9.
47. Quoted in Tim Wu, *The Master Switch: The Rise and Fall of Information Empires* (New York: Vintage, 2011): 37.
48. McChesney, *The Political Economy*, 158.
49. Quoted in Briggs and Burke, *A Social History*, 155.

50. Quoted in Wu, *The Master Switch*, 74.
51. Quoted in Starr, *The Creation*, 338.
52. Wu, *The Master Switch*, 74–85.
53. McChesney, *The Political Economy*, 161.
54. Starr, *The Creation*, 356.
55. Ibid., 352.
56. Quoted in McChesney, *The Political Economy*, 162.
57. Quoted in Wu, *The Master Switch*, 41.
58. Quoted in Briggs and Burke, *A Social History*, 201.
59. Briggs and Burke, *A Social History*, 201–204.
60. Wu, *The Master Switch*, 85.
61. Starr, *The Creation*, 362–363.
62. Ibid., 373.
63. Quoted in McChesney, *The Political Economy*, 189, 199.
64. Quoted in Pickard, *America's Battle*, 9.
65. Pickard, *America's Battle*, 14–15.
66. Quoted in Pickard, *America's Battle*, 28.
67. Briggs and Burke, *A Social History*, 216–217.
68. Quoted in Briggs and Burke, *A Social History*, 196.
69. Quoted in Robin Mansell and Kaarle Nordenstreng, "Great Media and Communication Debates: WSIS and the MacBride Report," *Information Technologies & International Development* 3, no. 4 (2006): 33.
70. Pedrinho A. Guareschi, *O Direito Humano à Comunicação: Pela Democratização da Mídia* (Petrópolis, RJ: Editora Vozes Limitada, 2013): 96.
71. Ladd, *Why Americans Hate*, 53.
72. Ignacio Ramonet, "Meios de Comunição: um Poder a Serviço de Interesses Privados?" in *Mídia, Poder e Contrapoder: da Concentração Monopólica À Democratização da Informação*, ed. Dênis de Moraes, 53–70 (São Paulo: Boitempo Editorial, 2013): 66.
73. Habermas, *The Structural Transformation*, 83, emphasis removed.
74. Philip M. Napoli, "The Marketplace of Ideas Metaphor in Communications Regulation," *Journal of Communication* 49, no. 4 (1999).
75. John Durham Peters, "'The Marketplace of Ideas': A History of the Concept," in *Toward a Political Economy of Culture: Capitalism and Communication in the Twenty-First Century*, ed. Andrew Calabrese and Colin Sparks, 65–82 (New York: Rowman and Littlefield, 2004): 66; Napoli, "The Marketplace of Ideas," 153.
76. Jürgen Habermas, "Political Communication in Media Society: Does Democracy Still Enjoy an Epistemic Dimension? The Impact of Normative Theory on Empirical Research," *Communication Theory* 16, no. 4 (2006): 420.

77. Raymond Williams, "The Existing Alternatives in Communications," *Monthly Review* 65, no. 3 (2013): 94.
78. Wu, *The Master Switch*, 122.
79. Quoted in Pickard, *America's Battle*, 106.
80. Wu, *The Master Switch*, 13.
81. Stanley Ingber, "The Marketplace of Ideas: A Legitimizing Myth," *Duke Law Journal*, no. 1 (1984): 17.
82. Clarke, *Journalism and Political*, 14–15, 49.
83. Ingber, "The Marketplace," 47.
84. Williams, "The Existing Alternatives," 101.
85. Herbert Marcuse, "Repressive Tolerance," in *A Critique of Pure Tolerance*, ed. Robert Paul Wolff et al., 1–12 (Boston: Beacon Press, 1969): 9.
86. Quoted in McChesney, *The Political Economy*, 78.
87. Pickard, *America's Battle*, 155–156.
88. Baker, *Media Concentration*, 2–3.
89. John D.H. Downing, "Media Ownership, Concentration, and Control: The Evolution of Debate," in *The Political Economy of Communications*, ed. Janet Wasko et al., 140–168 (New York: Wiley-Blackwell, 2011): 145.
90. Hardy, *Critical Political*, 65.
91. Pickard, *America's Battle*, 152–189.
92. Baker, *Media Concentration*.
93. Ibid., 13–16.
94. Daniel E. Ho and Kevin M. Quinn, "Viewpoint Diversity and Media Consolidation: An Empirical Study," *Stanford Law Review* (2009). However, see Baker, 1992, 2133–2135.
95. Nancy J. Moore, "Is the Appearance of Impropriety an Appropriate Standard for Disciplining Judges in the Twenty-First Century?" *Loyola University Chicago Law Journal* 41, no. 2 (2009): 300.
96. Baker, C. Edwin, "Ownership of Newspapers: The View from Positivist Social Science" (Research Paper R-12, Joan Shorenstein Center—Press, Politics, Public Policy, Harvard University John F. Kennedy School of Government, 1994).
97. Baker, *Media Concentration*, 25.
98. Tom Rosenstiel and Amy Mitchell, "Does Ownership Matter in Local Television News: A Five-Year Study of Ownership and Quality," Project for Excellence in Journalism, Washington, DC (2003).
99. Ben H. Bagdikian, *The New Media Monopoly* (Boston: Beacon Press, 2014).
100. Benjamin M. Compaine and Douglas Gomery, *Who Owns the Media? Competition and Concentration in the Mass Media Industry* (New York: Routledge, 2000).

101. Dwayne Winseck, "The Political Economies of Media: The Transformation of the Global Media Industries," in *The Political Economies of Media: The Transformation of the Global Media Industries*, ed. Dwayne Winseck and Dal Yong Jin, 3–48 (New York: Bloomsbury Academic, 2011): 20.
102. Winseck, "The State of Media," 36.
103. For example, Compaine, *Who Owns the Media?* Vizcarrondo, "Measuring Concentration."
104. Baker, *Media Concentration*, 60.
105. Eli Noam, *Media Ownership and Concentration in America* (Oxford: Oxford University Press, 2009): 62–74, 89, 143, 287, 378.
106. Winseck, "The State of Media," 37.
107. McChesney, *Blowing the Roof*, 229.
108. Andrew Calabrese and Colleen Mihal, "Liberal Fictions: The Public–Private Dichotomy in Media Policy," in *The Political Economy of Communications*, 229.
109. Guareschi, *O Direito Humano*, 51, translation mine.
110. Curran, *Media and Power*, 229.
111. Robert B. Horwitz, "On Media Concentration and the Diversity Question," *The Information Society* 21, no. 3 (2005): 185.
112. Baker, *Media Concentration*, 43–44.
113. Hamilton, *All the News*, 163–165. This process was the target of the darkly satirical 1976 film *Network*.
114. Natalie Fenton, "Deregulation or Democracy? New Media, News, Neoliberalism and the Public Interest," *Continuum: Journal of Media & Cultural Studies* 25, no. 1 (2011): 63–72; McChesney, *The Political Economy*, 123.
115. McChesney, *Blowing the Roof*, 160.
116. Robert G. Picard, "The Future of the News Industry," in *Media and Society*, ed. James Curran, 365–379 (New York: Bloomsbury, 2010): 372.
117. Ibid., 373.
118. Charles Lewis, *935 Lies: The Future of Truth and the Decline of America's Moral Integrity* (New York: PublicAffairs, 2014): 168.
119. Jesse Holcomb, "News Revenue Declines Despite Growth from New Sources," Pew Research Center's Journalism Project (April 3, 2014).
120. Jesse Holcomb and Amy Mitchell, "The Revenue Picture for American Journalism," Pew Research Center's Journalism Project (March 26, 2014).
121. Ladd, *Why Americans Hate*, 72.
122. Picard, "The Future of the News," 376.
123. Janine Jackson, "A Better Future for Journalism Requires a Clear-Eyed View of Its Present," in *Will the Last Reporter Please Turn Out*

the Lights, 204; Pew Research Center, "State of the News Media 2014: Overview" (March 2014).
124. Hardy, *Critical Political*, 130.
125. Robert W. McChesney and John Nichols, *The Death and Life of American Journalism: The Media Revolution That Will Begin the World Again* (New York: Nation Books, 2011): 290.
126. Cameron, Glen T., Lynne M. Sallot, and Patricia A. Curtin, "Public Relations and the Production of News: A Critical Review and Theoretical Framework," *Annals of the International Communication Association* 20, no. 1 (1997): 111–155.
127. Hamilton, *All the News*, 176–185.
128. Ladd, *Why Americans Hate*, 88–89.
129. Ladd, *Why Americans Hate*, 1.
130. Joan Pedro, "The Propaganda Model in the Early 21st Century (Parts I & II)," *International Journal of Communication* 5 (2011): 1876.
131. Clarke, *Journalism and Political*, 179, 215, 227, 266.
132. Ladd, *Why Americans Hate*, 197.
133. Sophia Kaitatzi-Whitlock, "The Political Economy of Political Ignorance," in *The Political Economy of Communications*, 469.
134. Lewis, *935 Lies*, 166.
135. Foster and McChesney, 2011, 19.
136. Clarke, *Journalism and Political*, 39–41.
137. Baker, *Media Concentration*, 112.
138. Hardy, *Critical Political*, 131.
139. Ibid., 150.
140. Hamilton, *All the News*, 30–31.
141. Baker, *Media Concentration*, 29–30.
142. Pickard, *America's Battle*, 213–214.
143. N. Gregory Mankiw, *Principles of Economics*, 7th ed. (Mason, OH: Cengage Learning, 2014): 215–217.
144. Hamilton, *All the News*, 28–29.
145. Baker, *Media Concentration*, 31–32.
146. See, e.g., Tony Lawson, *Economics and Reality* (New York: Routledge, 2006).
147. Dani Rodrik, *Economics Rules: The Rights and Wrongs of the Dismal Science* (New York: W. W. Norton & Company, 2015).
148. Timothy Besley and Andrea Prat, "Handcuffs for the Grabbing Hand? The Role of the Media in Political Accountability," *American Economic Review* 96, no. 3 (2006).
149. Jimmy Chan and Wing Suen, "Media as Watchdogs: The Role of News Media in Electoral Competition," *European Economic Review* 53, no. 7 (2009).

150. David Strömberg, "Mass Media Competition, Political Competition, and Public Policy," *The Review of Economic Studies* 71, no. 1 (2004).
151. Giacomo Corneo, "Media Capture in a Democracy: The Role of Wealth Concentration," *Journal of Public Economics* 90, no. 1 (2006).
152. Maria Petrova, "Inequality and Media Capture," *Journal of Public Economics* 92, no. 1 (2008).
153. Ferguson, *Golden Rule*, 402.
154. Ibid., 402–403, references removed.
155. Francisco Gil-White, "Let the Meme Be (a Meme)," in *Culture, Nature, Memes*, ed. Thorsten Botz-Bornstein, 158–190 (New York: Cambridge Scholars, 2008): 174.
156. Thomas E. Patterson and Wolfgang Donsbach, "News Decisions: Journalists as Partisan Actors," *Political Communication* 13, no. 4 (1996).
157. Ibid., 463.
158. S. Robert Lichter et al., *The Media Elite* (Bethesda, MA: Adler & Adler, 1986): 63–71.
159. See, e.g., Jim A. Kuypers, *Press Bias and Politics: How the Media Frame Controversial Issues* (Westport, CT: Praeger, 2002): 205; Tim Groseclose, *Left Turn: How Liberal Media Bias Distorts the American Mind* (New York: Macmillan, 2011): 100.
160. Hamilton, *All the News*, 72–73.
161. Ladd, *Why Americans Hate*, 79–81.
162. Schudson, *The Power of News*, 6.
163. Ibid., 7; S. Lichter et al., *The Media Elite*, 13–19, 29–31, 41–42.
164. David Croteau, "Challenging the 'Liberal Media' Claim," *Extra!* 11, no. 4 (1998); David Croteau, "Examining the 'Liberal Media' Claim: Journalists' Views on Politics, Economic and Social Policy (Including Health Care), and Media Coverage," *International Journal of Health Services* 29, no. 3 (1999).
165. Lichter et al., *The Media Elite*, 22–23.
166. A. Kent MacDonald, "Boring from Within the Bourgeois Press: Part One," *Monthly Review* 40, no. 6 (1988); A. Kent MacDonald, "Boring from Within the Bourgeois Press: Part Two," *Monthly Review* 40, no. 7 (1988).
167. Edward S. Herman, and Noam Chomsky, *Manufacturing Consent: The Political Economy of the Mass Media* (New York: Pantheon, 2002).
168. Kuypers, *Press Bias*, 244.
169. Groseclose, *Left Turn*, 152–156.
170. Ibid., 137.
171. Ibid., 161–168.
172. Ibid., 178–191.

173. Uscinski, *The People's News*, 31.
174. Pickard, *America's Battle*, 19, 126.
175. Lichter et al., *The Media Elite*, 43–44.
176. Columbia Journalism Review and The Pew Research Center, "Self Censorship: How Often and Why," The Pew Research Center for the People & the Press (March 30, 2000).
177. Rita Colistra, "Power Pressures and Pocketbook Concerns: Perceptions of Organizational Influences on News Content in the Television Industry," *International Journal of Communication* 12 (2018).
178. Joseph E. Uscinski, *The People's News: Media, Politics, and the Demands of Capitalism* (New York: NYU Press, 2014): 95–97.
179. David Edwards and David Cromwell, *Guardians of Power: The Myth of the Liberal Media* (London: Pluto Books, 2006).
180. Sandra J. Ball-Rokeach and Melvin L. DeFleur, "A Dependency Model of Mass-Media Effects," *Communication Research* 3, no. 1 (1976); Wayne Wanta et al., "Agenda Setting and International News: Media Influence on Public Perceptions of Foreign Nations," *Journalism & Mass Communication Quarterly* 81, no. 2 (2004); and Cui Zhang and Charles William Meadows III, "International Coverage, Foreign Policy, and National Image: Exploring the Complexities of Media Coverage, Public Opinion, and Presidential Agenda," *International Journal of Communication* 6 (2012).
181. Matthew A. Baum and Philip B.K. Potter, "The Relationships Between Mass Media, Public Opinion, and Foreign Policy: Toward a Theoretical Synthesis," *Annual Review of Political Science* 11 (2008).
182. Philip J. Powlick and Andrew Z. Katz, "Defining the American Public Opinion/Foreign Policy Nexus," *Mershon International Studies Review* 42, no. Supplement 1 (1998).
183. Valentino Larcinese et al., "Partisan Bias in Economic News: Evidence on the Agenda-Setting Behavior of US Newspapers," *Journal of Public Economics* 95, no. 9 (2011).
184. Ralph Miliband, "Communications in Capitalist Society," *Monthly Review* 65, no. 3 (2013).
185. Schudson, *The Power of News*, 5.
186. S. Robert Lichter et al., *The Media Elite*, 6–7, 43–44.
187. Schudson, *The Power of News*, 182–185.
188. Lippmann, *Public Opinion*, 101.
189. Jeffrey Friedman, "Public Opinion: Bringing the Media Back In," *Critical Review* 15, no. 3–4 (2003): 239–260.
190. Benjamin I. Page et al., "Democracy and the Policy Preferences of Wealthy Americans," *Perspectives on Politics* 11, no. 1 (2013).
191. Delli Carpini and Keeter, *What Americans Know*, 242–243.

192. Hamilton, *All the News*.
193. Hamilton, *All the News*, 154–159.
194. Uscinski, *The People's News*, 63–70.
195. Hamilton, *All the News*, 12.
196. Ibid., 139, 141.
197. Ibid., 151.
198. Uscinski, *The People's News*, 21.
199. Baumeister et al., "Bad Is Stronger Than Good."
200. Baker, *Media Concentration*, 92.
201. Walter Lippmann and Charles Merz, "A Test of the News," *New Republic* 23, no. 296 (1920): 3.
202. David Robert Grimes, "On the Viability of Conspiratorial Beliefs," *PloS One* 11, no. 1 (2016).
203. Herman and Chomsky, *Manufacturing Consent*.
204. Eric Herring and Piers Robinson, "Too Polemical or Too Critical? Chomsky on the Study of the News Media and US Foreign Policy," *Review of International Studies* 29, no. 4 (2003): 556.
205. Oliver Boyd-Barrett, "Judith Miller, the New York Times, and the Propaganda Model," *Journalism Studies* 5, no. 4 (2004): 436.
206. McChesney, *The Political Economy*, 129–130.
207. Pickard, *America's Battle*, 130.
208. Serrano, "Democracia e Liberdade," 77.
209. Karl Marx and Frederick Engels, *The German Ideology* (New York: International Publishers, 2010): 64–65.
210. Miliband, "Communications in Capitalist Society," 88.
211. Quoted in Danny Schechter, *The More You Watch, The Less You Know: News Wars/(Sub)Merged Hopes/Media Adventures* (New York: Seven Stories Press, 1999): 53.
212. Edwards and Cromwell, *Guardians of Power*, 148.
213. Manning, *News and News Sources*, 37.
214. Pedro, "The Propaganda Model," 1892.
215. See, e.g., Schudson, *The Power of News*, 4; Uscinski, *The People's News*, 29.
216. Kurt Lang and Gladys Engel Lang, "Noam Chomsky and the Manufacture of Consent for American Foreign Policy," *Political Communication* 21, no. 1 (2004); in response, see Jeffery Klaehn and Andrew Mullen, "The Propaganda Model and Sociology: Understanding the Media and Society," *Synaesthesia: Communication across Cultures* 1, no. 1 (2010): 33–34.
217. John Corner, "The Model in Question: A Response to Klaehn on Herman and Chomsky," *European Journal of Communication* 18, no. 3 (2003).

218. Andrew Mullen, "Twenty Years On: The Second-Order Prediction of the Herman-Chomsky Propaganda Model," *Media, Culture & Society* 32, no. 4 (2010).
219. Hardy, *Critical Political*, 44–46.
220. Sparks, "Extending and Refining," 69, 81–82.
221. Herman and Chomsky, *Manufacturing Consent*, xii.
222. Pedro, "The Propaganda Model," 1909; Klaehn and Mullen, "Sociology," 27; and Peter Thompson, "Market Manipulation? Applying the Propaganda Model to Financial Media Reporting," *Westminster Papers in Communication and Culture* 6, no. 2 (2009).
223. See, e.g., Robert M. Entman, *Projections of Power: Framing News, Public Opinion, and Us Foreign Policy* (Chicago: University of Chicago Press, 2004): 147–162; Mullen, "Twenty Years On."
224. Herman, "The Propaganda Model," 111.
225. McChesney, *The Political Economy*, 33.
226. Clarke, *Journalism and Political*, 92.
227. Lichter et al., *The Media Elite*, 297.
228. Pedro, "The Propaganda Model," 1915–1916.
229. See, e.g., Aeron Davis, "Investigating Journalist Influences on Political Issue Agendas at Westminster," *Political Communication* 24, no. 2 (2007).
230. Alexander Dyck and Luigi Zingales, "The Media and Asset Prices," Working Paper, Harvard Business School, 2003.
231. Clarke, *Journalism and Political*, 93–94.
232. Ibid., 250–251.
233. Guareschi, *O Direito Humano*, 82; Schudson, 1995, 24–25.
234. Manning, *News and News Sources*, 150.
235. Ina Howard, "Power Sources," FAIR, May 1, 2002, http://fair.org/extra-online-articles/power-sources/.
236. Manning, *News and News Sources*, 167.
237. Clarence R. Wyatt, *Paper Soldiers: The American Press and the Vietnam War* (University of Chicago Press, 1995): 15–17, 170–179.
238. Lewis, *935 Lies*, 253–259.
239. Chiara de Franco, *Media Power and the Transformation of War* (New York: Palgrave Macmillan, 2012): 177.
240. Herring and Robinson, "Too Polemical," 557.
241. W. Lance Bennett, "Toward a Theory of Press-State Relations in the United States," *Journal of Communication* 40, no. 2 (1990).
242. Scott L. Althaus et al., "Revising the Indexing Hypothesis: Officials, Media, and the Libya Crisis," *Political Communication* 13, no. 4 (1996).
243. Entman, *Projections of Power*, 153.

244. John Zaller and Dennis Chiu, "Government's Little Helper: US Press Coverage of Foreign Policy Crises, 1945–1991," *Political Communication* 13, no. 4 (1996).
245. Andre Billeaudeaux et al., "News Norms, Indexing and a Unified Government: Reporting During the Early Stages of a Global War on Terror," *Global Media Journal* 2, no. 3 (2003).
246. See, e.g., Brian McNair, "From Control to Chaos: Towards a New Sociology of Journalism," *Media, Culture & Society* 25, no. 4 (2003).
247. W. Lance Bennett, et al., "None Dare Call It Torture: Indexing and the Limits of Press Independence in the Abu Ghraib Scandal," *Journal of Communication* 56, no. 3 (2006).
248. Jonathan Matusitz and Gerald-Mark Breen, "An Examination of Pack Journalism as a Form of Groupthink: A Theoretical and Qualitative Analysis," *Journal of Human Behavior in the Social Environment* 22, no. 7 (2012).
249. Wolfgang Donsbach, "Psychology of News Decisions: Factors Behind Journalists' Professional Behavior," *Journalism* 5, no. 2 (2004): 138–139.
250. Hamilton, *All the News*, 22–23, 28.
251. Donsbach, "Psychology of News," 140–142.
252. See, e.g., Tsan-Kuo Chang and Jae-Won Lee, "US Gatekeepers and the New World Information Order: Journalistic Qualities and Editorial Positions," *Political Communication* 10, no. 3 (1993).
253. Maurice Murad, "Shouting at the Crocodile," in *Into the Buzzsaw: Leading Journalists Expose the Myth of a Free Press*, ed. Kristina Borjesson, 77–102 (Amherst, NY: Prometheus Books, 2002): 88.
254. Edwards and Cromwell, *Guardians of Power*, 37–41.
255. Clarke, *Journalism and Political*, 79–85; 202–203.
256. Aeron Davis, "Mediation, Financialization, and the Global Financial Crisis: An Inverted Political Economy Perspective," in *The Political Economies of Media*.
257. Marc-André Pigeon, "The Wizard of Oz: Peering Behind the Curtain on the Relationship Between Central Banks and the Business Media," in *The Political Economies of Media*.
258. David Miller, "Information Dominance: The Philosophy of Total Propaganda Control," in *War, Media, and Propaganda: A Global Perspective*, ed. Yahya R. Kamalipour and Nancy Snow, 7–16 (New York: Rowman & Littlefield, 2004): 10.
259. Uscinski, *The People's News*, 11–17.
260. Quoted in Pickard, *America's Battle*, 132.
261. Curran, *Media and Power*, 224.

262. Simeon Djankov et al., "Who Owns the Media?" *Journal of Law and Economics* 46 (2003): 357.
263. Baker, "Advertising," 2139, 2167; Hardy, *Critical Political*, 144–147, 152–154.
264. Baker, "Advertising," 2142, 2154.
265. Ibid., at 2156–2157.
266. Serrano, "Democracia e Liberdade," 73.
267. Baker, "Advertising," 2174.
268. Lewis, *935 Lies*, 142–144.
269. Quoted in Pedro, "The Propaganda Model," 1886.
270. Baker, *Media Concentration*, 38–41.
271. Lawrence R. Jacobs and Benjamin I. Page, "Who Influences US Foreign Policy?" *American Political Science Review* 99, no. 1 (2005).
272. Baker, "Advertising," 2153–2164.
273. Carl Bernstein, "How America's Most Powerful News Media Worked Hand in Glove with the Central Intelligence Agency and Why the Church Committee Covered It Up," *Rolling Stone* (October 22, 1977): 56.
274. Loch K. Johnson, "The CIA and the Media," *Intelligence and National Security* 1, no. 2 (1986): 145.
275. Lewis, *935 Lies*, 158–159.
276. Bernstein, "How America's," 65.
277. Johnson, "The CIA and the Media," 158.
278. Bernstein, "How America's," 66.
279. Shlomo Shpiro, "The Media Strategies of Intelligence Services." *International Journal of Intelligence and CounterIntelligence* 14, no. 4 (2001): 485–502.
280. Miller, "Information Dominance," 7.
281. Robin Brown, "Spinning the War: Political Communications, Information Operations and Public Diplomacy in the War on Terrorism," in *War and the Media: Reporting Conflict 24/7*, ed. Daya Kishan Thussu and Des Freedman, 87–100 (London: Sage, 2003); de Franco, *Media Power*, 180.
282. Michael Pfau, "Embedded Reporting During the Invasion and Occupation of Iraq: How the Embedding of Journalists Affects Television News Reports," *Journal of Broadcasting & Electronic Media* 49, no. 4 (2005).
283. Roslyn Fuller, *Beasts and Gods: How Democracy Changed Its Meaning and Lost Its Purpose* (London: Zed Books, 2015): 315–317.
284. Associated Press, "Pentagon Sets Sights on Public Opinion," *MSNBC* (February 5, 2009).
285. Baker, *Media Concentration*, 201–202.

CHAPTER 7

Comparing Media Systems: What a Difference Supply Makes

"*The free press is the ubiquitous vigilant eye of a people's soul, the embodiment of a people's faith in itself, the eloquent link that connects the individual with the state and the world, the embodied culture that transforms material struggles into intellectual struggles and idealises their crude material form. It is a people's frank confession to itself, and the redeeming power of confession is well known. It is the spiritual mirror in which a people can see itself, and self-examination is the first condition of wisdom.*"
—Karl Marx, "On Freedom of the Press"

In the century and a half since one of the world's best-known journalists wrote these words, the media has become ever more an indispensible "link that connects the individual with the state and the world." The Prince of Machiavelli's day has been replaced by the Electronic Prince, enjoying a hegemonic role in modern societies. As Pedro Gilberto Gomes observes, "it is increasingly the case that for something to be recognized as real, it must first be mediatized."[1]

The central position of the media in modern politics makes it a political issue of foremost importance. The media is the "locus of societal understanding,"[2] it is the infrastructure of the public sphere. A malfunctioning media guarantees a malfunctioning public sphere, makes democracy impossible, and vitiates the promise of self-government. Venício de Lima writes:

Without the right to a public voice – the right to speak and be heard – the free citizen does not exist. Without a democratic public opinion, the principle of popular sovereignty cannot be established. ... The failure to constitute a *democratic* public opinion is a central impasse today, because it structurally affects the formation of democratic legitimacy in all areas requiring decisive historical changes.[3]

This perspective hardly differs from that of Thomas Jefferson, who recognized that since a democracy is guided by the will of the people, that will must be enlightened—not manipulated, manufactured, or unduly influenced by one voice or chorus that drowns out all others.[4]

For democracies, the question is only *how* to provide the free and open public sphere democracy requires. Whether these ends are best achieved by the media's absolute freedom from government, or from government regulation of the media, is beside the point. Yet we cannot rule out that innate cognitive limitations prevent *any* type of media system from producing an informed citizenry. Our flawed psychology may make such a standard unrealistic. To address this possibility, we must examine the variety of media systems that exist today and their effects.

1   What Democracy Needs from Its Media

"*I know no safe depositary of the ultimate powers of the society but the people themselves; and if we think them not enlightened enough to exercise their control with a wholesome discretion, the remedy is not to take it from them, but to inform their discretion by education. This is the true corrective of abuses of constitutional power.*"
—Thomas Jefferson writing to William C. Jarvis, 1820

Nearly a century ago, Walter Lippmann wrote:

The world about which each man is supposed to have opinions has become so complicated as to defy his powers of understanding. ... What men who make the study of politics a vocation cannot do, the man who has an hour a day for newspapers and talk cannot possibly hope to do. He must seize catchwords and headlines or nothing.[5]

Today, the world has become more complicated, and in addition to newspapers, we have television and the internet to take up our free time and defy our powers of understanding. This being the case, what are we to make of the "informed citizen" as a requirement of democracy? Just how much information would one need to be "informed"—and can we realistically expect a media system to provide it?

Some media scholars suggest that democracy can exist even with a largely uninformed citizenry and a media that does not provide ample politically relevant information or a broad range of debate. John Zaller has argued for a "burglar alarm" standard for the media: Instead of attempting to provide a steady stream of information about every politically relevant topic, journalists should preferentially cover issues that require urgent attention.[6] Likewise, Doris Graber has argued for a "monitorial citizen" standard, in which citizens do not need to be fully informed, but only to survey the political scene with enough attention to detect major threats.[7] In doing so, "monitorial citizens" paying attention to "burglar alarms," but remaining largely ignorant about the political realm, can still fulfill the duties of democratic citizenship by using heuristics, or rules of thumb, to make voting decisions.[8] From this perspective, even a low-information media diet can sustain a healthy democracy. Citizens merely need to pay attention when the media raises the alarm about serious threats; during normal times, citizens can simply pick up information here and there to decide their votes. (For instance, hearing that a candidate is "pro-business" is not much information, but even without reading the candidate's political platform, with this minimal information one might accurately surmise that the candidate wants to lower taxes, weaken unions, and reduce regulation.) Even if the media does not provide a wide range of informed opinions, this is not a serious problem: after all, only those within the political mainstream have a chance of enacting their ideas into law, hence, these are the ideas that citizens most need to know. Given that our brains have limited information-processing capabilities, might this reduced standard suffice?

Critics have noted that this is a very U.S.-centered perspective (making it seem like apologetics for the unusual and historically high levels of ignorance in the United States compared to Western Europe), and that information matters tremendously for political decision-making, such that even the cleverest of heuristics cannot serve as a substitute.[9] Moreover, the "burglar alarm" or "monitorial citizen" standard is set up in opposition to a straw man: no one argues that citizens become the human equivalent of Google, responding to political queries with nearly all information in existence. Furthermore, the U.S. media already operates in burglar alarm mode, blaring away not only at serious threats in the political environment, but also to attract attention to sensationalistic stories about disasters, lurid reports on crime, and whatever else maximizes advertising revenue. The media is not putting people to sleep with an overabundance of information, but acting like the boy who cried wolf and losing the trust of audiences. Instead of the "burglar alarm" or "monitorial citizen" standard, the media should try to approximate the "full news" ideal, covering all events and decisions that may affect quality of life.[10]

A great deal of research demonstrates that heuristics cannot play the same political role as knowledge. When asked to describe what major political parties stand for, only knowledge of hard news correlates strongly with being able to correctly identify party positions. Knowledge of soft news is *negatively* associated.[11] This poses serious problems when voting: for instance, U.S. conservatives with low levels of political knowledge believe that the Republican Party supports government regulation of the economy as much as the Democratic Party.[12] This inaccuracy alone can frustrate their ability to cast an informed vote. A statistical analysis of political opinions and knowledge found that opinions are strongly dependent on information—to the extent that if all citizens were equally well informed about politics, one of every five policy issues would likely have a different collective preference.[13]

Naturally, one's opinion on political issues involves many factors, including education, class, personal, and family history. Although levels of education are a primary factor in how much political information people pick up from their media environment, TV news helps reduce knowledge gaps between those with high and low levels of education.[14] The policy-specific information the media provides is particularly important, as a series of experiments demonstrated: even (and especially) among those with high levels of general political knowledge, exposure to policy-specific information produces a significant influence on judgments.[15] Another experimental study found that the effects of education and political sophistication are greatly reduced, if not eliminated, by exposure to specific, diagnostic policy information.[16] Other factors like class and personal history can also be overwhelmed by a lack of information, as another study found: as a group, the highly informed held a variety of different opinions consonant with their backgrounds, while the uninformed showed little difference in opinion despite a variety of differences in background.[17] In other words, without information about a policy, we are unable to turn our predispositions into dispositions or recognize our interests.

An economic analysis of over 100 countries found that government performance and corruption were powerfully influenced by the presence of free and regular elections, and how well-informed the citizenry is. The study's authors explained that "the presence of a well-informed electorate in a democratic setting explains between one-half and two-thirds of the variance in the levels of governmental performance and corruption"—a greater effect than even a country's relative economic development.[18] A subsequent study found that this effect occurs over several election cycles: a well-informed citizenry learns which policies are in their favor and which politicians are corrupt, and votes accordingly, improving government in the long run.[19]

Political information is particularly essential regarding foreign policy, where one's education is unlikely to provide relevant guidance.[20] An experiment on support for foreign military intervention came to this conclusion, with those exposed to specific information on the intervention expressing less support than the uninformed.[21] Furthermore, the experiment's participants who had received relevant information demonstrated more stable opinions about the intervention over time, while still adjusting their opinions as reports about the conflict trickled in.

We cannot expect any media system to produce omniscient citizens. Nonetheless, we know that a country's population can be better informed than the U.S. population. Therefore, Graber is correct that one should not view "the media through the rose-colored glasses of an ideal but quite impossible world,"[22] and expect more than human cognitive limitations permit. But given the closer-to-ideal, contemporary European experience of a less commercialized, more regulated media system leading to a better-informed citizenry—no rose-colored glasses are needed. Perhaps we, as Graber observes, should not "ignore the fact that most U.S. media are commercial enterprises that must be concerned with attracting the kinds of clienteles and advertisers that allow them to make substantial profits."[23]

2 Commercialism and Its Discontents

"The proposal of any new law or regulation which comes from [businessmen], ought always to be listened to with great precaution, and ought never to be adopted till after having been long and carefully examined, not only with the most scrupulous, but with the most suspicious attention. It comes from an order of men, whose interest is never exactly the same with that of the public,

> *who have generally an interest to deceive and even to oppress the public, and who accordingly have, upon many occasions, both deceived and oppressed it."*
> —Adam Smith, *An Inquiry into the Nature and Cause of the Wealth of Nations*

If commercialism tends to push media systems farther from the democratic ideal, this problem is hardly limited to the United States. Policymakers in the U.S. and U.K. have demonstrated a primary concern with the business interests of media companies, the result of successful lobbying and a textbook case of regulatory capture.[24] In Europe generally, commercial interests have had more of a challenge, as European governments' initial media policies were to implement public service rather than commercial systems. However, over the past decades Europe's media systems have been largely opened to commercial TV, and where once countries had only a few public service channels, today there are nearly 9000. Just as Markus Prior demonstrated within the U.S., Europe is starting to evince the same "mo' media, mo' problems" phenomena: fewer viewers catching newscasts inadvertently, tuning into one of the more prevalent entertainment options and thereby producing greater gaps in political knowledge.[25] Simultaneously, commercialization and the reduction of subsidies in the European newspaper system are threatening papers that serve segments of society other than business or attract anything besides the broadest audience with a bland, uncontroversial style.[26] Unfortunately, this trend is global.[27]

To some, this is unobjectionable or even praiseworthy.[28] The news media is an institution comprising professionals who cannot work without a salary; funding for the media must come from somewhere, and where better than the advertising market? Funding from the government could come with strings attached, jeopardizing the objectivity and neutrality of the news. The threat of government censorship would increase alongside financial reliance on government funding. Commercial funding, on the other hand, comes from hundreds and thousands of dispersed businesses, which would need seemingly improbable coordination to exert a similar censoring pressure.

Nevertheless, commercial funding brings its own dangers. When the First Amendment was written, printing presses were relatively cheap and the number of active, literate citizens was roughly the same as the number of citizens who could afford to engage in publication.[29] Since there were no mass-circulation newspapers dominating the market, anyone's pamphlet or news-sheet could compete. (Even personal—not yet "private"—letters could be freely quoted in colonial-era newspapers.)[30] Today, however, costs of entering the contemporary newspaper market are out of reach for the overwhelming majority of active, literate citizens. Broadcast television and radio are by their technological nature constrained by the scarcity of the electromagnetic spectrum—so even if cost were no object, spectrum scarcity would limit entrants. While spectrum scarcity does not apply to satellite, cable, or internet television, the cost of entry in these markets is even greater than newspapers. Whether scarcity is caused by technological or financial limitations, the results are the same.[31] The U.S. Supreme Court has held (regarding technological scarcity) that barriers to entering media markets can produce a situation of "unlimited private censorship," as the few who do own media companies can transmit only views they agree with, effectively censoring others.[32]

Unlimited private censorship has emerged as a structural feature of the modern media. As Stanley Ingber explains:

> No one today seriously would argue that picketing and leafleting are as effective communication devices as newspapers and broadcasting. Access to the mass media is crucial to anyone wishing to disseminate his views widely. Nevertheless, monopolistic practices, economies of scale, and an unequal distribution of resources have made it difficult for new ventures to enter the business of mass communications. Restriction of entry to the economically advantaged quells voices today that might have been heard in the time of the town meeting and the pamphleteer. The media consequently carry great power to suggest and shape articulated thought. Media owners and managers, rather than the individuals wishing to speak, thus determine which persons, facts, and ideas shall reach the public.[33]

The advertising alternative to government funding, with its danger of government censorship, is not absolute independence, but an alternate form of dependence.[34] Dependence on advertising increases the danger of private censorship, at the least muting or diluting critical reporting on business. Ironically, since large media companies depend on good relations with governments to receive favorable regulation, private control of the media can produce the same effects as government censorship. This interpenetration of private and government power prompted one legal scholar to argue:

Analogies to the military-industrial complex can now be found in our media industry. Large media interests control profitability though their unique political and social influence, just as armament companies have been able to control profitability through their ties to the military. Indeed, the phenomenon might be called a media-political complex.... Due to powerful gatekeeping ability and dazzling agenda-setting power, media conglomerates have an enormous potential to shape political decision in their favor, often without public awareness.[35]

While some libertarians might be relieved to find the insignia of a private security firm rather than a national flag on the uniform of the jack-booted thugs who break down their door, most of us feel differently. Likewise with media censorship: what does it matter if the censor is a government employee applying a propaganda strategy or a private employee carrying out a business plan? As the constitutional and communications law professor Jerome Barron notes:

> If freedom of expression cannot be secured because entry into the communication media is not free but is confined as a matter of discretion by a few private hands, the sense of the justice of existing institutions, which freedom of expression is designed to assure, vanishes from some section of our population as surely as if access to the media were restricted by the government. ...The constitutional admonition against abridgment of speech and press is at present not applied to the very interests which have real power to effect such abridgment.[36]

Although Americans take great pride in the First Amendment, it was written to provide a free press in a radically different media environment. Doris Graber notes that today, the "media are not structured to perform the functions that America's founders expected of them."[37] Nonetheless, belief in a free press persists; it is useful and necessary for politicians, provides credibility and status for journalists, and is psychologically comforting for citizens.[38] Jan Oberg's suggestion rings true: "Perhaps we must begin to question the concept of a free media, if the main freedoms the most influential media choose to practice are the freedom to not investigate and not to question the war system of their own society, the freedom to be as biased as they please, and the freedom not to investigate what is not officially stated."[39]

Variations of the problem of commercial pressures vitiating freedom of the press and freedom of expression exist in all countries with commercialized media systems. The fundamental cause is explained by the Brazilian jurist Fábio Konder Comparato:

> It never hurts to reiterate that the public is in opposition to the private [viz., that which is owned]. The *public* is what pertains to all. The *private* is what pertains exclusively to one or some. The community or society is the exact opposite of private property. In this sense, one could say that freedom of expression, as a fundamental right, cannot possibly be the object of anyone's property ownership, because it is an essential attribute of the human person, a right common to all. Now, if the freedom of expression is currently exercised through the necessary mediation of the mass media [the means of communicating with the masses], then these cannot, logically speaking, be the object of corporate ownership in the private interest.[40]

Without the ability to *be* one of the few voices talking, or at least influencing what they say, we are practically deprived of our right to speak *to* society. If anyone proposed that we allocate speech rights through a pricing system, whereby only those who command the highest price for their speech are awarded the *right to speak*, we would consider this undemocratic. Yet this is the status quo in commercialized media systems—except worse, because its actual participants, advertisers, determine the pricing market for speech rather than the audience.[41] As Clifford Christians and Kaarle Nordenstreng conclude:

> Under such conditions we cannot speak of the will of the people; this is merely a reflection, an echo of the message originated by a small group of privileged individuals who exercise control over the channels of power, influence and communication. When this is the case, the so-called free market economy, which calls itself a society of free choice, is not entitled to look down on so-called totalitarian societies.[42]

In addition to the tension between commercialized mass media and freedom of expression, there are concrete, practical deficiencies in how the commercial media transmits important political information. The more commercialized media systems are particularly threatening for younger generations, who disproportionately ignore highly informative programming and opt for entertainment.[43] And even highly informative, hard news programming has been observed to be turning softer and less informative under the pressure of commercialization.[44]

Coverage of government actions tends to focus on "human impact" anecdotes in lieu of serious analysis of policies' content and consequences, and more time is devoted to "news" about the entertainment industry.[45] Visuals in TV news come to be used less to convey information and more to promote and legitimize the newscast itself.[46] While the use of vapid, largely information-free "image bites" is common to the media systems of the U.S. and Europe, their use on commercial vs. public stations is more widespread.[47]

Even the internet, which many hope to be the *deus ex machina* generating a happy ending after these troubling developments, is not (yet) up to the task. Most netizens' entry point to the internet is Google, whose algorithm favors news outlets with scale and established brand presence.[48] Furthermore, journalism on the internet comes predominantly from existing newspaper and TV news companies,[49] and links to their websites exhibit a "power law" distribution: "the rich get richer" as more people link to well-established news websites, drawing more traffic and leading to still further links driving still more traffic.[50]

Given the evidence, it is hard to dispute Natalie Fenton's conclusion that "[r]elying on fully commercial enterprises for the deliverance of news and current affairs journalism that purports to be for the public good and in the public interest has failed."[51] Our historically understandable but dangerously myopic focus on the danger of *government* censorship has distracted us from equally threatening private censorship. As Edmund Burke warned, we would be wise to treat both forms of censorship the same, regardless of the words we use to describe them:

> Wise men will apply their remedies to vices, not to names; to the causes of evil which are permanent, not to the occasional organs by which they act, and the transitory modes in which they appear. Otherwise you will be wise historically, a fool in practice. ... You are terrifying yourselves with ghosts and apparitions, whilst your house is the haunt of robbers.[52]

3 Commercialism Does Not Guarantee Pluralism

Once it is recognized how "private censorship" can exist within a commercialized media system, it is easier to see why the commercial media fails to provide the kind of pluralistic debate required for democracy. Media companies are often conceived of as vendors in a marketplace of ideas, a metaphor which implies the same diversity of perspectives as there is a diversity of goods offered in a thriving market. But a marketplace does not necessarily entail diversity. Unfortunately, as media economist Wayne Fu points out, "[v]iews that market operation can promote social objectives are plagued by ignorance about the viability of the presumed causal link between market structure and these prescribed performances."[53] While there are bazaars, street markets, and mega-malls that sell every imaginable item, there are also commissaries, company stores, and government-operated shops selling a frustratingly limited set of wares. Hence, the provision of diversity is a question not of *whether* a market exists, but what *kind* of market exists.

The degree of pluralism of a commercial media marketplace is not the direct result of the degree of concentration within the market. This point can be confused by indexes of media diversity which merely count the *number* of media outlets rather than the diversity of their contents and viewpoints.[54] Even a perfect media monopolist would feel commercial pressure to differentiate its products to capture all niches in the market; and in a perfectly competitive market with countless media outlets, the competition to attract the most desirable audience segments could lead to little more than a profusion of derivative, copycat products.[55] In fact, the intense competition in a highly populated media market might make it less likely that any outlet will take on costly investigative reporting, investigations, and analyses, or try out any risky innovations.[56]

Neither is pluralism coterminous with press freedom nor democratic governance. As one study of 9/11 coverage found, media presentations in *less* democratic countries were actually more pluralistic, offering wider, more diverse interpretations, than those in more democratic countries.[57] Of course, there are other reasons besides media pluralism to support press freedom, democratic governance, and an unconcentrated, open news media market. The point here is simply that these may help, or they may even be necessary, but they are not *sufficient* on their own.

There are good reasons to believe that an open and competitive market will produce diversity in the overall content provided by media companies, but there is less reason to believe that this diversity will extend to the political opinions and perspectives offered.[58] The media market produces competitive pressure for widely-attractive contents with high fixed costs, favoring duplication and economies of scale in place of myriad differentiated products. This makes a commercial media system less likely to exhibit *external* diversity, where each outlet may have an ideological bent but the market on the whole represents the full spectrum of ideological diversity. Nor are market mechanisms likely to produce ideological diversity *internal* to a given outlet. While many basketball fans may also appreciate football and tennis, there are far fewer socialists who also appreciate monarchy and fascism, or conservatives who also appreciate anarchism and communism. A media company seeking to attract basketball fans can also provide coverage of football and tennis without losing its target audience—however, a media company seeking to attract socialists or conservatives may well lose its target audience if it also provides perspectives from vastly different political outlooks.

A lack of pluralism in the media can be produced not only by commercial pressures, but as discussed earlier, by journalistic culture or professionalism as well. This has been called a "regime of objectivity," and it is typified by a reliance on official sources whose views are only challenged if a separate official source can be found with contrary views.[59] This produces unintended ideological consequences, usually in a conservative or status quo-maintaining direction. Nelson Rodrigues, a Brazilian journalist, called those following this sort of journalistic professionalism "objectivity idiots" for their inability to exercise independent judgment.[60] As the columnist Molly Ivins argued:

> There is no such thing as objectivity, and the truth, that slippery little bugger, has the oddest habit of being way to hell off on one side or the other: it seldom nestles neatly half-way between any two opposing points of view. … [M]ost stories aren't two-sided, they're seventeen-sided at least. In the second place, it's of no help to either the readers or the truth to quote one side saying, 'Cat,' and the other side saying, 'Dog,' while the truth is there's an elephant crashing around out there in the bushes.[61]

The regime of objectivity is particularly dangerous when political elites are largely in agreement on a given issue; when this occurs, an "objectivity idiot" would refuse to seriously question the elite consensus for lack of opposing "official sources" to quote, and out of fear of being labeled "ideological" or "unprofessional."[62] Such fear may be justified; Walter Lippmann explained that "the reporter, if he is to earn his living, must nurse his personal contacts with the eye-witnesses and privileged informants. If he is openly hostile to those in authority, he will cease to be a reporter unless there is an opposition party in the inner circle who can feed him news. Failing that, he will know precious little of what is going on."[63] As understandable as this behavior may be, it amounts to a serious form of intellectual corruption, whereby journalists refuse to provide a check on government and act as a mere extension of it, legitimizing their negligence by appeal to professional conventions.[64]

Whether caused by deficiencies in media markets, a flawed conception of what professional journalism should be, or some combination of the two, the conclusion remains that commercialized media systems are failing to provide the pluralism of opinions and perspectives that democracy requires. And as Venício de Lima notes, "[w]ithout a media functioning within a 'polycentric structure' that provides a public debate where all voices are heard, one cannot speak of freedom of the press as the guarantor of democracy."[65] To find out what sort of media system *is* capable of providing the pluralism democracy requires, we will need to look more closely at the variety of media systems in the world today.

4   Three-Media System Models

One of the best attempts to provide a framework for understanding the variety of media systems around the world is Daniel Hallin and Paolo Mancini's three models of media and politics.[66] Their models were designed to cover only North America (excluding Mexico) and Western Europe, but they provide a starting point for future extensions.

The main features of countries fitting the Mediterranean or *Polarized Pluralist Model* (Greece, Spain, Portugal, Italy, and France) are: an elite-oriented press with low circulation; the historically late development of freedom of the press and commercial media; dominance of electronic media; "political parallelism," whereby media outlets take partisan stances and identify with a political party; public broadcasting that tends to be directed by the government or parliament; professional journalism being conceived less according to objectivity and more as a form of political activism; and a media system that has recently been transitioning rapidly to commercialism or experiencing "savage deregulation." The countries typified by the North/Central European or *Democratic Corporatist Model* (Denmark, Sweden, Finland, Norway, Netherlands, Austria, Belgium, Germany, and Switzerland) are characterized by: a mix of partisan or interpretationist and neutral or information-oriented journalism; the historically early development of press freedom and newspapers catering to political parties and other organized social groups, which persist alongside a purely commercial press; high newspaper circulation; a high degree of journalistic professionalism and formal organization;

public broadcasting which tends to be more autonomous from government but with parties and social organizations involved in governance; and a trend toward commercialization balanced by the persistence of a strong public service media. The characteristics of media systems in the North Atlantic or *Liberal Model* (Ireland, Canada, USA, and the UK) are: a historically early development of press freedom and high-newspaper circulation; low levels of political parallelism and a high degree of commercialism; a high degree of journalistic professionalism, though less organized than the Democratic Corporatist countries; and a weak regulatory role for government.

The Polarized Pluralist countries share historical similarities relevant to their contemporary media systems. With the exception of France, they had relatively low literacy rates until the twentieth century, which retarded the emergence of mass-circulation newspapers. Instead, radio was the first mass media to develop, and the electronic media continues to be the primary source of news. Today, political parties heavily influence public television, with countries such as France and Italy instituting formal systems to give parties equal access. Journalists in Polarized Pluralist systems have attempted to win greater independence from media proprietors, with limited success; however, their levels of autonomy are still lower than in other systems. Newspapers, particularly economically marginal, partisan papers, enjoy relatively high levels of state subsidies to ensure external diversity and a pluralistic public debate. The historically wide range of political ideologies in these countries, from royalism to communism, has been a boon to the partisan press and an impediment to the development of media independent from politics. The frequency of legal proceedings against media owners in Southern Europe and the ease with which governments can use selective enforcement of tax laws and other regulations against media companies has further reduced the media's independence from politics. Recently, the Polarized Pluralist countries (with the exception of France) have been hit with "savage deregulation," provoking a "commercial deluge" more sudden and with fewer restraints than in Northern Europe.

The Democratic Corporatist countries (and Britain) pioneered press freedom, led by publications linked to political and religious struggles and incipient merchant capitalism. The historically early victory of liberal capitalism over feudalism and Protestantism over Catholicism led to the development of a broad, literate middle class that formed the large market supporting high-circulation newspapers. The historical weakness of the Right and the landed aristocracy in Northern Europe left these forces unable to resist pressure from the Left, merchants, and the independent peasantry for liberal institutions like the free press. The development of Protestantism, which required a mastery of critical debate about religious beliefs and supported a culture of reading, reasoning, and defending ideas, helped spread this culture to the political sphere. Today, a balance between pure market forces and democratic-socialist planning typifies the Democratic Corporatist model.[67] Countries with Democratic Corporatist media systems (with the exception of Switzerland and Germany) use direct subsidies to support the press, and all of them use a variety of indirect subsidies to support different forms of media.[68] These have helped to reduce the effects of the global trend toward commercialism in Northern Europe.

Like the Democratic Corporatist countries, the media systems of the Liberal countries also benefitted from the early development of liberal capitalism and Protestantism, leading to an early expansion of literacy and a large newspaper market.[69] Commercialized journalism first developed here, although from the beginning the commercial media was dependent on indirect state subsidies and was never completely independent of political parties and business interests. Although an adversarial attitude toward government was a founding aspect of journalistic culture in Liberal countries, ironically they also feature a strongly institutionalized relationship between government officials and journalists, along with the idea that the production of news be structured around the information and interpretations provided by government officials. "As a result of these relationships, news content is powerfully shaped by information, agendas, and interpretive frameworks originating within the institutions of the state."[70] This facet of the Liberal countries may be related to the status of Britain and the U.S. as world powers: that these states have more to lose from a vigorously independent news media could have created structural pressures to restrain it. As opposed to Democratic Corporatist and Polarized Pluralist systems, public television in the Liberal countries is separated from political parties and managed by neutral independent professionals. The historical dominance of liberalism in these countries meant that diverse ideological divisions did not have the opportunity to develop; socialism, for instance, arose in opposition to feudalism and capitalism, so it did not spread as widely in countries like the U.S. without experience with feudalism, or in the other Liberal countries where liberalism became dominant early. Although the Liberal media system has become a model for countries worldwide, it is heavily criticized within Liberal countries, it is less trusted than the media systems of continental Europe, and its rates of newspaper circulation are lower than those of the Democratic Corporatist system.

Other media scholars have attempted to extend Hallin and Mancini's typology beyond North America and Western Europe. For instance, Boguslawa Dobek-Ostrowska has placed Poland's media system between the Polarized Pluralist and Liberal models. Poland shares a low level of newspaper circulation and a variety of partisan papers in common with the Polarized Pluralist countries, but a wide variety of tabloid and free newspapers with the Liberal countries.[71] Unusually, the leading private TV news channel offers more information and news than Poland's own public television and the private networks of neighboring countries. Public TV and radio have visibly favored the ruling party since Poland's transition from communism, while the commercial media has demonstrated greater independence from government. However, while the Polish-owned commercial media does not tend to toe any party's line, it reflects its owners' ideologies; foreign-owned private media companies tend to be more neutral.

In the nearby Baltic countries, elements of all three media systems can be found.[72] As in the Polarized Pluralist model, newspaper circulation is low, journalistic professionalism developed late, and patterns of clientelism and instrumentalization of the media are apparent. Similar to the Democratic Corporatist model, the Baltic States feature institutionalized systems of media self-regulation with political and ideological independence. And as in the Liberal model, Baltic media is highly commercialized and profit-driven, with only a weak public service media sector. In Lithuania, for instance, it is common for businesses to bribe media outlets to suppress negative publicity or promote positive material. Professional autonomy for journalists is threatened by the fear of losing one's job, which can occur in retaliation for publishing negative information about major advertisers, for instance.

In Western Asia, pan-Arab satellite channels like Qatar's Al-Jazeera have overshadowed national television systems. The primary players in pan-Arab satellite TV are Saudi Arabia and Lebanon, with Saudi moguls providing the financing and Lebanese journalists, producers, and managers creating content.[73] Saudi Arabia is the most important advertising market in the Arab world and its broadcast system is controlled by the government, while Lebanon has only a small advertising market and its media system—along with the Saudi-financed pan-Arab satellite television system—is closest to the Polarized Pluralist model. The ideological spectrum represented by pan-Arab satellite television follows the division between liberals and conservatives in Saudi Arabia. Thus, not only does Saudi Arabia's rich advertising market skew media content toward Saudi preferences, but its financial control of satellite channels allows them to be instrumentalized for Saudi political purposes. Lebanese journalists have traditionally enjoyed greater autonomy than their Saudi counterparts, but Saudi funding exerts a controlling influence. However, to some extent these models, which were developed from studies of North American and Western European systems, cannot be easily applied to the systems of the rest of the world.[74]

5 Testing the Three Models of Media Systems

Lisa Müller has made an impressive attempt to quantify key components of the three-media models and measure 47 countries' performance according to these components.[75] First, she splits indicators between those measuring features of structure and those measuring content. The *structural* features include "access to information" (newspaper circulation, radio, and TV sets per capita, and the number of computers and internet users as a percentage of the population), "quantitative diversity" (number of newspaper titles, newspaper imports as a percentage of GDP, TV stations, and percentage of households receiving foreign or international channels), and "qualitative diversity" (the ideological balance of politically-aligned newspapers, share of politically-neutral newspapers' circulation, and the strength of the public broadcaster). The *content* features include "amount of critical political information" (share of newspaper articles on politics and share of articles on the government and parliament mentioning malpractice), "balance of political information" (balance of coverage of the constitutional branches and public administration), and "platform for diverse interests" (equality in mentions of political parties, *vote-proportional* frequency in mentions of political parties, share of articles mentioning more than one party, and average number of parties mentioned per article). These concepts are only partially encompassed by the measurements used to grasp them, but they provide a good first approximation.

Concerning structural features, Western and Central European media systems like those of Austria, Germany, and Switzerland perform best for all three dimensions.[76] The Scandinavian, Anglo-Saxon countries, and Japan perform particularly well on the "access to information" dimension, while small European countries such as Cyprus, Luxembourg, and Switzerland perform well in "quantitative diversity." For "qualitative diversity," a broader array of countries performs well, including France, Finland, India, and Israel. In terms of content, Müller faced significant data limitations, cutting her analysis to newspapers in ten countries. Within this limited sample, Liberal media systems do best in terms of "amount of critical political information," while Democratic Corporatist countries do fairly well on the "balance of political information" dimension while shining in terms of providing a "platform for diverse interests." Overall, Müller's empirical analysis provides support for Hallin and Mancini's typologies on the structural level, but differed significantly on the content level.

More interesting than how well the theory fits empirical data, however, are the effects of the structural and content-based features of different media systems.[77] Access to information is correlated strongly with political participation and, to a lesser degree, so is quantitative diversity. *Equality* of political participation was not significantly affected by any of the three-structural measures, after accounting for political interest. (Though interest in politics may be a partial product of qualitative and quantitative diversity in the abstract, beyond their data-limited measurements.) How well political views of representatives match those of the citizenry, and the inclusion of minority groups in government, are positively correlated with all structural media system measurements: access to information, quantitative diversity, and qualitative diversity. (Qualitative diversity exerts a positive effect on adequacy of representation over time, as citizens are exposed to a broad variety of perspectives and develop their own.) Corruption is negatively related, and the strength of political and public interest group organization is positively related, to access to information and quantitative diversity. Müller's analysis reveals that structural features of media systems exert significant influence on democratic functioning. The closer media systems come to the democratic ideal of providing ample and diverse political information and opinions, the closer society comes to the democratic ideal of an active citizenry engaging in responsible self-government.

6 THE BEEB VS. MADISON AVENUE: DO PUBLIC SERVICE OR COMMERCIAL MEDIA OUTPERFORM IN INFORMING?

Over 250 studies and statistical analyses have revealed that public service media outperform commercial media in every respect (with the possible exception of war reporting).[78] When well-trained journalists are given a salary and guidance from editors independent of political and commercial pressures, and told to report the news to best inform their fellow citizens about the political realm—that is most commonly what happens. Study after study comparing commercial and public service media, most in the U.S. and Europe, comes to this conclusion. Public service media has also been found to support democratic outcomes in countries transitioning from military dictatorships in Latin America and authoritarian governments in Eastern Europe.[79] Generously funded public service media attracts a large share of the audience (between 30% and 50% in Europe)[80] and its influence, alongside that of content and structural regulations, makes commercial news media do a better job too. Nor is this a new pattern; it was in evidence since the rise of television.[81] The key factor that can prevent public service media from performing this beneficial role is political interference. Still, as an analysis of 36 democracies demonstrated, *de jure* independence from government—that is, legislation protecting managers and editors from political interference—is largely successful at providing true, *de facto* independence.[82]

Well-funded, independent public service media positively influence commercial players in the media system. In Britain, Rupert Murdoch has so far proven unable to "Fox-ify" his Sky News channel. The impediment? Partly it is Britain's public service regulations for commercial stations, but it is also the influence of the BBC on British audiences, which has raised standards and fostered a demand for impartial, high-quality reporting.[83] This trend holds for 13 European countries: while there is a tendency for commercial media to negatively influence their public service counterparts, the greater trend is for public service media to positively influence their commercial counterparts.[84] Strong public service media do not push commercial media out of the hard news market[85]; instead, they raise the bar. For instance, when Sweden introduced commercial television in 1991, the new commercial channel attracted young and less-knowledgeable viewers, and it increased their political knowledge—most likely thanks to the high journalistic standards set by Sweden's public service media.[86]

Public service media with a dominant position in a country's media market can produce other benefits besides. They can help produce national political integration by providing a virtual public sphere in which a majority of citizens are exposed to the same information and debates, preventing partisan segmentation and polarization.[87] As an analysis of 13 countries found, the effects of strong public service media in less fragmented media systems are positive: they increase aggregate levels of political information and engagement, and reduce knowledge gaps between socioeconomic strata.[88] These effects occur not only through exposure to strong public media outlets, but also the "two-step flow" of information, as everyday conversations become more permeated with news content. This point was reinforced by a separate study of 12 European countries plus Israel, which found that countries with more competitive (fragmented) media systems provide lower levels of political information than countries with fewer channels.[89]

In Britain, public broadcasters feature more hard news on foreign affairs, politics, and social/economic issues than their commercial counterparts, which focus to a greater degree on sport, crime, entertainment, and human-interest stories.[90] In France, Britain, and Germany, public service media give greater coverage to elections than commercial media.[91] The public service media of several Northern European countries provide more election coverage than the more commercialized media systems of the U.S. and U.K., particularly during peak time when more people are watching television.[92] Sound bites allotted to candidates are longer in these European countries than in the U.S., and within the European countries, public service media provided longer sound bites than commercial media. Sound bites for candidates in the U.S. commercial media have shortened considerably over time and only a small proportion of these contain substantive content.[93]

Another key facet of news presentations is how stories are framed. Are stories put into a wider context (thematic framing) or presented without contextual information as if they were one-off events (episodic framing)? The relationships here are striking: European public service media spent most of their time providing thematic rather than episodic coverage, while commercial media in Europe and the U.S. spend greater time on episodic coverage.[94] These variations occur systematically according to the *type* of media (public service vs. commercial) across countries, rather than according to country.

Scheduling is another important aspect of news presentations, since news programming during peak times will attract more inadvertent viewers. European public service media schedule more news programming during peak times than the U.S. commercial media.[95] (This helps explain why even the most popular TV news program in the U.S. attracts only 3% of the population.)[96] Among European countries, those with the most public-service-oriented systems offer the widest "windows of opportunity" for citizens to learn about politics, with more peak time slots devoted to news than countries with more commercialized media systems.[97] Furthermore, within these peak-time news programs, public service media feature a greater proportion of hard versus soft news than their commercial rivals.[98]

7 Spreading Knowledge: Public Service vs. Commercial Media

While the evidence shows that viewers of public service media are better informed about politics than commercial media viewers, this *could* be because smarter or better-educated people disproportionately prefer public service media. Greater income equality is important too, since political knowledge gaps between those with high and low levels of education are smaller in more equal countries.[99] However, a study of 14 E.U. member states found that even after controlling for a battery of factors (gender, education, age, income, ideology, and political interest), in 10 of 14 countries a preference for public service media was still strongly correlated with knowledge about politics.[100] Using statistical techniques to mimic a real-world experiment, a study of six countries representing North America, Europe, and Asia concluded that exposure to public service media increases political knowledge to a greater extent than commercial media, but only where funding and other mechanisms guaranteed public broadcasters independence.[101] (Commercial media produce more knowledge only where government heavily influences public service media.)[102]

Political knowledge also correlates strongly with political interest; however, in public service media systems, this correlation is weaker than in commercial media systems. As Shanto Iyengar and colleagues explain, in commercial systems "political knowledge depends heavily upon political interest; in public service systems, however, it is possible for the less interested to overcome their motivational handicap because of the greater availability of news programming."[103] Greater availability and supply of hard news in public service media systems means those without high levels of education or political interest are inadvertently exposed and thereby become informed about the political realm.[104] This applies particularly to ethnic minorities: in the commercialized U.S. system, minorities are less exposed and knowledgeable about hard news, while in the more public service-oriented British system, there are no such gaps.[105]

Tests of international affairs knowledge have demonstrated that on average, Americans are strikingly more ignorant than the publics of all European G7 nations: for instance, 57% of U.S. citizens answered only one or none of a five-question knowledge proxy correctly, while 58% of Germans answered all or four of five questions correctly.[106] A similar comparison found Americans to be significantly more ignorant about world affairs than the Swiss, who benefit from a public service media system.[107] (On some hard news questions, Swiss high school dropouts performed better than American college graduates.) Television news in the U.S. not only provides less information about the world than European TV news, but two-thirds of it is focused on countries with heavy U.S. military or diplomatic involvement, rendering much of the rest of the world invisible.[108] (Americans are similarly more ignorant of domestic politics than Europeans—this is again in line with the reduced provision of political information in the U.S. commercial media.)[109] This same pattern of more knowledge about the world following a greater supply of international news was found in a study of 11 countries across 5 continents, with more commercialized media systems performing worse than public service media systems.[110]

Overall, evidence shows that public service media do a better job than commercial media in providing foreign coverage.[111] TV news in public service-dominated European countries offers an average of between 16 and 10 minutes of foreign coverage per day, while the two leading commercial broadcasters in the United States provide a combined daily total of *four* minutes.[112] Within European countries, public service media tend to outperform commercial media in providing foreign news. For instance, in Germany, public service broadcasting covers slightly more foreign news than commercial media, but both provide better presentations than the U.S. commercial media.[113] However, there is a pattern throughout national media systems to present international news from an "ego-centric," national perspective that concentrates only on domestic and foreign elites.[114]

Although some have argued that the U.S. media provides such limited coverage because Americans are less educated and familiar with the rest of the world, Christian Kolmer and Holli Semetko ask: "But what came first – the lack of education or the lack of information in US television news?"[115] A large part of the explanation must be the differences between the United States' commercialized media system and Europe's public service media systems, with their heavily funded, market-leading public broadcasters. "Thus, in [the European] system, the citizen watching a popular channel needs to actively choose to avoid information about public affairs. In the [U.S.] system, the citizen watching a popular channel needs to actively seek out this information."[116] Levels of *interest* in international news are high in the U.S., more so than many other countries with a greater supply of international news.[117] However, there is a glaring mismatch between what news editors choose to cover and what the public wants.[118] Regardless, as Cass Sunstein explains, without access to an alternate media system "the broadcasting status quo cannot, without circularity, be justified on the basis of [current] preferences. Preferences that have adapted to an objectionable system cannot justify that system."[119] Moreover, it makes little sense to think of American or any other culture as stable and unchanging, with fixed preferences the media can only adapt to, but not influence.[120]

Revealingly, differences in coverage between commercial and public service media have been found to affect opinions on immigration, currently a hot topic in the U.S. and Europe. Europeans who primarily watch commercial TV news have stronger anti-immigration views, while those who watch public broadcasts are less opposed; this correlation remains significant even after controlling for education, age, gender, and political interest.[121] The likely explanation? On commercial channels, immigration coverage tends to be sensationalistic, with immigrants treated as a threat, while public television provides more information and a better-balanced picture.

In a study of five European countries and the U.S., viewers of public television news in four of the five European countries were better able to correctly place their countries' parties on a political position scale than viewers of commercial TV news; surprisingly, U.S. viewers of commercial TV news were no better than non-viewers at placing their (two) political parties on a political position scale.[122]

Exposure to public service media has been shown to correlate with political knowledge and trust in the political system, even after controlling for education.[123] Exposure to commercial media, however, has mixed results, and its effects disappear or diminish when education is included in the analysis. Interestingly, exposure to U.S. commercial TV news may *decrease* political knowledge, while increasing trust in the (poorly-understood) political system.[124]

Since greater knowledge is associated with political participation, it makes sense that more informative media produce higher rates of participation. A comprehensive study of 74 democracies found that countries with public service media systems had higher levels of voting than countries with commercialized media systems. For every 1% increase in audience share for public broadcasting, there is a .15% increase in voter turnout—among advanced democracies, a .21% increase.[125] Greater density of media options is also correlated with "correct" voting (choosing candidates that match voters' policy preferences) across dozens of countries.[126] Political and ideological pluralism in the media system also produces more participation, particularly for newspapers but also for television.[127] Here, one democratic goal—a broad, pluralistic media system—serves as an effective means to another, the participation of citizens in political decision-making.

In conclusion, public service media systems outperform commercial media systems across the board[128]—even online.[129] Public service media systems are better at providing hard news, covering elections, and producing a knowledgeable citizenry that votes. Public service media also tend to be more trusted and provide broader and more critical coverage of politics.[130] The only area where public service media systems do not have a clear lead over commercial media systems is in coverage of foreign war and conflict—at least insofar as studies of Iraq war coverage have found.[131] Still, while during wartime both types of media too "often function as nothing less than 'critique filters,' catching much of the material that might shake accustomed perspectives on world politics,"[132] the BBC opened its critical eye once the war started, at least—unlike its commercial competitors.[133] The public service media systems of France and Germany also did comparatively well.[134]

8 Conclusion

"*We have the impression that the American people do not realize what has happened to them. They are not aware that the communications revolution has occurred. They do not appreciate the tremendous power which the new instruments and the new organization of the press place in the hands of a few men. They have not yet understood how far the performance of the press falls short of the requirements of a free society in the world today.*"
—Hutchins' Commission Report (1947)

The U.S. media system is experiencing a foundation-shaking crisis.[135] On its own, the internet is having mixed effects: it is hurting the revenue streams of newspapers, but providing a pluralistic source of news and debate for those with the skill and ability to use it. However, the majority of news reporting online comes from the same media companies that are in crisis.[136] (At least on news websites; on social media and blogs, a greater diversity is on offer.)[137] Those who attempt to bypass old media online and access alternative media find themselves in an information ecology clogged with junk memes and misinformation.[138] However, this is in comparison with legacy media outlets, which provide the opposite ecological deficiency: an ideological monoculture (or "bi-culture," with primarily liberal perspectives on social issues and primarily conservative perspectives on economic and foreign policy issues). Hence, as Catie Snow Bailard points out,

> the proper point of comparison is not the content of information online in a world where critics must compete with pro-government propaganda relative to some sort of ideal world of perfect information online that is completely free of distortion. Rather, the meaningful comparison is the sort of information that the Internet, with all its shortcomings, provides to citizens relative to the sort of information that was available for public consumption before the Internet existed.[139]

While television is still the top choice for news in the U.S.,[140] there is a wide generation gap: nearly two-thirds of Millennials get their news from internet social media, while Baby Boomers get theirs (in roughly the same proportion) from local TV.[141] This gap may be a cause of ideological gaps between generations in the U.S., as demonstrated by the Bernie Sanders primary campaign.[142] The internet's influence on political opinions can be split into "mirror-holding" and "window-opening" effects. Mirror-holding refers to how the internet "provides a larger and more diverse array of political information than the traditional media system could provide," offering a fuller picture of the political realm in one's country; and window-opening refers to the international diversity on the internet, offering a more inclusive picture of global politics.[143] Not only do mirror-holding and window-opening shape different political opinions, but they can also, as a recent meta-analysis found, lead to greater political engagement, particularly as internet penetration and use increase over time.[144]

Regardless of what internet media *may* change, there is a clear need for reform of the U.S. media system (and other countries'). This is the goal of several organizations within the United States (and around the world), such as Free Press and Media Alliance. Collectively, their goal is to democratize the media, whether reforming the governance structures of media outlets, creating alternative outlets, or improving regulation.[145] Besides "democratizing the media," activists conceive of their task as guaranteeing a free press or freedom of expression, upholding a right to communication, improving the cultural environment, or fighting for media justice.

Resisting the media democratization movement are media corporations, their associations, and an assortment of political and intellectual allies like libertarians.[146] What Walter Lippmann wrote in 1920 remains relevant: "Those who are now in control have too much at stake, and they control the source of reform itself. Change will come only by the drastic competition of those whose interests are not represented in the existing news-organization."[147] Luckily for the media democratization movement, journalists are quickly joining the ranks of those whose interests are not represented in the existing media system.[148] And from a strictly economic point of view, so are the owners of newspaper companies.

The *need* for media democratization is pressing. Walter Lippmann's 1920 prophesy—that in "a few generations it will seem ludicrous to historians that a people professing government by the will of the people should have made no serious effort to guarantee the news without which governing opinion cannot exist"[149]—has been proven correct. The current situation is ludicrous; we have attempted to provide the public good of political information and pluralistic debate through market means, but since no individual consumer has a sufficient incentive to pay for the benefits, collectively *we* do not pay and the market produces insufficient information.[150] Certainly, if the sorry state of the contemporary U.S. media system had been caused by government orders to fire half the nation's journalists, replace their reporting with PR releases, close foreign bureaus, give up investigative journalism, and ignore massive financial bubbles until they pop, then we would be up in arms.[151] When the same result occurs through market failure instead of government fiat, however, it is harder to see the problem (or its solution) for what it is. We fear government control of media so much we are blind to what Raymond Williams observed: That "the control claimed as a matter of power by authoritarians, and as a matter of principle by paternalists, is often achieved as a matter of practice in the operation of the commercial system."[152]

What we need from our media system—full political information and pluralism—is in economic terms an *externality* of media companies' operations and goes beyond and sometimes against these companies' rational, profit-maximizing considerations.[153] As self-regulation has demonstrably failed, the only remaining option is government intervention. Pascual Serrano writes:

> We are faced with a new challenge: to find a way for citizens to reclaim our right to information *through* the State, *from* which we need to demand the enforcement of its duty to guarantee it. We, citizens, must give power to the State, and the State, for its part, must give us control. This is the true freedom of the press in a democracy.[154]

As Judge Learned Hand poignantly expressed it, democracy is based on the supposition that "right conclusions are more likely to be gathered out of a multitude of tongues, than through any kind of authoritative selection. To many this is, and always will be, folly; but we have staked upon it our all."[155] And there are many good reasons to consider this supposition, on which we truly have staked our all, to be folly. We have not evolved a psychology matching the liberal ideal, and the psychology evolution *has* produced is rife with bias. These biases incline us toward ideas that confer individual or group advantages, or reinforce ideas we have already accepted—*not* toward "right conclusions," whatever they are. John Durham Peters argues that "the ultimate danger of the 'marketplace of ideas' is not political but ethical. The notion offers a bogus reassurance, too easy a theodicy for truth, too facile an understanding of evil. The kind of thinking it encourages gives us little fortification against disappointment by hard structural facts or against the lotus lands of egotism and hedonism."[156]

Skeptics, who like John Stuart Mill consider it "a piece of idle sentimentality" to hope that true opinions would have any inherent advantage over false opinions in a free and diverse public sphere, take a perfectly tenable position.[157] Opinions that are "true"—in the sense that if their preferred policies were implemented they would produce the positive outcomes predicted by the opinion—have no such inherent advantage on their own. Political opinions are so many estimates about how the world operates, and which interventions will improve its operation. As such, they are fundamentally constructed out of facts, whether accurate or inaccurate; that is to say, opinions are constructed out of the available information. This reveals the profundity of Walter Lippmann's insight, "In going behind opinion to the information which it exploits, and in making the validity of the news our ideal, we shall be fighting the battle where it is really being fought."[158] The proposals of the media democratization movement do precisely this: allow and even encourage the widest possible variety of opinions, but ensure that the information which they exploit is sound.

Notes

1. Pedro Gilberto Gomes, *Filosofia e Ética da Comunicação na Midiatização da Sociedade* (São Leopoldo, RS: Editora Unisinos, 2006): 135, translation mine.
2. Ibid., 121, translation mine.
3. Venício A. de Lima, "Normas Legais da Comunicação Social: Interesse Privado vs Interesse Público," in *Em Defesa de uma Opinião Pública Democrática*, ed. Venício A. de Lima et al., 169–196 (São Paulo: Paulus, 2014): 10–12, translation and emphasis mine.
4. Sean Michael McGuire, "Media Influence and the Modern American Democracy: Why the First Amendment Compels Regulation of Media Ownership," *Cardozo Public Law, Policy and Ethics Journal* 4 (2006): 690.
5. Walter Lippmann, *Liberty and the News* (La Vergne, TN: BN Publishing, 2012): 22–23.
6. Ibid.
7. Doris Graber, "Mediated Politics and Citizenship in the Twenty-First Century," *Annual Review of Psychology* 55 (2004).

8. Doris Graber, "The Media and Democracy: Beyond Myths and Stereotypes," *Annual Review of Political Science* 6, no. 1 (2003).
9. Toril Aalberg and James Curran, "How Media Inform Democracy: Central Debates," in *How Media Inform Democracy: A Comparative Approach*, ed. Toril Aalberg and James Curran, 3–14 (New York: Routledge, 2012): 11–12.
10. W. Lance Bennett, "The Burglar Alarm That Just Keeps Ringing: A Response to Zaller," *Political Communication* 20, no. 2 (2003).
11. Anders Todal Jenssen et al., "Informed Citizens, Media Use, and Public Knowledge of Parties' Policy Positions," in *How Media Inform Democracy*: 146–147.
12. Jesper Strömbäck et al., "The Financial Crisis as a Global News Event: Cross-National Media Coverage and Public Knowledge of Economic Affairs," in *How Media Inform Democracy*: 173.
13. Scott L. Althaus, "Information Effects in Collective Preferences," *American Political Science Review* 92, no. 3 (1998).
14. Jerit et al., "Citizens, Knowledge."
15. Gilens, "Political Ignorance."
16. James H. Kuklinski et al., "The Political Environment and Citizen Competence," *American Journal of Political Science* 45, no. 2 (2001).
17. Barbara Geddes and John Zaller, "Sources of Popular Support for Authoritarian Regimes," *American Journal of Political Science* (1989): 341.
18. Alicia Adserà et al., "Are You Being Served? Political Accountability and Quality of Government," *Journal of Law, Economics, and Organization* 19, no. 2 (2003): 479.
19. Gabor Toka, "Citizen Information, Election Outcomes and Good Governance," *Electoral Studies* 27, no. 1 (2008).
20. Somin, "Knowledge about Ignorance," 274–276.
21. Cigdem V. Sirin, "Examining the Effects of Political Information and Intervention Stages on Public Support for Military Interventions: A Panel Experiment," *Acta Politica* 46, no. 3 (2011): 285.
22. Graber, "Mediated Politics," 551.
23. Ibid.
24. Des Freedman, *The Politics of Media Policy* (New York: Polity, 2008): 78–79, 104.
25. Toril Aalberg, et al., "Media Choice and Informed Democracy: Toward Increasing News Consumption Gaps in Europe?" *The International Journal of Press/Politics* 18, no. 3 (2013).
26. Daniel C. Hallin and Paolo Mancini, *Comparing Media Systems: Three Models of Media and Politics* (Cambridge: Cambridge University Press, 2004): 292–294.

27. Kalyani Chadha and Anandam Kavoori, "Beyond the Global/Local: Examining Contemporary Media Globalization Trends across National Contexts," in *Media and Society*, ed. James Curran, 210–229 (New York: Bloomsbury Publishing, 2010).
28. See, e.g., Brian C. Anderson and Adam D. Thierer, *A Manifesto for Media Freedom* (New York: Encounter Books, 2008).
29. Lee C. Bollinger, *Uninhibited, Robust, and Wide-Open: A Free Press for a New Century* (Oxford: Oxford University Press, 2009): 56–57.
30. Peters, "Into the Air," 165.
31. Bollinger, *Uninhibited*, 54–64.
32. Ibid., 32–33, quoting from the *Red Lion Broadcasting Co. v. FCC* decision.
33. Ingber, "The Marketplace," 38–39.
34. Frank Blethen and Ryan Blethen, "The Wall Street-Based Absentee Ownership Model of Our News Is Broken," in *Will the Last Reporter Please Turn Out the Lights*: 9.
35. McGuire, "Media Influence," 710–711.
36. Jerome A. Barron, "Access to the Press. A New First Amendment Right," *Harvard Law Review* (1967): 1649, 1656.
37. Graber, "The Media," 147.
38. W. Lance Bennett, *News: The Politics of Illusion*, 8th ed. (New York: Pearson Education, 2009): 268–270.
39. Jan Oberg, "The Iraq Conflict and the Media: Embedded with War Rather than with Peace and Democracy," in *Democratizing Global Media: One World, Many Struggles*, ed. Robert A. Hackett and Yuezhi Zhao, 185–203 (New York: Rowan & Littlefield, 2005): 201.
40. Fábio Konder Comparato, "Prefácio," in *Liberdade de Expressão x Liberdade da Imprensa: Direito à Comunicação e Democracia*, 2nd ed., by Venício A. de Lima, 11–18 (São Paulo: Publisher Brasil, 2012): 14.
41. Cass R. Sunstein, *Democracy and the Problem of Free Speech* (New York: Free Press, 1995): 57–58.
42. Christians and Nordenstreng, "Social Responsibility," 5.
43. Lance W. Bennett, "Changing Societies, Changing Media Systems: Challenges for Communication Theory, Research and Education," in *Can the Media Serve Democracy? Essays in Honour of Jay G. Blumler*, ed. Stephen Coleman et al., 151–163 (New York: Palgrave Macmillan, 2015): 154.
44. Stephen Cushion, *The Democratic Value of News: Why Public Service Media Matter* (New York: Palgrave Macmillan, 2012): 68.
45. Sunstein, *Democracy*, 59.
46. Michael Griffin, "Looking at TV News: Strategies for Research," *Communication* 13, no. 2 (1992): 139.

47. Frank Esser, "Dimensions of Political News Cultures: Sound Bite and Image Bite News in France, Germany, Great Britain, and the United States," *The International Journal of Press/Politics* 13, no. 4 (2008): 419.
48. Justin Schlosberg, *Media Ownership and Agenda Control* (New York: Routledge, 2017): 122.
49. McGuire, "Media Influence," 716.
50. Katherine Ognyanova and Peter Monge, "A Multitheoretical, Multilevel, Multidimensional Network Model of the Media System: Production, Content, and Audiences," *Communication Yearbook* 37 (2013): 16.
51. Natalie Fenton, "Deregulation or Democracy? New Media, News, Neoliberalism and the Public Interest," *Continuum: Journal of Media & Cultural Studies* 25, no. 1 (2011): 70.
52. Edmund Burke, *Reflections on the French Revolution, Vol. XXIV, Part 3* (New York: PF Collier & Son, 1909–14): 242.
53. Wayne Fu, "Applying the Structure-Conduct-Performance Framework in the Media Industry Analysis," *International Journal on Media Management* 5, no. 4 (2003): 275.
54. Freedman, *The Politics*, 219.
55. McGuire, "Media Influence," 717–718.
56. Marina Popescu and Gabor Tóka, "Public Television, Private Television and Citizens' Political Knowledge," *EUI Working Papers RSCAS* 66 (2009): 6.
57. Joshua Woods, "Democracy and the Press: A Comparative Analysis of Pluralism in the International Print Media," *The Social Science Journal* 44, no. 2 (2007).
58. Michele Polo, "Regulation for Pluralism in the Media Markets," in *The Economic Regulation of Broadcasting Markets: Evolving Technology and the Challenges for Policy*, ed. Paul Seabright and Jürgen von Hagen, 150–188 (Cambridge: Cambridge University Press, 2007).
59. Robert Hackett and William Carroll, *Remaking Media: The Struggle to Democratize Public Communication* (New York: Routledge, 2006): 34.
60. Afonso de Albuquerque, "Another 'Fourth Branch': Press and Political Culture in Brazil," *Journalism* 6, no. 4 (2005): 494.
61. Quoted in Chris Hedges, "The Disease of Objectivity," in *Will the Last Reporter Please Turn Out the Lights*: 209.
62. McChesney, "A Real Media," 8.
63. Lippmann, *Liberty*, 25.
64. Clifford Christians and Kaarle Nordenstreng, "Social Responsibility Worldwide," *Journal of Mass Media Ethics* 19, no. 1 (2004): 17.

65. Venício A. de Lima, *Liberdade de Expressão x Liberdade da Imprensa: Direito à Comunicação e Democracia*, 2nd ed. (São Paulo: Publisher Brasil, 2012): 42.
66. Hallin and Mancini, *Comparing Media*, 73–75, 93–186.
67. Anker Brink Lund, "Media Markets in Scandinavia: Political Economy Aspects of Convergence and Divergence," *Nordicom Review* 28 (2007): 128.
68. Hallin and Mancini, *Comparing Media*, 161–162.
69. Ibid., 199–249.
70. Ibid., 234.
71. Boguslawa Dobek-Ostrowska, "Italianization (or Mediterraneanization) of the Polish Media System? Reality and Perspective," in *Comparing Media Systems: Beyond the Western World*, ed. Daniel C. Hallin and Paolo Mancini, 26–50 (Cambridge: Cambridge University Press, 2012): 31–38.
72. Auksė Balčytienė, "Culture as a Guide in Theoretical Explorations of Baltic Media," in *Comparing Media Systems*: 62–70.
73. Marwan M. Kraidy, "The Rise of Transnational Media Systems: Implications of Pan-Arab Media for Comparative Research," in *Comparing Media Systems*: 178–198.
74. See, e.g., Afonso de Albuquerque, "On Models and Margins: Comparative Media Models Viewed from a Brazilian Perspective," in *Comparing Media Systems*; Katrin Voltmer and Rüdiger Schmitt-Beck, "New Democracies without Citizens? Mass Media and Democratic Orientations—A Four-Country Comparison," in *Mass Media and Political Communication in New Democracies*, ed. Katrin Voltmer, 226–250 (New York: Psychology Press, 2006).
75. Müller, *Comparing Mass Media*, 65–81.
76. Ibid., 106–155.
77. Ibid., 182–203.
78. Cushion, *The Democratic Value*, 12, 205.
79. Katrin Voltmer and Rüdiger Schmitt-Beck, "New Democracies without Citizens? Mass Media and Democratic Orientations—A Four-Country Comparison," in *Mass Media and Political Communication in New Democracies*, ed. Katrin Voltmer, 226–250 (New York: Psychology Press, 2006): 238–240.
80. Hallin and Mancini, *Comparing*, 43.
81. Raymond Williams, *Communications*, 3rd ed. (New York: Penguin Books, 1976): 64–66.
82. Chris Hanretty, "Explaining the De Facto Independence of Public Broadcasters," *British Journal of Political Science* 40, no. 1 (2010).

83. Stephen Cushion and Justin Lewis, "Towards a 'Foxification' of 24-hour News Channels in Britain? An Analysis of Market-Driven and Publicly Funded News Coverage," *Journalism* 10, no. 2 (2009); Stephen Cushion and Bob Franklin, "Public Service Broadcasting: Markets and 'Vulnerable Vales' in Broadcast and Print Journalism," in *Can the Media Serve Democracy? Essays in Honour of Jay G. Blumler*, ed. Stephen Coleman et al., 65–75 (New York: Palgrave Macmillan, 2015): 68–69.
84. Frank Esser et al., "Political Information Opportunities in Europe: A Longitudinal and Comparative Study of Thirteen Television Systems," *The International Journal of Press/Politics* 17, no. 3 (2012): 261; Cushion, *The Democratic Value*, 89–90.
85. Popescu and Tóka, "Public Television," 16.
86. Andrea Prat and David Strömberg, "Commercial Television and Voter Information," CEPR Discussion Paper No. 4989 (2005): 23–24.
87. Elihu Katz, "And Deliver Us from Segmentation," *The Annals of the American Academy of Political and Social Science* (1996).
88. Lilach Nir, "Public Space: How Shared News Landscapes Close Gaps in Political Engagement," *Journal of Broadcasting & Electronic Media* 56, no. 4 (2012).
89. Esser et al., "Political Information Opportunities," 261.
90. Cushion, *The Democratic Value*, 67.
91. Frank Esser, "Dimensions of Political News Cultures: Sound Bite and Image Bite News in France, Germany, Great Britain, and the United States," *The International Journal of Press/Politics* 13, no. 4 (2008): 412.
92. Peter van Aelst et al., "The Political Information Environment During Election Campaigns," in *How Media Inform Democracy*: 58, 62.
93. Sunstein, *Democracy*, 61.
94. Tove Brekken et al., "News Substance: The Relative Importance of Soft and De-Contextualized News," in *How Media Inform Democracy*: 75.
95. Curran et al., "Media System," 19–20.
96. Brekken et al., "News Substance," 77.
97. Esser et al., "Political Information Opportunities."
98. Cushion, *The Democratic Value*, 73.
99. Kimmo Gronlund and Henry Milner, "The Determinants of Political Knowledge in Comparative Perspective," *Scandinavian Political Studies* 29, no. 4 (2006).
100. Christina Holtz-Bacha and Pippa Norris, "'To Entertain, Inform, and Educate': Still the Role of Public Television," *Political Communication* 18, no. 2 (2001).

101. Stuart Soroka et al., "Auntie Knows Best? Public Broadcasters and Current Affairs Knowledge," *British Journal of Political Science* 43, no. 4 (2013).
102. Popescu and Tóka, "Public Television," 18.
103. Shanto Iyengar et al., "Cross-National versus Individual-Level Differences in Political Information: A Media Systems Perspective," *Journal of Elections, Public Opinion and Parties* 20, no. 3 (2010): 303.
104. Kyu S. Hahn et al., "Does Knowledge of Hard News Go With Knowledge of Soft News? A Cross-National Analysis of the Structure of Public Affairs Knowledge," in *How Media Inform Democracy:* 135–136.
105. Curran et al., "Media System," 17–21.
106. Michael Dimock and Samuel L. Popkin, "Political Knowledge in Comparative Perspective," in *Do the Media Govern*, ed. Shanto Iyengar and Richard Reeves, 217–224 (London: Sage, 1997): 219.
107. Shanto Iyengar et al., "'Dark Areas of Ignorance' Revisited: Comparing International Affairs Knowledge in Switzerland and the United States," *Communication Research* 36, no. 3 (2009).
108. James Curran et al., "News Content, Media Consumption, and Current Affairs Knowledge," in *How Media Inform Democracy:* 85.
109. Ibid., 86–89.
110. Toril Aalberg et al., "International TV News, Foreign Affairs Interest and Public Knowledge: A Comparative Study of Foreign News Coverage and Public Opinion in 11 Countries," *Journalism Studies* 14, no. 3 (2013).
111. Curran et al., "Media System," 11–12.
112. Brekken et al., "News Substance," 74.
113. Christian Kolmer and Holli A. Semetko, "International Television News: Germany Compared," *Journalism Studies* 11, no. 5 (2010).
114. Hafez, *The Myth*, 24–39.
115. Kolmer and Semetko, "International Television," 712.
116. Ibid., 199.
117. Aalberg et al., "International TV News," 397.
118. Zixue Tai and Tsan-Kuo Chang, "The Global News and the Pictures in Their Heads: A Comparative Analysis of Audience Interest, Editor Perceptions and Newspaper Coverage," *International Communication Gazette* 64, no. 3 (2002).
119. Sunstein, *Democracy*, 74.
120. Williams, *Communications*, 106.
121. Zan Strabac et al., "News Consumption and Public Opposition to Immigration across Countries," in *How Media Inform Democracy:* 182–183.

122. Anders Todal Jenssen et al., "Informed Citizens, Media Use, and Public Knowledge of Parties' Policy Positions," in *How Media Inform Democracy:* 152, 155.
123. Kees Aarts et al., "Media, Political Trust, and Political Knowledge," in *How Media Inform Democracy:* 113–117.
124. Ibid., 112–114; Kees Aarts, email message to author, May 21, 2015.
125. Mijeong Baek, "A Comparative Analysis of Political Communication Systems and Voter Turnout," *American Journal of Political Science* 53, no. 2 (2009): 383–384.
126. Lau, Richard R., Parina Patel, Dalia F. Fahmy, and Robert R. Kaufman, "Correct Voting Across Thirty-Three Democracies: A Preliminary Analysis," *British Journal of Political Science* 44, no. 2 (2014).
127. Hetty van Kempen, "Media-Party Parallelism and Its Effects: A Cross-National Comparative Study," *Political Communication* 24, no. 3 (2007).
128. Toril Aalberg and James Curran, "Conclusion," in *How Media Inform Democracy:* 193.
129. Cushion, *The Democratic Value*, 91–122, 190–205.
130. Rodney Benson, "Public Funding and Journalistic Independence: What Does Research Tell Us?" in *Will the Last Reporter Please Turn Out the Lights*: 315–316.
131. Cushion, *The Democratic Value*, 147.
132. Hafez, *The Myth*, 42.
133. Cushion, *The Democratic Value*, 148.
134. Oberg, "The Iraq Conflict," 194.
135. Paul Starr, "An Unexpected Crisis: The News Media in Postindustrial Democracies," *The International Journal of Press/Politics* 17, no. 2 (2012).
136. McChesney, "A Real Media," 10; McGuire, "Media Influence," 716.
137. Scott Maier, "All the News Fit to Post? Comparing News Content on the Web to Newspapers, Television, and Radio," *Journalism & Mass Communication Quarterly* 87, no. 3–4 (2010).
138. Delia Mocanu et al., "Collective Attention in the Age of (Mis) Information," *Computers in Human Behavior* 51, Part B (2015).
139. Catie Snow Bailard, *Democracy's Double-Edged Sword: How Internet Use Changes Citizens' Views of Their Government* (Baltimore, MD: Johns Hopkins University Press, 2014): 55.
140. Lydia Saad, "TV is Americans' Main Source of News," *Gallup* (July 8, 2013).
141. Amy Mitchell et al., "Millennials and Political News: Social Media—The Local TV for the Next Generation?" *Pew Research Center, Journalism & Media* (June 1, 2015).

142. Peter Beattie, "Where Did the Bernie Sanders Movement Come From? The Internet," *Naked Capitalism* (May 25, 2016). Available at https://www.nakedcapitalism.com/2016/05/where-did-the-bernie-sanders-movement-come-from-the-internet.html.
143. Bailard, *Democracy's Double-Edged Sword*, 5.
144. Shelley Boulianne, "Does Internet Use Affect Engagement? A Meta-Analysis of Research," *Political Communication* 26, no. 2 (2009).
145. Hackett and Carroll, *Remaking Media*, 52, 65, 78–79.
146. Ibid., 140; Anderson and Thierer, *A Manifesto*.
147. Lippmann, *Liberty*, 59–60.
148. Hackett and Carroll, *Remaking Media*, 201.
149. Lippmann, *Liberty*, 8.
150. Sunstein, *Democracy*, 70.
151. Robert W. McChesney and John Nichols, "Down the News Hole," in *Will the Last Reporter Please Turn Out the Lights*: 106.
152. Williams, *Communications*, 133.
153. Fu, "Applying," 278.
154. Serrano, "Democracia," 82, translation and emphasis mine.
155. *United States v. Associated Press*, 372.
156. Peters, "The 'Marketplace'," 80.
157. Ibid., 69–70.
158. Lippmann, *Liberty*, 41.

CHAPTER 8

Conclusion: The Invisible Hand and the Ecology of Information

"The people in the sense in which Lincoln used the term, as referring to the electorate, is an organized body, but it is not of as high a type as a beast, for a beast, even though vaguely, has a consciousness of its unity, its selfhood. The people, the organized body of the citizenship has a unity, a selfhood, but it is no more conscious of it than are the coördinated cells of a cabbage leaf of their unity. The people is not a great beast. The people is a great vegetable."
Edward J. Ward, *The Social Center*

In Robert Dahl's conjecture, the key requirement for a plebiscitary democracy to be functionally equivalent to totalitarian rule was elites' ability to "plug in," hypodermic-needle fashion, desired opinions into the minds of the electorate. We can now review the evidence on whether this plugging-in ability exists, or in what form it might.

We started out asking how the invisible hand operates in the contemporary marketplace of ideas, dependent on the crooked timber of human psychology and the broken fourth branch of government, the media. The accumulated evidence recalls Shiping Tang's statement that "any framework on social evolution that does not explicitly admit power as a critical selection force is incomplete."[1] Yorgos Lanthimos' film *Dogtooth*, an allegory on fascism, patriarchy, and paternalism, provides an illustration. In the film, three grown-yet-infantile children are kept inside the boundaries of their hedge-fenced yard by their parents, who cow them into immobilizing fear with lies about the dangers of the outside world. These lies are not "white" or superficial, they are foundational: they

© The Author(s) 2019
P. Beattie, *Social Evolution, Political Psychology, and the Media in Democracy*, https://doi.org/10.1007/978-3-030-02801-5_8

are memes that *create* the world outside which the children will never experience. ("Sea," which the children will never see, is defined as a "leather armchair"; one of the daughters sees the word "pussy" on a videocassette case, and her mother tells her it means a "large lamp.") They are told they can leave their home only when one of their canine teeth, a "dogtooth," falls out, signifying the onset of maturity required to survive in the outside world. Toward the end of the film, the male child is commanded to rape one of his sisters, and he does; anticipating future rapes, she later smashes out one of her dogteeth with a dumbbell to attempt an escape. As Voltaire wrote: "You believe in incomprehensible, contradictory and impossible things because we have commanded you to; now then, commit unjust acts because we likewise order you to do so."[2]

To a circumscribed but still discomforting extent, the U.S. media system echoes the parents of *Dogtooth*, with the citizenry as their adult but infantilized children, whose pictures-in-the-head of the outside world are distorted, limited, and artificial. Power operating in the realm of social evolution produces these artifices, limitations, and distortions. Not the *intentional* exercise of power as in *Dogtooth*, but the unintentional, multifarious varieties of power comprising the political economy of media in interaction with the ecology of human psychology. Through the news media, the U.S. public is told that their form of government, which their government's military exploits are supposed to encourage globally, is "democracy" and that its military and covert operations are to ensure "security" and protect the "national interest." Indeed, those who can make you believe absurdities can make you commit atrocities.

The beginning of an understanding of this process lies in recognizing the physical nature of information and how it evolves. Information, in genes or brains, inheres in the organization of physical matter. Sources of variation (mutation, recombination; ideation, idea-blending) introduce new variants, which are computed by the surrounding environment: variants that survive longer and spread more widely are "selected," incrementally ratcheting up the complexity or "fit" of the information to aspects of the environment. In the realm of social evolution, there are three interpenetrating levels: the biological, the cultural, and the social, each with their own selection pressures. At the biological and cultural levels, schema research shows that we process incoming information to complement our existing information, sometimes distorting it in the process, making for a bias toward the status quo and the conservation of beliefs. At the social level, social representations research illustrates how socially-shared understandings—similar bundles of memes—emerge and spread, principally through the media but also through other institutions, and how these understandings affect politics. To understand social evolution, we must understand the environment: the demand-side pressures in the human brain and supply-side pressures from institutions.

The first place to look for demand-side pressures in the human brain is in its evolutionary history. Our species was partially created through climate change (and, ironically, we may destroy the species through anthropogenic climate change), which transformed our environment and created a new set of selection pressures. We adapted in an unusual way: by evolving a "theory of mind," joint intentionality, and language, overcoming the ever-present lure of self-interested, selfish behavior through a powerful psychological aversion to domination—an "egalitarian syndrome"—undergirding and reinforcing social norms and practices to discourage or eliminate bullies and would-be alphas. We became the first non-insect *eusocial* species in the animal kingdom. In the process, an evolutionarily stable strategy or equilibrium was reached, with some of the population having characteristics of the psychological Right (a desire for tradition and continuity, an acceptance of hierarchy) and some with characteristics of the psychological Left (a desire for change and novelty, for egalitarianism). Together, this "strategy" would allow for the evolutionary algorithm to apply at the social level, with the Left introducing variations and the Right preserving past variations. Differences in the *psychological* Left and Right extend to morality, with leftists valuing care and fairness more than rightists, and rightists valuing respect for authority, sanctity, and loyalty more than leftists. In total, these products of our evolutionary history produce a separate set of demand-side biases for the psychological Left and Right.

Liberalism as a (predominant) political philosophy views human beings as innate reasoners capable of meeting a relatively high standard of rationality in thinking about politics. Yet the accumulated evidence of human irrationality in the political domain overwhelms this view, revealing:

- Automatic, unconscious moral decisions justified by *ad hoc* rationalizations, a vast area of cognition (System 1) to which we have no conscious access, and *persuasion* that occurs through unconscious, System 1 processing;
- A mental architecture favoring cognitive consistency and low anxiety over accuracy and moral principle;

- Groupishness aroused by the most arbitrary and meaningless group distinctions, biasing us in favor of our in-group and against out-groups;
- We demonstrate ideological biases in memory, gullibly accept incoming information, and fail to revise discredited beliefs;
- We exhibit a tendency to justify and desire the status quo, regardless of its flaws, and to ignore dire problems in proportion to their urgency and complexity;
- Weak arguments do not weakly persuade, but rather inoculate us against accepting a strong version of the same argument, making weak balance in the media more manipulative than no balance at all;
- The myriad ways in which evil actions can be rationalized, removed from their context, or ignored, particularly in the case of war;
- The "interpreter" mechanism in our minds that produces self-deception by bringing only flattering information and motives into conscious awareness, while leaving ulterior motives and unflattering information in the dark;
- Stark differences in cognitive development, with a small minority developing a systematic style of thought analogous to the liberal ideal, while a majority develop only a linear or sequential style incapable of the complex reasoning democracy requires.

Media systems must therefore be calibrated to counteract or mute our demand-side, psychological biases; otherwise, even a fair and balanced media can produce irrational effects on public opinion, owing to our suboptimal psychology. A psychologically appropriate media system would be pluralist and open, favoring a diversity of perspectives and speakers, and seeking to frustrate distortions like in-group bias and system justification.

Psychological biases would be of little concern to a media system that produces minimal effects. This is not the case: the media produces large effects, which only seem minimal when opposing messages largely cancel each other out. Not only political messages, but also advertising and cultural programming affect opinions and influence socialization. The cognitive conservatism of our brains' design makes snowballing effects likelier than deep revisions of previously held beliefs, giving an absorption-advantage to information consonant with dominant social representations. Whether through priming, framing, agenda-setting, or direct persuasion, decades of research have revealed the media to be a powerful force in shaping public opinion. Hence, to a large extent elites do have the *ability* to plug in their preferences through the media to get what they want out of the system, though the metaphor of a plug suggests a degree of ease that is somewhat lacking. The "socket" is a moving target, and not always yielding.

The plug—the media system itself—has been recognized as a powerful force throughout its history and treated as such by governments for most of it. Yet at a pivotal juncture—the development of radio and then television—the United States government made the fateful decision to turn the broadcast media over to commercial enterprises, which used it for the narrow goal of fat profits. This is the first of several biases skewing media content: toward the perceived desires of women and young adults, including sensationalism, a liberal take on social issues, and more lifestyle or sports coverage. Journalists themselves tend to be left-of-center on social issues, and centrist or right-of-center on economic issues, and there is evidence of renewed ownership pressure on journalists to avoid coverage damaging to their parent companies' or advertisers' interests. Additional filters influence what information appears in the mass media: the code of journalistic professionalism removing context from stories in a quixotic quest for objectivity, source bias and indexing privileging the powerful, pack journalism and social influences from those whom journalists cover, advertiser pressure and flak, and even direct influence from the government. The cumulative result is that the media system "plug" gives preference to perspectives and interests of the economic and political elite, echoing the status quo-supporting biases of human psychology. Biases of both demand and supply skew toward the status quo, slowing social evolution by reducing sources of novelty and variation. The inputs "plugged in" to the system do not produce perfectly predictable outputs, but the media system allows certain inputs to be blocked, thereby impeding certain outputs. The answer to Dahl's conjecture seems to be that if the plebiscitary democracy of the United States is not strictly the functional equivalent of totalitarian rule, it is a worryingly close approximation.

Looking around the world at other media systems, the struggle to avoid the pap of commercialism and the propaganda of government control is universal. The media systems closest to approximating the democratic ideal are those of northern Europe, the Democratic Corporatist model. These retain a strong, well-funded public service media that does a far better job than commercial media of informing the electorate (and even influences commercial media in a positive direction, along with content regulations). In the presence of legal mechanisms to weaken government influence over public media, government-funded public service media is a force tending toward a more knowledgeable (and more *equally* knowledgeable) citizenry, one better able to identify its various interests and match them to political policies. The accumulated evidence makes unavoidable the conclusion that the U.S. media system (along with others) is an impediment to a system of government in which all people exercise equal political power.

Which political memes are prevalent among the U.S. electorate? That is, what information do voters get delivered to them by the predominant provider of information logistics, the media? An observer is likely to first notice that they are few in number. The electorate may not be stupid, but it is unarguably ignorant—and ignorant of the extent of its ignorance. For an observer aware of the breadth of the *global* political spectrum and the variety of ideologies around the world, the second most likely observation is that the Right and Left in the United States are surprisingly similar. Disagreements on social and religious issues run deep, but some of the most central issues of politics—how to produce and distribute goods and services, and interact with the rest of the world—are only fleetingly debated, as would be expected of a population ignorant of the variety of perspectives. So what does it mean for the voters to *decide* on economic or foreign policy, for instance, or to choose representatives to carry out their will? To ask the question is to answer it.

Nonetheless, the evidence does not allow for a strict deterministic reading: inputs do not *determine* outputs. Input from the media determines what information will be widely held, but not how that information will be processed and acted on. Conceptual blending can produce kaleidoscopic effects: a character or storyline from a movie or novel can blend with the anemic information provided by the media to create radically divergent ideas about a politician or political policy. For instance, the characters in *House of Cards* or *In the Loop* can blend with mere horserace coverage of politics to create a deeply cynical attitude toward politicians, even if they are generally presented positively in the media (creating arguably more-accurate knowledge even in the absence of much relevant information). Yet despite the important distinction between *determining* and *influencing*, it does little to reduce the democratic deficit. Leaving the formation of an accurately informed citizenry up to their own creativity is a crapshoot, with as great a likelihood of success as tossing paint against a canvas and hoping to create a painting to rival Jackson Pollock's.

1 Social Evolution: Observations for Epistemology

"Nothing is so passionate as a vested interest disguised as an intellectual conviction."
—Sean O'Casey, "The White Plague"

The meme's eye view, or the perspective of social evolution, is cause for a great deal of epistemic skepticism. It points out the arbitrariness and contingency of our beliefs, as being the result of memes which happened to reproduce themselves in our brains. It forces the uncomfortable recognition that each of us would have entirely different beliefs had we merely inhabited a different environment (as Montaigne would say, on the other side of a mountain). It demands that we engage in foundationally critical thinking; in light of our suboptimal rationality and the contingency of our beliefs, we must make constant good-faith attempts to debunk our own beliefs. That is, we must apply a falsificationist strategy against our beliefs, actively seeking out evidence that may undermine them—in effect, consciously swimming against the stream of our evolved psychology, which seeks to confirm our own beliefs.

There is no avoiding that even the most well-read among us are radically ignorant and that the realm of unknown unknowns dwarfs that of what we know and even what we know we do not know. Since our brains evolved to exhibit cognitive conservatism, treating our beliefs like prized possessions we are loathe to give up or replace, we must realize that our feeling of confidence in our beliefs is a universal illusion and only rarely well-founded. And as Macaulay might have argued, whose opinion is to decide which beliefs are well-founded, and whose confidence in their beliefs is a deception? This epistemic quandary would be bad enough even if our brains were bias-free blank slates from birth; it is made worse in light of our evolved political predispositions, our Left or Right psychology, our elective affinities for ideas promising equality and change or hierarchy and tradition.

Our ideas about any political issue are inherently contestable: a definitive answer to any of them is vanishingly unlikely, if only because social evolution is rarely in stasis. A definitive, correct answer at one moment is likely to be incorrect at the next moment in direct proportion to the change occurring in the interim. Adjudicating even the simplest political question is prey to radical ignorance, different sets of information held by opposing sides, the incommensurability of even the same (disembodied) information stored in different brains with emotional memories tied to it, and our evolved political predispositions. Every political argument shares in common the fate of every *legal* argument: "but the other side can argue that…" As in law, so in politics: the argument that carries the day is not necessarily the best-supported, but the one favored by the relevant authority, whether a judge or jury, the majority of voters or the government. And as Jonathan Swift wrote, lawyers "take special Care to record all the Decisions formerly made against common Justice and the general Reason of Mankind. These, under the name of *Precedents*, they produce as Authorities to justify the most iniquitous Opinions; and the Judges never fail of decreeing accordingly."[3] Likewise, the dead hand of political history produces its own sort of iniquitous precedents, the basic beliefs, and self-serving historical myths into which we are socialized. In the face of this, a retreat into radical relativism or epistemological skepticism, even cynicism, is understandable.

Yet an absolute epistemological skepticism is unwarranted. Just as the process of motivated reasoning is impeded by so-called knowledge constraints (we cannot completely ignore contrary evidence, and at critical mass it forces us to revise our beliefs), so too our political beliefs encounter reality constraints. We can no sooner believe that submission to the directives of an intergalactic empire is the best political-economic system than we can believe that the moon is made of Brie. Still, this is little comfort; the reality that can constrain our beliefs is too distant and immense to have any ideas *about* other than spooks. However, even with its distance and immensity, over time reality has asserted itself against our more fanciful political ideas, from the divine right of kings to the inferiority of certain "races" as created by God or nature. History is a graveyard of our more egregious spooks.

The epistemology suggested by the evolution of ideas can offer little guidance as to choosing accurate beliefs. But the banal, law student observation that "a different argument could be made" warrants only a tired nod of assent; it does not warrant radical relativism or all-encompassing epistemological skepticism. The question is not *whether* an argument could be made—of course, one *could* be made, an infinite number of different arguments can *always* be made—but whether an argument is better supported than any contrary argument. Of course, there are no judges on intellectual Mount Olympus who can observe the totality of relevant evidentiary support and unerringly rule in favor of the best-supported argument. We have only radically ignorant human judges. Yet in spite of our unavoidably, immutably radical ignorance, our brains were "designed" to argue: millions of years of evolution have produced a species of innate lawyers, capable not only of crafting arguments using the information one has, but also of choosing the most accurate and beneficial understandings of reality—again, given the information one has. Since our radical ignorance precludes us from choosing only the wisest and best among us to decide political questions, we are left with government by public opinion. Our only hope of making public opinion into a fine governor is to inform it. And since we know that we cannot be certain in the veracity of our own political beliefs, to *inform* public opinion can only mean to expose it to a diversity of political beliefs.

Even so, this provides little guidance; it is merely saying that we are dexterous enough to pick them up after we "let the cards fall where they may"—only it is requiring that we use a full deck. But the evidence of demand-side, psychological biases provides something more. It cannot suggest which ideas are more likely to be true, but it does suggest which ideas are *less* likely to be true. Absent some mystical principle by which our evolved psychological biases actually incline us toward Truth (a wildly contradictory Truth—truths which are true only on one side of a mountain, and false on the other), we can confidently use them to determine which of our ideas deserve greater *skepticism* than others. As in constitutional jurisprudence, where different laws are given varying levels of scrutiny according to the interest of the state and their risk of encroaching upon fundamental rights, we can use our knowledge of psychological biases as a guide to determine our level of skepticism toward certain ideas. Exposing the pedigree of an idea may undercut some— the pedigree of the "race" meme being the most obvious example— but exposing the psychological bias *supportive* of an idea is more widely applicable. Once our skepticism has been heightened with regard to an idea, we should expend greater effort in attempting to refute it, or in finding and considering someone else's refutation.

All psychological biases are irrational, compared to a liberal ideal, but some can be socially beneficial. We have biases toward equality and change or hierarchy and tradition, and while these are irrational to the extent that they derive from genetic endowments rather than analysis of evidence, they may be beneficial. In fact, these biases may be the cornerstone of social evolution: Left psychology provides a source of novel variation, and Right psychology provides longevity for the variants of the past. Nonetheless, we are likely to adopt and adhere to some ideas, to some extent, due to our psychological Left and Right biases. We would do well to submit ideas favored by our Left or Right psychology to greater scrutiny.

Other psychological biases are both irrational and harmful. In-group bias, while evolutionarily important in the abstract for its role in facilitating cooperation, is rationally indefensible in the majority of its manifestations. Being born in Borneo, Taiwan, or on a space station are all irrelevant—just as irrelevant as the color of one's eyes, skin, hair, or clothes—to a determination of individual or group worth. The fact that in-group bias makes us likely to treat such irrelevant, arbitrary distinctions as important in determining political questions must give us pause: it is a rational error despite its evolutionary pedigree. *Is* does not imply *ought*. Rather, it demands suspicion: we must apply strict scrutiny to ideas that make our in-group, whether national, partisan, ideological, ethnic, or any other sort, seem praiseworthy. *Ceteris paribus*, we are more likely to adopt an idea if it paints our in-group in a pleasing light; hence, all ideas we are exposed to which make us feel good about our in-group deserve suspicion. And *only* suspicion: in-group bias is only one force among many influencing our adoption of ideas, and there are plenty of true ideas that also make our in-groups look good. The United States was an inspiration for democrats the world over, despite its historical failure to live up to the ideal; Britain outlawed the practice of widow-burning in India, despite causing untold misery there and throughout its empire; and the Japanese empire freed millions from European colonialism, despite yoking them under its own domination.

The system justification tendency is another irrational bias demanding the application of strict scrutiny. (System justification itself could be conceived as the application of strict scrutiny to proposals for system *change*, thereby irrationally favoring the status quo.) Ideas with a Panglossian air, those that support whatever status quo one happens to be living in, deserve more suspicion then ideas critical of it. *Ceteris paribus*, ideas supportive of one's government or political and economic system have an (irrational) advantage over critical ideas; apologetics are stickier than critiques. Hence, we should apply extra scrutiny to defenses of the status quo (and only scrutiny: an irrational *inclination* does not imply the absence of any rational reasons).

Studies of gene-culture coevolution have uncovered a "prestige bias" tending to push us into irrationally adopting ideas simply because they are held by those with wealth or high status. As with in-group bias, this has a clear evolutionary rationale: adopting ideas from highly-regarded fellow tribe members likely was an adaptive strategy for most of human history. Someone able to win the approbation of aggressive egalitarians likely had some useful ideas about food, predators, or social life. After the Lucky Sperm Club arose along with sedentary mass societies, however, high status from wealth went to a much broader class of people, whose ideas are just as likely to be beneficial as harmful, brilliant as moronic. (Think of the political ideas of Henry Ford or Kim Kardashian.) *Ceteris paribus*, the spooks of the rich are no better than the spooks of the poor or middle-class—yet we are more likely to adopt them under the influence of prestige bias (not to mention supply-side biases). Ideas favored by those with wealth or high status therefore deserve stricter scrutiny.

These sorts of irrational psychological biases are important for epistemology, the study of knowledge, and may also help explain its opposite: "agnotology," or the study of ignorance.[4] While awareness of psychological biases can help *improve* epistemic practices in politics, they (along with supply-side biases) *explain* much about agnotology. The cigarette industry sowing doubt about the link between tobacco and cancer is primarily an example of a supply-side bias: tobacco companies funding and disseminating research meant to persuade people that cigarettes might *not* be harmful. It also involved demand-side bias: smokers were more likely to accept manufactured doubt about the danger of the drug they used (through cognitive dissonance reduction, confirmation bias, and the pull of addiction). Both forms of bias produced widespread ignorance of the very real link between cancer and cigarettes.

Another example is that of climate change.[5] Military-funded research in the 1940s predicted dangerous global warming, but military secrecy kept these findings from being publicly disseminated (a supply-side bias).[6] As other scientists and institutions began to openly publish similar findings, demand-side biases (cognitive consistency, system justification) entered the picture: believers in free-market ideology opposed the science because it suggested government intervention into the economy to solve a dire problem caused by the free market itself. This then fed back into a supply-side bias, as free-market fundamentalists took a page from Big Tobacco's playbook and began funding and disseminating research meant to cast doubt on climate change.

Of course, ignorance is rife in the political realm, which Jeffrey Friedman describes as "a cacophony of confident voices that unwittingly express factual ignorance, theoretical ignorance, ignorance of logic, ignorance of their own possible ignorance, ignorance of their opponents' possible ignorance; and, in consequence, dogmatism, demagoguery, and demonization."[7] But the ignorance of agnotology is of a yet another sort, suggesting partially-hidden or submerged knowledge on the demand side—a result of self-deception—and conscious attempts to spread ignorance (or doubt) on the supply side (facilitated by other psychological biases, like in-group bias).[8] Charles Mills has explored agnotology in liberal political philosophy, demonstrating how classical liberals displayed a shocking degree of ignorance about how their purportedly universal philosophy was in practice applied only to Whites.[9] He has identified the key variable of political epistemology and agnotology as *power*:

> [T]he conceptual array with which the cognizer approaches the world needs itself to be scrutinized for its adequacy to the world, for how well it maps the reality it claims to be describing. If the society is one structured by relations of domination and subordination (as of course most societies in recent human history have been), then in certain areas this conceptual apparatus is likely going to be shaped in various ways by the biases of the ruling groups.[10]

Indeed, economic and political power is the preponderant influence in the ecology of information. It brings with it its own demand biases, which readily enter supply as well. Perhaps Mark Twain should have written instead that whenever you find yourself on the side of the *powerful*, it is time to pause and reflect.

2 Power

> *"There is something about power that distorts judgments more or less. The chances that a powerful person will make an error are much greater than those of a weak person. Power has recourse to its own resources. Weakness must draw on reason. All other things being equal, it is always true that those who govern have opinions which are less just, less sane, less impartial than those whom they govern."*
> —Benjamin Constant, *Principles of Politics Applicable to All Governments*

In a free, commercial media system whose output mimics that of a government-controlled propaganda system, evil outcomes are not the result of evil intentions. They are the result of an invisible hand: the aggregate forces, pressures, and tendencies in a certain type of human ecology, whether the business world, the foreign policy establishment, or the media system. Adam Smith's "unseen hand" referred both to the force of self-interest and the force of morality, which Smith conceptualized as the desire to conform to the judgments of others in the society.[11] Smith wrote during a time when corporations were banned in England (in reaction to the Enron of the day, the South Sea Company's collapse); he recognized that the professional managers of corporations would not run their businesses in the way a baker or butcher (or partnership) would—they would lack the pressure of moral conformity.[12] Just as psychopaths do not intuitively *feel* our evolved sense of morality that produces conformity to social norms, psychopathic institutions lack structural features that might impose conformity to social morality. Institutions *with* such features would obviate any worry about psychopathic individuals within them: their individual (immoral) intentions would matter less once constrained by countervailing institutional pressure. This pressure would ensure that to do well, one would have to do good—regardless of motives and intentions. Defending Marcus Aurelius against the charge of narcissism, "that all his life he was just, laborious, beneficent out of vanity, and that his virtues served only to dupe mankind," Voltaire wrote: "Dear god, give us often such rascals!"[13]

But even in the face of morally appropriate institutional design, power remains a force capable of skewing the ecology of information and producing immoral outcomes. Power often is the creation of institutions: it is what control of an institution grants an individual. As such, it is both a supply-side bias (the institution and its effects once wielded) and a demand-side bias, since it affects our psychology in profound ways. The science fiction writer Douglas Adams observed: "It is difficult to be sat on all day, every day, by some other creature, without forming an opinion about them. ... On the other hand, it is perfectly possible to sit all day, every day, on top of another creature and not have the slightest thought about them whatsoever."[14] This is supported by psychological research: power reduces our ability to understand how others see the world, adopt others' perspectives, take into account others' knowledge or lack thereof, and intuit others' emotions.[15]

Like all psychological biases, that produced by power is invisible, subconscious. Max Weber was correct "that in every such situation he who is more favored feels the never ceasing need to look upon his position as in some way 'legitimate,' upon his advantage as 'deserved,' and the other's disadvantage as being brought about by the latter's 'fault.' That the purely accidental causes of the difference may be ever so obvious makes no difference."[16] Psychological bias is immune to the obvious.

If power is defined as the ability to exercise one's will, then in market societies where most everything one desires may be purchased, wealth is a rather direct proxy for power. Unsurprisingly, the psychological effects of wealth mimic those of power: wealth reduces our ability to empathize with others,[17] leading to a style of moral judgments[18] similar to that of psychopaths.[19] It makes us feel more entitled and leads to greater narcissism.[20] A study of lottery winners found that a sudden windfall of money made them less egalitarian and more supportive of right-wing political parties, in direct proportion to the amount of money won.[21]

Little wonder then, given the demand-side bias of wealth and power, that the wealthiest 1% in the USA has starkly different political beliefs than those of the 99%. They are more concerned about government deficits, more favorable to cutting taxes and social welfare programs (health care, the earned income tax credit, social security, minimum wage, government jobs programs, education), less favorable to increasing government regulation of corporations and redistributing wealth or income, and less concerned with inequality.[22] And in the U.S. political system, the wealthy mostly get what they want, while the government is non-responsive to the desires of the non-wealthy.[23] Evidence shows that elected officials do not even bother learning what the electorate wants.[24] Why should they: wealth can buy elections *to* Congress,[25] and votes *in* Congress.[26] Insufficient money is ever so much a bar to holding public office in the United States as the "wrong" ideology is in Iran or China.[27]

Private power is not *greater* than public power so much as it *constitutes* public power; government is a Leviathan to the people, a tool for the wealthy.[28] The demand-side bias produced by power fashions the link between class interest and ideology, and the disproportionate influence the wealthy exert over the media, political, and education systems creates supply-side biases influencing elections. Of course, the electorate has *proximate* power over the government through the vote. But the voters are the owners of the country in the same sense that shareholders are the owners of a corporation whose CEO presents them with annual reports giving them misleading or fraudulent information. Voters are the proximate owners; the ultimate owners are those who control the supply of information voters can easily, cheaply access. And policy-relevant information is cheaper for businesses to obtain, since voters must pay in time and money for it, while businesses acquire it in the daily course of operations.[29] Information drives a wide gap between proximate and ultimate control, explaining why the government does not serve the "median voter" but only those investment blocs that can afford the exorbitant costs of campaigning; without money, reason, discussion, and persuasion avail one nothing.[30] "The electorate is not too stupid or too tired to control the political system. It is merely too poor."[31] Delving into the byzantine array of recent campaign finance records, Tom Ferguson concludes: "What both major investors and candidates have long known intuitively— that a relatively small number of giant sources provide most of the funding for successful major party candidates—is true. The relatively thin stream of small contributions simply does not suffice to float (conventionally managed) national campaigns, and all insiders know it."[32]

The power of wealth exerts its pull in politics and the media, and also in the academy. Supply-side biases enter through grants from foundations and institutes named after their philanthropist founders (and funders), resulting in the production of analyses that seem less like political *science* and more like apologetics for the status quo.[33] In international relations scholarship, power pulls more directly.[34]

Of course, poverty does not grant wisdom, and wealth does not guarantee a distorted ideology. Malevolent motives or character do not need to be imputed; again, the ecology of our minds (psychology) interacting with the ecology of information (media, schools) produces its effects with or without human intentionality. Hence, not only are we more likely to adopt ideas of the powerful due to "prestige bias" operating within our psychology; we are also more likely to adopt the ideas of the powerful due to their influence over supply. *Ceteris paribus*, ideas favored and promoted by the powerful must be given stricter scrutiny.

3   Economics

"¡La economía es de gente, no de curvas!"—*"Economics is about people, not curves!"*
—Graffiti on a Madrid campus

To create a distinction between good ("supporting" of the ideals it purports to embody) and bad ("undermining" of the ideals it purports to embody) propaganda, the philosopher Jason Stanley took a step back to acknowledge that judgments about propaganda are unavoidably ideological: "If a neutral stance means a stance without ideological belief, then the neutral stance is a myth."[35] We all have ideological beliefs, spooks:

> The fact that there is no neutral stance cannot lead us to political paralysis, or to skepticism about political and moral reality. It is an error to try to evade the facts of our epistemic limitations by adopting metaphysical anti-realism. We must come to terms with the fact of our limited perspective while occupying that very perspective. There is simply no other way.[36]

So too this book must perforce occupy an ideological perspective. There is no objective perspective possible—only the objectivity of idiots (in the classical Greek sense of one who is removed from public affairs).

To some readers, this entire argument is a tempest in a teapot. "Sure," they might say, "there are problems with our media systems, and they might not be ideal – but what tragedy have they caused?" It is for this reason that the majority of media critics occupy a position to the right or left of the ideological spectrum in the media system.

We have already seen how media reports on economic issues hew closely to economic orthodoxy, particularly to the views of financial market participants and central bankers. This would be less of a problem if economic orthodoxy were like dominant paradigms in the natural sciences. But as Robert Sidelsky explains, economics is different: "much more so than in physics, the research agenda and structure of power within the profession reflect the structure of power outside it. They have the character of ideologies."[37] Holders of economic power have no interest in shaping physics or chemistry, but the science of the source of their power is another matter.[38] This reflection of the power outside economics forces us to ask:

> Who finances the institutions from which ideas spring? Who finances the dissemination of ideas in popular form – media, think tanks? What are the incentives facing the producers, disseminators, and popularisers of ideas even in a society in which discussion is 'free'? In short, what is the agenda of business? It is reasonable to see business as the hard power behind the soft power of ideas, not because the business community speaks with one voice, or because there are not other centres of hard power

(e.g. government) but because it is the main source of the money without which the intellectual estate would wither and die.[39]

This hard selection pressure (among others) has shaped economics since its inception. Robert Babe observes: "At every stage of its evolution, mainstream economics has been aligned with, and has doctrinally served, a class interest."[40] Or, when the interests of businesses in a country were sufficiently uniform, national interest would subsume class interest as the master of economics. For example, Sophus Reinert traces a forgotten British protectionist treatise through time and translations into several European languages from an explicitly evolutionary perspective.[41] First published in 1695, John Cary's *Essay on the State of England* argued for the encouragement of high value-added domestic manufacturing by imposing tariffs on foreign goods and restrictions on exports of raw materials; while this could increase prices of manufactured goods, it was compensated by an increase in wages.[42] Once implemented, this policy served England well, turning it into a manufacturing powerhouse. Yet England refused to preach what it practiced; instead, the British government kicked away the ladder, promoting the idea that only free trade and open markets brought wealth.[43]

By the nineteenth century, "'free trade' simply meant England's freedom to export manufactured goods in exchange for foreign raw materials, a practice oxymoronically known as 'free trade imperialism.'"[44] Yet British economists like Adam Smith and David Ricardo pointedly ignored the reality that Britain's success was owed to protectionism, along with its imperial depredations. (As Michael Hudson archly observes, "gunboats do not appear in Ricardian trade theory," and "[w]hen the Native Americans refused to submit to the plantations system and its personal servitude, armed appropriation of their land drastically reduced their 'factor proportions.'")[45] Economic ideas evolve to serve power, including by avoiding information that cannot be used for the purpose. When England needed to catch up, Cary's protectionism held sway; when England held a lead, protectionism continued in practice but was jettisoned in theory, and a new crop of economists preached to the world "do as we say, not as we do." Luckily for several other European countries such as Germany, these new economic doctrines were ignored (until, following England's example, they became sufficiently developed to afford free trade and preach it to less-developed others).

As time went by, even Smith and Ricardo lost favor. They and other classical economists adhered to the labor theory of value, which Karl

Marx later used as the foundation of his theory that capitalist profits comprised surplus value expropriated from laborers.[46] Even worse, Marx tied the labor theory of value and classical economics to a prediction that economic evolution would inevitably proceed to socialism.

> The use to which Marx put Ricardo's labor theory of value rendered it anathema... After the 1870s, just as Europe initiated a new colonialist expansion that culminated in World War I, orthodox economists stopped theorizing about the stages of development and its foreign-policy aspects. So inextricably had Marx identified the evolution of capitalism with the emergence of socialist institutions that the minds of orthodox economists snapped shut. A kind of fatalism, epitomized by the factor endowment view of comparative advantage, supplanted doctrines of active government development strategy. In advocating the avoidance of active government policy, economists dropped their concerns with technology and productivity. Henceforth their theories were marginal in a pejorative sense.[47]

The labor theory of value was replaced by the theory of "marginal utility," which was far more soothing to the wealthy. Instead of value deriving from labor, the theory posited that value derived from subjective preferences. As such, there could be no unjust expropriation of labor in the economy, since the marketplace merely expressed the aggregate desires of interchangeable individuals and compensated everyone in accordance with how well they met the desires of other market participants.[48] Neoclassical economics was born and as if in reward for its services, endures to this day.

Politics entered into the battle of paradigms in economics.[49] At the turn of the century, economists whose work pointed out problems with capitalist economies were denounced as traitorous socialists, denied jobs, or forced to resign; some became neoclassicists. At the beginning of the twentieth century, the neoclassical school included a focus on the distribution of income and material welfare instead of "preferences." But after a brief spell during which the Great Depression forced some reality on the Pollyannaish neoclassical vision of capitalism, and World War II demonstrated the effectiveness of massive government intervention into the economy, the field retrenched in an ideological fantasyland. With the beginning of the Cold War, government and private funding for economics favored apologetics for capitalism, to be used in ideological warfare against the Soviets.

[I]t was not an improvement of knowledge or tools that led to the shift from classical and institutional economics to today's "antigovernment-neoclassical-rational choice" mainstream. It was the result of a redefinition of what economics should be concerned with – from a fair to an efficient allocation of resources – an effort that was generously funded by businessmen and the military in the name of cementing the power and legitimacy of their selves and their beliefs within society in a post-1929 Depression ideological Cold War world.[50]

Today, neoclassical economics has received withering (and unanswered) criticism from many quarters, from within and without the field,[51] and a mix of heterodox approaches has recently challenged its dominance.[52] Fundamentally, its worse-than-worthlessness is a consequence of its limited methods.[53] Mainstream economics has not yet found an equilibrium between Panglossian irrelevance and catastrophic failures.

Yet the failures this methodological kneecapping has produced may continue, since the selection pressure of needing to be ideologically congenial to the wealthy has proven stronger than the selection pressure for a science capable of providing policy guidance for an equitable and sustainable economy. After all, from the perspective of those benefitting from the financialization of the economy, the epistemic failure of mainstream economics is not a bug—it is a feature.[54] As two economic historians put it, "[t]he price for maintaining such a view has always been to ignore or deny all significant social problems and all significant social conflicts"—an attractively low price for those unaffected by such problems and conflicts—while "[t]he reward for maintaining this view is, of course, that one can sit back and relax, forget all the unpleasantness of the world, and enjoy one's dreams of the beatific vision and eternal felicity."[55] And, one should add, wealth.

Not only does mainstream economics have a track record of failure for the non-wealthy (and a record of success for the minority benefitting from financialization), but merely *studying* it has been shown to produce "debased" moral behavior and attitudes.[56] Furthermore, the negative effects of earning a degree in economics are long lasting; one study found that U.S. Congress members with an economics degree were significantly likelier to engage in corrupt practices than their peers.[57]

Regardless, the most pernicious effect of mainstream economics may be in crowding out alternative ideas. Take the issue of government debt, which the U.S. media in recent years has presented as if it were the equivalent of household borrowing.[58] If a household borrows more than it can repay, bankruptcy awaits; this suggests that a similarly dire fate might await governments with too much debt ("look at Greece!"). Yet a government like that of the United States, which produces its own sovereign currency (unlike Greece), can never run out of the money it creates with a keyboard.[59] It does not even need to borrow, since like private banks, but without even solvency or capital adequacy restrictions, the government creates money *ex nihilo*. As Michael Hudson observed about the Great Recession bailouts:

> If there was a silver lining to all this, it has been to demonstrate that *if the Treasury and Federal Reserve can create $13 trillion of public obligations – money – electronically on computer keyboards, there really is no Social Security problem at all, no Medicare shortfall, no inability of the American government to rebuild the nation's infrastructure.* ... Even more remarkable is the attempt to convince the population that new money and debt creation to bail out Wall Street – and vest a new century of financial billionaires at public subsidy – cannot be mobilized just as readily to save labor and industry in the "real" economy.[60]

This attempt to convince the population of an absurdity is all the worse in light of two considerations: the suffering and even death attributable to the crisis[61] and the existence of plausible solutions. The media never tires of propagating scare stories about "entitlements" driving the U.S. into bankruptcy[62]—whatever that would mean for a sovereign issuer of fiat currency.[63] At least in the most accessed medium, television, there is no discussion of proposals for a universal basic income, a government job guarantee, or doing again what was done during World War II: re-tooling factories *en masse*, this time to produce a fully renewable energy system. Ideas that deserve mere *awareness*, plus critical scrutiny, are absent from the U.S. media—much like ideas about Iraq's actual military capabilities and Iraqis' opinions on an invasion in 2002–2003. If mere facts have no wings, then entire economic theories and policy proposals do not either.

One proposal a democratic electorate might be interested in is called the Chicago Plan. To understand it would require an understanding that contrary to economics textbooks,[64] private banks do not intermediate between savers and borrowers and banks are not constrained in their lending by the loanable funds savers have deposited.[65] Instead, banks create

8 CONCLUSION: THE INVISIBLE HAND ... 329

money *ex nihilo*, constrained only by solvency and capital requirements—but most powerfully, their own assessments (prone to the bias of "animal spirits") of profitability and solvency. And when banks create money via loans, they create deposits. As two IMF economists explained, "[t]he quantity of reserves is therefore a consequence, not a cause, of lending and money creation."[66] This is not how the monetary system is described in economics classes or the media. But the unavoidable conclusion is that "private banks are almost fully in control of the money creation process"—that is, "privately created deposit money ... plays the central role in the current U.S. monetary system, while government-issued money plays a quantitatively and conceptually negligible role."[67]

The Chicago Plan would reverse this, putting private banks into the role of a saver-borrower intermediary they are already falsely believed to play, and government into the role of primary credit creator. First proposed in the wake of the Great Depression, the Chicago Plan won wide support among economists, but was never implemented due to resistance from private banks.[68] After detailing their analysis along with a simulation, the IMF economist-authors conclude that the benefits of the plan would exceed even those imagined when it was proposed nearly a century ago:

> The Chicago Plan could significantly reduce business cycle volatility caused by rapid changes in banks' attitudes towards credit risk, it would eliminate bank runs, and it would lead to an instantaneous and large reduction in the levels of both government and private debt. It would accomplish the latter by making government-issued money, which represents equity in the commonwealth rather than debt, the central liquid asset of the economy, while banks concentrate on their strength, the extension of credit to investment projects that require monitoring and risk management expertise.[69]

Regardless of whether this argument or that put forth by banks to retain their exorbitant privilege of money creation would be found convincing, the point is that the electorate cannot deliberate on an argument it has never been exposed to. That is, in an economy drowning in debt, stagnant wages, and underemployment, rutted into secular stagnation and regular crises, the citizenry is denied the opportunity to even learn about a proposal intended to solve these problem and others (government credit creation could be directed toward renewable energy and climate change mitigation). The information ecology or the marketplace of ideas is impoverished or distorted as a result. Again, the normatively indefensible selection pressure of power leaves its mark.

4 What This Perspective Suggests About Contemporary Politics

The election of the United States' first reality TV star president recalls how, ever since television became the predominant source of political information, U.S. politics itself has been uncomfortably close to a reality TV show. It was the *first* reality TV show, to the extent that access to the airwaves has been limited to a narrow ideological spectrum, restricting the options citizens have to choose from. In this sense, the "show" of politics is produced by those who control this means of communication—as A.J. Liebling quipped, "freedom of the press is guaranteed to those who own one." Real power is exerted behind the scenes, although viewers do get to vote on the occupant of *The Real World: 1600 Pennsylvania Avenue*.

It stands to reason from the perspective in this book that someone with a lot of TV exposure would have a good chance of being elected by a largely politically ignorant electorate (particularly when profit-seeking television networks discovered that he attracted a great many eyeballs to sell to advertisers). His widely disseminated persona as a successful businessman resonated in a society taught in schools and by the news media to believe that free-market capitalism is the best system of economic organization, if not one prescribed by God. And while many immersed in economic memes from reputable media outlets pointed out that by several objective measurements (like the most commonly used unemployment rate, GDP, and the federal deficit), the economy had recovered from the Great Financial Crisis, other objective measurements (median real wages, wealth and income concentration, inter-generational mobility, labor force participation, and household debt) indicated a great deal of economic suffering and anxiety among broad swaths of the electorate—fertile soil for a "change" candidate, even (or especially) one who breaks the rules of political decorum and strays outside of the ideological center—but an unfriendly environment for an establishment candidate.

Trump either devised or stumbled on an effective strategy: repeat memes from right-wing media outlets (not just Fox, but further right, fringe outlets), even if the memes are considered false and the outlets deemed disreputable by the ideological mainstream. As a Harvard study of the online ecosystem concluded, a "sustained campaign of materially misleading political messaging ... leverag[ing] basic psychological features of memory and belief formation ... generated a pool of memes that could be recombined for mutual reinforcement ... made into stories that created a folklore, reinforcing in-group identity and denigrating the out-group."[70] By repeating these memes and folklore, Trump seemed forthright and fearless to audiences of the same outlets, a rare truth-teller among a sea of lying politicians. So too with statements that crossed taboos against speech considered racist and sexist by the political elite—not only would these resonate with voters harboring racist and sexist ideas (memes about ethnic out-groups being genetically or culturally inferior and promoting the relegation of women to subordinate social roles), but also among those with ideas explaining their own economic woes as the fault of immigrants and "mooching" minorities (due to ignorance of accurate, more complex explanations, and facilitated by in-group bias). In-group bias under one of its many guises, partisanship, did the rest, with Republicans overwhelmingly voting for the Republican; the hypothetical median voter was not a factor.

The ultimate source of these ideas is the right-wing media, which has grown prodigiously since the late 1980s.[71] As this book's perspective would predict, in contradistinction to the view that media outlets merely adapt to citizens' (somehow) endogenously formed opinions, first came the rise in right-wing media and then came increased polarization in Congress and among the electorate.[72] This second wave of right-wing media, less intellectual and more entertainment-oriented than the first wave in mid-century, did not simply send ideas into the ether—it transported physical bits of information into tens of millions of brains. The recipients of such information were free to disregard it or reinterpret it in myriad ways, but the stark increase in political polarization (particularly on the Right) suggests that many chose to accept ideas from the newly opened right-wing floodgate, and shaped their political worldviews out of it. The estimated combined weekly audience for conservative television, cable, and (overwhelmingly) radio programming, 115 million, is over 50% larger than the combined weekly audience of nearly 75 million for centrist and liberal programming.[73] (The ratings data this back-of-the-envelope calculation used do not allow discounting for viewers/listeners of multiple shows; hence, the total weekly audience for all broadcast TV and radio political programming is undoubtedly smaller.) Hence, conservative and liberal views on social issues, but only conservative and centrist views on economic and foreign policy issues, were easily, cheaply accessible. For left-wing views on economics and foreign policy, one would have to scour the blooming, buzzing overabundance of the internet. Yochai Benkler and colleagues explain that:

> [T]he highly asymmetric architecture of the media ecosystem precedes [Trump], as do the asymmetric patterns of political polarization, and we think it more likely that his success was enabled by a political and media landscape ripe for takeover rather than that he himself upended the ecosystem. Trump, as both candidate and president, was both contributing cause and outcome, operating on the playing field of an already radicalized, asymmetric media ecosystem. (Benkler et al., *Network Propaganda*, 19–20)

Yet Trump, as the logical (if large) extension of existing trends,[74] was not the most interesting phenomenon in the 2016 election. More interesting was how electoral propaganda and legacy media outlets were shown to have lost a great deal of their influence (at least influence from the analysis the media provides, if not influence from the airtime granted to eyeball-grabbing candidates). Had they kept the influence they enjoyed a decade or two ago, Clinton would have defeated Trump (had Jeb Bush, the winner of the early dollar vote, not already beaten him for the Republican nomination) on the strength of her support from most newspapers and TV channels and her significant advantage in ad spending. As many to the Left and Right of the political center have long hoped, the dominance of legacy mass media outlets over public opinion was eclipsed—pleasing the Left, by more participatory forms of media (social media, blogs, etc.), and pleasing the Right, by more conservative, partisan, but still commercial media outlets (Fox, talk radio, the websites of the newly christened "alt-Right," etc.—all of which could extend their reach through social media).

Much attention has focused on the role of social media and "fake news" in the 2016 election. Given the tiny margins by which Trump won, they belong on a long list of *necessary* causes: sexism, racism or "racial resentment," turnout by non-college-educated, older, and rural voters, insufficient turnout by ethnic minorities, working-class distress, battlefield casualties, James Comey, the DNC emails, automation, a last-minute surge in dark money, neoliberal economic policies, voter suppression and disenfranchisement, the Clinton campaign's strategy, and more (possibly even including inept Russian facebook posts). Yet as the authors of a Columbia Journalism School study observe, fake news is a distraction from the larger issue that the structure and the economics of social platforms incentivize the spread of low-quality content over high-quality material. Journalism with high civic value—journalism that investigates power, or reaches underserved and local communities—is discriminated against by a system that favors scale and shareability.[75]

This is merely familiar commercial bias operating in a different media ecosystem, social media, where editors at legacy media outlets are replaced with new editors: those in one's online social network. Meanwhile, the panic over "fake news" is currently pressuring tech companies to tweak their algorithms to reshape the internet ecosystem in the image of the legacy media. Media researcher Jonathan Albright predicts that this "next era of the infowars is likely to result in the most pervasive filter yet: it's likely to normalise the weeding out of viewpoints that are in conflict with established interests."[76] The more things change, the more they (may) stay the same.

The other contender for most interesting development was the overperformance of the Bernie Sanders campaign. One need not go back as far as the days of the Red Scare to find disbelief that a self-described democratic socialist could nearly win a major party's nomination; early 2016 would do. His eventual loss is easily explainable: most regular voters in Democratic Party primaries are among the (relatively) politically knowledgeable, whose main lifeline to the realm of politics is the agenda-setting media, which favored the establishment frontrunner. The anomaly was his unexpected success. Like Trump, he was doubtless helped by an economy failing broad swaths of the population and a message closely calibrated to this reality, but he also seemed uniquely helped by the internet. Not only did he dominate on social media platforms, but he won a higher share of the vote in states with a higher proportion of netizens and in counties with greater broadband internet availability.[77] Since the internet provides a significantly different ecology of information than television and newspapers,[78] it should produce different effects on the formation of political opinions.[79] The vast breadth of the internet provides a greater variety of facts (and lies), arguments (sound and specious), perspectives (worthwhile and worthless), and interpretations (considered and kooky) than any television station or newspaper could *hope* to offer. Those who turn to the internet for political information have a greater chance of being exposed to ideas one may never find in the legacy media, including ideas like democratic socialism the U.S. legacy media has long considered verboten. The

2016 U.S. election (further) demonstrated that the internet has vastly changed the ecology of political information; if recent experience can justify any prediction of the future, it would be to expect the unexpected.

In Europe, the same prediction is sensible. While proponents of the European Union expected it to reduce the likelihood of the violent conflict that has soaked European history in blood, ironically some features of the E.U.'s design are recreating the conditions that led to Europe's last orgy of bloodletting. In the 1930s, applied liberal economic ideology created severe economic pain for majorities of Europeans, leading many to support fascist governments that rejected economic liberalism and used the state to intervene heavily in the economy to employ the unemployed and produce public goods.[80] Today's eurozone was designed according to similar liberal economic principles—namely the belief that capitalist economies produce a felicitous equilibrium if left without government interference[81]—and has reproduced similar economic pain. In this fertile soil, nationalist, xenophobic ideas are spreading, threatening the breakup of the E.U. if not renewed violence between nations. If history is any guide, to avoid the rise of the nationalist Right will require abandoning liberal economics for a more active state role (necessary also to transition from the current cyanide pill of an economy[82] to an indefinitely sustainable one). The problem then and now is that liberal economics is particularly attractive to those with wealth and disproportionate power over systems of government, media, and education. Liberal economics, thought by many at the time to have been delivered a fatal blow by the Great Depression and subsequent government-spending-fueled recovery,[83] has come back to dominance in the academy—helped by funding from those with enough wealth to find it palatable—and from there, to the minds of public officials and the highly educated.[84] Here again, the internet and the way it has reshaped the ecology of information may prove helpful for alternative economic ideas that threaten the relative wealth of a few and promise a reduction in pain for many. Until they spread more widely, the (near) future for the nationalistic, xenophobic European Right is bright.

5 Outline of an Ideal Media System

According to the liberal view, an ideal media system might look the same as the status quo in the United States. All are free to start their own media outlet, with government restrictions on this liberty limited to media like television and radio facing scarcity from the laws of physics. Freedom of the press is guaranteed (to all who own one). Media corporations or individual proprietors compete for audience share and audiences choose from among their products, voting with their dollars and eyeballs. Government-funded media exists, but the majority of its revenues come from private donors, and its audience share is small. From a liberal perspective, this is a system suited for rational, self-interested, utility-maximizing individuals: competition in the market should produce a plethora of options citizens are free to choose from, the best defense against manipulation, deception, and propaganda. In a functioning marketplace, manipulative, deceitful, and propagandistic products should be weeded out in favor of more honest sources (how this happens without making the assumption of perfect information common in neoclassical economic models is unclear).[85] The result is that no one can beat the market; that is, no politician, party, corporation, interest group, etc. can evade critical scrutiny from a free market for media companies. There will always be some media outlet to recognize the opportunity to make money by doing good: exposing corruption and criticizing bad policy will be valued and rewarded by the marketplace. Doing bad for political actors will be prohibitively expensive.

Yet to believe that this accurately describes the contemporary U.S. media requires mere assumption; a look at media systems in other countries or even a few hours of channel surfing reveals just how few options the U.S. mass media offers (for political perspectives). Reporting on foreign policy rarely strays from the perspectives of the U.S. foreign policy elite and reporting on economic issues rarely strays from mainstream Republican and Democratic Party positions—which is far narrower than what is available in several other countries (and online). The liberal view does not obtain; the free market for media companies has failed, and the felicitous equilibrium it should produce is nowhere in sight. Instead, we have a distorted market: non-consumers receive benefits they have not paid for and consumers pay for benefits they do not receive; a funding model for television in which viewers are not the customers, but advertisers, skewing incentives; and political-economic power exercising a clear selection pressure over which ideas make it into the mass media. Instead of fulfilling the role imagined in the liberal ideal, the news media tends toward a free-market version of a propaganda system, with a variety of political-economic pressures in place of government diktat.

Perhaps one benefit of Trump's election was that it provided a clear illustration of the dangers inherent in the U.S. media system. Referring to the reality TV star's candidacy in early 2016, the CEO of CBS infamously said: "It may not be good for America, but it's damn good for CBS."[86] (Half a century earlier, a former CBS news director made a similar point with the opposite valence: that "[t]elevision makes so much [money] at its worst that it can't afford to do its best.")[87] A free market is theorized to allocate resources in the most efficient manner to best meet consumers' needs; yet this free market for media companies resulted in nearly $5 billion in free coverage lathered on Trump.[88] In addition to the studies of foreign policy and economic coverage discussed in Chapter 5, U.S. media coverage of the 2016 election contradicts the liberal view and confirms the view argued here. Commercial pressures in a commercial media system resulted in an inordinate amount of free coverage to arguably the least qualified presidential candidate in U.S. history. What was bad for the country was good for media companies—and the latter won out.

The U.S. media system does not produce the beneficial outcomes predicted by the liberal view due partially to supply-side deficiencies, but other failures come from the demand side. Our minds are "designed" to accept and build on information we have absorbed as schemas; media stories that contradict widely held beliefs are likelier to be rejected, ignored, or distorted. If human beings more closely approximated the liberal ideal of rational thinkers, the present U.S. media system might work. However, contrary to this ideal, when the truth matches our accumulated knowledge, we desire it—but when it does not, we desire alternative facts. What then would an ideal media system look like, one calibrated to the minds we have, and which could provide the free market of ideas required for democracy better than the free market for media companies currently does?

Before proceeding, it may be helpful to conceptualize two evils we seek to avoid: Nicholas Garnham's "pap and propaganda"—the commercial dreck of the present U.S. media system, and the overt, intentional propaganda present in several media systems around the world where the state has taken power without granting democratic control—or Phillip Pettit's *dominium* and *imperium*, un-freedom caused by private or state domination. Domination is produced when one agent has the power of interference on an arbitrary basis over another: when an agent has "sway over the other, in the old phrase, and the sway is arbitrary."[89]

The media as a collective agent has the power of interference on an arbitrary basis over the citizenry, simply by omitting perspectives and information citizens would otherwise choose to obtain. This form of private domination is an evil to be avoided, and state domination, *imperium*, is an even clearer evil. Pettit notes, "almost all the main figures [in the classical republican tradition] treat the question of which institutions do best by freedom as an open, empirical issue, not as a question capable of a priori resolution."[90] In the realm of the media too, the appropriateness of freedom (as governmental non-interference) is an open, empirical issue. We need not consider state domination an evil so great that we must open ourselves to private domination, or private domination an evil so great that we must open ourselves to government domination. We can plan to avoid both.

Perhaps we should follow the authors of the U.S. Constitution and tame this source of concentrated power through democratic control and checks and balances: turning the media into a *de jure* branch of government, under democratic oversight.[91] A government body, like the Federal Communications Commission, could be removed from the executive branch and established as an independent, fourth branch of government: the Democratic Media Commission (DMC). Its goal would be to ensure that the public enjoys a free market of ideas and information to inform its decisions, without any actor exercising domination through disproportionate sway. It could be governed by a board of commissioners, like the FCC, except with a total of nine: five of its commissioners elected by working journalists and four through elections using rank-order voting open to all citizens.

The DMC's remit would include analyzing news reports to check for bias and levying fines for misleading reports, persistent ideological bias, or lack of ideological diversity.[92] Ensuring great breadth of ideological perspective would be of the utmost importance: if some perspectives were excluded from "popular information and the means of acquiring it," then the goal of a free market of ideas, free of domination by any actor, would not be reached. This fourth branch of government would exercise power (granting the citizenry control) over media outlets reaching above a certain number of people—especially outlets that serve as the sole or primary source of news for a significant portion of the population. For smaller media outlets, with fewer resources to devote to providing a balance of diverse opinions, governmental interference would have to be different. Since the founding of the U.S., a strongly partisan, small-scale press has facilitated a lively political culture, and today it adds to the overall diversity of ideological perspectives. However, it threatens ideological self-segregation and the absorption of biased, inaccurate information that is held unperturbed in an environment walled off from challenge. To avoid this outcome, such media outlets could be required to provide rebuttal space for journalists from opposing sides of the political spectrum. People could still choose to ignore the airtime or column inches devoted to rebuttals, but to ignore would require an active decision, rather than the passive operation of our psychology.

This proposal would add a more stringent layer of regulation, albeit regulation over which the citizenry would have some representative-democratic control. The commercial structure of the media would remain. The pressures of advertiser, owner, and source bias previously discussed would still be in operation. Media companies would then be trapped between the financial pressures of a competitive marketplace and the financial pressures of a new regulatory scheme using fines to punish non-adherence. This is not what the news media needs, especially at a historical juncture when the current newspaper business model is facing extinction and no viable replacement is on the horizon. Forcing media companies to take expensive measures (hiring additional journalists to provide a breadth of ideological diversity) by threat of fines will not work when journalism is flirting with economic extinction.

However, the current economic weakness of the news media can inform our proposal. Firstly, since the inception of the republic news media been subsidized by the government, and early television news was considered an important public service to be provided by the networks, a loss leader that would increase a network's prestige and build brand loyalty. It would not represent a reckless leap to revisit subsidizing the provision of political information. Secondly, the most widely blamed cause for the present crisis of journalism is the threat of the internet to its profit model. And what is the nature of this threat? For one, the internet has reduced the marginal cost of journalistic product to near zero. In other words, once a newspaper article has been written or a news program recorded, producing additional units costs nearly nothing. The internet has turned journalism into an economic activity with all the characteristics of a public good: zero marginal cost, non-rivalry in consumption, and non-excludability.

Since the internet has turned journalism as an economic activity into a public good, we have three options: ban the internet, allow market failure in journalism, or *treat* journalism as a public good. Despite the ridiculous or pernicious implications of the first two options, the third might still come as an unpleasant proposal for the owners of the news media, but with eminent domain law requiring adequate compensation to be paid for acquired property, only those bullish on the news media's economic future would have cause for great distress. The DMC could be

8 CONCLUSION: THE INVISIBLE HAND ... 339

authorized to use eminent domain to buy distressed media companies (primarily newspapers), leaving commercially viable and successful companies alone.

Inspired by James Curran's proposal, the DMC would oversee the entry of several major new players into the media system, in addition to the newly regulated commercial sector.[93] First, failing newspapers bought by the DMC contain valuable assets: primarily, journalists and editors. These would be given funding, autonomy, and control, allowing them to choose whether to continue as online-only newspapers or to branch out into other journalistic projects online or on television. Second, organized political groups, from parties to activist organizations, would receive government grants (following the Dutch model) from the DMC to operate their own media outlets. Third, ethnic and political minority groups would also receive grants from the DMC (following the Scandinavian model) to fund publications and television programs to air on government-funded or commercial channels. Fourth, the DMC would create an independent television and radio station funded generously by government, which would hire only experienced journalists from around the world to govern television and radio station themselves, setting editorial policy without interference. (Additionally, all media outlets receiving government funding could be required to hire a certain percentage of foreign journalists to impede parochial, nationalist biases.) These four new entrants to the media system would need to have funding guarantees, indexed to inflation, so that neither the DMC nor Congress could use its purse strings to exert control.

Turning a large portion of journalism into a public utility would bring us back to the problem of a tyranny of the majority and government *imperium*. What we would need for a well-functioning journalistic public utility is a specifically republican institutional form. We would need safeguards to prevent a tyranny of the majority from exercising domination through a publicly owned media. The first mechanism would be having five commissioners elected by working journalists, with the other four being elected by the citizenry. Yet we would need a contestatory mechanism—in place of direct democratic control—for those whose interests are not being served by the media to remedy grievances.

A Media Ombudsman's Office (press council) led by an elected official could be instituted as a contestatory mechanism for those who feel the media and DMC are not tracking their interests.[94] The remit of the

Ombudsman would *not* be determining what is "better" or desirable, but ensuring maximum diversity including views some will unavoidably consider "worse" and undesirable. What is important is determining whether a perspective on an issue is in good faith or if someone is clamoring for space in the mediatized public sphere merely to propagandize in bad faith in furtherance of their interests. Like any system, one organized around providing maximum diversity can be gamed: one could define individual perspectives in such a way as to create an unmanageable number of them or to create an artificially low number. Drawing inspiration from the Declaration of Independence's "decent respect to the opinions of mankind," this problem can be avoided: political perspectives, philosophies, or worldviews commanding the allegiance of some significant fraction of the world's population would make the list. Within each of these broad trends of thought, diversity would remain essential: no one strand or sect would be allowed to define the overall trend, but instead, each would be represented by proponents who may disagree on finer points. This design could evade attempts to game the system by, for instance, a group with the goal of enlisting the U.S. to overthrow a foreign government creating half a dozen "competing" perspectives all arguing for military intervention, but with spurious areas of disagreement designed to generate an illusion of diversity and to crowd out or dilute anti-war perspectives. The Ombudsman's Office would be tasked with determining whether an excluded perspective is in good faith and is sufficiently unique and valuable to warrant inclusion.

The DMC could be instituted via constitutional amendment laying out the principles it is tasked with maintaining; if the commissioners and the ombudsman fail to live up to their duty of maintaining a free marketplace of ideas, citizens could bring suit in the courts to compel changes in keeping with the letter and spirit of the constitutional amendment. Citizens would thereby retain their freedom to choose the news that fits their preferences and fight for the inclusion of their preferred perspective(s); they would only gain additional freedom in the form of greater options in ideological perspective to choose from and be exposed to.

Objections of all sorts might be made to this proposal, but two are most likely. First, the expense: the Newspaper Association of America last reported $37.6 billion in annual revenue, the three top 24-hour cable news channels $4 billion, local TV stations $9.3 billion from news programs (roughly half of their total revenue of $18.6 billion), and network news programs $1.1 billion (estimated from their reported $809 million in the first three-quarters of 2015).[95] We can use the S&P 500 average price-sales ratio of 2 (historically high) to calculate a rough estimate of fair market value from revenue data: $104 billion, from combined annual revenues of $52 billion. Hence, a democratization of the core of the US news media system would amount to a one-time expense of $104 billion and an annual expense of $52 billion (or roughly one-twelfth of the declared military budget). Second, the issue of social planning: this proposal *is* social planning, but it is merely replacing one set of managers and directors—the electorate itself and professional journalists—for another: private investors, media company owners, CEOs, and their undemocratically appointed managers and editors. There is no Edenic ideal threatened with defilement at the hands of an unruly mob; there is a broken, plutocratic system facing a proposal for democratic reform and renewal. Bree Nordenson points out, "[t]o survive, journalism and journalists need to let go of their aversion to Uncle Sam."[96] And as Tom Ferguson describes his "Golden Rule" as it applies to the provision of information in democracies: "In politics, you get what you pay for. Or someone else does."[97] The alternative to government as sugar daddy is not free sugar; influence will instead come from private sources more difficult to bring under democratic control.

Another objection deserves attention: if the profusion of options ushered in via cable led to many people avoiding politics altogether in favor of entertainment—and even the devolution of news programming into "journo-tainment" could not stop the tide—then in the modern, internet-heavy media environment would a democratic media system focusing on hard news and analysis from a variety of ideological perspectives simply turn off even greater numbers? This is possible, but by no means certain: there is evidence that many are turned off by the news media *because* it has devolved into journo-tainment.[98] Regardless, nudging viewers into watching the news and increasing opportunities for incidental exposure can stem the tide toward greater political apathy and ignorance. The commercial entertainment media can be enjoined to set aside a significant fraction of ad time for advertisements for news programming on DMC-funded channels, and entire commercial breaks can be granted to DMC-funded news shows to present five-minute summaries of the day's news coverage. In this way, even the most politically apathetic television viewer would be goaded several times a day into tuning into news programming. This would reduce revenue for television stations and advertisers, but the net result for society—just from a reduction in advertising, not including the increase in levels of political knowledge—may be positive.[99]

These reforms have dealt with the supply side of the equation, but an ideal media system would also have to address the demand side. Among the features of our psychology least likely to be corrected, persuasion and processing through the peripheral route (System 1) stand out. Television is a limited tool, and ensuring our undivided attention during news programs is not one of its capabilities. Making news programs visually bland (Sovietizing rather than Foxifying) may stimulate central, effortful processing, but may also stimulate channel switching. However, one negative aspect of peripheral processing can inspire a good reform: if our System 1 is likelier to accept statements from an attractive person, perhaps television pundits should not be selected for their looks.

Given that the rational ideal is wrong about how we tackle moral questions (deliberate on reasons before making judgments), what can media outlets do to stimulate conscious, critical reflection on our gut-instinct moral responses? One possibility is that when making arguments for a political position that implicates morality, journalists should paint with all five colors of the moral palette. That is, to invoke care, fairness, loyalty, authority, and purity when presenting the case for any political argument, even if it associated with the Left. (This strategy has received experimental support in application to environmental issues.)[100] Debate moderators and talk show hosts can remind the audience from the beginning that the discussion is likely to engage their gut moral instincts and urge them to critically interrogate their reactions. At the end of the program, viewers could be given examples of how moral gut reactions were found over the course of the debate to be inadequate and where they would need to be thought through.

Due to the phenomenon of attitude inoculation, media outlets cannot provide balance to a story by giving the majority of the focus to one perspective (e.g., the President's), and a small amount to critics. Instead of weak balance being better than nothing, it may be worse. Media outlets need to be aware of this psychological feature and ensure that good-faith, well-supported arguments are given equal focus; even, or especially, when one side of an argument enjoys greater prestige and newsworthiness.

A more serious psychological maladaptation (in the modern era) is groupishness, our in-group and out-group biases. It is the bloody thread connecting wars, religious violence, ethnic conflict, and criminal gangs,

8 CONCLUSION: THE INVISIBLE HAND ... 343

yet it also provides the psychological basis for solidarity and cooperation. The media can shape its presentations to mute our groupishness and readapt it to a globalized, interconnected world of mass societies. First, we know groupishness manifests in language with the linguistic intergroup bias—and that this linguistic bias can spur in-group bias when thinking about what we are reading or listening to. Journalists must be educated about the linguistic intergroup bias and learn to avoid it. Editorial writers and pundits especially should avoid "us" and "them" language, and journalists should refer to in-groups in the third person. News articles and television scripts should use specific language when describing the actions of governments; the "United States" has never bombed anyone, but the United States Air Force has. When describing in-groups, journalists should take pains to include negative information (which may be easier to do when many of one's co-workers are foreign nationals and likely members of different ethnic and religious groups). When describing out-groups, journalists should emphasize points of similarity with the audience's in-group(s) and out-groups' internal diversity: Muslims follow a variety of interpretations of their faith, as do Christians and Buddhists; Iraqis had many different perspectives on their government as well as the United States'; Russians run the gamut from authoritarian to liberal, and so on. Crime reports should avoid groupishness-piquing adjectives: what benefit is there in describing an accused murderer as a *Black* man, a rape victim as a *White* woman, or a drug trafficker as *Hispanic* (except in a local news report on a dangerous criminal at large)? Lastly, the media should emphasize the superordinate in-group *humanity*, making arbitrary national and ethnic boundaries subordinate and less salient.

Presenting negative information about audiences' in-group(s) is likely to arouse cognitive dissonance, along with any information that challenges widely held beliefs—prompting motivated, meaning-maintaining, *irrational* reasoning to reduce it. To encourage more rational responses, the news media can affirm the audience's self-image before presenting negative information about an in-group. For instance, before a report on evidence of torture in U.S. Army prisons, audiences could be reminded of U.S. government diplomatic support for political prisoners in some countries, or the U.S. government role in forging the Geneva Conventions; a report on the pedophilia scandal in the Catholic Church could follow a reminder of the good work that Catholic Charities performs around the world, and so on. To provide knowledge constraints on motivated reasoning about domestic and international politics, schools would be better positioned than the news media. Parents who feel uncomfortable cognitive dissonance from textbooks that describe domestic and foreign evils perpetrated by their government should have no power to reject textbooks on the basis of their negative affect. With a fuller and fairer picture of the negative aspects of their country's history, citizens would be socialized with knowledge constraints that can impede motivating reasoning about current events, particularly those in which their government acts in ways that contradict widely held values (like self-determination in the case of coups and electoral interference, human rights in the case of U.S. government-supported dictatorships, etc.). Media audiences could even be encouraged by news anchors, pundits, and editorial writers to imagine the opposite of what they believe to avoid psychological biases the news may exacerbate. Here, journalists would need to popularize knowledge about psychological biases that affect our thinking about politics.

System justification tendency is another politically significant bias that the news media should mute or reduce. Criticisms of existing systems—of political and economic organization, criminal justice, wealth distribution, racial disparities, international relations, etc.—need to be given a great deal of sustained coverage and analysis. Otherwise, *ceteris paribus*, they will be ignored by a human psychology that finds acknowledging them painful. Before such critiques, to minimize cognitive dissonance and prevent irrational avoidance strategies, media audiences can be reminded that injustice has been a constant of human history; today, some of the grosser injustices such as feudal despotism and plantation slavery have been overcome, but every generation has the opportunity to bring society closer to justice. Positive aspects of existing systems can be emphasized and proposed fixes for their negative aspects discussed (including whichever small actions individual viewers and readers can take), to emphasize that problems are surmountable.

In covering war and threats of war, the media must heighten its sensitivity to psychological bias. It must avoid distortions arising from intergroup bias.[101] Media audiences must hear from a range of voices in "enemy" nations or groups: those supportive of their government and those opposed, along with a sampling of the variety of ideological perspectives in the population (e.g., Christian Iraqis opposed to Hussein, but fearful that a U.S. military invasion would be worse). Points of commonality between portions of the "enemy" out-group and the audience's in-group(s) should be emphasized. Above all, war must never be sanitized; psychological discomfort at the sight of a mangled body is an inestimably lesser evil than the violence that turned a human being into a mangled body. Before and during a war, audiences must be reminded that war inevitably means death, disfigurement, rape, torment, and destruction affecting innocents along with combatants, no matter how smart the bombs used. Lastly, audiences must be reminded of relevant history—the Gulf of Tonkin and Iraqi WMD—whenever a case for war is being made in response to an alleged act of aggression, existential threat, or atrocity.

Lastly, an ideal media system would work hand in glove with the education system to stimulate a more complex, systematic style of thought among viewers and readers, to create the citizens democracy requires. Currently, little is known about what factors facilitate the development of systematic thought; however, in the media context, we could do worse than to apply Goethe's hypothesis that "when we treat man as he is, we make him worse than he is; when we treat him as if he already were what he potentially could be, we make him what he should be." Instead of catering to the lowest common denominator, the media should present complex political issues in their complexity, but breaking them down into more easily comprehensible parts. Pundits and editorial writers should provide models of systematic thought, while making their best efforts to *present* systematic arguments in an easily digestible manner. This may frustrate those who have developed only a linear or sequential style of thought, but over time, it may help spur additional development. Overall, the media is likely to be able to play only a supporting role in facilitating a systematic thinking style among the population; schools, parents and workplaces must do the heavy lifting. Nonetheless, if a supporting role can be played, it should.

6 Final Remarks

"It does not take the ghost of a Marie Antoinette to realize that when the few declare war on the many, the millinery business is headed for bad times."
—Gore Vidal, "Clinton-Gore II"

Sandra Braman is correct in pointing out that information provides the backbone for all of power's other forms: instrumental, structural, and symbolic. Part of information's power lies in ignorance: what we are ignorant of cannot *inform* our decisions. The absence of information influences our decisions in different ways, but no less than the *presence* of information. Hence the awesome power of the media: it can provide information for informed decisions, the backbone of democratic power, or it can withhold it. Facts, theories, proposals, and perspectives lack wings. Although our minds have an impressive ability to combine and create ideas, this cannot make up for a lack of specific information. Creativity cannot serve as a replacement to an informed understanding of politics.

Deaths totaling *several* 9/11s occur every day around the world due to a lack of food, billions endure the suffocation of poverty, the organized mass murder of war rages on, our economic system pushes our environment to uninhabitability, and every second we remain a computer glitch or human error away from nuclear apocalypse. These problems stand no chance of being solved if the means of mass communication are used to deliver information not about them, but circuses. (Bread sold separately.)

Our species has been astoundingly successful in spreading from a corner of Africa to conquering the planet. 252 million years ago, another species enjoyed similar success: *Methanosarcina*, a microbe that evolved a way to turn oceanic carbon into energy, converting it into methane.[102] So successful was this microbe that over the next few million years, its methane waste had exterminated 96% of species in the ocean and 70% of vertebrates on land. *Homo sapiens* is currently on pace to match this record; if our carbon emissions continue unabated and a climate tipping point is reached, we could even break it. Liberal democratic societies, as they have from their beginning, can "be fairly described as an organized assault on nature."[103] And in this war, we are "winning." I can imagine intelligent, *informed* life elsewhere in the galaxy, constrained by something like *Star Trek's* Prime Directive of non-interference, observing our planet from afar. Perhaps we are on a reality TV show, *Quasi-Intelligent Species of the Galaxy*, with alien bookies taking bets on our survival over decades. Being an Earthian, I would be ineligible to place a bet—but I wonder about the odds.

Since information is the foundation of power, without *popular* information and the means of attaining it cheaply and easily, we are guaranteed a tragic farce of a society. Like everyone, I am prey to informational biases of demand and supply; my beliefs are the result of gene-environment development interacting with the ecology of information I have inhabited. Like everyone else, I am radically ignorant: what I know is only an infinitesimal fraction of what I do *not* know, and my *unknown unknowns* are just as numerous as anyone's. Among the little I do know are spooks about grave threats to the species (itself a spook), along with spook solutions to these problems. I believe my ideas are accurate descriptions of the world and what could be done to improve it—but so too does everyone. My truths are false on the other side of the mountain (in the U.S., I would not need to go further than my front door to cross the true-false border). As a Marine Corps' sergeant instructor once yelled at me, "excuses are like assholes: we all got 'em, and they all stink!" We all have memes, and since many of them contradict each other, they cannot all be true. Yet our radical ignorance prevents us from correctly separating the true from the false. No *one* of us can.

A Native American story has it that:

> A young child was greatly frightened by her dream, in which two wolves fought viciously, growling and snapping their jaws. Hoping for solace, she described this dream to her grandfather, a wise and highly respected elder. The grandfather explained that her dream was indeed true: "There are two wolves within each of us, one of them benevolent and peace-loving, the other malevolent and violent. They fight constantly for our souls." ... At this, the child found herself more frightened than ever, and asked her grandfather which one wins. He replied, "The one you feed."[104]

For a folktale, this is a fairly accurate depiction of the Janus-faced, competitive and cooperative nature evolution has produced; and of our capacity for good and evil.

Since none of us can determine the truth, we cannot know what food to feed which wolf. I see no other option than to follow Judge Learned Hand and presuppose "that right conclusions are more likely to be gathered out of a multitude of tongues." Is it "too easy a theodicy for truth" to expect that right conclusions *will* be gathered out of a multitude of tongues? Almost certainly. But are they *likelier* to be gathered out of a multitude of tongues than a restricted set? The choice is not between a proven failure and guaranteed success, but a proven failure and an alternative with no guarantee. I would stake upon it my all.

Notes

1. Tang, *The Social Evolution*, 24.
2. Quoted in Norman L. Torrey, *Les Philosophes: The Philosophers of the Enlightenment and Modern Democracy* (New York: Capricorn Books, 1961): 277.

3. Jonathan Swift, *Gulliver's Travels* (San Francisco: Ignatius Press, 2011): 279–280.
4. Robert N. Proctor, "Agnotology: A Missing Term to Describe the Cultural Production of Ignorance (and Its Study)," in *Agnotology: The Making and Unmaking of Ignorance*, ed. Robert N. Proctor and Londa Schiebinger, 1–33 (Stanford, CA: Stanford University Press, 2008).
5. Naomi Oreskes and Erik M. Conway, "Challenging Knowledge: How Climate Science Became a Victim of the Cold War," in *Agnotology*.
6. Proctor, "Agnotology," 19.
7. Jeffrey Friedman, "Popper, Weber, and Hayek: The Epistemology and Politics of Ignorance," *Critical Review* 17, no. 1 (2005): xxiii–xxiv.
8. Cohen, *States of Denial*, 4–5.
9. Mills, *The Racial Contract*.
10. Charles W. Mills, "White Ignorance," in *Agnotology*: 236.
11. Wolin, *Politics and Vision*, 298, 398–399.
12. Bakan, *The Corporation*, 6, 37.
13. Voltaire, *Philosophical Dictionary*, 400.
14. Douglas Adams, *Dirk Gently's Holistic Detective Agency* (New York: Gallery Books, 2014): 5.
15. Adam D. Galinsky et al., "Power and Perspectives Not Taken," *Psychological Science* 17, no. 12 (2006); Dacher Keltner et al., "Power, Approach, and Inhibition," *Psychological Review* 110, no. 2 (2003): 265–284.
16. Max Weber, *Law in Economy and Society: An Outline of Interpretive Sociology*, ed. Guenther Roth and Claus Wittich (Berkeley, CA: University of California Press, 1978): 953.
17. Michael W. Kraus et al., "Social Class, Contextualism, and Empathic Accuracy," *Psychological Science* 21, no. 11 (2010).
18. Stéphane Côté et al., "For Whom Do the Ends Justify the Means? Social Class and Utilitarian Moral Judgment," *Journal of Personality and Social Psychology* 104, no. 3 (2013).
19. Michael Koenigs et al., "Utilitarian Moral Judgment in Psychopathy," *Social Cognitive and Affective Neuroscience* 7, no. 6 (2012).
20. Paul K. Piff, "Wealth and the Inflated Self: Class, Entitlement, and Narcissism," *Personality and Social Psychology Bulletin* 40, no. 1 (2014).
21. Nattavudh Powdthavee and Andrew J. Oswald, "Does Money Make People Right-Wing and Inegalitarian? A Longitudinal Study of Lottery Winners," Institute for the Study of Labor, Discussion Paper No. 7934 (January 2014).
22. Benjamin I. Page et al., "Democracy and the Policy Preferences," 67.
23. Larry M. Bartels, "Economic Inequality and Political Representation," in *The Unsustainable American State*, ed. Lawrence Jacobs and Desmond King,

167–196 (New York: Oxford University Press, 2009); Gilens and Page, "Testing Theories."
24. David E. Broockman and Christopher Skovron, "What Politicians Believe about Their Constituents: Asymmetric Misperceptions and Prospects for Constituency Control," Working Paper, University of California Berkeley and University of Michigan (2015).
25. Fuller, *Beasts and Gods*, 95–96.
26. Thomas Stratmann, "Can Special Interests Buy Congressional Votes? Evidence from Financial Services Legislation," *Journal of Law and Economics* 45, no. 2 (2002).
27. Fuller, *Beasts and Gods*, 10.
28. Wolin, *Politics and Vision*, 255–256.
29. Ferguson, *Golden Rule*, 29.
30. Ibid., 60, 381–406.
31. Ibid., 384, emphasis removed.
32. Ferguson et al., "Party Competition," 19.
33. Ferguson, *Golden Rule*, 9.
34. Perry Anderson, *American Foreign Policy and Its Thinkers* (London: Verso, 2015): 155–157.
35. Stanley, *How Propaganda Works*, 77.
36. Ibid., 77–78.
37. Robert Skidelsky, "The Crisis of Capitalism: Keynes versus Marx," *Indian Journal of Industrial Relations* 45, no. 3 (2010): 323.
38. H.L. Mencken, "The Dismal Science," in *Prejudices: A Selection* (Baltimore: Johns Hopkins University Press, 1996): 151.
39. Sidelsky, "The Crisis," 324.
40. Robert E. Babe, "Political Economy of Economics," in *Media, Structures, and Power: The Robert E. Babe Collection*, ed. Edward A. Connor, 388–393 (Toronto: University of Toronto Press, 2011): 389.
41. Sophus A. Reinert, *Translating Empire: Emulation and the Origins of Political Economy* (Boston: Harvard University Press, 2011): 9, 232.
42. Ibid., 210.
43. See, e.g., Ha-Joon Chang, *Kicking Away the Ladder: Development Strategy in Historical Perspective* (London: Anthem Press, 2002).
44. Reinert, *Translating Empire*, 279–285.
45. Michael Hudson, *Trade, Development, and Foreign Debt: How Trade and Development Concentrate Economic Power in the Hands of Dominant Nations* (Kansas City, MO: ISLET, 2009): 29, 116.
46. E.K. Hunt and Mark Lautzenheiser, *History of Economic Thought: A Critical Perspective* (New Delhi: PHI Learning, 2011): 276–279.
47. Hudson, *Trade, Development*, 206, 219.
48. Babe, "Political Economy," 391–392.

49. Norbert Häring and Niall Douglas, *Economists and the Powerful: Convenient Theories, Distorted Facts, Ample Rewards* (New York: Anthem Press, 2012): 8–46.
50. Ibid., 25.
51. For a selection, see Friedman, *Power Without Knowledge*, Chapter 4.
52. John B. Davis, "The Turn in Economics: Neoclassical Dominance to Mainstream Pluralism?" *Journal of Institutional Economics* 2, no. 1 (2006); however, see Frederic S. Lee, "The Research Assessment Exercise, the State and the Dominance of Mainstream Economics in British Universities," *Cambridge Journal of Economics* 31, no. 2 (2007).
53. Lawson, *Economics and Reality*, 282; for a defense of neoclassical methodology that ends up reinforcing the methodological critiques, see Rodrik, *Economics Rules*.
54. Michael Hudson, *Killing the Host: How Financial Parasites and Debt Destroy the Global Economy* (Kansas City, MO: ISLET-Verlag, 2015).
55. Hunt and Lautzenheiser, *History of Economic Thought*, 396.
56. Amitai Etzioni, "The Moral Effects of Economic Teaching," *Sociological Forum* 30, no. 1 (2015).
57. René Ruske, "Does Economics Make Politicians Corrupt? Empirical Evidence from the United States Congress," *Kyklos* 68, no. 2 (2015).
58. Stanley, *How Propaganda Works*, 83–86.
59. Thomas Ferguson and Robert Johnson, "A World Upside Down? Deficit Fantasies in the Great Recession," *International Journal of Political Economy* 40, no. 1 (2011): 12.
60. Michael Hudson, "Free Money Creation to Bail Out Financial Speculators, but Not Social Security or Medicare," *Naked Capitalism* (June 17, 2011).
61. Marina Karanikolos et al., "Financial Crisis, Austerity, and Health in Europe," *The Lancet* 381, no. 9874 (2013).
62. Ferguson and Johnson, "A World Upside Down," 33–35.
63. See, generally, L. Randall Wray, *Modern Money Theory: A Primer on Macroeconomics for Sovereign Monetary Systems* (London: Palgrave Macmillan, 2012).
64. For example, Mankiw, *Economics*, 556–558, 684–686.
65. Richard A. Werner, "Can Banks Individually Create Money Out of Nothing?—The Theories and the Empirical Evidence," *International Review of Financial Analysis* 36 (2014): 1–19; Zoltan Jakab and Michael Kumhof, "Banks are Not Intermediaries of Loanable Funds—And Why This Matters," Bank of England Working Paper No. 529 (May 29, 2015).
66. Ibid., 3, 28.
67. Jaromír Beneš and Michael Kumhof, "The Chicago Plan Revisited," IMF Working Paper No. 12/202 (August 2012): 10–11.

8 CONCLUSION: THE INVISIBLE HAND ... 351

68. Ibid., 19.
69. Ibid., 55–56.
70. Robert Faris et al., "Partisanship, Propaganda, and Disinformation: Online Media and the 2016 U.S. Presidential Election," Berkman Klein Center Research Publication 2017–6 (August 2017): 129. Available at: https://ssrn.com/abstract=3019414.
71. John Halpin et al., "The Structural Imbalance of Political Talk Radio," Joint Report by The Center for American Progress and Free Press (June 22, 2007); Nicole Hemmer, *Messengers of the Right: Conservative Media and the Transformation of American Politics* (Philadelphia: University of Pennsylvania Press, 2016): 252–276.
72. James Moody and Peter J. Mucha, "Portrait of Political Party Polarization," *Network Science* 1, no. 1 (2013); Pew Research Center, "Political Polarization in the American Public: How Increasing Ideological Uniformity and Partisan Antipathy Affect Politics, Compromise and Everyday Life" (June 12, 2014).
73. Jamie Turner and Shenaz Lilywala, "Do Conservatives or Liberals Own the Airwaves?" *60 Second Marketer* (February 9, 2014). Available at: https://60secondmarketer.com/blog/2014/02/09/conservative-vs-liberal-media-usage/.
74. Chris Wells et al., "How Trump Drove Coverage to the Nomination: Hybrid Media Campaigning," *Political Communication* 33, no. 4 (2016): 669–676.
75. Emily J. Bell et al., "The Platform Press: How Silicon Valley Reengineered Journalism," *Columbia Journalism Review* (March 2017): 10.
76. Jonathan Albright, "Stop Worrying about Fake News. What Comes Next Will Be Much Worse," *The Guardian* (December 9, 2016). Available at: https://www.theguardian.com/commentisfree/2016/dec/09/fake-news-technology-filters.
77. Beattie, "Where Did."
78. The Pew Research Center, "New Media, Old Media: How Blogs and Social Media Agendas Relate and Differ from the Traditional Press" (May 23, 2010).
79. For example, Choi and Lee, "Investigating"; Yphtach Lelkes, Gaurav Sood, and Shanto Iyengar, "The Hostile Audience: The Effect of Access to Broadband Internet on Partisan Affect," *American Journal of Political Science* 61 (2015); Lu Wei and Douglas Blanks Hindman, "Does the Digital Divide Matter More? Comparing the Effects of New Media and Old Media Use on the Education-Based Knowledge Gap," *Mass Communication and Society* 14, no. 2 (2011).
80. For example, Werner Abelshauser, "Germany: Guns, Butter, and Economic Miracles," in *The Economics of World War II: Six Great Powers*

in International Comparison (Cambridge: Cambridge University Press, 1998): 122–176.
81. For example, Lavoie, Marc. "The Eurozone: Similarities to and Differences from Keynes's Plan," *International Journal of Political Economy* 44, no. 1 (2015): 3–17.
82. For example, Jeremy Grantham, "The Race of Our Lives Revisited," GMO White Paper (August 2018). Available at: https://www.gmo.com/docs/default-source/research-and-commentary/strategies/asset-allocation/the-race-of-our-lives-revisited.pdf.
83. Angus Burgin, *The Great Persuasion: Reinventing Free Markets Since the Depression* (Cambridge, MA: Harvard University Press, 2012); Carroll Quigley, *Tragedy and Hope: A History of the World in Our Time* (New York: MacMillan, 1966): 497–555.
84. Haring and Douglas, *Economists and the Powerful.*
85. Colin Hay, "Ideas and the Construction of Interests," in *Ideas and Politics in Social Science Research*, ed. Daniel Béland and Robert Henry Cox, 65–82 (New York: Oxford University Press, 2011).
86. Eliza Collins, "Les Moonves: Trump's Run Is 'Damn Good for CBS'," Politico, February 29, 2016.
87. Quoted in Uscinski, 2014, 110.
88. Mary Harris, "A Media Post-mortem on the 2016 Presidential Election," mediaQuant (November 14, 2016).
89. Pettit, *Republicanism*, 52.
90. Ibid., 100.
91. For example, Ignacio Ramonet, "Meios de Comunição: um Poder a Serviço de Interesses Privados?" in *Mídia, Poder e Contrapoder: da Concentração Monopólica À Democratização da Informação*, ed. Dênis de Moraes, 53–70 (São Paulo: Boitempo Editorial, 2013): 99.
92. For example, Michele Polo, "Regulation for Pluralism in the Media Markets," in *The Economic Regulation of Broadcasting Markets: Evolving Technology and the Challenges for Policy*, ed. Paul Seabright and Jürgen von Hagen, 150–188 (Cambridge: Cambridge University Press, 2007).
93. Curran, *Media and Power*, 240–247.
94. For example, Roger Simpson, "'Our Single Remedy for All Ills' The History of the Idea of a National Press Council," *American Journalism* 12, no. 4 (1995).
95. Pew Research Center, "State of the News Media 2016."
96. Bree Nordenson, "The Uncle Sam Solution: Can the Government Help the Press? Should It?" *Columbia Journalism Review* 46, no. 3 (2007): 41.
97. Ferguson, *Golden Rule*, 355.
98. For example, Clarke, *Journalism and Political*, 179, 215, 227, 266.

99. See, e.g., Hannah Holleman, Inger L. Stole, John Bellamy Foster, and Robert W. McChesney, "The Sales Effort and Monopoly Capital," *Monthly Review* 60, no. 11 (April 2009); Ron Roberts, *Psychology and Capitalism: The Manipulation of Mind* (Washington: Zero Books, 2015): 71–81.
100. Christopher Wolsko, Hector Ariceaga, and Jesse Seiden, "Red, White, and Blue Enough to Be Green: Effects of Moral Framing on Climate Change Attitudes and Conservation Behaviors," *Journal of Experimental Social Psychology* 65 (2016).
101. Yoram Peri, "The Impact of National Security on the Development of Media Systems: The Case of Israel," in *Comparing Media Systems: Beyond the Western World*, ed. Daniel C. Hallin and Paolo Mancini, 11–25 (Cambridge: Cambridge University Press, 2012): 22–24.
102. Morris, *Foragers, Farmers*, 261–262.
103. Wolin, *Politics and Vision*, 283.
104. David P. Barash, "Evolution and Peace: A Janus Connection," in *War, Peace, and Human Nature: The Convergence of Evolutionary and Cultural Views*, ed. Douglas P. Fry, 25–37 (Oxford: Oxford University Press, 2013): 37.

Index

A
Abelson, Robert P., 141, 162
Adaptations, 68
Advertising, 168, 172, 173, 224, 227, 228, 256, 342
advertisers, 256, 330
Affect, 32, 44, 186
affective dimension, 34
affective reaction, 146
Africa, 64, 66, 68, 73, 188, 221
Agenda-setting, 185, 188, 189, 312
Aggressive egalitarianism, 76–78, 97, 99
Agnotology, 319, 320
Agriculture, 66, 83
Algorithm, 127, 282, 333
Alphas, 77, 78, 85, 96, 311
Altruism, 69, 70, 75, 76
American Revolution, 223
Amygdala, 90
Anchoring, 124
Anger, 68
Anthropology, 33
Anxiety, 133, 180
Appetitive system, 181

Argumentation, 75
Attitude inoculation, 145, 342
Availability heuristic, 123, 172
Aversive system, 181

B
Bacon, Francis, 127
Baker, Edwin, 220, 259
Bandura, Albert, 176, 182
Basic beliefs, 182
Behavioral flexibility, 64
Belief, 42
Belief persistence, 129, 139
Beliefs as possessions, 141
Bias, 124, 244
Biased assimilation, 146
Biocca, Frank, 169
Boehm, Christopher, 76
Bonds, 81
Boulding, Kenneth, 40
Braman, Sandra, 51, 345
British Broadcasting Company (BBC), 228, 291
Burglar alarm standard, 275

Burke, Edmund, 222, 230, 282
Buying mood, 256, 257

C
Capitalism, 38, 39, 83, 246, 249, 255, 326, 330
Capture, 239
Care, 98
Censorship, 3, 116, 222, 232, 278, 282
Central route, 125, 184
Change and equality, 93, 94
Change blindness, 1, 68
Chaos, 80, 246
The Chicago Plan, 328, 329
Children, 91, 93
Chimpanzees, 63, 74, 75, 77, 84
China, 42, 67, 80, 84, 91, 221
Chomsky, Noam, 242, 249, 251
Climate change, 10, 64, 66, 71, 181, 187, 319
Code of journalistic professionalism, 251
Cognitive conservatism, 312, 315
Cognitive consistency, 131, 311
Cognitive dissonance, 130, 131, 343, 344
Collaboration, 65
Collective representations, 22, 26
Commercial bias, 333
Commercialized media systems, 281, 296
Commercial media, 229, 283, 291, 313, 320
Commission on the Freedom of the Press, 233
Commodity value, 233
Communication, 65
Competing frames, 188
Competition, 73, 74, 76, 283
Concentration, 233–235, 239, 245, 283

Conceptual blending, 27, 314
Confirmation bias, 127, 129, 130
Conservatism, 22, 80, 92, 115, 139
Consolidation, 233
Conspiracy, 4, 248, 249, 250
Constellation, 45, 46
Converse, Philip, 201
Cooperation, 41, 65, 69, 72–76, 80, 96
Copying fidelity, 29
Corruption, 285, 290
Crisis in journalism, 236
Cultivation theory, 175, 185

D
Dahl, Robert, 169, 309, 313
Darwin, Charles, 19, 20, 67, 68
Dawkins, Richard, 24, 25, 41
de Chardin, Pierre Teilhard, 14, 26
de Forest, Lee, 226, 229
de Lima, Venício, 178, 273, 285
Demand, 6, 311, 317, 319, 336, 342
Democracy, 4, 52, 115, 126, 144, 171, 201, 255, 274, 275
Democratic Corporatist Model, 285, 313
Democratic ideal, 219
Democratic Party, 276, 333, 335
Democratizing the media, 298
Democrats, 143, 187, 253
Demographic characteristics, 255
Deregulation, 285, 286
Descartes, René, 140
de Tocqueville, Alexis, 223
Disgust, 90
Distorted market, 335
Diversity of opinions, 76, 289
Domestication, 82
Domination, 336
Dunning–Kruger Effect, 157
Durkheim, Emile, 22

E

Ecology, 42, 51, 80
Ecology of information, 6, 43, 52, 220, 246, 249, 254, 259, 321, 334
Economic crisis, 235
Economic determination hypothesis, 255
Economic ideologies, 43
Economic orthodoxy, 324
Economic policies, 148
Economics, 120, 123, 124, 136, 172, 180, 186, 192, 231
Economists, 122, 126, 256
Education, 276
Egalitarianism, 64, 66, 67, 76, 96
Egalitarian syndrome, 78, 311
Elaboration likelihood model of persuasion (ELM), 183
Election, 170, 188, 228, 230
Elective affinities, 7, 51, 91
Electoral campaigns, 194
Ellul, Jacques, 167, 168, 196, 204
Embedding, 258
Embodied information, 32
Emergent phenomena, 44, 84, 120
Empire, 12
Endowment effect, 124
Entertainment, 236
Entman, Robert, 172, 191
Entropy, 19
Environmental influences, 93
Environment of evolutionary adaptation (EEA), 68
Environments, 93
Epidemiology, 23, 41
Epigenetic changes, 85
Epigenetics, 72, 84, 88
Episodic framing, 292
Epistemology, 30, 123, 131, 316, 319
Ethereal ideas, 48
Ethnic groups, 176

Ethnocentrism, 80, 97, 182
Ethos of intractable conflict, 148
Europe, 11, 91, 94, 120, 221, 222, 242, 277, 278, 289, 291, 294, 295, 334
Eusociality, 7, 73, 154, 311
Evolutionarily stable strategy, 7, 95, 311
Evolutionary algorithm, 18, 24, 25, 27–29
  substrate-neutrality of, 27
Evolutionary economist, 25, 45
Evolutionary perspectives, 23
Evolutionary psychologists, 68
Evolutionary psychology, 70, 71
  criticism, 71
Evolutionary theory, 7, 52
Evolved nature, 67
Exaptations, 68, 81, 97
Externality, 238, 299

F

Fairness, 96
Fake news, 332, 333
False consciousness, 142, 144
Fan, David, 192
Fear, 87, 90
Ferguson, Tom, 199, 240, 323, 341
Filters, 249, 250, 257
Fitness, 69, 75
Flak, 257
fMRI scans, 90
Foreign policy, 50, 126, 257, 259, 277, 335
Fourth branch, 165, 230, 337
Fox News, 191, 193, 330
Framing, 124, 146, 180, 185, 186, 292, 312
Freedom from oppression, 93, 94
Freedom of the press, 280
Free market, 233

358 INDEX

Freud, Sigmund, 118
Friedman, Jeffrey, 46, 51, 158, 245, 320
"Full news" ideal, 276

G
Gazzaniga, Michael, 123, 125, 151
Gene-behavior linkage studies, 89
Gene-culture coevolution, 7, 80, 94, 98, 319
Genes, 20, 27, 52, 64, 69, 72, 84, 87, 310
Genetic evolution, 82
    analogy to, 25, 26
Genome-wide association, 89
Gilbert, Daniel T., 140, 162
Good Samaritan, 131
Graber, Doris, 180, 190, 195, 208, 275, 277, 280
Gramsci, Antonio, 13, 142, 178
Gresham's Law, of political information, 200
Groseclose, Tim, 243
Group context, 70
Groupishness, 70, 135, 312, 342
Groups, 81
Gut instinct, 121
Gut reaction, 91, 121

H
Habermas, Jürgen, 225, 231
Hallin, Daniel, 285, 288, 290
Hamilton, James, 225, 246, 247
Hand, Learned, 299, 347
Heritability, 86, 88
Herman, Edward, 242, 249, 251
Heuristics, 123–125, 201, 276
Hicks, Bill, 134
Hierarchical social structure, 64
Hierarchy, 67, 77, 96, 98, 181, 230
Holmes, Oliver Wendell, 116

Homo sapiens, 66, 67, 82, 99, 119, 346
Homosexuality, 69, 70, 97
Hudson, Michael, 325, 328, 349, 350
Human mirror-neuron system, 90
Human nature, 4
Hunter-gatherer societies, 77
Hypocognition, 48
Hypodermic needle, 8, 169, 309

I
Ideas, 2
Ideology, 37, 48, 88, 90, 91, 93, 94, 197, 232, 244, 250, 286, 322
    ideological diversity, 337
    ideological perspective, 340
    ideological segregation, 197
    ideological self-segregation, 196
Ignorance, 9, 45, 199–201, 238, 247, 315, 320, 330
Image, 40
Imaginability, 172
Imitation, 22, 28, 31
Immigration, 87, 136, 295, 331
Indexing, 253, 313
Inequality, 78, 142, 230, 240
Influencing machine, 169, 170
Information, 2, 6, 10, 17, 19, 25, 28, 30, 34, 40, 50, 127, 133, 140, 179, 219, 240, 248, 310
    informational power, 51
    information costs, 199
    information ecology, 51
    information logistics, 50
    information theory, 18
    information *vs.* Meaning, 18, 29
    physical basis, of information, 31
    physical information, 49
Ingber, Stanley, 231, 232, 279
In-group bias, 35, 97, 135, 318, 331, 342
Inoculation, 145, 312

INDEX 359

Institutions, 42
Intelligence, 92
Interest, 51, 97, 201, 322
Intergroup bias, 135, 138, 344
International relations, 126, 323
Internet, 188, 190, 195, 197, 227, 235–237, 254, 258, 282, 297, 333, 334, 338
Interpreter mechanism, 123, 125, 151, 312
Intransitivity of explanations, 44
Investigative journalism, 225, 253
Invisible hand, 309, 321
Iraq, 3, 138, 143, 173, 190, 193, 248, 253–255, 296, 328

J
James, William, 19
Jefferson, Thomas, 126, 224, 274
Joint goals, 74
Joint intentionality, 65, 311
Journalism, 338
Journalistic professionalism, 233, 313
Journalists, 236, 298

K
Kingdoms, 67
Kin selection, 69, 70, 73
Knowledge, 30
Knowledge constraints, 130
Knowledge gap, 180, 198, 200, 201, 276, 292

L
Labor theory, 326
laissez faire, 94, 193, 231, 245
Lamarckian evolutionary entities, 27
Language, 65, 66, 148, 221, 311
Large-game hunting, 77
Lawyers, 121, 122

Lazarsfeld, Paul, 169, 229
Left and Right psychological orientations, 95
Leftwing ideology, 87
Liberal economics, 71, 116, 231
Liberalism, 7, 117, 247, 287
Liberal Model, 286
Liberals, 92, 115, 139
Linear style, 312, 345
Linear thinking, 152
Linguistic bias, 136
Linguistic intergroup bias, 343
Lippmann, Walter, 51, 154, 166, 167, 175, 219, 245, 268, 274, 284, 298, 300
Logistics, 50
Loyalty, 97

M
Magic bullet, 169
Mainstreaming, 176
Major transitions in evolutionary history, 73, 79
Mancini, Paolo, 285, 288, 290
Manning, Paul, 225
Marginal cost, 338
Marginal utility, 326
Market determination hypothesis, 246–249, 251
Market failures, 117
Marketplace of ideas, 9, 13, 116, 117, 153, 165, 231
Marx, Karl, 51, 52, 142, 246, 249, 273, 325, 326
Marxism, 73
Materialism, 176
Meaning maintenance, 133, 134, 343
Means of communication, 167, 202
Media, 37, 50, 52, 93, 94, 99, 126, 146, 148, 149, 153, 165, 178, 182, 230, 248
Media bias, 241, 245

360 INDEX

Media democratization, 298
Media dependency theory, 179
Media effects, 169
Media power, 2, 8, 173
Media systems, 285, 288
Media Tenor, 253
meios de communicação, 167
Memeplex, 26
Memes, 14, 20, 24–28, 31–33, 40, 42–45, 48, 53, 297, 315
Meme theory
 critiques of, 26, 29
Memory, 32, 128, 138, 150, 312
Mergers, 233, 235, 236
Methodology, 36, 128, 238
Milgram, Stanley, 147
Miliband, Ralph, 244, 249
Mill, John Stuart, 13, 116, 231, 300
Minimal effects, 169–171, 174, 312
Minimal group paradigm, 138
Mirror-neuron system, 29, 98
Misinformation, 200, 249
Monitorial citizen standard, 275
Moral, 148, 182
Moral considerations, 69
Morality, 70, 78, 91, 95, 121, 125
 care, 98
 categories of, 96
 fairness, 96
 loyalty, 97
 respect for authority, 96
 sanctity, 97
Moscovici, Serge, 23, 34, 36, 40
Motivated reasoning, 129, 187, 316
Motivation, 142, 343
Müller, Lisa, 289, 290

N
Naïve realism, 47
Narrative, 175, 180, 185, 186
Nationalist, 52, 138

Natural selection, 68, 79, 83
Nature *vs.* nurture, 88
Neanderthal, 66
Neoclassical economics, 238, 326, 327, 335
Neoclassical logic, 240
Neural network, 29
Neuronal level, 46
Neuronal network, 28
Neuroscience, 78
Newspapers, 189, 194, 221, 223, 236, 239, 247, 278, 332

O
Objective press, 225
Objectivity, 184, 251, 284, 313
Objectivity idiot, 284
Obtrusive issues, 189
Oligarchy, 169
Oligopoly, 232
Ombudsman's Office, 339
Ontological claims, 29
Opinion leaders, 170
Opinions, 179
Out-group, 135, 142, 182, 331, 342
Ownership, 234, 244, 245, 256, 298

P
Pack journalism, 254, 313
Partisan journalism, 251
Partisan media, 197
Partisan news, 194
Partisan opinion shows, 171
Partisan press, 224, 225
Partisan programming, 171
Partisanship, 256
Perception, 47
Peripheral route, 125, 184
Perloff, Richard, 183
Personality, 87, 92, 93, 147

Persuasion, 125, 141, 171, 182
Pettit, Phillip, 336
Philosophy, 30
Planck Principle, 129
Pluralism, 282–284, 296, 297, 299
Pluralistic ignorance, 201
Polarization, 171, 192, 239
Polarized Pluralist Model, 285
Political bias, 242
Political ideology, 45, 87
Political ignorance, 199, 201
Political information, 292, 299
Political knowledge, 293, 296, 342
Political liberalism, 117
Political nature, 85, 98
Political participation, 194, 290, 296
Political parties, 295
Political psychology, 38
Political science, 34
Politics, 3, 85
Power, 4, 5, 44, 191, 221, 321, 322
Power of information, 50
Prejudice, 132, 133, 135, 137, 150
Press freedom, 283
Primates, 63
Priming, 184, 185, 312
Printing press, 12, 221
Prior, Markus, 213, 215, 216, 278
Process value, 233
Professionalism, 284
Profitability, 246
Propaganda, 3, 4, 39, 167, 172, 175, 253, 320, 332, 335
Propaganda model, 248–251, 255
Protection from threat, 93, 94
Proximate explanations, 67
Psychological Left, 7, 93, 94, 311, 318
Psychological Right, 7, 93, 94, 311, 318
Psychology, 67, 87, 118
Psychopathy, 98, 132, 321

Public good, 238, 338
Public media, 250
Public opinion, 165, 167, 168, 187, 189, 191, 192, 198, 222, 317, 332
Public relations, 65, 236, 258
Public service media, 291, 292, 296, 313
Public sphere, 9, 39, 165, 220, 223, 231, 248, 253, 259, 273, 340
Public utility, 339

R
Races, 21, 85, 115, 316, 317
Racial status, 44
Racism, 176
Racist, 138
Radical press, 224
Radio, 226, 279
Rational ideal, 153
Rationality, 124, 165
Rational moral psychology, 117
Rawls, John, 117
Reason, 116
  defined, 21
Regulation, 274, 286, 338
Regulatory capture, 278
Replicating entities, 24
Replication, 41, 44, 119, 120
Representativeness, 123
Republican Party, 171, 276, 335
Republicans, 143, 187, 191, 253, 331
Respect for authority, 96
Revealed consumer preferences, 225
Revealed preferences, 201
Revenue, 236, 237
Rightwing media, 331
Risk averse, 124
Risk seeking, 124
Rosenberg, Shawn W., 164

S
Sanctity, 97
Sanders, Bernie, 333
Santayana, George, 118, 120
Schema, 31–34, 40, 43, 44, 46, 53, 130, 180, 181, 187, 189
Science, 5, 128
Scientific "laws", 43
Scientific method, 118
Scientific realism, 43
Search Engine Manipulation Effect (SEME), 215
Selection pressure, 53, 83, 325
Selective investment theory, 75
Selects, 69
Self-deception, 149, 150
Self-interest, 43, 245
Sequential style, 152, 312, 345
Sexual dimorphism, 64
Sexuality, 68
Sexual recombination, 27
Sexual selection, 74
Smith, Adam, 321, 325
Snowball effect, 254
Social Darwinism, 20, 21
Social evolution, 25, 27, 79, 80, 84, 99
social evolution theory, 23, 49
Socialism, 52, 333
Socialist, 333
Social media, 258, 297, 332, 333
Social network, 43, 182, 196
Social-psychological pressures, 254
Social psychological research, 119, 120
Social psychology, 118, 126, 254
Social representation, 34, 38–40, 42–44, 48, 51, 53
definition of, 36
Social representations theory, 34
Soft news, 276, 293
Solomon, Miriam, 120
Soul, 30, 116, 117

Sound bites, 292
Source bias, 252, 253, 313
Spandrels, 69, 72
Speech, 82
Spencer, Herbert, 20
Sperber, Dan, 28, 41, 42, 44
Spinoza, Baruch, 140
Spiral of silence, 195
Split-brain research, 122, 123
Stanley, Jason, 167, 324
Status quo, 126, 136, 142, 143, 145, 259, 312, 323
Stereotypes, 135, 137, 175, 176
Stirner, Max
  "spooks", 48, 91, 141, 316, 324, 346
Stress, 196
Structural violence, 98
Subsidy, 200, 223, 238, 278, 338
Supply, 6, 311, 319, 322, 336, 342
System 1, 124, 125, 129, 140, 311, 342
System 2, 124, 125, 129, 140, 143
Systematic style, 152, 312, 345
System justification, 35, 130, 142, 145, 151, 318, 344

T
Talking drum, 221
Tarde, Gabriel, 20, 21
Taylor, Kathleen, 48, 180
Technology, 66, 79, 98
Teleological social evolution, 22
Television, 2, 191, 198, 229, 279, 330, 332
Thematic coverage, 292
Thematic framing, 292
Theory of mind, 65
Third-person effect, 193
Tradition and inequality, 93, 94
Trump, Donald, 330–333, 335, 336

Trust, in press, 237
"Truth wins", 76
Twins, 86
Twin studies, 87–89

U
Ultimate explanations, 67
Underemployment, 329
Unemployment, 190, 193, 330
Unobtrusive issues, 190, 193

V
Values, 179, 188, 200, 201
Variation, 310
Veblen, Thorstein, 63
Violence, 82, 147, 173, 342
Violent competition, 64
Voltaire, 147, 259, 310, 321
Voter turnout, 198

W
War, 3, 11, 39, 70, 124, 134, 138, 139, 143, 148, 167, 173, 186, 193, 221, 249, 253, 254, 257, 296, 312, 344
Wealth gaps, 71
Weber, Max, 51, 321
Western, Educated, Industrialized, Rich, and Democratic (WEIRD), 119
Williams, Raymond, 299
Wilson, Edward O., 72
Writing technologies, 41

Z
Zaller, John, 170, 191, 213, 275